D1194135

Custer and the Battle of the Little Bighorn

Custer and the Battle of the Little Bighorn

An Encyclopedia of the People, Places, Events, Indian Culture and Customs, Information Sources, Art and Films

by THOM HATCH

McFarland & Company, Inc., Publishers
Jefferson, North Carolina, and London

British Library Cataloguing-in-Publication data are available

Library of Congress Cataloguing-in-Publication Data

Hatch, Thom, 1946–
    Custer and the Battle of the Little Bighorn : an encyclopedia
of the people, places, events, Indian culture and customs,
information sources, art and films / by Thom Hatch.
      p. cm.
    Includes index.
    ISBN 0-7864-0154-0 (library binding : 50# alk. paper) ∞
    1. Little Bighorn, Battle of the, Mont., 1876—Encyclopedias.
2. Custer, George Armstrong, 1839–1876—Encyclopedias.
I. Title.
E83.876.H37   1997
973.8'2—dc20
                                          96-34688
                                            CIP

©1997 Thomas Raymond Hatch. All rights reserved

*No part of this book, specifically including the index, may be reproduced
or transmitted in any form or by any means, electronic or mechanical,
including photocopying or recording, or by any information storage and
retrieval system, without permission in writing from the publisher.*

Manufactured in the United States of America

McFarland & Company, Inc., Publishers
  Box 611, Jefferson, North Carolina 28640

To my wife, Lynn,
and daughter, Cimarron,
for their inspiration and encouragement

Contents

List of Maps

All maps were created by the author

List of Illustrations

Nearly all of the photographs and other illustrations are courtesy of the Little Bighorn Battlefield National Monument; the remainder are from the author's collection.

Introduction

Generations of historians, novelists, painters, and television and movie producers have elevated Brevet Major General George Armstrong Custer into this country's most enigmatic and controversial soldier and the Battle of the Little Bighorn into one of the most analyzed conflicts. Consequently, there exists a cultlike attraction to Custer and the battle that made him famous.

This fascination stems primarily from the fact that the battle itself is swathed in intrigue. To study the Battle of the Little Bighorn is to enter a maze without a verifiable outlet. What exactly happened in this engagement between the 7th U.S. Cavalry and the Sioux and Cheyenne Indians on that Sunday afternoon—June 25, 1876—is largely a mystery. Countless theories abound. In fact, there are so many of them that the Custer bibliography is one of the largest in American history.

Considering that voluminous bibliography, the vast number of colorful characters, and the paradoxical particulars involved, this new work acts as a comprehensive guide to assist the interested reader in gathering the relevant information—fact, theory, and speculation—into a manageable perspective.

Topics for entries include people; places; significant social, political, cultural, and historical events of the time; military campaigns, battles, terminology, and equipment; Plains Indian culture and customs; noteworthy source books, articles, and authors; famous artists and artwork; popular movies; and other consequential subject matter associated with the life and career of Custer and with the Battle of the Little Bighorn.

Additionally, because of an overlapping of events and characters from this era, entries have been included for other notable Great Plains military campaigns and their participants from the 1864 Sand Creek Massacre to the 1890 Battle of Wounded Knee.

How to Use This Encyclopedia

Entries are listed in alphabetical order. The keyword or phrase, which represents the form most familiar to the reader, appears in bold type at the beginning of the entry. Common abbreviations are never used as the keyword. A detailed index has been provided in the event no appropriate keyword exists for a topic that a reader wishes to locate.

Cross-references, indicated by small capital letters within the body of text, and "see" or "see also" within or at the end of the text, guide the reader to additional relevant information pertaining to that particular subject.

Following the text of most entries is a listing of sources for further study: those books, articles, or periodicals that will provide extensive information. These references have been for the most part listed in alphabetical order, except where one or two specific sources are deemed particularly significant.

The Encyclopedia

A Company, Seventh Cavalry This company was commanded during the Battle of the LITTLE BIGHORN (LBH) by Capt. Myles M. MOYLAN with 1st Lt. Charles C. DERUDIO second in command (on temporary duty from E Company). The company's other officers were on temporary duty: 1st Lt. Algernon SMITH commanding E Company; and 2nd Lt. Charles A. VARNUM in charge of the Indian scouts. Company A was part of Maj. Marcus RENO's Battalion, and participated in RENO'S VALLEY FIGHT and the RENO-BENTEEN DEFENSE SITE. It lost 8 killed and 7 wounded, and 3 members were awarded the MEDAL OF HONOR for their actions.

Adams, Mary ("Maria") Custer's black cook from spring 1873 until his death. She accompanied him on the YELLOWSTONE EXPEDITION OF 1873— where she and Custer drew the ire of Col. Alfred SULLY because of their cast-iron stove—and the LITTLE BIGHORN CAMPAIGN. Her controversial affidavit, executed January 16, 1878, stated that she overheard Gen. Alfred TERRY tell Custer on the night of June 21, 1876, or the next morning to "Use your own judgment and do what you think best if you strike the trail." This contradicted those claiming Custer disobeyed Terry's orders at LBH. An entire chapter of *The Custer Myth: A Source Book of Custeriana*, by W. A. Graham (Harrisburg, PA: Stackpole, 1953), is devoted to the examination of this affidavit. *Sources for further study include:* "Custer's Cooks and Maids," by John Manion, in *Custer and His Times*, 2, edited by John M. Carroll (Fort Worth, TX: Little Bighorn Associates, 1984).

Alexis, Grand Duke The 19-year-old third son of Russian Czar Alexander II visited the United States in January 1872 and received VIP treatment from the government and the military. Generals, Russian admirals, ambassadors, and other dignitaries as well as a flock of reporters followed the grand duke everywhere. The highlight of his trip was a Nebraska buffalo hunt—the most famous sport in the United States at the time— with escort and guide Custer, Buffalo Bill CODY, and about 100 SIOUX Indians led by SPOTTED TAIL, who brought along his 16-year-old niece: CRAZY HORSE's first cousin. Custer's former enemy from the HANCOCK EXPEDITION OF 1867, PAWNEE KILLER, also joined the entourage. The hunting party roughed it on Red Willow Creek—called "Camp Alexis"—living in tents with plush accouterments, and freely flowing champagne. Entertainment included Indian war dances, races, and bow and arrow exhibitions. Alexis killed his first buffalo with a pistol shot to the head when he and Custer charged the herd on horseback. The grand duke dispatched a runner into North Platte 50 miles away with instructions to cable the czar in Russia with the triumphant news. Custer and his wife Libbie, whose company the grand duke greatly enjoyed, were permitted by Gen. Phil SHERIDAN (at the behest of Alexis) to accompany his personal entourage, which then traveled to Denver, St. Louis, then back East, and finally to New Orleans where it departed on board the Russian fleet. *Sources for further study include:* "Red Carpet for a Romanoff," by John I. White, *American West* 9 (January 1972); and "Custer, Cody and the Grand Duke Alexis," by Elizabeth Bacon Custer and John Manion, *Research Review: The Journal of the Little Big Horn Associates*, 4 (January 1990).

Allison Commission *see* BLACK HILLS

American Horse (Oglala Sioux) (ca. 1800–September 9, 1876) This cousin of RED CLOUD was one of CRAZY HORSE's closest friends and top lieutenants. He participated in the late 1860s fights between the SIOUX and the U.S. Army over the BOZEMAN TRAIL, including the FETTERMAN MASSACRE (he claimed to have personally stabbed Capt. Fetterman to death), the WAGON BOX FIGHT, and the HAYFIELD FIGHT. In 1870 American Horse was a member of Red Cloud's peace delegation to Washington, D.C. However, he was a participant in the Battle of the LITTLE BIGHORN in June 1876. On September 9, 1876, American Horse was residing in the village at SLIM BUTTES when troops under Gen. George CROOK attacked. The village was completely destroyed and American Horse was killed. Numerous SEVENTH CAVALRY items, including a gauntlet (glove) belonging to Capt. Myles KEOGH as well as his I Company guidon were found inside the tepee belonging to American Horse.

American Horse (Oglala Sioux) (1840–1908) American Horse was the son-in-law of RED CLOUD and probably the nephew of AMERICAN HORSE the elder. He participated in the FETTERMAN MASSACRE, but after the FORT LARAMIE TREATY OF 1868 went to live on the reservation at Red Cloud Agency. He was a spokesman for peace during the Ghost Dance fascination that led to the

Battle of WOUNDED KNEE in 1890, and led a delegation to Washington, D.C., the following year to speak about that event and the treatment of his people. In later years he toured with Buffalo Bill CODY's Wild West Show and drew a pictographic history of the Oglala Sioux.

American Indian Movement (AIM) Indian rights organization. Led by activist Russell Means, AIM occupied Wounded Knee, SD, in 1973 to demand that the U.S. government live up to the rights of the SIOUX under the FORT LARAMIE TREATY OF 1868. In 1976 they disrupted centennial ceremonies at LITTLE BIGHORN BATTLEFIELD NATIONAL MONUMENT. Members pounded on drums, dragged an inverted American flag, intimidated the audience, and threatened to set fire to the museum. This protest was staged to bring attention to the overall plight of American Indians.

Ammunition Resources of Cavalrymen at the Battle of the Little Bighorn The theory that the cavalrymen ran out of ammunition, a factor that led to Custer's defeat, has been popular over the years, beginning with newspaper accounts and the RENO COURT OF INQUIRY. Each cavalryman carried into battle one hundred .45/55 caliber cartridges, 50 each in his cartridge belt and saddlebags. That gave Custer's command over 20,000 available shots. Prior to engaging the Indians, Custer dispatched at least 2 orderlies with specific instructions to bring up the pack train of ammo as quickly as possible. Obviously, the status of ammunition was on his mind from the start. The Indians realized that extra ammo supplies were kept in saddlebags, and concentrated on running off the cavalry mounts by shooting the horse holders and waving blankets. Many soldiers, especially those on CUSTER HILL and CALHOUN HILL, however, shot their horses for breastworks, which would have given them access to their ammo. Archaeological evidence from the battlefield is inconclusive, partially due to relic hunters who over the years have removed unknown numbers of casings from unknown locations. Regardless, the evidence that does exist certainly does not show that anywhere near 20,000—or even 10,000 if every horse was run off—shots were fired by the cavalrymen that day. It is likely that the soldiers were simply overwhelmed and killed before they could expend all available rounds.

Arapaho Indians High Plains Indian tribe whose traditional territory was between the Platte and Arkansas rivers to the front range of the Rocky Mountains. Northern Arapaho warriors helped RED CLOUD fight the army over the BOZEMAN TRAIL that led to the FORT LARAMIE TREATY OF 1868. Southern Arapaho, with allies the CHEYENNE and KIOWA, attacked the SEVENTH CAVALRY's camp supply during the HANCOCK EXPEDITION OF 1867. Company F under Capt. George YATES lost 1 man in the skirmish. The Arapaho signed a treaty at MEDICINE LODGE in 1867, and agreed to move south onto a shared reservation with the Cheyenne. However, few obeyed, and the tribe—both southern and northern elements—continued to raid with their allies. During the Battle of WASHITA, southern Arapaho warriors exited from villages downstream from BLACK KETTLE's village on the Washita River, and participated with Cheyenne and Kiowa in killing Maj. Joel ELLIOTT and his men, who were separated from main force. They had abducted a white woman, Mrs. Clara BLINN, and her son on the Arkansas River in Colorado, October 1868. The bodies of the 2 recently killed captives were found on the WASHITA CAMPAIGN in an abandoned Kiowa camp downstream sometime after the battle. In late January 1869 Custer located and, without a shot fired, forced the surrender of 65 lodges under Chief Little Raven in the Wichita Mountains. Members of this tribe had taken part with the Cheyenne in the capture of 2 white captives in Kansas whom Custer rescued in March 1869. (See WASHITA CAMPAIGN OF 1868–69.) The tribe was then forced to the reservation in Indian Territory near FORT COBB. The northern Arapaho were eventually settled on the Wind River Reservation in Wyoming. *Sources for further study include: The Arapahoes, Our People,* by Virginia Cole Trenholm (Norman: University of Oklahoma Press, 1973).

Archaeological Excavations at LBH Battlefield When a grass fire swept across 600 acres of the 640 acre battlefield in August 1983, Superintendent James V. Court obtained National Park Service approval (but no funding) for an examination of the area by archaeologist Douglas D. Scott, Richard A. Fox, Jr., and about 100 volunteers. The CUSTER BATTLEFIELD HISTORICAL AND MUSEUM ASSOCIATION financed that initial dig, which lasted about 5 weeks. It produced over 4,000 artifacts—from brass buttons to casings and cartridges—but there were no major discoveries, other than a complete skeleton they named "Trooper Mike." Historical novelist A. B. Guthrie was opposed to the work, but famed forensic anthropologist Clyde Snow gladly participated. There have been subsequent digs in various areas in and around the battlefield. *Sources for further study include: Archaeological Insights into the Custer Battle: A Preliminary Assessment,* by Douglas D. Scott and Richard A. Fox, Jr. (Norman: University of Oklahoma Press, 1987), *Archaeological Perspectives on the Battle of Little Bighorn,* by Douglas D. Scott, Richard A. Fox, Jr., Melissa A. Conner, and Dick Harmon (Norman: University of Oklahoma Press, 1989); and *Archaeology, History and Custer's Last Battle: The Little Bighorn Reexamined,* by Richard A. Fox, Jr. (Norman: University of Oklahoma Press, 1993).

Arikara (Ree) Indians Blood enemies of the SIOUX, and friendly toward the white man. About 60 served

at one time or another as SEVENTH CAV-ALRY scouts during the Custer era. Their name, meaning "antlers," came from the way in which they had originally arranged their hair around two bones rising from the head like horns or antlers. They were visited by Lewis and Clark in the early nineteenth century, and were considered friendly. They were called "Corn Indians," from living in permanent villages and planting crops such as corn, pumpkins, and squash. The practice of farming is the reason they were despised by the Sioux. It was the Ree scouts—the most famous of whom was BLOODY KNIFE—who claimed that shortly before the march to the LITTLE BIGHORN, Custer visited their camp and was said to have boasted that this was to be his last campaign before going to Washington and becoming the "Great Father." Many have since interpreted that statement as Custer's ambition to become president of the United States. However, the veracity of the episode remains in question. Notable scouts Bloody Knife, Little Scout, and Bobtailed Bull were killed during RENO'S VALLEY FIGHT at the Battle of the LITTLE BIGHORN. *Sources for further study include: The Arikara Narrative of the Campaign against the Hostile Dakotas, June 1876,* edited by O. G. Libby (Bismarck: North Dakota Historical Society, 1920).

Artwork Relating to Custer and the LBH Battle

Many well-known and countless obscure artists have interpreted the Battle of the LITTLE BIGHORN. The first depiction of the battle was a woodcut by William de la Montagne Cary that ran in the *New York Graphic Illustrated* newspaper on July 19, 1876. The impressive work shows Custer's command with SABERS, the one swashbuckling weapon that inspires artists, but sabers were not present at the battle. Another early illustration was *Custer's Last Fight* by A. K. Waud, which was included in Frederick

Whittaker's *A Complete Life of Gen. George A. Custer* (New York: Sheldon, 1876). Currier and Ives also offered *Custer's Last Charge* in 1876. An early favorite was *Custer's Last Rally*, painted in 1881 by John Mulvany. This work, measuring 20' by 11', was completed after the artist had visited the battlefield to sketch the terrain and had studied military dress and equipment, as well as portraits of Custer and his officers. The rendering is huge, heroic, and impressive—in spite of the fact that Custer grips a saber. The last known owner was the H. K. Heinz Company of Pittsburgh, PA. Vinnie Ream Hoxie—Lincoln's sculptor—was an acquaintance for whom Custer sat while in Washington in early 1876. A marble bust of him was completed by her in the fall of 1881, and widow Libbie scraped together enough money (with a little help from her friends) for the purchase.

Perhaps the most famous work of its time due to the locations where it was displayed was *Custer's Last Fight* by Otto Becker, adorning saloon walls nationwide in the late nineteenth century. The Anheuser-Busch Brewing Company distributed 150,000 copies of this lithograph as an advertising poster, and more than 1 million were printed. The original, painted by Cassilly Adams in 1885 (see illustration, opposite) measured 9'6" by 16'5" and hung in a St. Louis saloon until 1888, when Anheuser-Busch acquired the saloon's assets. Adolphus Busch had the painting re-created by Otto Becker, then lithographed in color, printed, and copyrighted in 1886. The Cassilly original was presented to the SEVENTH CAVALRY at FORT RILEY, and was lost in frequent moves until found at Fort Bliss, TX, in 1925. It was destroyed by fire on June 13, 1946. Edgar S. Paxton's *Custer's Last Stand*, which measures 5' by 9', was painted after 20 years' research. This work portrays 36 members of Custer's command painted from photographs.

Opposite: Custer's Last Fight by Cassilly Adams.

Rufus Zogbaum's illustration *The Last Stand* can be found in the April 1890 issue of *Harper's*. The cofounder of the original Taos Society of Artists, Ernest L. Blumenschein, created a full-page illustration called *We Circled All Round Him* that was published in the September 1898 issue of *McClure's* magazine. Frederic Remington created a small pen and ink drawing in 1890 titled *Custer's Last Stand*, which he presented to Custer's wife Libbie. It was reproduced in the July 1891 issue of *Cosmopolitan*. Charles M. Russell interpreted the battle twice in 1903. The first, *Custer's Last Stand*, shows the troopers in battle; it can be found in the December 1904 issue of *Outing*. His second rendering, *The Custer Fight*, is a watercolor that pictures Indians riding into battle, and is owned by the National Cowboy Hall of Fame in Oklahoma City. O. C. Seltzer, a student of Russell, painted a series of seven depictions of events surrounding the battle, such as *Sitting Bull Making Medicine*, and *Trumpeter John Martin Bringing His Famous Last Message from Custer to Major Benteen*. Popular magazine illustrator N. C. Wyeth's *Custer's Last Stand* appeared in an advertisement for Lucky Strike cigarettes in 1932 with the catch phrase "Nature in the Raw Is Seldom *Mild*." Elk Eber, whose father was German and mother a Sioux, painted *Custer's Last Stand* (1926) from his mother's eyewitness account. Another *Custer's Last Fight* (1939) by W. R. Leigh, which measures 6'6" by 10'6" depicts Custer somewhat obscured by dust and smoke while firing a revolver. Harold Von Schmidt's *Custer's Last Stand* was a color foldout in the September 1950 issue of *Esquire*. His son, Eric, created the 1976 *Here Fell Custer*, which portrays the final moments of the battle (the artist appears near Capt. Tom CUSTER). Michael Gentry began in the 1970s painting Native Americans, including one titled *Custer's Nemesis* that shows Sioux Joseph WHITE BULL shooting at Custer. The most haunting paintings of the subject have been rendered by

Don Griffiths, whose *Destiny* displays the battlefield at the bottom with portraits of participants in the sky; and *Libbie's Vision*, which refers to the premonition of Custer's wife. J. K. Ralston's series on the subject, including *Call of the Bugle*, have become very popular. Perhaps the most unusual painting may be *Custer's Last Supper* by Lynn Cahill, an imitation of da Vinci's masterpiece that replaces the original images with Custer, his officers, and scouts, with Reno in place of Judas. Other excellent modern re-creations include *Souvenirs of Little Bighorn* by Michael Donahue; Michael Gentry's *Long Hair's Last Sunday*; Ralph Heinz's accurate portrayals of battle events such as *With Their Backs to the Wall*; *Reno's Retreat* and others by Jack Hines; *Custer's Last Stand* among others by Mort Kunstler; Mike Schreck's numerous historical paintings including the 1993 *Sgt. Butler*; Jeanie Southworth's *Reflections of Custer's Last Stand*; Robert Sticker's *Far West*; and *Here Fell Son of Morning Star* by Dan Taylor.

It should be noted that numerous Indians created pictographs with their interpretation of the battle. They include: High Bull (Cheyenne); Kicking Bear drew *Custer's Last Stand*; Chief Red Horse (Sioux) drew *Indians Leaving Battleground* and *Sioux Charging Soldiers*, as well as many others in the 1880s; Joseph White Bull (Sioux); White Bird (Cheyenne) produced *Custer's Fight*, *Battle of the Little Big Horn* (see illustration on page 9) and *Reno's Retreat*; WOODEN LEG (Cheyenne); and Amos Bad Heart Bull (Sioux). If you consider photographs artwork, the following two books contain an impressive collection: *Custer in Photographs* by D. Mark Katz (Gettysburg, NY: Yo-Mark Production, 1985), and *The Custer Album* by Lawrence A. Frost (Norman: University of Oklahoma Press, 1990). *Sources for further study include:* The Custer Reader edited by Paul Andrew Hutton (Lincoln: University of Nebraska Press, 1992); and the Smithsonian Institution.

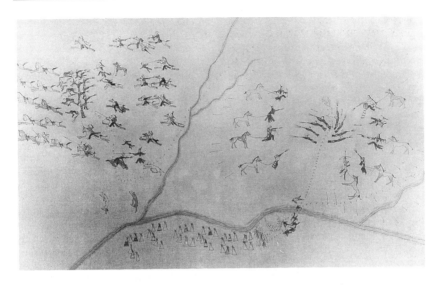

Battle of Little Big Horn by **White Bird (Cheyenne)**

Ash Creek, MT (aka Sundance Creek; Reno Creek) A tributary flowing into the Little Bighorn River that whites renamed RENO CREEK. Indians under SITTING BULL were camped on Ash Creek on June 16, 1876, when word reached them that Gen. George CROOK and his command were approaching. Rather than wait for Crook to attack the camp, the Indians rode off to initiate their own attack. See ROSEBUD, BATTLE OF THE.

Audubon Club This organization was one of the recipients of Custer's impressive accumulation of personally mounted game heads, horns, hides, fossilized animal and fish parts, and petrified wood collected from the Great Plains. See also CENTRAL PARK ZOO; BLACK HILLS EXPEDITION OF 1874.

B Company, Seventh Cavalry This company was commanded during the Battle of the LITTLE BIGHORN by Capt. Thomas M. McDOUGALL. The company's other officers were on temporary duty: 1st Lt. William T. Craycroft on detached service at headquarters, De-

partment of Dakota; 2nd Lt. Benjamin H. HODGSON was assigned as adjutant to Maj. Marcus RENO. B Company was the packtrain escort, and participated in the RENO-BENTEEN DEFENSE SITE. It lost 2 killed and 4 wounded, and 5 members were awarded the MEDAL OF HONOR for their actions.

Bacon, Daniel Stanton (Judge) (December 12, 1798–March 18, 1866) Bacon was the father of Custer's wife, Elizabeth C. BACON CUSTER (Libbie), and a leading citizen of Monroe, MI. This descendant of the Plymouth colony had at one time or another been a farmer, a schoolteacher, a member of the Territorial Legislature, losing candidate for Michigan lieutenant governor in 1837, a probate judge, and director of a bank and a railroad. At the age of 38 he married 23-year-old Eleanor Sophia Page of Grand Rapids, MI, in September 1837. The couple had 4 children: 2 girls died in infancy and a boy, Eddy, died at 8 of a childhood disease. That left Elizabeth—Libbie, the future Mrs. Custer—to be doted upon. However, when Libbie was 12 her mother passed away. He sent the child off to boarding school, rented out their house, and took a room at the Exchange Hotel. In early 1860 he married a widow, Rhoda Wells Pitts. When Custer asked for Libbie's hand in the fall of 1863, the judge wrote to Custer stating that he might ponder the matter for "weeks or even months." He did not approve of his daughter marrying a common military man. However, Custer's frequent correspondence and heroic exploits in the Civil War helped convince the judge of his future son-in-law's worthiness and so he gave his blessing to the union. Bacon once said: "Elizabeth [Libbie] has married entirely to her own satisfaction and to mine. No man could wish for a son-in-law more highly thought of." He died of cholera after a long illness.

Bacon, Elizabeth C. *see* CUSTER, ELIZABETH B.

Barnitz, Albert (March 10, 1835–July 18, 1912) Major, 7th Cavalry. His military career began when he volunteered for the 2nd Ohio Infantry in 1861, and pursued Quantrill and other guerrilla units on the Kansas frontier. He later served in the 3rd Division commanded by Custer, and participated in battles in the Shenandoah Valley. Barnitz married Jennie Platt in early 1866, and was appointed captain in the SEVENTH CAVALRY in November of that year. He was severely wounded at the Battle of WASHITA (November 27, 1868), where he was awarded brevet of full colonel for "distinguished bravery." The wound occurred during a personal duel with an Indian whom he killed but from whom he received a bullet in the abdomen that was at the time believed fatal. He recovered, but was retired from the service on medical disability (1870). He wrote for newspapers until his death: the autopsy revealed the cause as a growth around the wound received at Washita. *Sources for further study include: Life in Custer's Cavalry: Diaries and Letters of Albert and Jen-*

nie Barnitz, 1867–68, edited by Robert M. Utley (Lincoln: University of Nebraska Press, 1977).

Barrett, Lawrence New York Shakespearean actor. Custer and his wife Libbie attended a performance of this famous actor starring in *Rosedale* at an exposition in St. Louis on their way to FORT RILEY, KA, in 1866 and went backstage to meet Barrett. They became close friends with the Barretts and frequent social companions whenever the Custers visited New York City. The former Civil War captain accompanied Custer on his tour with President Johnson in 1866, and again on the January 1872 buffalo hunt in honor of Grand Duke ALEXIS of Russia. He was invited to join the BLACK HILLS EXPEDITION OF 1874 but prior obligations prevented it. Barrett gave a benefit performance shortly after the Battle of the LITTLE BIGHORN to help raise funds for a Custer memorial. Mrs. Barrett accompanied Libbie Custer to West Point, NY, on October 10, 1877, on the occasion of Custer's reinterment. When Lawrence Barrett passed away March 20, 1891, Libbie was at the side of Mrs. Barrett.

Bates, Col. Charles Francis Author of several Custer-related books. Col. Bates assisted in the recovery of the original of Custer's last order at LITTLE BIGHORN—"Benteen. Come on..."—carried by orderly John MARTIN to Capt. F. W. BENTEEN. Thought lost since 1879, the message had been in the possession of a New Jersey collector when Bates noticed it advertised for sale at an auction. He arranged with the owner to have it secured by the U.S. Military Academy at West Point.

Battle Ridge (aka Custer Ridge) It was along this elevation above the eastern side of the Little Bighorn River that most of the troops in Custer's 5 companies fought and died at the Battle of the LITTLE BIGHORN. Battle Ridge is bordered by CALHOUN HILL on the south and CUSTER HILL on the north.

Bear Butte An extinct volcano on the northern fringe of the BLACK HILLS that was a special gathering place where the SIOUX nation met to trade, share news, and participate in religious ceremonies. Custer halted his column here to write his official report at the completion of the BLACK HILLS EXPEDITION OF 1874. This location is also notable as the birthplace of CRAZY HORSE in the fall of 1841.

Beecher's Island, Battle of (September 17, 1868) While guarding the railroad up the SMOKY HILL ROAD (Kansas), Maj. George A. FORSYTHE and 50 seasoned scouts were attacked on the Arikara Fork of the Republican River by a superior force of CHEYENNE and SIOUX Indians led by ROMAN NOSE, who was killed the first day. The men dug in on an island in the dry stream bed and fought back the siege. Finally, after 9 days, the 10th Cavalry's black "BUFFALO SOLDIERS" came to their rescue. *Sources for further study include: The Battle of Beecher Island and the Indian War of 1867–1869*, by John H. Monnett (Niwot: University Press of Colorado, 1992).

Belknap Scandal William W. Belknap, former Civil War general, secretary of war in the Grant administration, was accused of corruption in the awarding of Western post traderships, and for that reason became the subject of impeachment hearings in early 1876. Custer became embroiled as a witness in the scandal that threatened his participation in the LITTLE BIGHORN CAMPAIGN.

Custer had investigated the circumstances at his post, FORT ABRAHAM LINCOLN, and concluded that Belknap was conspiring with the local trader in a kickback scheme. In the summer of 1875 Secretary Belknap was scheduled to visit Fort Lincoln. Under normal circumstances such a distinguished visitor would be greeted with great ceremony. Prior to the visit the post trader delivered several bottles of wine to Custer for use in entertaining Belknap. The gift was returned with the remark that Custer did not drink. Upon arrival, Belknap was in effect snubbed by Custer, the acting commanding officer, who refused to properly greet the secretary at the edge of the reservation. He instead waited at his door, then hastily retired to his quarters after formalities had been completed. Custer later excused his behavior by claiming that he had heard rumors that the secretary's visit was for the purpose of assisting the traders in smuggling whiskey across the Canadian border.

James G. Bennett, Jr., publisher and editor of the *New York Herald* newspaper and political friend of Custer, regularly printed anti–Grant material, some supplied by Custer (who, it was rumored, had been a paid informant), including exposés of corruption at Western forts and trading posts. In his edition on February 10, 1876, Bennett accused Belknap of selling traderships and called for a full congressional investigation. He further implicated Orvil GRANT, the president's brother, and in doing so wondered how much profit Orvil had "made in Sioux country starving squaws and children."

The Democrat-controlled Congress viewed this growing scandal as an ideal opportunity to embarrass President GRANT. Heister Clymer, chairman of the House Committee on Expenditures in the War Department, decided to hold investigative hearings into the matter in early 1876. Belknap resigned on March 2, 1876, to avoid impeachment, but the hearings continued. Orvil Grant admitted that his brother, the president, had given him license to 4 posts in 1874. Eventually, a pattern of questionable activity emerged. Orvil apparently was making a profit in various behind-the-scenes activities—middleman in giving out licenses, supplies said to be delivered to authorized recipients that were not but then were resold elsewhere—all simply due to his influence with the president. It appeared that a split of the profits was funneled to Belknap's wife.

Custer was called to testify in late March. He related how upon his arrival at Fort Abraham Lincoln he had requested the removal of the resident trader, S. A. Dickey, for various infractions, including introducing alcohol to the Indians. The new trader, Robert C. Seip, had admitted to Custer that he delivered two-thirds of his profits to representatives of Secretary Belknap. Custer also spoke in opposition of the 1870 law that put the appointment of post traders under the control of the secretary of war. This practice, he said, increased prices of goods at frontier posts, which caused a hardship on the troops. Custer, however, did not stop there. In addition to supplying incriminating *hearsay* knowledge about Belknap, he went on to implicate Orvil Grant in the tradership kickback scheme. Custer's testimony caused some cynics to point out that Custer saw nothing wrong or contradictory about fighting against the Indians as well as those who cheated them. Custer's high-profile presence—which added more in publicity than in substance to the hearings—was completed on April 4.

Custer expected to return to Fort Lincoln and prepare for the upcoming campaign against the SIOUX and CHEYENNE. The president, however, was infuriated by Custer's testimony, and decided to punish his impudent officer by refusing to allow him to accompany the Dakota Column. Custer was devastated. He visited the White House on 3 occasions to make amends, but Grant refused to see him. The *New York Herald* and other newspapers reported that Custer was being disgraced for speaking the truth, an abuse of power by Grant.

Custer's popularity at the time can be evidenced by the fact that in early 1876 he considered a lucrative offer from the Redpath Lyceum Bureau, a New York talent agency. The contract called for him to lecture 5 nights a week for 4–5 months

at $200 per night: a considerable amount of money in those days. He had turned down the opportunity because it would conflict with his preparations for the Little Bighorn Campaign.

Custer impatiently waited while the SEVENTH CAVALRY—temporarily commanded by Maj. Marcus RENO—prepared for the march. On May 6—likely under the direction of Gen. Alfred TERRY—Custer sent the following telegram to the president:

I have seen your order transmitted through the General of the Army directing that I not be permitted to accompany the expedition to move against hostile Indians. As my entire regiment forms a part of the expedition and I am the senior officer of the regiment on duty in this department I respectfully but most earnestly request that while not allowed to go in command of the expedition I may be permitted to serve with my regiment in the field. I appeal to you as a soldier to spare me the humiliation of seeing my regiment march to meet the enemy and I not share its dangers.

Following respectful persuasion from generals SHERMAN, SHERIDAN, and TERRY, who realized the need for their experienced Indian fighter, the president grudgingly relented on May 8 and gave permission for Custer to join the march for the Little Bighorn. *Sources for further study include:* "Report on Management of the War Department, Rep. Heister Clymer, Chairman of Committee," *House Reports* no. 799, 44th Congress, 1st Session, serial no. 1715 (1876), vol. 8; *Nation* (New York), March 16, 1876; "Custer's Last Meeting with Secretary of War Belknap at Fort Abraham Lincoln," by Eric Brigham, *North Dakota History* 9 (August 1952); *New York Herald*, May 2, May 10, July 6, 1876; *Army and Navy Journal*, May 27, 1876; *The Custer Tragedy*, by Fred Dustin (Ann Arbor, MI: Edwards Brothers, 1939); and *Tales from Buffalo Land*, by Usher L. Burdick (Baltimore: Wirth Brothers, 1940).

Bell, James M. (October 1, 1837–September 17, 1919) 7th Cavalry Officer. Bell earned a master's degree at Wittenburg College (Pennsylvania) in 1862. His military career began when he was appointed captain in the 13th Pennsylvania Cavalry in October 1863. He participated in 16 major Civil War engagements, including the Wilderness, Spottsylvania, and Ream's Station, earning brevets to major. He was appointed a second lieutenant in the SEVENTH CAVALRY in 1866; and first lieutenant in 1867. He served as quartermaster from 1867–69, and distinguished himself at the Battle of WASHITA by reaching Custer in timely fashion with a critical resupply of ammunition. Bell was a frequent social guest of the Custers. He was on an authorized leave of absence during the LITTLE BIGHORN CAMPAIGN, and received his captaincy as a result of the death of Capt. George YATES. He was awarded brevet to lieutenant colonel for the Battle of Canyon Creek against the NEZ PERCÉ (1877); commanded a regiment in the Cuban Campaign of the Spanish-American War (1898–99); and as brigadier general led a brigade in the Philippines. Bell retired to Pasadena, CA, as a brigadier general in the regular army (1901).

Benteen Baseball Club This athletic organization was composed of SEVENTH CAVALRY enlisted men from FORT ABRAHAM LINCOLN around 1875–76. Many of the ballplayers were assigned to Capt. F. W. BENTEEN's H Company, hence the name. The team played baseball against area civilian and military teams. One particular game was played July 31, 1874, on the BLACK HILLS EXPEDITION OF 1874 between the Actives of Fort Lincoln and the Athletes of FORT RICE: the Actives beat the Athletes 11–6. One starting player, second baseman Pvt. William Davis, was killed and 4 other regulars were wounded at the Battle of the LITTLE BIGHORN. 1st Sgt. Joseph McCurry, who was wounded in the battle, was team captain, treasurer, and star pitcher; his ENLISTED MAN'S PETITION has become a source of controversy. The club's activities were drastically curtailed following the battle.

Benteen, Frederick William (August 24, 1834–June 22, 1898) Captain, 7th Cavalry (see illustration below), commander of Company H from 1866–82. Benteen was a capable and admired officer who has become notorious as Custer's most outspoken critic as well as the recipient of Custer's last order at the Battle of the LITTLE BIGHORN.

A Southerner with Virginia roots, he surprisingly entered the Civil War in September 1861 as a lieutenant on the side of the Union with the 10th Missouri Cavalry. This greatly displeased his father, T. C. Benteen, who allegedly stated, "I hope the first bullet gets you!" Benteen was appointed captain in October 1861. By that time the elder Benteen was employed as chief engineer on a Mississippi riverboat that was captured by Capt. Benteen's unit on August 18, 1862. The

Frederick W. Benteen, 1885

other civilian crew members were soon released. Inexplicably, perhaps on account of his son's influence, T. C. Benteen was imprisoned for the duration of the war. Benteen was appointed major in December 1862, and lieutenant colonel in October 1864. He fought in 18 major Civil War engagements, including Wilson's Creek, Pea Ridge, and the siege of Vicksburg, and was awarded brevets up to lieutenant colonel in the regular army.

Following the Civil War, he served as colonel of the 138th U.S. Colored Volunteers (July 1865–January 1866). He received his regular army commission in September 1866 and was assigned to the SEVENTH CAVALRY.

Benteen took an immediate dislike to Custer, who was younger in age yet senior in rank and nationally famous. One public confrontation between the two occurred following the Battle of WASHITA, and concerned Maj. Joel ELLIOTT and his men, who were later found dead. Elliott's tragic death provided Benteen, his friend and former Civil War superior, fodder for which to create a controversy that continued beyond Custer's death at the LITTLE BIGHORN. Benteen wrote a letter that was highly critical of Custer's conduct at Washita, especially in "abandoning" Elliott. The letter was sent to a former Benteen Civil War comrade in St. Louis who, apparently without permission, gave the letter to the *St. Louis Democrat* newspaper where it was published. A copy of the letter found its way to Custer while the 7th Cavalry campaigned against CHEYENNE Indians in Oklahoma. He had "officer's call" sounded, and in his tent displayed the newspaper and threatened to horsewhip the author. Benteen readily admitted authorship, which shocked and befuddled Custer. One account reported that Custer exited the tent without a word; another states he stammered that he would see Benteen again, and dismissed the officers. Custer scholars have debated reasons for Custer's passive response to Benteen without concurring on a definitive

answer. Theories tend to be presented along loyalty lines. Those who favor Custer claim he backed off for the good of the outfit; detractors question Custer's courage. Benteen said that he later returned to the commanding officer's tent with a newspaperman as witness, and at that confrontation Custer "wilted like a whipped cur." (Benteen's letter as well as a complete chapter devoted to Benteen material can be found in *The Custer Myth: A Source Book of Custeriana*, by W. A. Graham [Harrisburg, PA: Stackpole, 1953].) The Elliott affair remained an open wound that for 8 years until Custer's death caused dissension among the officers of the regiment.

Custer, as far as anyone can document, never spoke in a disparaging manner about this officer who never missed a chance to insult or ridicule his commanding officer. In fact, in his book, *My Life on the Plains; Or, Personal Experiences with Indians* (New York: Wheldon, 1874)—a book that Benteen referred to as "My *Lie* on the Plains"—Custer related an incident from the Battle of Washita when Benteen, in a benevolent gesture, made every effort to convince an Indian boy to surrender rather than fight, but was eventually forced to kill the young brave.

Benteen, the senior captain and third in command of Custer's cavalry at the Battle of the LITTLE BIGHORN, was sent to the left to scout a line of ridges with a battalion composed of companies D, H, and K—about 125 men—while Custer, Reno, and 8 companies plus the packtrain headed north toward the Indian village. While on this unproductive scout, Benteen received Custer's last known order. The message, hastily scribbled on notepaper by Adj. 1st Lt. W. W. COOKE, and delivered by John MARTIN, read: "Benteen. Come on. Big village. Be Quick. Bring Packs. W. W. Cooke. P. bring pacs." Benteen, however, inexplicably did not "come on." He instead chose to lollygag along the way. Some scholars theorize that if Benteen had immediately responded to the message and hurried his troops he could have arrived on the field in time to assist Custer's command.

Benteen eventually halted his battalion at the request of Maj. Marcus RENO, and took up a hilltop defensive position on what is presently known as the RENO-BENTEEN DEFENSE SITE, some 4 miles south of CUSTER HILL. Benteen, who was wounded in the thumb as he walked about exposing himself to SIOUX and CHEYENNE Indian sharpshooters, distinguished himself by assuming de facto command of the pinned-down, outnumbered troops who endured a murderous siege for two days following the destruction of Custer's troops. Benteen's coolness and bravery clearly had a large part in saving Reno's beaten command (and his own) from perhaps total annihilation at the hands of the same Indians who had defeated Custer.

When Gen. Alfred TERRY and reinforcements arrived two days after the battle, Benteen was told that Custer lay dead 4 miles to the north. He was surprised, and remarked that he had speculated that Custer had gone off and abandoned his command as at the Battle of Washita. Terry told him to go and see for himself. Benteen obliged, and returned in a disturbed state. An officer who accompanied the captain reported that Benteen looked down on Custer's body and passionately said, "There he is, God damn him, he will never fight anymore!"

Benteen and his wife Catherine lost 4 children to spinal meningitis, a disease that, according to Benteen, he also contracted. They had 1 son, Fred, who became a major in the army.

Benteen fought against the NEZ PERCÉ in 1877; and was promoted to major in 1882 with the 9th Cavalry. While serving as commander of Fort Duchesne, UT, in 1886 he faced a court-martial and was found guilty of various offenses, ranging from "drunkenness on duty" to "exposing his person." He was dismissed from the service as punishment. This sentence was later amended by President Cleveland to a one-year suspension in respect for Benteen's excellent record. He was granted disability retirement at the end of the served suspension.

Benteen retired to Atlanta, GA, and was awarded a brevet to brigadier general in 1890 for his actions at the Little Bighorn and Canyon Creek against the Nez Percé in 1877. He died of paralysis from a stroke, and was buried in Arlington National Cemetery. See also ENLISTED MEN'S PETITION; BATES, COL. C.

Sources for further study include: The *Benteen-Goldin Letters on Custer and His Last Battle*, edited by John M. Carroll (New York: Liveright, 1974), offers a look at Benteen's bitterness toward those with whom he had served, Custer in particular; *Gray Head and Long Hair: The Benteen-Custer Relationship*, by Karol Asay (New York: John M. Carroll, 1983); *Camp Talk: The Very Private Letters of Frederick Benteen of the Seventh U.S. Cavalry to His Wife, 1871 to 1888*, edited by John M. Carroll (Bryan, TX: J. M. Carroll, 1983); *Cavalry Scraps: The Writings of Frederick W. Benteen*, edited by John M. Carroll (East Stroudsburg, PA: Guidon Press, 1979); and *Harvest of Barren Regrets: The Army Career of Frederick William Benteen, 1834–1898*, by Charles K. Mills (Glendale, CA: Arthur H. Clark, 1985).

"Benzine Boards" This nickname was given to review boards that were established in 1870 at the direction of the War Department for the purpose of reducing the officer corps. Commanders were requested to recommend for discharge those officers considered incompetent, unfit, or simply undesirable. Officers from the SEVENTH CAVALRY whose names were submitted included E. GODFREY, E. MATHEY, Algernon SMITH, and T. WEIR, none of whom were dismissed.

Bismarck Tribune The newspaper known for vigorously promoting the opening of the BLACK HILLS, "the El Dorado of America," to gold miners. *Tribune* reporter Mark KELLOGG perished with Custer at the Battle of the LITTLE BIGHORN. The paper published details of Custer's defeat in an extra edition on July 6, 1876.

Black Army Regiments Four regiments composed of black Americans were authorized by a congressional act in 1866. The units were segregated from the rest of the army, and dispatched to fight Indians on the Plains. Led by white officers, these regiments were respected as capable opponents by the Indians. See also BUFFALO SOLDIERS; BEECHER'S ISLAND, BATTLE OF. *Sources for further study include: The Buffalo Soldiers: A Narrative of Negro Cavalry in the West,* by William F. Leckie (Norman: University of Oklahoma Press, 1967).

Black Elk (Oglala Sioux) (1863–1950) Student of CRAZY HORSE; medicine man; noted expert on SIOUX culture. Black Elk participated in the Battle of the LITTLE BIGHORN at age 13, and scalped a soldier who was still alive. He described the incident in *Black Elk Speaks: The Life Story of a Holy Man of the Oglala Sioux,* edited by John G. Neihardt (New York: William Morrow, 1932): "He had short hair and my knife was not very sharp. He ground his teeth. Then I shot him in the forehead and got his scalp." He took the scalp to his mother who honored him with a shrill tremolo. After Crazy Horse was killed in 1877, his family fled to Canada and joined SITTING BULL. He became a respected shaman during his stay above the border, and eventually returned to the Pine Ridge Reservation. In 1886–89 Black Elk toured with Buffalo Bill CODY's Wild West Show, once performing for Queen Victoria of England. *Sources for further study include: Black Elk: The Holy Man of the Oglala,* by Michael F. Steltenkamp (Norman: University of Oklahoma Press, 1993).

Black Hills, D.T. This mountainous wilderness area along the Dakota-Wyoming border runs roughly 100 miles north to south and 60 miles east to west, and was within the boundaries of the GREAT SIOUX RESERVATION as awarded in the FORT LARAMIE TREATY OF 1868. The Black Hills became a matter of contention between the SIOUX Indian tribe and the U.S. government, a dispute that led to the LITTLE BIGHORN CAMPAIGN.

The Sioux probably reached the Black Hills somewhere around the time of the American Revolution (1775). They had pushed aside the CHEYENNE who apparently had earlier pushed aside the KIOWA who had pushed aside the COMANCHE who had pushed aside the CROW. The Black Hills area, called *Paha Sapa* by the Sioux, was primarily used as a hunting ground and a place to camp or hide out after raiding parties. The Fort Laramie Treaty of 1868 that ended war with RED CLOUD over the BOZEMAN TRAIL set aside the area as a reservation for the Sioux (see map on page 17).

It was the panic of 1873, however, that caused the U.S. government to begin considering the Black Hills in terms of mineral deposits. The public outcry for admittance to the forbidden territory for the purpose of prospecting became overpowering. It was decided that the military should explore this unknown region in order to determine a spot in which to possibly establish a fort and to secretly search for gold. Custer led such an expedition in the summer of 1874. (See BLACK HILLS EXPEDITION OF 1874.) Upon his return, Custer became a leading advocate of opening the Black Hills to settlers, miners, loggers, and for any other practical purposes. He reasoned in a message to the War Department that the Sioux were not using the area, so it was basically ripe for the plucking. Newspapers jumped on the bandwagon, and speculation began about how to relieve the Sioux of the land they had been promised by treaty. Soon the U.S. government

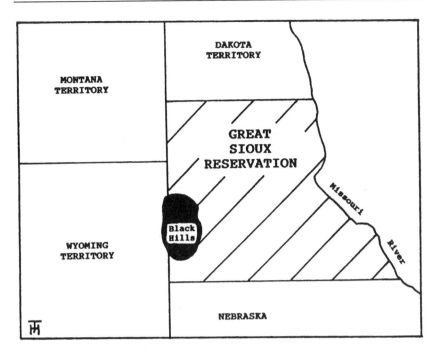

Black Hills in relation to the Great Sioux Reservation

began making overtures toward the Sioux to sell the Black Hills.

The Sioux were split over the proposal to sell. Most reservation Indians approved of the idea, thinking that they would be paid handsomely. Another faction, led by SITTING BULL and CRAZY HORSE, vowed to sell the land only over their dead bodies. Red Cloud, SPOTTED TAIL, and other chiefs were invited to Washington, D.C., in the summer of 1875, the reason for which, to their surprise (they considered this their chance to complain about agency business), was to sign over title to the Black Hills. They refused, saying they lacked authority. Soon after, Spotted Tail visited the Hills and decided the land was worth somewhere between $7 and $40 million and enough provisions to keep the Sioux content for 7 generations.

The Allison Commission, chaired by Iowa senator William B. Allison, was convened in September 1875 near Red Cloud Agency to discuss the issue. The members were greeted with a show of hostility over the Black Hills. Those Indians who rejected the idea of parting with the Hills staged a protest. These were mainly the younger warriors from Sitting Bull's bands who arrived from the Hills to disrupt the proceedings, and to threaten severe reprisal against any Sioux chief who accepted the proposal of the commissioners and signed a treaty. The commission then recommended that Congress simply offer what it considered fair value for the region. If the Sioux refused to sell, rations and provisions at the reservations would be terminated.

The frustration over the Black Hills and the hostile Sioux who had been raiding in the unceded territory finally came to a head when President Grant decided that all Indians must report to reservations by January 31, 1876, or suffer the consequences. The consequences began the LITTLE BIGHORN CAMPAIGN portion of the GREAT SIOUX WAR of 1876–77 that led to the army being dispatched in an effort to force those Indians who disregarded the order onto reservations.

Following the Great Sioux War, to the victors went the spoils. Congress passed an appropriation bill in 1877 that provided that the Sioux would receive rations and goods only after they gave up the Black Hills. The commission returned to complete the formalities: Sioux chiefs grudgingly signed the treaty and *Paha Sapa* became U.S. property.

In 1980 the U.S. Supreme Court ordered that the Sioux be compensated for the loss of their land, but the tribe has steadfastly refused to accept nothing less than the land itself.

The Black Hills is presently a tourist destination and recreation area. Within its boundaries is national forest; Mount Rushmore; the CRAZY HORSE Memorial; and numerous visitor attractions including Deadwood, SD, known for its legalized gambling.

Sources for further study: Follow the BLACK HILLS EXPEDITION OF 1874 entry.

Black Hills Expedition of 1874
This expedition, led by Custer, departed from FORT ABRAHAM LINCOLN on July 2, 1874, on a mission to explore the BLACK HILLS region of Dakota Territory, which was part of the GREAT SIOUX RESERVATION. The published purpose of the expedition was to identify Plains Indians' escape trails as well as likely locations for military posts. However, it was a poorly kept secret that Custer was also seeking to verify claims of valuable mineral deposits. Gold was indeed discovered, which began an influx of miners in violation of the FORT LARAMIE TREATY OF 1868. This invasion intensified hostilities between the SIOUX and the U.S. government, and led to the GREAT SIOUX WAR OF 1876–77, which included the LITTLE BIGHORN CAMPAIGN.

The column consisted of 10 companies of the SEVENTH CAVALRY; 2 infantry companies; 3 GATLING GUNS; scouts; interpreters; teamsters with 110 wagons; the scientific corps under Capt. William Ludlow, including a geologist, Newton Winchell; a paleontologist, George Bird GRINNELL; a photographer, W. H. Illingworth; a botanist, A. B. Donaldson; professional miners, Horatio Ross and William McKay; observer Lt. Col. Fred GRANT, the president's son; and numerous journalists—more than 1,000 participants.

It was July 20 when the expedition actually entered the Black Hills using a well-worn Indian trail. On July 22, 1874, at Inyan Kara, an extinct volcano on the western edge, some of the ARIKARA and Santee Indian scouts advised Custer to turn back and not invade the Sioux domain. They warned that if he did enter they would not accompany him for fear of Sioux retaliation. Custer doubted that the scouts had much information to offer anyway, since they had never been to the region before so he released them; BLOODY KNIFE, however, chose to remain with the column.

From then on, Custer personally rode ahead and blazed the trail throughout the expedition, and had the reputation of having the ability to always find a passage through even the most difficult terrain (see map on page 19). Their route eventually led to a resplendent valley that gave the botanist a field day. Custer did not exaggerate when he named the place Floral Valley. Nearly every account, diary, or letter home carried a description of the beauty of the abundant wildflowers and overall serenity that pervaded in the valley, written in terms normally considered alien to hardened cavalrymen. The scientists were also impressed by the plentiful fossils they discovered along the way.

The Sioux Indians had been sending up smoke signals to indicate that they were aware of the presence of troops, but had chosen not to attack the intruders traveling the route that they referred to as the Thieves Road. In late July, however, the army encountered a small hunting

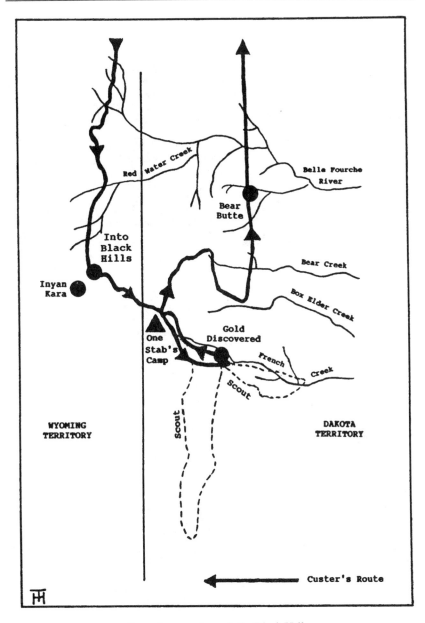

Custer's route through the Black Hills

party of Sioux under Oglala Chief One Stab from Red Cloud Agency. The 5 lodges of Indians were camped in Castle Creek Valley, and the 27 occupants were quite surprised to come face to face with the 7th Cavalry. Custer smoked the peace pipe with the chief and invited his people to visit the army camp for some free

Black Hills Expedition of 1874: Custer's camp along French Creek.

coffee, sugar, and bacon, which they accepted. Custer's Indian scouts, however, were not as accommodating; they wanted to kill their Sioux enemy. When the Sioux were ready to depart, Custer ordered a detail of 15 men to accompany them for safekeeping. The Sioux were not comfortable with that arrangement, and galloped away with the troopers in pursuit. During the chase—although Custer had ordered no violence—one of the Sioux was shot, possibly by one of the Scouts. The Sioux camp had been abandoned by the time the troops arrived. Chief One Stab, however, had remained with Custer as either captive or guest. Custer wrote: "I have effected arrangements by which the Chief One Stab remains with us as a guide." One Stab remained with Custer for several days, guiding the expedition into the southern hills. And, contrary to rumors spreading across the reservation that he had been killed, the chief was released unharmed.

On July 30, 1874, along the upper part of the French Creek near a glade that Custer had named Custer Park after himself, miners Horatio Ross and William McKay first found what they had been seeking: gold deposits (see illustration above). The troops had been

passing the time playing baseball or cards, writing letters, catching up on their sleep, or exploring the surroundings until the miners reported that panning for gold might net a prospector as much as $75 a day. French Creek was soon lined with anxious soldiers, 20 of whom later staked a claim as the Custer Park Mining Company.

Custer spent much of the time hunting and accumulating a menagerie of snakes, rabbits, and birds. He proudly reported to his wife Libbie that during the permanent camp on French Creek, the site of present-day Custer City, SD, he attained what he considered his greatest feat as a hunter: he had killed a grizzly bear (see illustration, page 21). It required an ambulance detail of 12 men under Fred Snow to adequately transport Custer's collection of flora, fauna, and fossils.

Scout "Lonesome Charley" REYNOLDS was entrusted with a message, dated August 2, 1874, with the first word about the discovery of gold. He traveled alone 100 miles in 4 nights to FORT LARAMIE through hostile country to deliver it. Custer had provided Reynolds with a canvas mail bag that had been inscribed: "Black Hills Express. Charley

Black Hills Expedition of 1874: Custer with the first grizzly he killed. From left: Bloody Knife; Custer; Pvt. Noonan; Capt. William Ludlow.

Reynolds, Manager. Connecting with All Points East, West, North, South. Cheap rates; Quick Transit; Safe Passage. We are protected by the Seventh Cavalry."

The expedition departed from the Black Hills on August 15. Ironically, Custer chose BEAR BUTTE, the birthplace of Sioux warrior CRAZY HORSE, as the location to halt the column and write his official report. The column arrived back at Fort Lincoln on August 30, 1874, after traveling 60 days and 883 miles, or 1,205 miles including those for reconnaissance.

Sources for further study include: Custer's Gold: The United States Cavalry Expedition of 1874, by Donald Jackson (New Haven, CT: Yale University Press,

1966); *Gold in the Black Hills,* by Watson Parker (Lincoln: University of Nebraska Press, 1982); for newspaper reports and official reports see *Prelude to Glory: A Newspaper Accounting of Custer's 1874 Expedition to the Black Hills,* edited by H. Krause and G. D. Olson (Sioux Falls: Brevet Press, 1974); for an officer's perspective see *With Custer in '74: James Calhoun's Diary of the Black Hills Expedition,* edited by Lawrence Frost (Provo, UT: Brigham Young University Press, 1979); for a trooper's perspective see *Private Theodore Ewert's Diary of the Black Hills Expedition of 1874,* edited by John M. Carroll and Lawrence Frost (Piscataway, NJ: CRI Books, 1976); "The Black Hills Expedition of 1874: A New Look," by Max E. Gerber, *South Dakota History* 8 (June–July 1970); *Black Hills/White Justice: The Sioux Nation versus the United States: 1775 to the Present,* by Edward Lazarus (New York: HarperCollins, 1991); "The Red Man and the Black Hills," by Charles F. Bates, *Outlook Magazine* 27 (July 1927); and *The Passing of the Great West: Selected Papers of George Bird Grinnell,* edited by John F. Reiger (New York: Winchester Press, 1972).

Black Kettle (Southern Cheyenne) (1803–November 27, 1868) This prominent chief was a well-known advocate of peace among his people. He signed the Treaty of Fort Wise (1861) pledging peace along the SANTA FE TRAIL, and the 1867 Treaty of MEDICINE LODGE. In spite of his peaceful intentions, he was the victim of 2 disastrous attacks by military forces—the SAND CREEK MASSACRE and the Battle of WASHITA—and the latter was where he was killed.

When the governor of Colorado invited all Indians in the area in the fall of 1864 to prove their friendliness by moving near the forts, Chief Black Kettle presented his tribe to FORT LYON. They were treated to supplies, and directed to spend a peaceful and safe winter at a place about 40 miles northeast called Sand Creek. At dawn on November 29 a

troop of Colorado militia under diabolic Methodist preacher Col. John Chivington attacked Black Kettle's unsuspecting village. Within an hour nearly 200 Cheyenne men, women, and children had been killed, many scalped and mutilated. Black Kettle barely escaped with his life.

It was almost 4 years to the day when Black Kettle's village on the Washita River was attacked by Custer's SEVENTH CAVALRY. Unknown to Custer, the chief had just returned from a meeting with Col. William B. HAZEN, who had the unenviable task of determining which Indian tribes were to be considered hostile or peaceful. Hazen was convinced that Black Kettle was peaceful, but told the chief to personally make peace with Gen. Phil SHERIDAN to ensure his safety. The general could not be located, so Black Kettle had returned home and was asleep in his lodge when the troopers stormed the village at dawn on November 28, 1868. This time Black Kettle was not so fortunate. He and his wife were shot and killed in the icy water of the Washita River as they attempted to escape on his pony.

The military defended its action by the fact that 2 white captives were present in the village, along with numerous items stolen from white settlements by Indian raiding parties. Others, including Indian agent Edward W. WYNKOOP who resigned his post in protest, condemned the destruction of Black Kettle's village.

Black Kettle probably was a peaceful Indian. However, he could not control the actions of the hot-tempered young warriors of his tribe, and eventually paid for that with his life.

Sources for further study include: The Fighting Cheyennes, by George Bird GRINNELL (Norman: University of Oklahoma Press, 1956); *The Southern Cheyennes,* by Donald J. Berthrong (Norman: University of Oklahoma Press, 1963).

Blackfeet Sioux Indians One of the SIOUX tribes camped in the village on the Little Bighorn River that participated in the Battle of the LITTLE BIGHORN. Their name was said to originate from wearing worn-out or fire-blackened moccasins. They are distinct from and should not be confused with their northern neighbor, the Blackfoot tribe. A prominent Blackfeet warrior who participated in the battle was Kill Eagle.

Blinn, Mrs. Clara Mrs. Blinn and her son, Willie, were captured and kept alive as slaves by CHEYENNE, KIOWA, and ARAPAHO Indians. They were taken on the Colorado plains while traveling by wagon train with her husband, Richard, to Franklin County, KA, in 1868. She smuggled a message out of an Indian camp addressed to "Kind Friend," which reads in part: "We were taken on the 9th of Oct. on the Arkansas below FORT LYON. I can't tell whether they killed my husband or not—My name is Mrs. Clara Blinn my little boy Willie Blinn, he is two years old." (This letter is on display at the National Frontier Trails Center, Independence, MO.) Both Clara Blinn and her son were killed by Kiowa Indians under SATANTA in a village downstream from BLACK KETTLE's village during the Battle of WASHITA (November 27, 1868). Custer agonized over his failure to save Blinn and her child. However, their deaths were significant in teaching Custer a lesson that he applied in the successful rescue of 2 white women the following year at Sweetwater Creek, TX, during the WASHITA CAMPAIGN OF 1868–69.

Bloody Knife (Arikara-Sioux) (ca. 1840–June 25, 1876) Custer's chief (and favorite) Indian scout. His mother was an ARIKARA (REE) and his father SIOUX. He lived his first 15–16 years with the Sioux, and was discriminated against because of his mixed blood. This caused him to develop a deep hatred for that tribe. He enlisted in the U.S. Army on May 1, 1868, with the rank of lance corporal, and soon acquired a serious drinking habit. During the BLACK HILLS EXPEDITION OF 1874, when most other Ree and Santee scouts refused to enter the hills for fear of Sioux retaliation, Bloody Knife decided to remain with Custer. At the Battle of the LITTLE BIGHORN, after a scout to the lookout area known as CROW'S NEST, he warned Custer that there were too many Indians to fight: a warning Custer brushed aside. Bloody Knife was killed that day in RENO'S VALLEY FIGHT. His death was significant in that he was shot in the head, his blood and brains splattering onto the face of Maj. Marcus RENO. This caused Reno to lose his nerve and panic, which began a series of actions that ended in disaster. In April 1879 a woman named She Owl appeared at FORT BERTHOLD claiming to have been married to Bloody Knife for 10 years, and wanted to collect the pay due to him. The army believed her story and paid her almost $100. *Sources for further study include: Bloody Knife!*, by Ben Innis (Fort Collins, CO: Old Army, 1973).

Bouyer, Minton "Mitch" (1837–June 25, 1876) Guide and interpreter. Bouyer was born to a French trader and SIOUX Indian mother, thus allowing him access to both cultures. He explored much of the West under Jim Bridger's tutelage, and was adopted in 1870 into the CROW Indian tribe. He was assigned from Col. John GIBBON's Montana Column to Custer's command 3 days prior to the Battle of the LITTLE BIGHORN because he knew the Rosebud and Little Bighorn valleys better than the ARIKARA scouts. It was Bouyer who first warned Custer that they would find more Indians than they could handle. Custer reputedly replied that Bouyer could stay behind if he was afraid. Bouyer stated that he would go wherever Custer went, and thus became the only army scout to perish with Custer's detachment. In 1987 it was announced that bone fragments discovered on the battlefield had been identified as belonging to Bouyer. A burial ceremony at LITTLE BIGHORN BATTLEFIELD NATIONAL MONUMENT Cemetery was held on July 25 of that year. *Sources for further study include: Custer's Last Campaign: Mitch Bouyer and the Little Bighorn Reconstructed*, by John S. Gray (Lincoln: University of Nebraska Press, 1991).

Bozeman Trail This shortcut to the Montana gold fields passed through traditional Sioux buffalo hunting ground which prompted the Indians to attack the intruders. The War Department was determined to protect the trail's travelers, and to that end dispatched army troops and began to build forts: Reno, C. F. Smith, and PHIL KEARNY. Persistent attacks and harassment by Sioux warrior RED CLOUD caused the trail and forts to be abandoned in accordance with the FORT LARAMIE TREATY OF 1868. Notable skirmishes along the trail were the FETTERMAN MASSACRE, the HAYFIELD FIGHT, and the WAGON BOX FIGHT. *Sources for further study include: The Bozeman Trail: Historical Accounts of the Blazing of the Overland Route into the Northwest and the Fights with Red Cloud's Warriors*, by E. A. Brininstool and G. R. Hebard, 2 vols. (Cleveland: Arthur H. Clark, 1922).

Bradley, James H. First lieutenant, U.S. 7th Infantry. As chief of scouts, Bradley had the dubious distinction while scouting ahead of the Terry-Gibbon Column of discovering the bodies of Custer's command at LITTLE BIGHORN 2 days after the battle. He was later killed in action against the NEZ PERCÉ at the Battle of the Big Hole, MT, on August 9, 1877. His daily diary is reprinted in *The March of the Montana Column: A Prelude to the Custer Disaster*, edited by Edgar I. Stewart (Norman: University of Oklahoma Press, 1961).

Brevet Rank Brevets were promotions that advanced an officer to an honorary rank as an award for achievement on the field of battle. Custer was usually addressed as "General" in respect of the brevet rank of major general that he earned in the Civil War, although his actual regular army rank following the war was lieutenant colonel.

Brisbin, James S. Major, 2nd Cavalry. Brisbin's unit was part of Col. John GIBBON's Montana Column during the LITTLE BIGHORN CAMPAIGN. Brisbin was known as "Grasshopper Jim" by the troops for his frequent analysis and pamphlets exhorting the future of Montana agriculture. Just prior to Custer's march for the Little Bighorn, Brisbin argued with Gen. Alfred TERRY that Custer was undermanned, and requested that his troops with GATLING GUNS—with Terry in command because Brisbin did not want to serve under Custer—be permitted to accompany the SEVENTH CAVALRY column. Custer refused the assistance, and Terry abided by that. Brisbin was also present at a meeting the day before Custer marched in which Terry offered instructions for the route and timing of the attack. Brisbin later claimed Custer disobeyed those orders. (See DISOBEDIENCE OF ORDERS BY CUSTER.) Brisbin was said to have been the ghostwriter of a first-person account under 1st Lt. Charles DeRUDIO's name in the *New York Herald* that dealt with DeRudio's actions during RENO'S VALLEY FIGHT. DeRudio claimed the piece was "colored" a good deal. Shortly before his death in 1892, Brisbin wrote a letter to Gen. E. S. GODFREY that was critical of an article Godfrey had written in *Century* magazine, entitled "Custer's Last Battle." Brisbin believed that the article, which was popular with the public, was too pro–Custer. The letter was printed as a chapter in *Troopers with Custer: Historic Incidents of the Battle of the Little Big Horn*, by E. A. Brininstool (Harrisburg, PA: Stackpole, 1952).

Brown, Eliza The Custers' cook 1863–69. This runaway slave was 17 years old when she "jined up with the Ginnel" during the Civil War, shortly before his marriage to Libbie. She was captured by the Confederate Army in June 1864, but escaped and made it back to friendly lines after dark the same day. During the June 1867 flood at FORT HAYS, Libbie and Eliza rescued more than one person from the powerful waters of the rising creek with a clothesline. Eliza served the Custers until, according to Libbie, she "got on a spree and was insolent," and was replaced by Mary ADAMS. She married, and renewed her friendship with Libbie after the LITTLE BIGHORN battle. *Sources for further study include:* "Custer's Cooks and Maids," by John Manion, in *Custer and His Times, 2* edited by John M. Carroll (Fort Worth, TX: Little Bighorn Associates, 1984).

Brulé Indians One of the SIOUX tribes camped along the Little Bighorn River that participated in the Battle of the LITTLE BIGHORN. Their name, Cu Brulé, meaning burnt buttocks, is derived from a prairie fire around 1763 when several tribe members were burned to death. The most prominent members of the tribe that participated in the battle were Crazy Bull and Crow Dog.

Buffalo Bill Cody *see* CODY, WILLIAM F.

Buffalo Hunting The most popular sport in the United States during Custer's time on the Plains. Custer participated in countless hunts, perhaps the most famous as escort and guide to ALEXIS, GRAND DUKE of Russia in 1872. The railroad made buffalo readily accessible to hunters who came in droves to accommodate the growing market for hides. By 1888 a herd of over 50 million had been culled to less than 1,000 on the hoof. Texas cattleman Charley Goodnight was instrumental in attempting to preserve the species.

Buffalo Soldiers Respectful term given to black soldiers by Plains Indians due to the resemblance between the black man's hair and the coat of a buffalo, which to them was a sacred animal. See also BLACK ARMY REGIMENTS; BEECHER'S ISLAND, BATTLE OF.

Burial of Custer and His Troops *see* INTERMENT

Burkman, John (1839–November 6, 1925) The Custers' loyal orderly, or striker, for 9 years. "Old Neutriment," a nickname bestowed upon him for his enjoyment of food, shared Custer's love for dogs and horses. Burkman had been detailed with the packtrain at the Battle of the LITTLE BIGHORN, and agonized the remainder of his life that he had not been with Custer. He was discharged from the army on May 17, 1879, and moved to Billings, MT, to remain close to the place where Custer had perished. In his old age he had related his memories of the Custers and frontier life, which led to a biography, *Old Neutriment* by Glendolin Damon Wagner (Lincoln: University of Nebraska Press, 1989). He finally committed suicide at his boarding house: a gun in one hand, a bag of candy in the other.

Butler, James Sergeant, L Troop, 7th Cavalry. Butler had served in the British Army, fought for the Union in the Civil War, and had been with the SEVENTH CAVALRY since its activation on July 28, 1866. He was killed at the Battle of the LITTLE BIGHORN. His body was found on the battlefield, surrounded by a large number of cartridge casings, in a position farthest away from Custer and closest to the RENO-BENTEEN DEFENSE SITE. This has brought about speculation that he carried a message from Custer to Maj. Marcus RENO or Capt. F. W. BENTEEN that was never delivered. It is believed that a skeleton surrounded by 19 shells discovered in 1928 on the battlefield by a CROW Indian could be the remains of Butler. These remains were later buried in the LITTLE BIGHORN NATIONAL MONUMENT Cemetery. Butler has been the subject of a painting, *Custer's Last Hope* by J. K. Ralston, and a novelette by

Usher L. Burdick, *Tragedy in the Great Sioux Camp* (1936).

C Company, Seventh Cavalry
This company was commanded during the Battle of the LITTLE BIGHORN by Capt. Thomas W. CUSTER with 2nd Lt. Henry M. HARRINGTON second in command. The company's other officer, 1st Lt. James CALHOUN, was on temporary duty as commander of L Company. Company C was part of Custer's detachment. It has been theorized that Capt. Custer was detailed as aide-de-camp to his brother, which left 2nd Lt. Harrington in charge. Everyone in Company C was killed, the bodies found in various locations along BATTLE RIDGE. Tom Custer's body was located near his brother on CUSTER HILL; Harrington's body was never found. Sgt. Daniel KANIPE had been sent with Custer's first message to hurry the packtrain, and survived the battle on the RENO-BENTEEN DEFENSE SITE.

Calhoun, Frederic S. (April 19, 1847–March 20, 1904) Lieutenant, 2nd Infantry. The brother of 1st Lt. James CALHOUN. Fred accompanied the YELLOWSTONE EXPEDITION OF 1873 as an employee of Custer's former West Point roommate Tom Rosser, who was chief surveyor for the NORTHERN PACIFIC RAILROAD. He spent the winter of 1873–74 at his brother's residence at FORT ABRAHAM LINCOLN. Custer thought enough of Fred to encourage him to seek an army commission, and endorsed the application: a vacancy in the SEVENTH CAVALRY was available. Calhoun accompanied the BLACK HILLS EXPEDITION OF 1874 as a civilian employee while he awaited word on his appointment. When the commission to second lieutenant arrived on March 10, 1875, it was not for the 7th Cavalry but for the infantry. Fred subsequently served in Utah, then in the fall of 1876 began campaigning with Gen. George CROOK during the GREAT SIOUX WAR OF 1876–77.

He was post adjutant at CAMP ROBINSON when on May 6, 1877, CRAZY HORSE surrendered. The Indian warrior was subsequently murdered by a member of Calhoun's F Company. After serving in a variety of posts around the West and Northwest, Calhoun was promoted to first lieutenant in February 1887. He became ill in 1888 with a disorder of the nervous system, and was medically retired in 1890.

Calhoun, James (August 24, 1845–June 25, 1876) First lieutenant, 7th Cavalry. Brother of Frederic S. CALHOUN; husband of Margaret "Maggie" Custer CALHOUN, Custer's sister. An Ohio native, "Jimmi" or "Jimmy" Calhoun served as an enlisted man with the 23rd U.S. Infantry from 1865 to 1867. He was commissioned second lieutenant in the 32nd Infantry on July 31, 1867, and soon transferred to the 21st Infantry. He met Custer's sister, Margaret, at FORT LEAVENWORTH in 1870, and the two became romantically involved. Custer must have taken to Calhoun as well: Calhoun along with 1st Lt. W. W. COOKE witnessed Custer's last will and testament in April 1870. Custer arranged to have Calhoun assigned to the SEVENTH CAVALRY in January 1871, as first lieutenant and commander of L Company. In a letter to Custer dated April 23, 1871, Calhoun expressed his appreciation: "I have just received my commission as 1st Lt. in the 7th Cavalry, and it reminds me more vividly than ever how many, many times I am under obligations to you for your very great kindness to me in my troubles. I shall do my best to prove my gratitude. If the time comes you will not find me wanting." Calhoun became Custer's brother-in-law on March 7, 1872, when he and Maggie were married in the Methodist Church in Monroe, MI. He was nicknamed "Adonis" due to his blond hair, good looks, and 6'1" height, and was relentlessly teased because of his seriousness. He ably served as Custer's regimental adjutant during both the YELLOWSTONE

EXPEDITION OF 1873 and the BLACK HILLS EXPEDITION OF 1874. His penchant for gambling (and losing) at cards caused great concern among family members. His brother Fred, as well as the Custers, tried to reason with him, explaining that he simply was not a good enough card player to compete with any success. It did little good. When Calhoun approached brother-in-law Tom CUSTER about a loan, he was told: "Relationships don't count in poker. Bunkey or no bunkey, keep your hand out of my haversack." The night before the 7th Cavalry marched for the valley of the LITTLE BIGHORN, June 21, 1876, Calhoun stayed up all night playing cards on board the docked steamer FAR WEST with Maj. RENO, Capt. KEOGH, Tom Custer, boat captain Grant MARSH, and a couple of infantry officers. At the Battle of the LITTLE BIGHORN Calhoun's L Company was deployed at the south end of BATTLE RIDGE—perhaps as the rear guard—while Custer and the others continued on north. Calhoun and his men perished on that hill above Deep Coulee, now known as CALHOUN HILL, when the forces of CRAZY HORSE from the north and GALL from the west combined to crush L Company between them. Calhoun's remains were removed from the battlefield and reinterred on August 3, 1877, at Fort Leavenworth, KA. His diary, kept during the BLACK HILLS EXPEDITION OF 1874, was published in book form, entitled *With Custer in '74: James Calhoun's Diary of the Black Hills Expedition*, edited by Lawrence Frost (Provo, UT: Brigham Young University Press, 1979). Frederick Whittaker in his imaginative 1876 biography, *A Complete Life of Gen. George Armstrong Custer* (New York: Sheldon, 1876), included a romantic version of the death of Calhoun.

Calhoun, Margaret Emma (January 5, 1852–March 22, 1910) Custer's younger sister from his father Emanuel's second marriage to Maria Ward Kirkpatrick CUSTER; wife of James CAL-

HOUN. Due to family finances at the time, Custer arranged to pay for Maggie's schooling at Boyd's Seminary (Libbie Custer's alma mater) in the late 1860s, where she became an accomplished pianist. Maggie often visited the Custers at their frontier posts. She met infantry 1st Lt. James Calhoun at FORT LEAVENWORTH in 1870, and the two became romantically attached. For this reason, Custer arranged to have Calhoun assigned to the SEVENTH CAVALRY in January 1871. Calhoun and Maggie were married at the Methodist Church in Monroe, MI, on March 7, 1872. She traveled to her husband's duty stations whenever possible, and along with sister-in-law Libbie, was at the center of Custer's "royal family." Maggie and Libbie Custer rode with the regiment as far as the Heart River when it left for the Little Bighorn. The two women returned to FORT ABRAHAM LINCOLN later that day with the paymaster. At the Battle of the LITTLE BIGHORN she lost not only her husband but 3 brothers and 1 nephew. When the officers detailed to inform the wives of the tragedy were departing after their task, Maggie ran after them and asked, "Is there no message for me?" There had been no message. Later, Capt. Hughes, from Gen. Alfred TERRY's staff, presented Maggie with some cartridges fired from her husband's revolver. Maggie, Libbie Custer, and Annie YATES departed from Fort Lincoln on July 30 on a special train provided by the NORTHERN PACIFIC RAILROAD. The memorial service for the fallen local cavalrymen held in Monroe on August 13 was conducted by Rev. James Venning, the same minister who had married Maggie and Jimmy. She was present when her husband's remains were reinterred at Fort Leavenworth, KA, on August 3, 1877. In 1880 she served as Michigan state librarian, and in 1887 toured the country as an actress and received favorable reviews. In 1903 she married John Halbert Maugham at Onteora Park, NY, in the Catskill Mountains. She and Libbie remained close friends until Maggie's death.

Calhoun Hill This hill above Deep Coulee on LITTLE BIGHORN BATTLE-FIELD was the southern end of the half-mile long BATTLE RIDGE that stretched to CUSTER HILL on the north. The L Company of 1st Lt. James CALHOUN fell here.

California Joe *see* MILNER, MOSES

Camp Robinson, NE This camp, located at the junction of White River and Soldier Creek near the Red Cloud Indian Agency, was established March 8, 1874, by Gen. Phil SHERIDAN to monitor the BLACK HILLS region. It was the scene of much military activity, due to its proximity to both the Red Cloud and Pine Ridge Indian agencies. Camp Robinson was the place where CRAZY HORSE was killed in 1877. It was abandoned in the late 1940s after having served as K-9 dog training center and a quartermaster's depot during World War II.

Camp Supply, I.T. Camp Supply, located where Wolf and Beaver creeks join to form the North Canadian River, was established November 18, 1868, as a supply depot for Gen. Phil SHERIDAN's winter WASHITA CAMPAIGN OF 1868–69. It was from here that Custer marched to attack BLACK KETTLE's village at the Battle of WASHITA. It was designated a fort in 1878 and abandoned in 1894.

Central Park Zoo This zoo located in New York City was the recipient of wildlife captured by Custer on his various expeditions to the South and Western United States. The donations included a badger, a bear, a jackrabbit, two marsh harks, a porcupine, and a number of rattlesnakes.

Cheyenne Indians The Cheyenne Indians split into two distinct bands about 1832 when one segment of the tribe

established residence along the Arkansas River and became known as the southern Cheyenne. The northern band settled around the North Platte River and became very much like their Plains neighbors and allies, the SIOUX. The tribe had 7 military societies, the Dog Soldiers becoming the most aggressive and feared. The Cheyenne constantly waged war on traditional Indian enemies as well as whites. However, their attacks on whites became more intense following the SAND CREEK MASSACRE in 1864. At that time, they aligned themselves with the Sioux leader RED CLOUD, and fought the U.S. Army in the conflict over the BOZEMAN TRAIL that led to the FORT LARAMIE TREATY OF 1868. During the HANCOCK EXPEDITION OF 1867, Custer and the SEVENTH CAVALRY pursued the CHEY-ENNE and their Sioux allies led by PAWNEE KILLER throughout western Kansas and into Colorado and Nebraska without much success. The Indians fought in retaliation for Gen. W. S. HANCOCK's senseless burning of their village on Pawnee Fork. The MEDICINE LODGE treaties in 1867 promised peace, and designated a shared reservation for the Cheyenne and ARAPAHOS. However, the peace did not last long. In September of that year Cheyenne warriors under ROMAN NOSE (who was killed) were involved in the Battle of BEECHER ISLAND. The following year Gen. Phil SHERIDAN launched the WASHITA CAMPAIGN OF 1868–69. On November 27, 1868, Custer and the 7th Cavalry attacked Chief BLACK KETTLE's village on the WA-SHITA River and killed nearly 100 Cheyenne, including Black Kettle, who had been known as an advocate of peace. Custer took women and children prisoner, one of them—a teenager named MONAHSETAH—was said in Cheyenne Indian oral tradition to have later borne Custer's child. The Cheyenne were defeated at the Battle of SUMMIT SPRINGS in March 1869, and many submitted to the reservation agreement. The next major conflict was the Sioux and Cheyenne victories in the GREAT SIOUX WAR OF 1876–77, which included the Battle of the LITTLE BIGHORN. However, after the DULL KNIFE FIGHT in November 1876 when Col. Ranald MACKENSIE and 1,000 troopers attacked 200 lodges, chiefs DULL KNIFE and LITTLE WOLF led their people to the reservation. The reservation in Indian Territory on the southern Plains was not to their liking; they had expected to share the Sioux Reservation near the BLACK HILLS. Some members of the tribe led by Dull Knife and Little Wolf decided to head north to their Old Tongue River stomping grounds. The army objected and pursued; few were successful in reaching Red Cloud Agency at Pine Ridge. Finally, the northern Cheyenne were granted their wish for a Tongue River Agency. However, by that time there were too few of them remaining to appreciate the gesture. See also TALL BULL; TWO MOON; WOODEN LEG. *Sources for further study include: The Southern Cheyennes*, by Donald J. Berthrong (Norman: University of Oklahoma Press, 1963); *The Northern Cheyennes*, by Verne Dusenberry (Helena, MT: 1955); *Cheyenne Memories*, by John Stands-in-Timber and Margot Liberty (New Haven, CT: Yale University Press, 1967); *The Fighting Cheyennes*, by George Bird GRINNELL (Norman: University of Oklahoma Press, 1956); and *Cheyenne Autumn*, by Mari Sandoz (New York: McGraw Hill, 1953).

Cody, William Frederick "BUFFALO BILL" (1846–1917) Prospector; pony express rider; Civil War soldier; buffalo hunter; army scout; and showman. Cody began his scouting career as chief of scouts for Gen. Phil SHERIDAN during the WASHITA CAMPAIGN OF 1868, and was later involved in the Battle of SUMMIT SPRINGS. His most famous (infamous) performance for the army, however, came just a few weeks after the Battle of the LITTLE BIGHORN. On July 17, 1876, Col. Wesley Merritt's 400-man 5th Cavalry with scout Cody ambushed

a force of perhaps 30 Cheyenne Indians—out of an estimated 800 that had left Red Cloud Agency—at Warbonnet, or Hat, Creek. The Battle of WARBONNET CREEK has become notable became it consisted merely of a duel between Buffalo Bill and a Cheyenne subchief named *Hay-o-wai* or Yellow Hair. Actually, it was not a duel as we know it. Cody shot the pony out from beneath Yellow Hair, rode the Indian down, then killed and scalped him. He then held up the bloody scalp for all to see, and announced that this was the "first scalp for Custer." The "duel" involving Custer's name became a popular part of his Wild West Show and a play, *The Red Right Hand, or Buffalo Bill's First Scalp for Custer*. SITTING BULL and other former Indian foes became a popular feature of Cody's shows. Cody attempted to meet with Sitting Bull in December 1890 to convince the Sioux chief to help calm the uprising caused by the Ghost Dance. He was not allowed access to Sitting Bull, and the chief was killed a few days later in a prelude to the Battle of WOUNDED KNEE. Of the myriad dime novels written about Cody in the late nineteenth century, one of the more absurd was *Buffalo Bill with General Custer*, by Prentiss Ingraham, in which the scout was depicted as the lone survivor of the Battle of the LITTLE BIGHORN. Bill, of course, was not even present at that battle. *Sources for further study include: Buckskins, Bullets, and Business: A History of Buffalo Bill's Wild West*, by Sarah J. Blackstone (Westport, CT: Greenwood, 1986); and *First Scalp for Custer: The Skirmish at Warbonnet Creek, Nebraska, July 17, 1876*, by Paul L. Hedren (Lincoln: University of Nebraska Press, Bison Book, 1987).

Comanche (Myles KEOGH's horse) This bay gelding was said to be the only living thing found on the field following the Battle of the LITTLE BIGHORN. Comanche came to the SEVENTH CAVALRY as part of a herd of mustangs purchased by 1st Lt. Tom CUSTER for the

Comanche, held by Pvt. Gustave Korn, 1878

army on April 3, 1868, from a trader at St. Louis and shipped to FORT LEAVENWORTH, KA, for processing. At that time, he was 5 years old, stood 15 hands high, weighed 925 pounds, and was described as 75 percent American and 25 percent Spanish. Although officers normally selected their horses from private stock, Capt. Myles KEOGH, in need of a second mount, purchased the animal from the government for $90. Comanche received his name after being struck in the right flank by a Comanche arrow near the Cimarron River in southwest Kansas on September 13, 1868, and was said to have squawked like a Comanche Indian. He was wounded again by a Comanche arrow in June 1870, and received an injury to his right shoulder in January 1871, in Kentucky. At the Battle of the Little Bighorn, Keogh was eventually shot off Comanche's back. The bullet passed through the forequarters of the horse, and upon emerging shattered the captain's

left leg. Comanche was found two days after the battle by 1st Lt. Henry NOWLAN, a friend of Capt. Keogh. The horse had been wounded 7 times and was in extremely poor condition. Nevertheless, the decision was made to try and save him. He was led 15 miles to the steamer, FAR WEST, where a stall was provided between the rudders. When the Far West reached FORT ABRAHAM LINCOLN, Comanche could not walk and had to be transported to the stables by wagon and once there supported with a sling. He was left in the care of Pvt. Gustave Korn, a blacksmith, who diligently nursed him back to health (see photo above). Col. S. D. STURGIS, commanding officer of Fort Lincoln, issued General Order no. 7 on April 10, 1878, which read:

1. The horse known as "Comanche" being the only living representative of the bloody tragedy of the Little Big Horn, Montana, June 25, 1876, his

kind treatment and comfort should be a matter of special pride and solicitude on the part of the 7th Cavalry, to the end that his life may be prolonged to the utmost limit. Though wounded and scarred, his very silence speaks in terms more eloquent than words of the desperate struggle against overwhelming odds, of the hopeless conflict, and heroic manner in which all went down that day.

2. The commanding officer of "I" troops will see that a special and comfortable stall is fitted up for Comanche. He will not be ridden by any person whatever under any circumstances, nor will he be put to any kind of work.

3. Hereafter upon all occasions of ceremony (of mounted regimental formation), Comanche, saddled, bridled, and led by a mounted trooper of Troop I, will be paraded with the regiment.

Thereafter, Comanche, draped in mourning, would lead Capt. Keogh's old troop during ceremonial occasions. Otherwise, he lived a life of privilege as the "2nd commanding officer" of the 7th Cavalry. His favorite pastimes were rooting through garbage pails and begging for buckets of beer at the enlisted men's canteen. The later habit had probably formed during the year of convalescence when he had been given a whiskey bran mash every other day. Comanche followed Gustave Korn around like a puppy, one time trailing the blacksmith into Junction City to the home of Korn's lady friend. The animal caused such a jealous ruckus on her front lawn that Korn was obliged to come outside and lead him back to his stall. Comanche lived contentedly until Pvt. Korn was killed at the Battle of WOUNDED KNEE. At that point he lost interest in everything except swilling beer, and his health began to fail. In spite of every medical effort to save him, on November 6, 1891, Comanche died at the age of 28. The officers of the 7th Cavalry responded positively to an offer from Professor L. L. Dyche, a naturalist at the University of Kansas, and decided to have Comanche mounted. Dyche agreed to do the work free of charge if the finished product would be donated to the University Museum at Lawrence. Comanche was exhibited at the World's Fair in Chicago in 1893, then went to stand in the museum—presently protected in a humidity-controlled glass case because souvenir hunters were constantly plucking hair from him. *Sources for further study include: Keogh, Comanche and Custer*, by Edward S. Luce (Ashland, OR: Lewis Osborne, 1974); *Comanche (The Horse That Survived the Custer Massacre)*, by Anthony A. Amaral (Los Angeles: Westernlore, 1961); *Comanche of the Seventh*, by Margaret Leighton (New York: Berkley, 1959); and *His Very Silence Speaks: Comanche—The Horse Who Survived Custer's Last Stand*, by Elizabeth Atwood Lawrence (Detroit: Wayne State University Press, 1989).

Comanche Indians This nomadic tribe, which was closely related to the Shoshoni Indians, lived on the southern Plains where they followed the great herds of buffalo. They were a warring people, fighting Indian enemies and the U.S. Army for many years before Custer moved west. They agreed to suspend hostilities by signing the MEDICINE LODGE treaties of 1867, which provided them a shared reservation with the KIOWA and KIOWA-APACHES, as well as provision and educational resources. In return the Comanches promised to cease their attacks on white travelers and settlements. Many of the tribe submitted to the reservation agreement. However, a number continued to participate in raiding parties with their allies the CHEYENNE, Kiowa, and ARAPAHO. Custer first encountered them during the HANCOCK EXPEDITION OF 1867, and the SEVENTH CAVALRY fought regular skirmishes with them in southwest Kansas. Comanches were camped downstream from BLACK KETTLE's village on the WASHITA River when Custer and the SEVENTH CAVALRY attacked. This decisive action by the army convinced many more Comanches to settle on the reservation. The hostile element remained aligned with Kiowa chief SATANTA, and concentrated its efforts farther south into Texas. This brought about an eventual showdown with the army under Col. Ranald MACKENSIE in what was known as the Red River War of 1874–75, and an end to Comanche freedom on the Plains.

Cooke, William Winer (aka "Cook" due to an administrative error when he joined the 7th Cavalry; May 29, 1846–June 25, 1876) "The Queen's Own" first lieutenant, 7th Cavalry.

This Canadian soldier of fortune was commissioned second lieutenant in the 24th New York Cavalry during the Civil War on January 26, 1864, and was promoted to first lieutenant on December 14. Cooke fought in several battles, including the Wilderness, Cold Harbor, Dinwiddie Court House, Sayler's Creek, and was wounded at Petersburg. He earned brevets to lieutenant colonel for gallant and meritorious service.

1st Lt. William W. Cooke, 1875

Cooke was appointed a second lieutenant in the SEVENTH CAVALRY on July 28, 1866, and made first lieutenant the following year (see photo). He served as regimental adjutant from December 1866 to February 1867 and again from January 1871 until his death at the Battle of the LITTLE BIGHORN. His appearance was quite distinctive inasmuch as he wore "dundrearies": long sidewhiskers extending to a sculpted point at his chest. The style of facial hair was named after Lord Dundreary, a character in the play *Our American Cousin* (which was playing at Ford's Theater the night President Lincoln attended and was assassinated). Cooke had the reputation as one of the best shots and fastest runners in the regiment.

Cooke was involved in several notable incidents during the HANCOCK EXPEDITION OF 1867. He was placed in charge of a 48-man detail to escort a wagon train in late June that had been ordered by Custer to FORT WALLACE for supplies. The squadron arrived at Fort Wallace without any problem. However, halfway back on their return trip to Custer's camp on the Republican River the wagon train, loaded with supplies, came under attack from about 600 to 700 hostile SIOUX Indians. A running battle ensued for several hours, with the soldiers keeping the Indians at bay. Finally, just as ammunition became critically low, the Indians mysteriously broke contact and disappeared. It was not long before Capt. Robert WEST arrived with a detachment of soldiers that had been detailed to relieve the escort. The cavalry had arrived in the nick of time to save Cooke and the beleaguered wagon train.

It was on July 7 that Cooke was involved in an incident that led to charges at Custer's court-martial. The column had halted at about noon to rest the horses when 13 troopers, 7 on horseback, deserted in plain view of the command. Custer noted: "I directed Major ELLIOTT and lts. [Tom] CUSTER, Cook[e] and Jackson, with a few of the guard, to pursue the deserters who were still visible, tho more than a mile distant, and to bring the dead bodies of as many as could be taken back to camp. Seven of the deserters, being mounted on our best horses, and having two miles' start, made their escape." Three deserters were wounded; one later died. No military charges were placed against Cooke or the other shooters since they were simply obeying Custer's orders. However, on January 3, 1868, Capt. West preferred civil murder charges against Cooke and Custer. On January 18 the judge cited lack of evidence and dismissed the case.

Another charge against Custer at his court-martial was that he ordered without proper authority a forced march on personal business of over 150 miles in 55 hours, taking along lts. Cooke and Tom Custer. Cooke became an unwilling witness at the official proceedings. (See CUSTER, GEORGE ARMSTRONG, for more detail.)

The 7th Cavalry attacked the village of CHEYENNE chief BLACK KETTLE on the Washita River on November 27, 1868, in what became known as the Battle of WASHITA. One report has Cooke disappearing from the battle site until the fighting was over, but the charge has never been substantiated and would have been highly out of character if true.

Cooke's bravery was demonstrated on March 15, 1869, at Sweetwater Creek, TX, when he and Custer put their lives on the line by brazenly entering a Cheyenne village alone and unannounced in order to parley. The KANSAS VOLUNTEER CAVALRY believed that those Indians held 2 white women who had been taken hostage in Kansas. In the chief's lodge they were introduced to ceremonies meant to intimidate them, with warnings that acts of treachery would result in Custer's entire command being killed. They managed to leave the village unharmed with confirmation of the presence of the captives; Custer later gained their release. (See WASHITA CAMPAIGN OF 1868–69.)

Cooke as adjutant delivered Custer's order to Maj. Marcus RENO that com-

menced the Battle of the LITTLE BIGHORN. Believing that the allied Indians were running away, Custer told Cooke to order Reno to move toward the village "and charge afterward, and you will be supported by the whole outfit." Cooke then returned to Custer across the Little Bighorn River. Reno failed to carry out those orders to the letter. (See RENO'S VALLEY FIGHT.)

Cooke is most notable for his scribbled message of Custer's last known order. The orderly assigned to take the order to Capt. F. W. BENTEEN was Pvt. John MARTIN (Giovanni Martini), a recent immigrant. Cooke wanted to make certain the order was understood so he wrote it on a piece of notepaper. "Benteen. Come on. Big village. Be Quick. Bring Packs. W. W. Cooke. P. bring pacs." The misspelled postscript demonstrates with what haste Cooke wrote. (See also BATES, COL. CHARLES.)

Cooke died alongside Custer and 40 others on CUSTER HILL. A Cheyenne Indian named WOODEN LEG claimed to have scalped one side of Cooke's face and tied the hair to an arrow shaft. He presented the unusual scalp to his grandmother, which was the custom, and she at first was frightened of it but later accepted the honored gift. However, at a dance two nights later she discarded the strange scalp.

Cooke's body was removed from the battlefield and reinterred in 1877 in Hamilton, Ontario.

Crazy Horse (OGLALA-BRULÉ SIOUX) (ca. 1842–September 5, 1877) Warrior Crazy Horse was one of the most revered figures in SIOUX Indian history. He participated in RED CLOUD's war over the BOZEMAN TRAIL; harassed Custer on the YELLOWSTONE EXPEDITION OF 1873; and was a major force in the GREAT SIOUX WAR OF 1876–77.

Early Years

Crazy Horse was born near BEAR BUTTE on the eastern edge of *Pa Sapa*, the

BLACK HILLS. He was named "Curly" due to his light, curly hair, which complemented his light complexion. His father was the Oglala Sioux Crazy Horse and his mother a Brulé Sioux—the sister of SPOTTED TAIL. His mother died when Curly was young, and his father then took her sister as his wife. Curly was patiently taught the skills to become a hunter and warrior, had a pony of his own, and had killed a buffalo by the time he was 11 years old.

At age 12 he was accompanying the men on raiding parties of emigrant trains around FORT LARAMIE. The Sioux believed they had little to fear due to the small garrison of soldiers at the fort. One soldier, however, a recent West Point graduate named Lt. John L. Gratten, apparently disregarded any presumed threat. On August 17, 1854, a cow from a Mormon wagon train was shot by a MINNICONJOU SIOUX named High Forehead, who had been staying at the Sioux camp east of Fort Laramie. Gratten decided to arrest High Forehead, and set out for the Indian camp with 29 troopers, an interpreter, a mountain howitzer, and a 12 pound fieldpiece. Negotiations for High Forehead's arrest quickly broke down, and artillery rained on the camp. The Indians attacked, killing every trooper except one. Gratten was found with 24 arrows in his body and a crushed face and skull. Curly had witnessed the incident, and it made an indelible impression on him regarding his future relations with the white man.

Soon after the Gratten fight Curly sought guidance by meditating on a mountaintop. He experienced a vision of a warrior who became invulnerable by following such rituals as painting his body with white hail spots and a lightning bolt. Curly from then on adopted the habit of painting white hail spots on his body and a streak of lightning down one cheek. He also tied a brown pebble behind each ear, tossed a handful of dust across his pony, and rode naked except for moccasins and a breechcloth.

The following year Curly killed his first human. A band of young Sioux warriors were out attempting to steal Pawnee horses when they happened upon some Omaha Indians who were hunting buffalo. The Sioux took several Omaha mounts, which caused the buffalo hunters to give chase. A fight ensued, and Curly spotted an Omaha in the bushes. He boldly charged to close with his enemy, and killed a woman. Although it was not shameful in Sioux culture to kill a woman, he was too upset to take her scalp and left it for someone else.

Late that year he returned to his Ash Hollow village from hunting and was shocked to find the entire village burned to the ground. Gen. W. S. Harney's army troops had been out punishing the Indians who were raiding along the Oregon Trail, and had attacked the village and killed 86 Sioux. Curly witnessed the destruction of another village in July 1857, this one occupied by CHEYENNE allies. These acts against his people made him realize that peace with the white man would be all but impossible.

Crazy Horse

In 1858—the year he became 16—Curly and some other young warriors planned a raid on an ARAPAHO village. They were discovered, and consequently attacked by the Arapahos. Curly charged the enemy many times, scoring coup after coup and taking many scalps, but received an arrow in the leg. His friend Hump removed the arrow and dressed the wound. Curly wondered why he had been wounded when in his vision he had been promised protection. Then he realized why—the warrior in his vision had taken no scalps. Thus, he would never again take a scalp. His accomplishments against the Arapaho were cause for celebration. Curly's father sang a song he had composed for his son, one that announced the boy's new name: Crazy Horse.

The years when the white man fought his Civil War was time Crazy Horse spent building his reputation among his people as a fearless warrior. There were raids against natural Indian enemies and the occasional small party of whites, but little contact with major military forces. That dramatically changed in 1865 when the BOZEMAN TRAIL brought an endless stream of emigrant wagon trains, gold seekers headed for Montana, and soldiers to protect them.

The U.S. government began building forts: PHIL KEARNY, Reno, and C. F. Smith. Under the generalship of Chief RED CLOUD, the Indians waged war. The Sioux harassed the forts, and attacked miners, wagon trains, and other travelers. Red Cloud wanted to destroy Fort Phil Kearny, but realized that direct assaults would be suicidal. He alternately skirmished with the troops, and deployed warriors to gauge their reaction when an attack was feinted.

On December 21, 1866, the drills were over, and an opportunity presented itself in what became known as the FETTERMAN MASSACRE. Crazy Horse led an attack, that included GALL and RAIN-IN-THE-FACE, on a wagon train of woodcutters from Fort Phil Kearny who were required to range some distance away in order to find a sufficient supply of wood.

Capt. William J. Fetterman set out from the fort with a detail of 80 men to rescue the woodcutters' train. His specific orders from post commander, Col. Henry Carrington, were to escort the train back to the fort, and especially, Carrington warned, they must not cross Lodge Trail Ridge. Crazy Horse, who had become a master of the decoy, lured Fetterman into disobeying orders and crossing Lodge Trail Ridge in order to chase his band of fleeing Indians. It was the oldest trick in the book of Plains Indian warfare—Crazy Horse's specialty—and Fetterman led his men directly into the trap. The soldiers were killed to a man.

On August 2, 1867, Crazy Horse and a large group of warriors attacked a woodcutting detail from Fort Phil Kearny in what became known as the WAGON BOX FIGHT. A total of 2 officers, 26 soldiers, and 4 civilians took shelter in a corral constructed from wagon beds. Crazy Horse and his men alternated sniping and charging the position, but were discouraged by the superior firepower from the soldiers. About 4½ hours later a detachment arrived from the fort. Crazy Horse prudently broke contact, taking with him captured horses and mules.

Red Cloud's efforts at waging war were successful enough to bring the U.S. government to its knees. The FORT LARAMIE TREATY OF 1868 specified that the army should abandon their forts along the Bozeman Trail.

Crazy Horse, who had refused to "touch the pen" to the treaty, became war chief of the Sioux. The whites rarely traveled the Bozeman Trail now, so Crazy Horse turned his warring attention toward the CROWS and Shoshonis. The next several years were spent enjoying the freedom of life and the adventure of war parties against Indian enemies.

Crazy Horse had vigorously courted Red Cloud's niece Black Buffalo Woman almost 10 years earlier. At that time, however, she had spurned Crazy Horse to marry a warrior named No Water. Village gossip told about how Crazy Horse had continued to see her when her husband was away. In the fall of 1871 Crazy Horse convinced Black Buffalo Woman to run off with him. No Water found the two in a tepee together, and shot Crazy Horse: the bullet entering at the nostril and fracturing his jaw. Crazy Horse was seriously wounded, and it was feared he would die. He slowly and painfully recovered. Both men were guilty in the eyes of the tribe—No Water for not allowing Black Buffalo Woman to live with whomever she wanted; and Crazy Horse for putting his own selfish desires ahead of that of the tribe. Black Buffalo Woman returned to No Water, and some months later gave birth to a child with light hair that was rumored to have been fathered by Crazy Horse.

Crazy Horse Meets Custer

Crazy Horse spent the early 1870s harassing and attacking Crow Indians and prospectors in the BLACK HILLS. He finally married a woman named Black Shawl in the summer of 1872, and she bore him a daughter, They-Are-Afraid-of-Her. Another peril, however, presented itself when Custer's SEVENTH CAVALRY entered Indian country on the YELLOWSTONE EXPEDITION OF 1873. The purpose of the military presence was to protect surveyors for the NORTHERN PACIFIC RAILROAD, the "Iron Horse" that threatened the Indian way of life. Crazy Horse and Custer first met on August 4 when Custer and about 90 men had halted at noon near the mouth of the Tongue River. The cavalry horses had been turned out to graze, the men were lazing around, and Custer was taking a nap. Little did the soldiers know that they were under surveillance by Crazy Horse and a group of Sioux and Cheyenne. Crazy Horse, the master of the decoy and ambush, sent or was perhaps part of a handful of mounted warriors who, whooping shrilly, brazenly charged the cavalry horses with intentions of stampeding them. The horse guards began firing and sounding the alarm, and the Indians tore off down the valley toward a stand of timber. The cavalrymen immediately gave chase, Custer and about 20 troopers in the lead. The remainder of the detachment advanced more slowly. Custer, however, became suspicious when the Indians led the soldiers near a heavy growth of timber that stood along a river bank. He halted his men and went forward with only 2 orderlies. He proceeded a few hundred yards in advance of the squadron, and kept a watchful eye on the timber. The Indians to his front also halted as if to tempt further pursuit. Custer had recognized Crazy Horse's plans for an ambush and knew he should not advance any further. The soldiers nervously waited for any sign of aggression. The wait was not long. Within moments Crazy Horse sent his 300 mounted warriors charging from the timber. Custer wheeled his mount and hightailed it back to where he had left his 20 men, and quickly arranged them into a skirmisher line. The cavalrymen rose from the tall grass and fired three point-blank volleys into Crazy Horse's onrushing warriors. The effective barrages discouraged any further mounted attacks. Crazy Horse tried to fire the grass but it burned out without covering any ground. Ammunition became dangerously low for the soldiers, but late in the afternoon the remainder of the troops arrived. Custer mounted a charge, and Crazy Horse was forced to break contact.

The Battle of the Yellowstone

Following that failed attempt at defeating Custer, Crazy Horse decided to move his village of 500 lodges to another location. Word reached him that the 7th Cavalry had followed, and was now camped near the mouth of the Bighorn River where the Sioux had recently crossed to the south bank of the Yellowstone. The river at this point was too deep and swift for the cavalry to cross. This afforded Crazy Horse the opportunity to attack while the soldiers were bogged down. At daybreak on August 11 Crazy Horse deployed his warriors in the cottonwoods 300 yards away on the opposite bank. He gave the order to fire, and the battle commenced. The women and children of the village, including Black Shawl and They-Are-Afraid-of-Her, had gathered on the bluffs behind their men to watch the action and to offer encouragement. With a base of fire in place, Crazy Horse and approximately 200 warriors swam the river above and below Custer's position and began to close in. Custer reacted quickly to the threat by deploying sharpshooters to return fire across the river and others to cover the bluffs of his side. Two companies were sent down the valley and two companies headed up the valley. Twenty men dropped off to defend a benchland.

Crazy Horse hit that position first, sending 4 Indian straight charges consisting of 100 warriors, but each was repulsed. Attacks on the other detachments were equally unsuccessful. Custer—who had his horse shot out from under him but commandeered another—mounted his entire 450-man command, signaled the regimental band to strike up "GARRYOWEN" and ordered a charge. Crazy Horse was not prepared for that tactic. The surprise action routed his warriors, who scattered in all directions. Custer chased them for 9 miles before he lost them when they recrossed the Yellowstone. Casualties were light, the exact number difficult to accurately report due to exaggeration by both sides.

The Black Hills

The U.S. government violated both treaty and trust by allowing the Sioux reservation in the Black Hills to be explored by Custer and his 7th Cavalry on the BLACK HILLS EXPEDITION OF 1874. Although there were no direct confrontations, the Sioux were well aware of the soldiers who traveled the Thieves Road into *Pa Sapa*. The expedition was but a spark. The real fire came when gold deposits were discovered and hordes of prospectors were soon ignoring feeble military protests to stake their claims and seek their fortune. The U.S. government began to negotiate with the reservation Indians over the sale of the Black Hills, which angered Crazy Horse, SITTING BULL, and other free-roaming Sioux. About this time Crazy Horse's daughter died of cholera while he was out fighting Crow Indians. The village had then moved some 70 miles from the child's burial scaffold. It was said that he tracked down the place and lay for 3 days beside his daughter's body. The death of his child had a profound effect on Crazy Horse. He began taking extreme chances in battle, disappeared for long spells, and grew strange to his people. The bodies of many unscalped miners were found in the Black Hills. It was widely thought, even by his own people, that this strange man was behind the violent acts. The U.S. government in late 1875 had dispatched runners to inform the Indians in the area of the Yellowstone that they must report to the reservation by January 31, 1876, or be considered hostile. In the case of their refusal to submit, the army would come and force them onto the reservation. The edict was ignored by Crazy Horse, Sitting Bull, and warriors such as Gall and Rain-in-the-Face, and Cheyenne allies under TWO MOON. The first indication that the military meant business came in mid–March when troops under Gen. George CROOK attacked and destroyed a Sioux-Cheyenne village on the Powder River. Crazy Horse came to their rescue that night during a raging snowstorm and recaptured the pony herd. However, the gauntlet had been thrown; the army must be fought.

Sun Dance

In early June, Sitting Bull and his followers camped in the Rosebud Valley and held a Sun Dance. The Indians arranged buffalo skulls and other ritual items and constructed an arbor with a pole in the middle. Strips of rawhide dangled to the ground from this center pole. Warriors would then have the skin of their chest slashed by a medicine man. A stick would be inserted inside the flesh, then attached to one strip of rawhide. The warrior would be lifted off the ground, and prove his fortitude by being supported solely by the strip of rawhide. He could not cry out or would be branded a squaw. Crazy Horse did not regard the Sun Dance as a proper manner in which to prove one's manhood, and declined to participate. Sitting Bull, on the other hand, directed his adopted brother to slice strips of flesh from his arms. Sitting Bull then commenced dancing until he passed out. Once revived, he told of a vision: a vision of dead soldiers falling from the sky into their camp. This was interpreted by his people to mean that they wold be victorious in battle against the army.

The Battle of the Rosebud

The first opportunity to verify Sitting Bull's vision came on June 17 when Crazy Horse led his warriors against Gen. George Crook's troops at the Battle of the ROSEBUD. Unknown to Crook, Sitting Bull's village lay directly in the path of the planned march, and the army had been under constant surveillance by Cheyenne scouts. When Crook finally broke camp on June 16 and headed down Rosebud Creek, the Indians became greatly concerned about the well-being of their families. They held a council and it was decided that instead of waiting for Crook to approach, Crazy Horse would strike the army with somewhere between 500 to 1,000 warriors—perhaps half the total number available—while the others remained behind to protect the village. Crook and Crazy Horse and their respective men were on the move during the early morning hours of June 17. Crazy Horse had the advantage because his scouts had located Crook, whereas Crook was unaware of the pursuing Indians. Crook called a halt at midmorning for coffee and to graze the horses in a valley of broken terrain dotted with trees, bushes, and rocks. Crazy Horse appeared and spotted the army at about the same instant that Crook's Crow Indian scouts spotted the hostile Indians. The scouts hightailed it for Crook, shouting out the warning as they rode for their lives. Crazy Horse departed from the customary tactics of circling around prey from a distance, and instead led a headlong charge into the surprised troopers. Due to the terrain, the fighting was fragmented: a battle of every man for himself with small, disorganized units. At one point Crook ordered the cavalry under Col. Anson MILLS to head downstream to search for and attack the Indian village that he correctly surmised was located there. Mills became apprehensive when the valley became narrower with abundant ambush sites. Crazy Horse, the master of decoy, had indeed deployed warriors in the ambush. Perhaps the decoy trick had been overused; Mills turned back and escaped disaster. After an undetermined period—possibly as long as 3 hours—of fierce fighting, the Indians massed for one final concentrated attack. Crook noticed this, and ordered Mills to regroup his cavalry and maneuver behind the Indians. Crazy Horse decided to break contact, and left the field to the amy. The army admitted to somewhere between 10 and 28 killed and 21 to 56 wounded. Although every soldier was not killed as foretold in Sitting Bull's vision, the results were sufficient enough to encourage the warriors that fighting rather than fleeing was the answer in dealing with the army.

The Battle of the Little Bighorn

Sitting Bull moved his village the following day down Reno Creek to the Little Bighorn River. The number of lodges had almost doubled in size—from 400 to nearly 1,000—bolstered by brethren from the reservation who had arrived for a summer of freedom. On June 24 the village was again moved, this time down the Little Bighorn about 2 miles below the mouth of Reno Creek. Custer and the 7th Cavalry attacked that village about noon on June 25, and the Battle of the LITTLE BIGHORN commenced. The outnumbered troopers were no match for the motivated Indians. Maj. Marcus RENO was quickly repulsed in RENO'S VALLEY FIGHT, and sent retreating to the RENO-BENTEEN DEFENSE SITE. Custer's detachment fared worse: they were all killed. Crazy Horse, his near-naked body painted with white hail spots and the lightning bolt on his cheek, with a brown pebble behind each ear, led a group of warriors who delivered the final murderous charge into the cavalrymen. He had ridden down the valley below the village, crossed the river, and attacked from the north. After crushing the troopers on CUSTER HILL, Crazy Horse swept southward down BATTLE RIDGE to deliver the final blow by forcing the soldiers on CALHOUN HILL into the clutches of Chief Gall's warriors.

Black Hills

Crazy Horse and his followers spent a month or so celebrating their victory with feasts and dances. Then, with less than 600 warriors, he headed for the Black Hills. Crazy Horse and his people camped at the place of his birth, Bear Butte, and began harassing the prospectors who had flocked to the hills in search of their fortune. In what amounted at times to a one-man war—his people were tired of fighting—Crazy Horse alone attempted to regain the land promised to the Sioux.

Slim Buttes

Gen. George Crook remained on the trail of Crazy Horse, but the army was weakened due to starvation and fatigue. Col. Anson Mills had been dispatched on a mission to procure food at Deadwood, D.T., when he came upon the Sioux village of SLIM BUTTES. He attacked the 37 lodges at dawn on September 9, and quickly gained control. The soldiers began destroying the village, while gorging themselves on the meat supply. Meanwhile, runners notified Crazy Horse, who was nearby. He arrived about noon, and counterattacked. The battle raged until late afternoon when Gen. Crook and reinforcements arrived and Crazy Horse was forced to break contact.

The Battle of Wolf Mountain

The Cheyenne had been severely beaten 2 months earlier in the Battle of DULL KNIFE, and had sought refuge with Crazy Horse. The winter had taken its toll, and many of these people were prepared to surrender. Gen. Crook had promised Crazy Horse a reservation if he, too, submitted. Crazy Horse subsequently opened talks with Gen. Nelson MILES to discuss terms. However, as the Cheyenne approached the Tongue River Cantonment, some of Miles's Crow scouts attacked them, killing 5 Sioux. The Indians fled, and hostilities continued. In

early January, Miles with about 350 troops were searching the Tongue River Valley when the Indians attempted to lure them into a trap. The ambush was sprung too early, and Miles was able to capture a number of Cheyenne women and children. Then 500 warriors under Crazy Horse attacked at dawn on January 8 with intentions of freeing the captives. Miles was well prepared, and bombarded them with artillery and skillfully deployed marksmen. The battle ended around noon when a blizzard obscured visibility and the Indians withdrew. Neither side sustained many casualties.

Surrender

On May 5, 1877, Crazy Horse led almost 900 of his brethren into CAMP ROBINSON to surrender. His people were hungry and weary, and more and more Sioux had accepted the reservation. Black Shawl had contracted tuberculosis, a major factor in Crazy Horse's decision. His presence at Red Cloud Agency had an effect on the young warriors who worshiped him, the older chiefs who resented him, and the army officers who grudgingly respected him. However, he was refused a reservation of his own; and in turn he refused to visit the "Great Father" in Washington, D.C. His aloof attitude began causing problems. Red Cloud and Spotted Tail conspired to discredit him, and Gen. Crook secretly intended to have him sent to prison in Florida. The NEZ PERCÉ had left their reservation, and Crook wanted Crazy Horse to scout for the army. He refused. Some said that scout Frank GROUARD, a former friend of Crazy Horse, misinterpreted Crazy Horse's answer to a question about the Nez Percé. Grouard related that the warrior had said he might fight *against* the white man rather than *with* the white man.

Death

Crook heard rumors that Crazy Horse was planning to lead his people in a rebellion, and so ordered his arrest. Crazy Horse fled with his family toward Spotted

Tail Agency. A $200 reward was offered to any Indian who could capture Crazy Horse. It was said that his former romantic rival, No Water, killed 2 horses in his haste to be the one. Crazy Horse explained at Spotted Tail Agency that he had not intended to fight the whites or cause an uprising. He had simply desired to leave Red Cloud Agency due to the turmoil that surrounded his presence there. Crazy Horse was returned to Red Cloud Agency on September 6, 1877. Upon his arrival he was stunned to learn that he would be incarcerated in the stockade. Crazy Horse pulled a knife, and was grabbed by childhood friend Little Big Man. Soldiers rushed forward, and Crazy Horse was struck in the abdomen by a bayonet. He died later that day from the wound. His father buried his body somewhere in his homeland in a place as yet undiscovered by the white man.

Memorial

The late Boston-born sculptor Korczak Ziolkowski began a project to carve a 563-feet high likeness of Crazy Horse mounted on his horse on a mountainside in South Dakota. Korczak (his professional name) won first prize at the 1939 New York World's Fair for a marble portrait, then helped carve the four presidents' faces into Mount Rushmore. He was asked by Chief Henry Standing Bear to create a monument to Crazy Horse, and began the project in 1948. Korczak passed away in 1982, but his work has been carried on by his widow, Ruth, and 6 of their 10 children. The sculpture, when completed, will stand 9 stories high from the horse's hooves to the tip of the 44-feet feather. This monument in progress, 12 miles from Mount Rushmore, includes a tourist center and Native American museum. The task of creating the likeness of Crazy Horse may be difficult inasmuch as no known photograph of him exists.

Sources of further study include: Crazy Horse and Custer: The Parallel Lives of Two American Warriors, by Stephen E.

Ambrose (Garden City, NY: Doubleday, 1975); *Crazy Horse: The Strange Man of the Oglalas*, by Mari Sandoz (Lincoln: University of Nebraska Press, 1942); *Red Cloud's Folk: A History of the Oglala Sioux Indians*, by George E. Hyde (Norman: University of Oklahoma Press, 1937); "Crazy Horse's Story of the Custer Battle," edited by Doane Robinson, *South Dakota Historical Collections*, 6 (1912); "Chief Crazy Horse, His Career and Death," by E. A. Brininstool, *Nebraska History* 12, no. 1 (1929); and "Oglala Sources on the Life of Crazy Horse," by Eleanor Hinman, *Nebraska History* 57, no. 1 (1976).

Crittenden, John J. (June 7, 1851– June 25, 1876) Second lieutenant, 20th Infantry. This Kentucky native graduated from West Point, a classmate of the SEVENTH CAVALRY's 2nd Lt. James STURGIS, and was commissioned a second lieutenant on October 15, 1875. He had been blinded in one eye shortly after graduation, but continued with his military career. Crittenden was on detached duty from the infantry serving as assistant commander of Calhoun's L Company at the time of the Battle of the LITTLE BIGHORN. He was part of Custer's detachment, and was killed along with the men of Company L. His body was found at the southern end of BATTLE RIDGE on what is known as CALHOUN HILL. His father requested that Crittenden's body be buried where he fell, thus becoming the only individual grave ever dug on that battlefield. The War Department unearthed Crittenden's remains in the spring of 1932 and transferred them to the nearby cemetery at LITTLE BIGHORN BATTLEFIELD NATIONAL MONUMENT.

Crook, George (1828–90) General, U.S. Army. Known as "Three Stars" to the Indians. This West Point graduate distinguished himself as an Indian fighter in the Pacific Northwest in the late 1850s, receiving a poisoned arrow in the hip in a battle with the Pitt River Indians. During the Civil War he commanded a cavalry division; he was captured in early 1865 but exchanged within a month. After the war he served with the 23rd Infantry in Idaho Territory and fought against the Paiutes before moving on to Oregon. Crook won his greatest acclaim and a brigadier general's star by subduing the Apaches in Arizona from 1871 to 1873. He developed the successful strategy of using surrendered Apaches to track renegade Apaches. He was assigned command of the Department of the Platte in time for the GREAT SIOUX WAR OF 1876–77. Crook presented the outward impression of a folksy yet eccentric man. He was an imposing figure, over six feet tall, braided his parted blond whiskers, wore canvas coveralls and moccasins rather than a uniform, and preferred a mule over a horse for riding. His column marched northward from Fort FETTERMAN in present-day Wyoming as part of the three-pronged attack force sent against SITTING BULL. The soldiers failed to reach their objective when CRAZY HORSE decided to turn the tables on them at the Battle of the ROSEBUD: a great embarrassment for Crook. He was inexplicably camped far south on Goose Creek at the time of the Battle of the LITTLE BIGHORN, although his column had been part of Gen. Alfred TERRY's overall plan. When Terry called an end in September to the LITTLE BIGHORN CAMPAIGN, Crook continued to pursue Crazy Horse's band toward the BLACK HILLS on what became known as the "Starvation March." His troops were exhausted and forced to eat their horses and mules. Crook's one victory during the campaign came in the Battle of SLIM BUTTES on September 9, 1876, when he reinforced Col. Anson MILLS's detachment to drive off Crazy Horse. Later that year, his forces destroyed provisions owned by CHEYENNE Chief DULL KNIFE. He then became supervisor of the Red Cloud Agency, and in 1882 was again sent against the Chiricahua Apache

in Arizona, duplicating his prior success. He became commanding general of the Department of the Missouri in 1888. *Sources for further study include: Campaigning with Crook*, by Charles King (Norman: University of Oklahoma Press, 1964); *With Crook at the Rosebud*, by J. W. Vaughn (Harrisburg, PA: Stackpole, 1956), and *General George Crook: His Autobiography* (Norman: University of Oklahoma Press, 1946).

Crow Indians (They called themselves *Absaroka*, which meant either Sparrowhawk People or Chosen People.) This Indian tribe of the Siouan linguistic group migrated to the Plains from the East in the seventeenth century and, after being pushed out of the BLACK HILLS by the CHEYENNE and SIOUX, settled along the Yellowstone River. At first they were hostile toward the U.S. government due to their resentment of white travelers along the Oregon Trail. Soon, however, they became allies of the whites, and many of their people began serving as scouts and guides for the U.S. Army. They fought with Gen. George CROOK at the Battle of the ROSEBUD, and the following year helped track the NEZ PERCÉ. Notable Crow Indian scouts that served with Custer—on loan from Col. John GIBBON—during the LITTLE BIGHORN CAMPAIGN were CURLY, Hairy Moccasin, Half-Yellow Face, Goes Ahead, White Man Runs Him, and White Swan. *Sources for further study include: Absaroka: Home of the Crows*, by M. I. Carrington (Lincoln: University of Nebraska Press, 1983); and *The Vanishing Race*, by Joseph K. Dixon (Garden City, NY: Doubleday, Page, 1913).

Crow King (Hunkpapa Sioux) This war chief, known as a trusted lieutenant of SITTING BULL, fought at the Battle of the LITTLE BIGHORN. He accompanied Sitting Bull to Canada, returning in January 1881. His story of the famous battle can be found in *The Custer Myth: A*

Sourcebook of Custeriana, by W. A. Graham (Harrisburg, PA: Stackpole, 1953).

Crow's Nest This traditional Plains Indian lookout afforded a fair view of the Valley of the Little Bighorn because of its topographical location rather than height. It was from this vantage point on the morning of June 25, 1876, that Custer's scouts first reported evidence of SITTING BULL's village, which was located some 15 miles away. See LITTLE BIGHORN, BATTLE OF.

Curly (Crow; aka "Curley"; ca. 1856–May 21, 1923) Curly was a scout with Custer during the LITTLE BIGHORN CAMPAIGN. Contrary to popular belief, he was not the lone survivor of the famous battle simply because he was not a participant. Many stories have been told—mostly by Curly himself—about his harrowing escape that day. He had fashioned his hair in the Sioux style and pretended to be a member of the tribe; he had hidden inside the carcass of a dead horse; or he had covered himself with a blanket and hid in a ravine. None of them were true. Curly and the other scouts, whose job was finding the Sioux not fighting them, were released by Custer before the battle began. He may have observed the beginning of the battle and realized what was about to take place. However, while Custer was being defeated Curly was traveling to the Bighorn and Yellowstone rivers where the steamship *FAR WEST* was waiting. He reported Custer's annihilation, but without an interpreter present was not understood. In 1886, at the tenth reunion of the battle, Curly was confronted by SIOUX war chief GALL. He called Curly a coward for leaving before the fight, and told him had he stayed he would now be dead. Curly did not answer Gall. He left the army on September 30, 1876, and eventually had a ranch near Crow Agency, MT. He was buried in the cemetery at LITTLE BIGHORN BATTLEFIELD NATIONAL MONUMENT. Curly's reservation cabin is on display at an attraction called Trail Town in Cody, WY. *Sources for further study include:* "Interview with Curly, September 18, 1908," in *Custer in '76: Walter Camp's Notes on the Custer Fight,* edited by Kenneth Hammer (Provo, UT: Brigham Young University Press, 1976); "Curley the Crow Scout Once More," in *Winners of the West* (St. Joseph, MO: National Indian Wars Veterans, July 1924); and "Statement of Curley the Scout," *The Tepee Book* (June 1916).

Custer, Boston (October 31, 1848–June 25, 1876) "Bos" was the fourth child born to Emanuel and Maria CUSTER, nearly 9 years younger than brother George Armstrong. Described as rather frail due to weak lungs, Bos was hired by his brother as a SEVENTH CAVALRY "guide" for the BLACK HILLS EXPEDITION OF 1874, regardless of the fact that this was his first trip west, he could not recognize one trail from another, and had been known to become easily lost. He quickly became the butt of his brothers' good-natured practical jokes. Brother Tom CUSTER gave him a rock that he swore was a "sponge-stone," and that if placed under water would become a useful sponge. Bos fell for it, much to the delight of his brothers. Once on the march Bos stopped to pick a rock from his horse's shoe. Custer and Tom rode ahead then hid and fired shots over Bos's head, which sent him galloping for help thinking it was an Indian attack. Bos was hired as "forage master" for the LITTLE BIGHORN CAMPAIGN. He wrote a letter to his mother dated June 21, 1876, from the 7th Cavalry's camp at the confluence of the Yellowstone and Rosebud.

My Darling Mother—The mail leaves to-morrow. I have no news to write. I am feeling first-rate. Armstrong [Gen. Custer's nickname] takes the whole command, and starts up the Sweet Briar on an Indian trail with the full hope and belief of overhauling them—which I think he will, with a little hard riding. ... I hope to catch one or two Indian ponies with a buffalo robe for [brother] Nev, but he must not be disappointed if I don't. ... Now don't give yourself any trouble at all as all will be well. ... Goodbye my darling Mother.

On the final approach into the Little Bighorn Valley on June 25, 1876, Bos was in the rear with the packtrain, and would have likely escaped death had he remained there. Bos, however, had heard about the impending fight and hurried forward to be with his brothers. His body was found along with Custer, Tom, and nephew Autie REED among the 40 on CUSTER HILL. Bos was reinterred in the Custer family plot in Monroe, MI, in 1877.

Custer, Elizabeth Clift Bacon ("Libbie"; April 8, 1842–April 6, 1933) The wife of George Armstrong Custer. She was 5'4" tall with chestnut brown hair and light blue-gray eyes (see photo this page).

Libbie grew up in Monroe, MI, the daughter of Judge Daniel S. BACON, one of the town's leading citizens. Her father was 38 when he married 23-year-old Eleanor Sophia PAGE of Grand Rapids, MI, in September 1837. The couple had 4 children—2 girls died in infancy and a boy, Eddy, died at age 8 of a childhood disease. That left Libbie to be doted upon. However, when Libbie was 12, her mother passed away from a disease that Judge Bacon described to his family as one the nature of which "physicians were unacquainted with." The judge had promised Libbie's mother on her deathbed that he would properly care for their only child. He sent Libbie off to boarding school at the Young Ladies' Seminary and Collegiate Institute—known as Boyd's Seminary—rented out their house, and took a room at a hotel. Libbie graduated from Boyd's in the spring of 1862, valedictorian of her class.

Custer was just an occasional resident of Monroe where he lived off and on with

Elizabeth (Libbie) Bacon Custer, 1874

his half sister, Lydia Ann REED. Due to that fact, and their differing social levels, the refined Miss Bacon and Custer, son of the town smithy in New Rumley, OH, did not meet as children. However, her first impression of him was to last a lifetime. She called it "that awful day." It occurred in October 1861 when Capt. Custer was home on leave from the army. He and a friend had visited a local tavern and imbibed to excess. The two drunks staggered through the streets of Monroe past the Bacon residence on their way toward the Reed home, half a mile south. Libbie and her father happened to observe the disgusting revelers. The incident, however, cured Custer of drinking alcohol for the rest of his life. (See LYDIA ANN REED.)

Custer and Libbie formally met at an 1862 Thanksgiving party at Boyd's Seminary. Custer was immediately smitten with her and courted her by showing up wherever she happened to be and calling on her at home. She, on the other hand, was not too sure about him. Her father and stepmother had raised her in the Presbyterian Church, and there was the social disparity. Besides, Libbie was not exactly wanting for suitors. Judge Bacon noticed Custer's growing interest in his daughter, and decided to put an end to the relationship. He did not fancy his only child married to a common military man. The judge made Libbie promise to not see Custer again or write to him after he had returned to duty in the Civil War.

Custer pledged his undying love to her, which she rebuffed, but she later wrote in her diary: "He is noble, brave and generous and he loves, I believe, with an intensity that few know of or as few ever can love. ... He tells me he would sacrifice every earthly hope to gain my love and I tell him if I could I would give it to him. I told him to forget me and he said he *never could* forget me and I told him I never should forget *him* and I wished to be his true friend through life but it is no use to offer myself as friend for he will never think of me otherwise than his wife. ... Oh, Love, love, how many are made miserable as well as happy by all the powerful influence." Meanwhile, back on duty, 23-year-old Gen. George Armstrong Custer was becoming a national celebrity due to his daring exploits. The prestigious *Harper's Weekly* had published a drawing of a classic Custer cavalry charge. Libbie had obeyed her father's wishes and refused to see or accept mail from Custer. A go-between, however, emerged. Nettie Humphrey, the future wife of Custer's adjutant, Jacob Greene, passed information through letters for the estranged couple. Libbie had by now fallen in love with Custer, and at a masquerade ball at the Humphrey house on September 28, 1863, she promised to marry Custer if her father consented to the union. Custer composed what he considered the most important letter of his life, asking Judge Bacon if he could merely correspond with Libbie. The judge relented—no doubt partially due to Custer's growing fame and regard—and allowed Libbie to write to her future husband. Her first letter began: "My more than friend—at last—Am I a little glad to write you some of the thoughts I cannot control?"

On February 9, 1864, Custer and Elizabeth Clift Bacon were married in the First Presbyterian Church of Monroe, MI, in a storybook wedding with a standing-room only congregation of witnesses. Libbie's former schoolmaster, Rev. Boyd, performed the ceremony. Custer, with short hair and wearing a coat that cost $100, chose his adjutant Jacob Greene as his best man. Libbie wore traditional white, and was given away by her father. The couple received such gifts as a silver tea service from the 7th Michigan Cavalry, a silver dinner service from the 1st Vermont Cavalry, and a Bible from Judge Bacon. Custer presented Libbie with a gold watch engraved "E.B.C."

Libbie faithfully followed her husband to each of his duty stations. She endured the hardships of frontier life without complaint, satisfied to be with the man she loved. Custer in turn was devoted to her, and even faced a court-martial to be at her side at the conclusion of the HANCOCK EXPEDITION OF 1867. (See CUSTER, Court-Martial.) Although childless, their marriage was a great love story. Her adventures and passion for Custer can be found in her three excellent memoirs: *"Boots and Saddles"; Or, Life in Dakota with General Custer* (New York: Harper and Brothers, 1885); *Tenting on the Plains; Or, General Custer in Kansas and Texas* (New York: Harper and Brothers, 1887); and *Following the Guidon* (New York: Harper and Brothers, 1890).

When Custer died at the LITTLE BIGHORN, Libbie became a widow at age 34. She returned to Monroe, MI, and contemplated her future. She found her calling in the debate surrounding the famous battle and Custer's actions. She worked tirelessly to protect his national image against those who would bring criticism. Her memoirs not only informed the public about her experiences on the frontier but furthered the heroic image of her husband. For the remainder of her life—57 years—she remained unmarried and vigorously defended Custer against any attack. She was instrumental in raising funds to erect memorials in Michigan and at West Point in Custer's honor. She traveled the world, and was much in demand as a public speaker. Libbie Custer died two days short of her ninety-first birthday, and was buried beside her husband at the U.S. Military Academy at West Point.

Sources for further study include: Excerpts from a sample of her correspondence can be found in *The Custer Story: The Life and Intimate Letters of General George A. Custer and His Wife Elizabeth,* edited by Marguerite Merington (New York: Devin-Adair, 1950). Biographies include: *General Custer's Libbie,* by Lawrence Frost (Seattle: Superior, 1976); and *Elizabeth Bacon Custer and the Making of a Myth,* by Shirley A. Leckie (Norman: University of Oklahoma Press, 1993).

Custer, Emanuel Henry (1806–November 27, 1892) Custer's father. Emanuel Custer was the village blacksmith, and for 12 years justice of the peace in New Rumley, OH. He had helped found the New Rumley Methodist Church, and was proud of his Pennsylvania Dutch ancestry. Emanuel's grandfather fought in the Revolutionary War, and he was a distant relative of Gen. George Washington. He regarded his loyalty to the Democratic party, which could be called nothing less than militant, to be as sacred as his church ties. He was also a prominent member of the New Rumley Invincibles, the local militia. Emanuel's first wife bore him three children during their six years of marriage before she passed away in 1835. Seven months later he married a widow from Burgettstown, PA, named Maria Ward Kirkpatrick (CUSTER), who brought three children of her own to the union. Their first two children died in infancy. Five healthy children were then born in or New Rumley, OH: George Armstrong, Nevin Johnson, Thomas Ward,

Boston, and Margaret Emma. From all accounts, Emanuel acted like a big kid when he was around his children. He would romp, wrestle, and play as aggressively as any of them, making them the target of practical jokes and dodging their pranks in return. Secretary of War Stanton and Emanuel were friends from the days when Custer had been a client of Stanton's law firm, which impressed son George Armstrong upon meeting the secretary in Washington during the Civil War. Son George Armstrong—a notorious believer in nepotism—hired Emanuel in 1866 to serve as "forage master" for the army division stationed in New Hempstead, TX. The extended family had a grand time horseback riding and hunting and playing practical jokes on each other. After the general's death at the LITTLE BIGHORN, Libbie arranged for Emanuel to have Custer's horse Dandy. The elder Custer for years was a common sight proudly riding his late son's favorite horse in parades. Libbie reflected on Emanuel Custer in the Detroit *Free Press* on December 11, 1892, two weeks after his death: "His warmest friends, his genuine admirers, were half of them opposed to his politics, but he loved dearly to have them oppose him; he challenged their thrusts and then invited them to a country dinner of fatted turkey after Michigan went Democratic two years ago, in order to show them how he valued their society in spite of what he thought their mistaken views."

Custer, George Armstrong ("Autie," "Armstrong"; December 5, 1838–June 25, 1876) Lieutenant colonel, 7th Cavalry. Custer stood nearly 6 feet tall and weighed about 170 pounds. He had blue eyes, and wavy blond hair—worn short for field duty and long in garrison—with a matching mustache and at times an imperial or beard. Nicknames through the years included: Autie; Armstrong; Cinnamon; Fanny; the Boy General; Old Curly; "nomad," Yellow Hair; Iron butt; and Son of the Morning Star.

Birth and Ancestry

Custer was born on December 5, 1839, in New Rumley, OH, to Emanuel H. and Maria Ward Kirkpatrick Custer, Emanuel's second wife. George Armstrong was the firstborn from this union. Three brothers followed: Nevin Johnson (1842); Thomas Ward (1845); and Boston (1848); and a sister, Margaret Emma (Maggie), born in 1852. There exists no conclusive documentation regarding Custer's ancestry. His father was proud of his Pennsylvania Dutch heritage, and was a distant relative of George Washington. His mother was of British origins. Custer wrote to wife Libbie from New York in the spring of 1876 telling her about a letter he had received from a man living in Scotland's Orkney Islands who believed they were from the same family with various spellings of the name: Cusiter, Cursider, and Cursetter.

Early Years

Emanuel was a farmer as well as the village blacksmith, and the boys—especially Armstrong—developed an early skill in horsemanship and an acceptance of hard work. The children attended school in New Rumley until moving to a log cabin in Harrison County and transferring to Creal School north of Scio. At age 10 Armstrong went to live with his half sister, Lydia Ann REED, who had married David Reed and moved to Monroe, MI. He returned after two years to help on the farm. However, it was felt that Monroe had advantages for him in schooling, and he was enrolled in Alfred Stebbins's Young Man's Academy there at age 14. Custer's deskmate at the academy enjoyed telling about Armstrong's habit of sneaking adventure novels into class and reading them instead of textbooks. Favorite titles included: *Tom Burke of Ours*, *Jack Hinton*, and *Charles O'Malley, the Irish Dragoon*, the latter also being a favorite of future 7th Cavalry comrade Capt. Myles KEOGH across the ocean in Ireland. He was hardly a bookworm, however, but a natural born leader on the sports field, a fun-loving yet aggressive youngster. Custer returned once more to New Rumley at age 16 to teach at the Beech Point School and later at the Locust Grove School between terms while attending McNeely Normal School in Hopedale. It was while at school in Hopedale that Armstrong wrote to the district's Whig representative, John A. Bingham, requesting an appointment to the U.S. Military Academy at West Point. Differing stories have been written about the manner in which Armstrong received the prestigious appointment from a man whose politics were contrary to those of the staunchly Democratic Custer family. Bingham later related that the "honesty" of Custer's letter "captivated" him. Others have speculated that the father of a girl whom Custer was sweet on pulled strings with the congressman in order to remove the boy from his daughter's life.

West Point

On July 1, 1857, Custer and 67 other plebes reported for duty at the U.S. Military Academy at West Point, NY (see photo next page). His record there can be summed up best by a statement he later made: "My career as a cadet had but little to commend it to the study of those who came after me, unless as an example to be carefully avoided." West Point graded their cadets with a system that called for a certain number of demerits for each offense. One hundred demerits in a 6-month period was grounds for dismissal. Custer came close on numerous occasions. However, his demerits were awarded for minor offenses, such as being out of uniform or tardiness. He was very popular with his classmates, and a leader whom they occasionally followed into the "skin book" of demerits: such as late-night forays to an off-limits place called Benny Havens. The class of 1861 was torn between loyalties. Southern states began to secede from the Union, which prompted many cadets from that region to resign and return home. Friendships nurtured over 4 years together would soon be tested as classmates would face each other as enemies on Civil War battlefields. Custer would eventually meet his roommate Tom Rosser when both were in charge of opposing divisions of cavalry. Custer nearly did not graduate with his class—and not due to excessive demerits. Only days before graduation Custer was officer of the guard, and disregarded his duty to stop a fistfight. Instead, he told the assembled crowd to stand back and let there be a fair fight between Cadet William Ludlow (chief engineer on the BLACK HILLS EXPEDITION OF 1874) and a plebe. 1st Lt. W. B. HAZEN, a West Point instructor and future Custer critic, appeared and placed Custer under arrest and subject to court-martial. Due to the war and the need for officers, Custer was let off with only a reprimand when during normal times he likely would have been dismissed. He graduated 34th in a class of 34. However, on July 17, 1861—2 days following his court-martial—2nd Lt. Custer reported for duty with the 2nd Cavalry. *Sources for further study include: "Skinned": Delinquency Record of Cadet George Armstrong Custer, USMA Class of June 1861,* edited by W. Donald Horn (Short Hills, NJ: 1980); and "Cadet Custer's Court-Martial," by Minnie Dubbs Millbrook, in *Custer and His Times,* edited by Paul A. Hutton (El Paso: Little Bighorn Associates, 1981).

Civil War Record

Today Custer is remembered due to his death at the Battle of the LITTLE BIG-HORN; however, in his day he was a national hero due to his Civil War exploits. On May 5, 1862, at Williamsburg, VA, he captured the first enemy battle flag taken by the Union Army, and on April 9, 1865, accepted the Confederate white flag of surrender at Appomattox. In between exists a series of intrepid acts of incredible proportion that earned him the rank of brigadier general at age 23: the

Cadet George Armstrong Custer, West Point, 1861

youngest in our country's history. He personally led electrifying cavalry charges that inspired his men and earned their adulation, and captured the fancy of newspaper and magazine writers and their readers. He began his military career in a less flamboyant manner as an aide-de-camp on the staffs of generals Phillip Kearny; W. F. Smith; Alfred Pleasanton; and commanding general of the Army of the Potomac, George Mc-Clellan—to whom Custer became very attached. McClellan said of Custer: "In these days Custer was simply a reckless, gallant boy, undeterred by fatigue, unconscious of fear; but his head was always clear in danger and he always brought me clear and intelligible reports of what he saw when under the heaviest fire." In the spring of 1862, during the siege of York-town, VA, Custer was assigned to duty as a military observer from a hot-air balloon. Custer usually ascended at night to a height of 1,000 feet for his reconnaissance with field glasses. With map and compass, he would note gun emplacements, count enemy campfires, plot the number of white tents, and sketch their locations in his notebook. Custer, however, desired action, and although assigned as a staff officer, he commanded respect for leading charges and rallying troops in the Peninsula, Antietam, and Chancellorsville campaigns. At Brandy Station on June 9, 1863—in the first and largest true cavalry engagement of the war—Custer had 2 horses shot out from under him and was cited for bravery. This led to his unexpected June 29, 1863, promotion from captain to brigadier general—leapfrogging major, lieutenant colonel, and colonel—and making him the youngest general in the Union Army. Custer made a memorable debut as commander of the Michigan Brigade one week later at the Battle of Gettysburg. Confederate forces under Gen. George Pickett were massing for an attack on the center of the Union lines. East of town, Rebel cavalry legend J. E. B. Stuart prepared his horsemen to support Pickett. Custer, with saber drawn, rode to the head of his troops, shouted "Come on, you Wolverines!" and twice led his in-

Brevet Major General George Armstrong Custer, 1865

spired troops directly into Stuart's soldiers. The Union cavalry defeated Gen. Stuart that day, denying him access to the Union rear, in what likely turned the tide at that bloody battle. Newspaper and magazine reporters saw a rising star, and the Custer legend was born. He made excellent copy: a young, dashing hero with golden curls, who wore an outlandish uniform highlighted by a bright red necktie. Custer continued to reap glory and respect with his brilliant, calculated charges and field generalship. At Yellow Tavern on May 11, 1864, another Custer charge resulted in the death of Confederate general James Ewell Brown (J. E. B.) Stuart. There were victories at Beaverdam Station, the Wilderness, and Winchester. On September 30, 1864, he was awarded his second star and command of the 3rd Cavalry Division under Gen. Phil SHERIDAN. A week later he faced his former West Point roommate, Confederate general Thomas Rosser, at Tom's Brook, VA. Custer's Union cavalry advanced toward the superior force of entrenched Rebels. When all was ready for battle, Custer—in an act of bravado—rode out in front of his command where he could be seen by both sides. He then removed his broad-brimmed hat and swept it across himself and down in a salute to his friend. Custer then commenced to hand the Confederates what Rosser later admitted was his worst defeat. His division distinguished itself during the Appomattox Campaign in the waning days of the war, playing a major role in the April 6, 1865, Battle of Sayler's Creek: known in the South as "Black Thursday" (see illustration this page). This was the final battle of the Civil War where the Confederates lost one-third of their army killed, wounded, or captured. Two days later Custer captured 4 Rebel railroad trains carrying vital supplies. Later that day, a Confederate messenger under a flag of truce approached Custer to ask that Gen. U. S. Grant be informed that Gen. Robert E. Lee desired a meeting to surrender his army. Lee surrendered to Grant at Appomattox Court House in Wilmer McLean's parlor at 3 P.M. on Palm Sunday to end the Civil War. The writing table on which the official papers were signed was purchased for $20 by Gen. Phil Sheridan. The next day he wrote the following note to Custer's wife Libbie: "I respectfully present to you the small writing table on which the conditions for the surrender of the Army of Northern Virginia were written by Lt. General Grant—and permit me to say, Madam, that there is scarcely an individual in our service who has contributed more to bring about this desirable result than your husband."

Sources for further study include: Custer Victorious: The Civil War Battles of General George Armstrong Custer, by Gregory J. W. Urwin (East Brunswick, NJ: Associated University Press, 1983); *Custer in the Civil War: His Unfinished Memoirs,* edited by John M. Carroll (San Rafael, CA: Presidio, 1977); *Personal Recollections of a Cavalryman with Custer's Michigan Brigade in the Civil War,* by J. H. Kidd (Grand Rapids, MI: Black Letter, 1969); *East of Gettysburg: Stuart vs. Custer,* by David F. Riggs (Bellevue, NE: Old Army, 1970); *From Winchester to Cedar Creek: The Shenandoah Campaign of 1864,* by Jeffry Wert (Carlisle, PA: South Mountain, 1987); *Last Hours of Sheridan's Cavalry: A Reprint of War Memoranda,* by Henry Edward Tremain (New York: Bonnell, Silver and Bowers, 1904); and *The Union Cavalry in the Civil War,* vol. 1: *From Fort Sumter to Gettysburg, 1861–1863,* and vol. 2: *The Union Cavalry in the Civil War in the East, from Gettysburg to Appomattox, 1863–1865,* by Stephen Z. Starr (Baton Rouge: Louisiana State University Press, 1979, 1981).

Marriage

On February 9, 1864, 24-year-old Brig. Gen. George Armstrong Custer married 21-year-old Elizabeth "Libbie" Clift Bacon in a standing-room only ceremony at the First Presbyterian Church in Monroe, MI. She followed him to duty stations on the frontier, and endured hardships without complaint. Libbie remained unmarried for the rest of her life—nearly 57 years—after Custer's death. She was devoted to defending the Custer image. The couple had no children. See CUSTER, ELIZABETH BACON.

Reconstruction Duty

The position of adjutant general of Mexico was offered to Custer by Benito Juárez, the Mexican president, in Spring 1866 with a salary of $18,000 in gold— twice his major general's pay. Custer would be required to lead the army against Emperor Maximilian, the French puppet. Although highly recommended by President GRANT, Gen. Phil Sheridan, and Secretary of War Stanton, Secretary of State Seward thought France might be offended and refused to allow Custer a leave of absence to accept the position. Custer's assignment in June 1865 was to command the Cavalry Division of the Military District of the Southwest, and to organize a cavalry division in Alexandria, LA, that would later be stationed in Texas. Right from the start, he encountered severe discipline problems with veteran troops who had fought in the Civil War but now wanted to go home. It was the first time in his career that soldiers under his command did not worship him, and it was here that Custer faced a rumored assassination attempt and squelched a mutiny. The unit moved to Hempstead, TX, in August and was finally garrisoned in Austin, headquartered at the Blind Asylum, from November 1865, until Custer's departure in February 1866. Although Custer and his troops were at odds throughout his tenure as commanding officer, on a personal basis he enjoyed his duty in Texas. Wife Libbie, cook Eliza BROWN, brother Tom, and even his father, Emanuel—employed as a forage agent—had accompanied him. The local society was extremely cordial, and the Custers spent their days riding, hunting, and simply catching up on life after the wartime separation. *Sources for further study include: Custer in Texas: An Interrupted Narrative*, by John M. Carroll (New York: Sol Lewis, 1975); *Tenting on the Plains: Or, General Custer in Kansas and Texas*, by Elizabeth Bacon Custer (New York: Harper and Brothers, 1887); "The Boy General and How He Grew," by Minnie Dubbs Millbrook, *Montana: The Magazine of Western History* 23 (Spring 1973); "A Better Time Is in Store for Us: An Analysis of the Reconstruction Attitudes of George Armstrong Custer," by William L. Richter, *Military History of Texas and the Southwest* 11 (1973).

Politics

Custer's initial foray into politics came while campaigning for Andrew Johnson, the man who had ascended to the presidency when Lincoln was assassinated. Custer and wife Libbie toured with Johnson in September 1866 in an attempt to win support for the president's Southern policy, which was a plea for voters in the fall to approve lenient treatment of the defeated people. Johnson likened the Union to a circle that had been broken and required mending, and therefore called his tour "Swinging Round the Circle." Newspapers speculated that Custer had been promised a colonelcy (not true, although he had requested one in writing), and attacked him vehemently for the first time in his career because he mingled with traitor Southerners, in particular the president who was much despised in the North. Even in Custer Country—Michigan, Indiana, and Ohio—the reception was unpleasant at best. He and Libbie left the presidential party before the end of the trip in order to escape the protesters and bad publicity.

7th Cavalry

The SEVENTH CAVALRY Regiment was one of four new regiments authorized by an act of Congress on July 28, 1866. It was assigned to FORT RILEY, KA, with the mission of protecting the KANSAS PACIFIC RAILROAD from hostile Indians.

Lt. Col. Custer, second in command to Col. A. J. SMITH, who spent much of the time on detached duty, made his first appearance on the evening of November 3, 1866. He was accompanied by wife Libbie, her friend, and their cook, Eliza BROWN.

Hancock Expedition

Maj. Gen. W. S. HANCOCK, commander of the Department of the Missouri, was chosen to lead an operation into Kansas—called the HANCOCK EXPEDITION OF 1867—to demonstrate the might of the military to the Plains Indians. Custer led 8 companies of the 7th Cavalry on this expedition, and chased the Indians across the Kansas Plains for several months. Detachments of his regiment were involved in harrowing escapes and minor skirmishes, which in the end accomplished little in coaxing the Indians to become peaceful. More notable than his exploits against the Indians were Custer's actions on this operation that led to charges against him at a court-martial in September.

Court-Martial

The incidents that led to this court-martial occurred during the Hancock Expedition of 1867. The court-martial of Brevet Maj. Gen. George Armstrong Custer convened at FORT LEAVENWORTH, KA, on September 15, 1867, at 11:00 A.M. A summary of the charges preferred by Col. A. J. Smith is as follows:

First Charge: Absence without leave from his command. Without proper authority Custer traveled from FORT WALLACE to FORT HAYS, a distance of about 275 miles, at a time when his command was expected to be actively engaged against hostile Indians.

Second Charge: Conduct to the prejudice of good order and military discipline. Immediately after his command had completed a long and exhausting march, when the horses were in an unfit condition, Custer and about 75 men with their horses executed a rapid march from FORT WALLACE, KA to Fort Hays without proper authority. Custer then procured at Fort Hays (2 ambulances and) 4 mules belonging to the United States, and did use such (ambulances and) mules for the conveyance to himself and part of his escort from said Fort Hays to FORT HARKER. Further, having received information that a party of Indians had attacked a small party detached from his escort near Downer's Station, KA, Custer failed to take proper measures for the repulse of the Indians, or the defense or relief of the detachment. After the return of the detached party of his command with a report that 2 of their number had been killed, Custer neglected to take any measures to pursue the Indians, or recover or bury the bodies of those of his command that had been killed.

Additional charges were preferred by Capt. Robert W. West, a member of Custer's command.

First Charge: Conduct prejudicial to good order and military discipline. While en route commanding and marching a column of his regiment, Custer, when ordering a party of 3 commissioned officers and others of his command in pursuit of supposed deserters who were then in view leaving camp, also ordered said party to shoot the supposed deserters down dead without trial; and did thus cause 3 men to be severely wounded. After the soldiers had been shot down and severely wounded, Custer ordered the said soldiers to be placed in a wagon, and to be hauled 18 miles without medical treatment. One deserter, Private Charles Johnson, was so severely wounded that he soon died.

Custer pleaded not guilty to all charges and specifications. However, after almost a month of testimony—including a lengthy written rebuttal by Custer—the court found him guilty on all counts. He was sentenced to be suspended from rank and command for one year, and to forfeit

his pay for the same time. Custer thought that the reviewing officer might overturn the verdict, but on November 18, 1867, Lt. Gen. William T. SHERMAN issued a brief statement that the "proceedings, findings and sentence in the case of Brevet Major General Custer are approved by President Grant." Custer was less than devastated by the findings. He considered himself persecuted as scapegoat for the failure of the Hancock Expedition. Some vindication came from Gen. Sheridan, who considered Custer unfairly treated, and offered the Custers complimentary use of his quarters at Fort Leavenworth during the suspension. The couple accepted Sheridan's offer, and spent an enjoyable winter social season there before leaving for home in Monroe, MI, the following spring.

Custer's Side of the Story

However, the question remains: why did Custer make his mad dash across Kansas? Custer, backed up by his wife Libbie in her memoirs, wrote:

Our [the expedition's] arrival at Fort Wallace was most welcome as well as opportune. The Indians had become so active and numerous that all travel over the SMOKY HILL route had ceased; stages had been taken off the route, and many of the stage stations had been abandoned by the employees, the latter fearing a repetition of the Lookout Station Massacre. No dispatches or mail had been received at the fort for a considerable period, so that occupants might well have been considered as undergoing a state of siege. ... We were over two hundred miles from the terminus of the railroad over which our supplies were drawn, and a still greater distance from the main depots of supplies. It was found that the reserve of stores at the post was well-nigh exhausted, and the commanding officer reported that he knew of no fresh supplies being on the way. ... Cholera made its appearance among the men, and deaths occurred daily. ... I decided to select upward of a hundred of the best mounted men in my command and with this force open a way through to Fort Harker a distance of two hundred miles, where I expected to obtain abundant supplies.

True, Fort Wallace would normally have been considered under a state of siege at that point in time. But the arrival of Custer's troops had certainly provided some relief in the way of reinforcements. It is questionable as to whether the news about the cholera epidemic had reached Fort Wallace at the time of Custer's arrival. Regarding supplies, conflicting reports indicate that only the quartermaster could say for sure.

An Unspoken Reason

One of the most plausible theories for the mad dash would be more credible if it hadn't been brought to light by Custer's nemesis, Capt. F. W. BENTEEN. Benteen claimed that Lt. Charles Brewster wrote an anonymous letter, possibly at the urging of Custer's servant, Eliza Brown, warning Custer that he had better return home and "look after his wife a little closer." Rumor had it that wife Libbie and Capt. Thomas WEIR were becoming an item. Weir had indeed been accompanying Libbie and other ladies around forts Hays and Harker, but it was not unusual on the frontier for temporarily unattached wives to be escorted by any available officer when their own husbands were on duty. And, as has been mentioned in various diaries and memoirs, officers' wives considered flirting one of the benefits of life in the frontier military where men outnumbered the women by astronomical numbers. Although it is doubtful that Libbie Custer had anything more than a flirtatious passing interest in Capt. Weir, it would be a romantic notion to think that Custer would have jeopardized his career just to see the woman he loved. Libbie remembered the occasion of her husband's surprise morning visit; it began when she

heard "The clank of a saber on our gallery and with it the quick, springing steps of feet, unlike the quiet infantry around us. The door behind which I paced uneasily, opened, and with a flood of sunshine that poured in, came vision far brighter than even the brilliant Kansas sun. There before me, blithe and buoyant, stood my husband!" And that visit inspired her to write: "There was in the summer of 1867 one long, perfect day. It was mine, and— blessed be the memory, which preserves to us the joys as well as the sadness of life!—it is still mine, for time and eternity." Benteen further stated that an angry Custer immediately confronted Weir upon his arrival at Fort Harker and had the captain begging for his life. Weir, it should be noted, was the officer who disobeyed orders at the Battle of the LITTLE BIGHORN and made the decision to move his company toward the distant sound of firing, which he likely suspected—and would have been correct to assume—was Custer's command in dire need of reinforcements. Why did Custer make his mad dash across Kansas? Only Custer knows for sure.

The Additional Charges

Capt. Robert West, a member of Custer's command, had preferred additional court-martial charges against Custer. West had apparently become disenchanted with Custer when, as officer of the day in May 1867, he was ordered by Custer to shave the heads of six men as punishment for an unauthorized visit to the store. Additionally, two of the deserters that Custer ordered shot on the Hancock Expedition were members of West's company. West also preferred civil murder charges against Custer and 1st Lt. W. W. COOKE on January 3, 1868, in connection with the shooting of the deserters. The two were arraigned on January 8 by Judge Adams, and discharged from custody due to a question of jurisdiction. On January 18 the judge cited a lack of evidence and dismissed the case. West, a capable officer when sober, had a history of letting the bottle get the better of him. He faced a court-martial on charges of drunkenness brought by Custer in early 1868 and was convicted and suspended from service for a period of two months. When Custer returned to duty from his suspension to prepare for the winter campaign of 1868–69, he was warmly greeted by his command, including Capt. West. Custer, however, refused to shake West's hand. West, perhaps beginning to read the writing on the wall, resigned his commission in early 1869 when he received the sutlership at the new Fort Sill. *Sources for further study include: Tenting on the Plains; Or, General Custer in Kansas and Texas,* by Elizabeth Bacon Custer (New York: Harper and Brothers, 1887); *My Life on the Plains; Or, Personal Experience with Indians,* by George A. Custer, edited by Edgar I. Stewart (Norman: University of Oklahoma Press, 1962); "The Court-Martial of Brevet Major General George A. Custer," by Milton B. Halsey, Jr., *Trail Guide* 13 (September 1968); and "The Court-Martial of General George Armstrong Custer," by Lawrence A. Frost (Norman: University of Oklahoma Press, 1968), *Annals of Wyoming* 36 (October 1964).

The Washita Campaign

The regiment remained for the most part in garrison throughout the winter of 1867–68 when cold weather kept the Indians idle. The peace commissioners worked to make treaties with the Plains tribes. However, when spring arrived the hostilities commenced. Following a summer of war waged by the Indians, Gen. Phil Sheridan knew he must take drastic action. On September 1, 1868, Brig. Gen. Alfred SULLY marched out of FORT DODGE with 11 companies of the 7th Cavalry under acting commander Maj. Joel ELLIOTT for the purpose of punishing the Indians. Sully soon returned to Fort Dodge, his expedition an embarrassing failure. Further vindication from Custer's court-martial came in the form of a telegram he received, dated September 24, 1868, from Maj. Gen. Phil Sheri-

dan, Headquarters, the Department of the Missouri, requesting that he report immediately for duty. Custer was back in the business of commanding the 7th Cavalry in the field, and the WASHITA CAMPAIGN OF 1868–69 commenced. This campaign, which included the controversial Battle of WASHITA—as well as numerous other controversial incidents—was a great success for the army and established Custer as the premier Indian fighter in the country.

Kentucky

In 1871 the 7th Cavalry was assigned in small detachments around the South in the states of Kentucky, Tennessee, and South Carolina. Custer and two companies were stationed from September 1871 until February 1873 at Elizabethtown, KY. Duties included keeping track of the Ku Klux Klan, local moonshiners, and purchasing horses for the army. Otherwise, he spent time at the horse breeding farms and racetracks, but longed to return to the action of the frontier. One respite from duty was his buffalo hunt with ALEXIS, Grand Duke of Russia, January–February 1872. *Sources for further study include:* "Custer's Kentucky: General George Armstrong Custer and Elizabethtown, Kentucky, 1871–1873," by Theodore J. Crakel, *Filson Club History Quarterly* 49 (April 1974); *Nomad: George A. Custer* in Turf, Field and Farm, edited by Brian W. Dippie (Austin: University of Texas Press, 1980); and *General Custer's Thoroughbreds: Racing, Riding, Hunting, and Fighting,* by Lawrence A. Frost (Bryan, TX: J. M. Carroll, 1986).

Yellowstone Expedition

In the spring of 1873 the regiment reassembled in Memphis, TN, for the journey to FORT RICE, D.T. From there, the column marched in June on the YELLOWSTONE EXPEDITION OF 1873 to provide security for the NORTHERN PACIFIC RAILROAD survey team, led by Custer's former West Point roommate and Civil War opponent Tom Rosser. Custer engaged in two notable skirmishes with SIOUX Indians under CRAZY HORSE, and again proved his skill as an Indian fighter. The regiment returned from the expedition on September 23 to their new home, FORT ABRAHAM LINCOLN, near Bismarck, D.T.

Black Hills Expedition

The military forces of the BLACK HILLS EXPEDITION OF 1874 marched out of Fort Lincoln July 2, 1874, with Custer commanding ten companies of the 7th Cavalry. Its mission was to explore the wilderness region in western Dakota known as the BLACK HILLS, which had been given to the SIOUX by treaty. By the time the expedition had returned on August 30 and settled in for the harsh Dakota winter, they had discovered gold deposits and had incited a growing hostility from the Sioux for their intrusion. This expedition and the subsequent invasion of the Black Hills by gold prospectors directly led to the GREAT SIOUX WAR OF 1876–77, which included the Battle of the LITTLE BIGHORN and the LITTLE BIGHORN CAMPAIGN.

Politics

The year 1875 was spent with garrison duty, routine drills, and dress parades. In early 1876 Custer was called to Washington, D.C., to testify before Congress about the sale of post tradership and associated corruption. He drew the ire of President GRANT when he spoke against the president's brother, who was involved in the illegal scheme. As punishment, Grant refused to permit Custer to accompany the Dakota column on the LITTLE BIGHORN CAMPAIGN. Grant eventually relented, and Custer was restored to duty. See BELKNAP SCANDAL.

Little Bighorn

Custer and the 7th Cavalry marched out of Fort Lincoln on May 17, 1876, to participate in the Little Bighorn Campaign. 1st Lt. (later Gen.) E. S. GODFREY, commander of K company, described Custer's appearance for the march:

Gen. Custer carried a Remington Sporting rifle, octagonal barrel; two Bulldog self-cocking, English, white-handled pistols, with a ring in the butt for a lanyard; a hunting knife, in a beaded fringed scabbard; and a canvas cartridge belt. He wore a whitish gray hat, with broad brim and rather low crown, very similar to the Cowboy hat; buck skin suit; with a fringed welt in outer seams of trousers and arms of blouse; the blouse with double-breasted military buttons, lapels generally open; turn down collar, and fringe on bottom of shirt. He rode "Vic," a sorrel with four white feet and legs and a blaze in the face.

The mission of the army was to force "hostile" Sioux and CHEYENNE Indians—those who had ignored an edict to surrender—onto their reservations. Custer's cavalry rode in a detachment called the Dakota Column under the command of Gen. Alfred TERRY. Two other forces were included: the Montana Column under Col. John GIBBON marched from Fort Ellis and the Wyoming Column led by Gen. George CROOK marched from FORT FETTERMAN. Terry's plan called for 3 columns to converge in a pincer movement designed to trap the Indians in between them. While Crook camped along Goose Creek in Wyoming and Gibbon with Terry approached as reinforcements, the 7th Cavalry was ordered to follow a fresh Indian trail. This trail eventually led to SITTING BULL's village on the Little Bighorn River. Without knowing the exact number of enemy or the terrain, Custer attacked on Sunday afternoon, June 25. Custer and about 225 of his troopers were all killed by a superior force of Indians in what became known as the Battle of the Little Bighorn. Custer had written just 2 months before the battle: "If I were an Indian, I often think I would greatly prefer to cast my lot among those of my people who adhere to the free open plains rather than submit to the confined limits of a reservation, there to be recipient of the blessed benefits of civilization, with its vices thrown in without stint or measure."

Burial

Two days following the battle, Custer's body was buried in a shallow grave where he fell. A year later his remains were exhumed, and on October 10, 1877, he was buried with full military honors at West Point. See also TILFORD, JOSEPH G. *Sources for further study include:* Custer was author of *My Life on the Plains; Or, Personal Experiences with Indians*, a compilation of his articles from *Galaxy* magazine, edited by Edgar I. Stewart (Norman: University of Oklahoma Press, 1962); and *Nomad: George A. Custer in* Turf, Field and Farm, a compilation of articles from *Turf, Field and Farm* magazine, edited by Brian W. Dippie (Austin: University of Texas Press, 1980). Excerpts from a sampling of his correspondence can be found in *The Custer Story: The Life and Intimate Letters of General George A. Custer and His Wife Elizabeth*, edited by Marguerite Merington (New York: Devin-Adair, 1950). Notable biographies include: *Crazy Horse and Custer: The Parallel Lives of Two American Warriors*, by Stephen E. Ambrose (Garden City, NY: Doubleday, 1975); *Son of the Morning Star*, by Evan S. Connell (San Francisco: North Point, 1984); *The Custer Album, a Pictorial Biography of General George A. Custer*, by Lawrence A. Frost (Norman: University of Oklahoma Press, 1990); *Favor the Bold*, by D. A. Kinsley, 2 vols. (New York: Holt, Rhinehart and Winston, 1967–68); *Custer: The Life of General George Armstrong Custer*, by Jay Monaghan (Boston: Little, Brown, 1959); *Cavalier in Buckskin: George Armstrong Custer and the Military Frontier*, by Robert M. Utley (Norman: University of Oklahoma Press, 1988); *Glory-Hunter: A Life of General Custer*, by Frederic F. Van de Water (Indianapolis: Bobbs-Merrill Co., 1934); and *A Complete Life of Gen. George A. Custer* by Frederick Whittaker (New York: Sheldon, 1876).

Custer, Libbie *see* CUSTER, ELIZABETH BACON

Custer, Margaret Emma *see* CALHOUN, MARGARET EMMA

Custer, Maria Ward Kirkpatrick (Mrs. Emanuel Custer) (1807–82) The mother of George Armstrong Custer. She had been a widow with three children when she became the second wife of Emanuel CUSTER in 1836. Mrs. Custer was usually referred to as being in ill health or an invalid for much of her life. It is probable that George Armstrong was her favorite, inasmuch as the first two Custer children died in infancy and George was an only child for his first three years. One thing is certain: Custer adored her and had never quite severed that invisible umbilical cord. Wife Libbie Custer wrote in *"Boots and Saddles"; Or, Life in Dakota with General Custer* (New York: Harper and Brothers, 1885): "The hardest trial of my husband's life was parting with his mother. Such partings were the only occasions when I ever saw him lose entire control of himself. ... She had been an invalid for so many years that each parting seemed to her the final one. ... The general would rush out of the house, sobbing like a child, and then throw himself into the carriage beside me, completely unnerved." Mother Custer was opposed to her son entering West Point, primarily because of the ominous threat of Civil War, but left that decision in God's hands. Her grief following the Battle of the LITTLE BIGHORN when she lost three sons was understandable. "How can I stand it?" she lamented. "All my boys gone."

Custer, Nevin Johnson (July 29, 1842–February 10, 1915) Nevin was the second son born to Emanuel and Maria Custer, three and one-half years younger than older brother George Armstrong. Nevin did not follow his brothers into the military. He reported to the Cleveland, OH, recruiting office to volunteer, but was physically disqualified due to chronic rheumatism. Nevin married, had five children, and took up farming. In early 1871 Custer sold some mining stock in order to send Nevin a down payment on a jointly purchased farm that would allow his brother to remain near their aging parents in Monroe, MI. Apparently, the venture was a struggle. Wife Libbie wrote to Custer in late August 1873 to say: "Mother Custer is in low spirits. She worries about Nevie. His poor crops, his poverty, his increasing family." Following Custer's death, wife Libbie auctioned off her portion of the farm: Nevin bid $775 to buy the 114 acres. Nevin died suddenly from an attack of gastritis, and the occasion of his funeral became Libbie Custer's final trip to Monroe, MI.

Custer, Thomas Ward (March 15, 1845–June 25, 1876) Tom was the third son born to Emanuel and Maria Custer, six years younger than brother George Armstrong whom he worshiped.

Civil War Record

Tom attempted to enlist at the outbreak of the Civil War in 1861, but his father had alerted the recruiter that Tom was only 16—2 years too young—and he was turned down. That had been in Monroe, MI. Across the border was the town of New Rumley, OH, where he had been born. On September 2, 1861, away from his father's watchful eye, Pvt. Tom Custer was sworn into Company H of the 21st Ohio Infantry. For the next 3 years Tom fought as a common foot soldier in such battles as Shiloh, Stones River, Chickamauga, Missionary Ridge, Chattanooga, and in the Atlanta Campaign. He distinguished himself enough to be assigned as orderly to Brig. Gen. J. S. Nedley, and was promoted to corporal in 1864. Regardless of his success with the infantry, Tom knew that the real glory was in the cavalry: as evidenced by his brother who, at age 23, had become the youngest general in history. Due to the influence of his brother, Tom Custer was commissioned as a second lieutenant on November 8, 1864, and was appointed to the

staff of Gen. Custer's 6th Michigan Cavalry. The older Custer showed no favoritism, and indeed regularly chose his brother for extra assignments. Nevertheless, the hardened veterans of the unit were highly skeptical of their new comrade who had been quickly promoted to captain.

Medal of Honor

In keeping with Custer tradition, Tom would distinguish himself and earn the respect of his comrades by leading a daring charge. On April 3, 1865, Gen. Robert E. Lee with 80,000 retreating men had passed just north of Gen. Custer's campsite, traveling west along the Appomattox River Valley. Gen. Custer followed, moving his troops cautiously along the Namozine Road until they reached Namozine Creek. The bridge had been destroyed, and Rebel fortifications could be observed on the far bank. Gen. Custer did not know it at the time, but his men were greatly outnumbered by the enemy. He ordered one troop to outflank the position by wading the stream while a cannon battered the breastworks. Men with axes were detailed to remove the fallen trees from the stream and thereby permit the remainder of the troops to easily cross and attack. Tom Custer, however, refused to wait for the stream to be cleared. He impatiently spurred his horse and brazenly charged across Namozine Creek toward the enemy position, a course of action that inspired the rest of the troops to follow. The enemy fired volleys at the onrushing cavalrymen, but soon broke as a result of the surprise maneuver. The battle became a running fight as the Rebels tried to elude their pursuers. When Capt. Custer's small force neared the Namozine Church, they found themselves facing a determined line of Confederate cavalry. Once more it was Tom who boldly led the charge, and was the first cavalryman to break through. He headed straight for the regimental color bearer, for that was the prize that he had set his sights on. It may seem odd, but nineteenth-century combatants considered the capture of enemy battle colors to be the highest measure of glory that could be bestowed upon an individual. This resulted from the belief that the loss of a regimental flag was a unit's greatest shame, and was therefore worth fighting and dying for. In truth, it was an act that assuredly took courage but had little military significance whatsoever. Tom's personal mission, however, was successful. He shot the color bearer from the saddle and snatched away the coveted regimental colors. He continued on, the banner streaming behind, to ride a dangerous obstacle course through the woods. Suddenly, he rode directly into a group of gray uniforms. He prepared to shoot his way out, but found it unnecessary. Instead of fighting, the beaten Confederates raised their arms to indicate surrender. When hostilities had cooled, an elated Capt. Custer presented his proud brother with the battle flag along with 14 prisoners, including 3 officers. Maj. Gen. Phil SHERIDAN recommended that Tom Custer be breveted to major and awarded the Medal of Honor for his valor.

Second Medal of Honor

A second opportunity to display his courage came just 3 days later. Early on April 6, Lee's exhausted army was approaching Farmville when the column inadvertently split into two detachments. Gen. Custer's opportunistic cavalrymen plunged right into the enemy at a place called Sayler's Creek. The hastily entrenched Confederates put up a gallant fight, and kept the division at bay for some time. Tom Custer was at the front of the 3rd Brigade when it led the charge against enemy lines. The Rebels held their fire behind the improvised breastworks until the last moment, then unleashed a furious barrage. The assaulting cavalrymen were undaunted, and soared over the fortifications with hooves flying, sabers slashing, and pistols smoking. Within minutes, the gray line was sent

scattering in the wake of the surging Federals. The Rebels continued to fight as they withdrew to the north. Now that the most serious fighting was over, Tom Custer was intent upon capturing one or more Rebel battle colors. He swooped down on a likely target, but the Confederate color bearer was not about to easily part with the prize and fired his pistol point-blank at the charging Custer's head. The bullet struck Tom in the cheek and exited behind his ear. His face was blackened with powder and blood spurted from the severe wound. The force of the blast threw him backward, flat against his horse's rump. He struggled to right himself and had the presence of mind to draw his own revolver. With a remarkably steady hand, he coolly shot and killed the standardbearer then grabbed the coveted banner. Blood poured down his damaged face as he wheeled his horse and galloped through the chaotic battlefield with one thought in mind. The wound was of minor consequence; he wanted to show off the trophy to his brother. Then Col. (and eventual Gen.) Henry Capehart, a future Medal of Honor winner himself, had witnessed Tom's actions and later said, "for intrepidity I never saw this incident surpassed." Tom jubilantly called to his brother, "the damned rebels have shot me, but I've got my flag!" The general took one look at his younger brother's gory injury and ordered Tom to go and have his wound dressed. Tom refused the command, stating that he would not leave the field until the battle had been won. He asked someone to look after his captured colors, and was about to ride off when his brother placed him under arrest. He was then escorted to the surgeon at a nearby plantation house being used as a hospital for necessary repairs. His heroic deeds throughout the battle and his demonstration of courage in capturing the enemy battle flag gained him a brevet of lieutenant colonel and his second Medal of Honor (see photo page 58). Thomas Ward Custer became the first

Capt. Thomas W. Custer, wearing his two Congressional Medals of Honor, 1870

person to be distinguished with two awards of our nation's highest military medal, and he was the only double honoree during the Civil War.

7th Cavalry

The 20-year-old was mustered out of the army on November 24, 1865. He received a regular army appointment as a second lieutenant in February 1866, and joined the SEVENTH CAVALRY in July as a first lieutenant. He participated in numerous engagements on the frontier, including the 1868 Battle of WASHITA, where he was wounded in the right hand and assumed command of Capt. Louis HAMILTON's C Company after the captain had been killed.

Wild Bill Hickok

Tom was a wild and reckless youth, an ardent gambler with cards who frequently drank to excess. The story is told about how he got on the wrong side of William Butler "Wild Bill" HICKOK in Hays City, KA, in 1869. A drunk Tom Custer rode his horse into a saloon, and was promptly dragged off and arrested by Wild Bill, then hauled before a justice of the peace and fined. Tom, incensed over the arrest, brought three soldiers with him on a later trip to town, and they cornered and disarmed Hickok. Physical revenge was about to be exacted when a bartender supplied Hickok with a pistol. Wild Bill quickly plugged the three soldiers (we don't know how seriously). Tom fled to FORT HAYS and reported the incident to Gen. Phil Sheridan, who ordered Hickok's arrest. Wild Bill hopped on a freight train and left town before being caught.

Rain-in-the-Face

As a first lieutenant, Custer accompanied his brother on both the YELLOWSTONE EXPEDITION OF 1873 and the controversial BLACK HILLS EXPEDITION OF 1874 into the BLACK HILLS region of South Dakota when gold was first discovered. An incident occurred between Tom and SIOUX Indian RAIN-IN-THE-FACE that has been the subject of some controversy. It began during the Yellowstone Expedition of 1873 when on August 4 three men attached to the 7th Cavalry were ambushed and killed by a Sioux war party near the mouth of the Tongue River. In December 1874 it was reported by scout Charley REYNOLDS to Gen. Custer that Rain-in-the-Face had been overheard bragging that he had been the one who had killed the men on the Tongue River the previous year. Custer decided that Rain-in-the-Face should face criminal charges for the murders. With temperatures reaching more than 50 below 0, Tom Custer was part of a detail assigned to capture the Indian and hold him for trial. They found Rain-in-the-Face in the Hatch Trading Store at Standing Rock Agency. Tom slipped behind Rain-in-the-Face and wrestled him to the floor. The fugitive was arrested and imprisoned at FORT ABRAHAM LINCOLN, but escaped during the night of April 18, 1875, with a little help from his friends. Rain-in-the-Face vowed revenge, promising to some day cut out Tom Custer's heart and eat it. Tom was killed in the Battle of the LITTLE BIGHORN, and singled out for the most brutal of mutilations. His body had been repeatedly stabbed, slashed, crushed beyond recognition, and riddled with arrows. He could be identified only by his tattoos: an American flag, an eagle with outspread wings, and the initials "T.W.C." The mutilation caused some to speculate that Rain-in-the-Face had taken his revenge. Capt. F. W. BENTEEN, however, swore that Tom's heart had *not* been removed. A Sioux Indian story explaining the mutilation theorized that because of one of Custer's tattoos—the eagle with outstretched wings, which signifies a leader in Indian tradition—many braves desired to strike the dead man whom they presumed to be the soldier chief. In addition, cannibalism was as repugnant to the Plains Indians as it was to the white man. Tom's sister-in-law, Libbie Custer, believed that Rain-in-the-Face had indeed committed the atrocity. She wrote in *"Boots and Saddles"; Or, Life in Dakota with General Custer* (New York: Harper and Brothers, 1885): "The vengeance of that incarnate fiend was concentrated on the man who had effected his capture. It was found on the battlefield that he had cut out the heart of that gallant, loyal, and lovable man, our brother Tom."

Little Bighorn

It has been speculated that Tom Custer, who was commander of C Company, had been assigned as aide-de-camp to his brother at the Battle of the Little Bighorn. Regardless, his body was found beside his brother on CUSTER HILL. The Custer brothers were temporarily buried side by side on that barren scab of land above the river the Plains Indians called Greasy Grass. On November 3, 1877, Tom's remains were removed and reinterred at FORT LEAVENWORTH, KA.

Custer Battlefield Historical and Museum Association (P.O. Box 902, Hardin, MT 59034) This former National Park Service cooperating association is dedicated to providing "both financial and moral support to the Little Bighorn Battlefield to the maximum extent."

Custer Battlefield National Monument *see* LITTLE BIGHORN BATTLEFIELD NATIONAL MONUMENT

Custer Battlefield Preservation Committee (P.O. Box 902, Hardin, MT 59034) This nonprofit organization, founded by former battlefield superintendent James Court, has purchased with donated funds hundreds of acres of land adjacent to LITTLE BIGHORN BATTLEFIELD NATIONAL MONUMENT for the purpose of protecting the integrity of the land.

Custer Hill It was here at the north end of CUSTER RIDGE on LITTLE BIGHORN battlefield that Custer and about 40 troopers made their last stand. A granite monument and marble slabs presently mark this location. See LITTLE BIGHORN, BATTLE OF.

"Custer's Last Stand" The name commonly used to refer to the Battle of the LITTLE BIGHORN. There were, in fact, a number of last stands during the battle. As the warriors pressed close to each individual pocket of resistance in the vicinity of BATTLE RIDGE—perhaps beginning with Custer's position and sweeping south towards companies F, I, and L—those desperate troopers would have fought until the last man fell. There is no evidence that Custer and his headquarters command on CUSTER HILL engaged in the thrilling last stand of legend and lore. In fact, many troopers from companies E and F that had assembled on Custer Hill in the latter stages of the battle were said to have fled toward the Little Bighorn River—in an attempt to either escape or attack—and were dispatched along the way. It has been speculated that Custer had been mortally wounded earlier in the battle on the initial charge down MEDICINE TAIL COULEE. Without knowledge of the exact location where Custer was killed, the question arises as to which Indian actually dispatched him. An endless parade of SIOUX and CHEYENNE candidates stepped forward in the years following the battle to confess. RAIN-IN-THE-FACE swore to a missionary on his death bed that he had committed the deed. TWO MOON made a likely candidate because he had a grudge against Custer. Brave Bear was given the distinction by the Cheyenne since he had survived Custer's attack at the Battle of WASHITA. White Bull was the subject of *The Warrior Who Killed Custer: The Personal Narrative of Chief White Bull*, translated and edited by James H. Howard (Lincoln: University of Nebraska Press, 1968). And then there was Hawk, Flat Hip, Scarlet Top, and Red Horse, who all claimed the honor as well. The allied Indians believed that the cavalry was led by Gen. George CROOK, whose command they had engaged at the Battle of the ROSEBUD a week earlier. It was later, when they had learned the identity of their famous foe, that the debate began. *Sources for further study include: Custer's Luck*, by Edgar I. Stewart (Norman: University of Oklahoma Press, 1955).

"Custer's Luck" Custer (and others) referred to the favorable events that occurred in his life as "Custer's Luck."

Custer Ridge *see* BATTLE RIDGE

D Company, Seventh Cavalry This company was commanded during the Battle of the LITTLE BIGHORN by Capt. Thomas B. WEIR with 2nd Lt. Winfield S. EDGERLY second in command. The company's other officer, 1st Lt. James M. BELL, was on a leave of absence. Company D was part of Capt. F. W. BENTEEN's scout, and participated in the RENO-BENTEEN DEFENSE SITE, where it lost 3 killed and 2 wounded.

Seven members were awarded the MEDAL OF HONOR for their actions.

Deep Ravine This drainage on LITTLE BIGHORN battlefield was north of MEDICINE TAIL COULEE, located near the end of the slope that ran from CUSTER HILL to the Little Bighorn River. Testimony from soldiers on the field 2 days after the battle stated that the bodies of 28 members of E Company were found and buried there, approximately 2,000 feet from Custer Hill. These bodies have subsequently eluded detection, perhaps due to a change in the course of the river.

DeRudio, Carlo (Charles Camilus) (August 26, 1832–November 1, 1910) First lieutenant, 7th Cavalry. DeRudio was a count, born in Bulluno, Italy, to a family of Venetian noblemen.

DeRudio graduated from the Royal Austrian Military Academy, and held a commission in Emperor Franz Joseph's army. However, he left the army to become a revolutionary and soldier of fortune, following Giuseppe Garibaldi to defend Rome against the French in 1849. It was in January 1858 that DeRudio participated with three others in a failed attempt to assassinate Napoleon III and Empress Eugénie with bombs at the Paris Opera. One man was sentenced to life imprisonment; DeRudio and the others received the death sentence. A last-minute reprieve saved DeRudio's life, and he was sentenced to life at the French penal colony on Devil's Island. In the fall of 1858 DeRudio and a dozen other men carved out a canoe from a tree and sailed to freedom in British Guiana.

He emigrated to the United States in 1864, and enlisted in the 79th New York Highlanders as a private. On October 17, 1864, he was commissioned as first lieutenant and assigned to the 2nd U.S. Colored Troops. He received an appointment to second lieutenant in the 2nd Infantry on August 31, 1867, but it was held up while the government investigated his

European criminal record, then finally restored.

On July 14, 1869, DeRudio was assigned to Company E of the SEVENTH CAVALRY. Just prior to the march to the LITTLE BIGHORN, he was transferred to assistant commander of A Company. The night before the battle, DeRudio and some other officers—BENTEEN, KEOGH, and PORTER among them—spent much of the night telling tales of thrilling escapes, but none of them topped those of the Italian soldier of fortune. Little did DeRudio know at the time that the following day he would add one more to his resumé.

It began during RENO'S VALLEY FIGHT, when Maj. Marcus RENO ordered the disastrous retreat from the timber to the bluffs across the Little Bighorn River. DeRudio, along with 2 scouts—Fred GERARD and Billy JACKSON—and a handful of troopers were cut off by the attacking Indians and left behind in the timber. The remainder of the command had either made it to the bluffs and dug in a defensive position (see RENO-BENTEEN DEFENSE SITE) or their bodies lay strewn along the bloody route the command had ridden. That night the stranded soldiers caught 2 horses, and 4 of the men, including DeRudio, rode to the river searching upstream for their comrades and a place to ford. Before long they were challenged by an Indian. The 2 scouts galloped away; DeRudio and a private named Thomas O'Neil hid on a small island. In the hazy light of dawn, DeRudio thought he observed the mounted command returning in the distance. He called out, thinking he had recognized Capt. Tom CUSTER. However, it was not Tom Custer or the 7th Cavalry, although the mounted men were clearly riding 7th Cavalry horses—they were Indians. The warriors fired at them, and they scampered away into the brush, only to run into more Indians. The 2 soldiers fired at those Indians, and took refuge behind a grouping of stumps and fallen logs. The Indians broke contact, allowing the cavalrymen to remain hidden. Later, they watched as a procession of Indians, mostly women and children, passed within 50 yards of their position heading south toward the Bighorn Mountains. When darkness arrived, DeRudio and O'Neil crawled to the river and quenched their great thirst. DeRudio decided they would walk out, down the Little Bighorn to the Yellowstone then to the Rosebud. But then he heard the braying of a mule, and knew that soldiers must be nearby. DeRudio and O'Neil approached the line on the bluffs, identified themselves, and were saved. The 2 scouts had appeared some time earlier in the evening.

Contrary to paintings and illustrations of the Little Bighorn Battle that depict the soldiers wearing a SABER, the troops had, in fact, left their sabers with the packtrain, except for possibly DeRudio (a European soldier would not consider himself completely dressed without his saber) and 1st Lt. E. G. MATHEY. DeRudio was promoted to captain on December 17, 1882, and retired a major in 1896.

Sources for further study include: Charles C. DeRudio, by Charles K. Mills (Bryan, TX: J. M. Carroll, 1983); "Interview with Charles DeRudio, February 2, 1910," in *Custer in '76: Walter Camp's Notes on the Custer Fight*, edited by Kenneth Hammer (Provo, UT: Brigham Young University Press, 1976); "Charles DeRudio (Carlo DeRudio) 1st Lt. 7th U.S. Cavalry," by Melville Stone, *Collier's Weekly*, May 15, 1920; and "Major DeRudio: A Man with a Charmed Life," *Washington Star*, October 16, 1910. According to DeRudio, the following publications attributed to him were actually written by Maj. James BRISBIN, 2nd Cavalry, who moonlighted as a newspaper correspondent, and were "colored" a good deal: "My Personal Story," *New York Herald*, July 30, 1876, and reprinted in the *Chicago Times*, August 2, 1876, and the *Frontier and Midland Magazine*, January 1934 (Montana State University, Missoula).

De Wolfe, Dr. James M. Acting assistant surgeon, 7th Cavalry. De Wolfe was an enlisted man during the Civil War, then on the frontier. He graduated from Harvard Medical School on June 26, 1875, one day short of a full year prior to the Battle of the LITTLE BIGHORN. Dr. De Wolfe was attached to the command of Maj. Marcus RENO during the battle. He was with the troopers who fled from the timber in an attempt to reach the bluffs across the Little Bighorn River during RENO'S VALLEY FIGHT. De Wolfe and his orderly made it as far as the bluffs, but chose the wrong ravine to climb and were halfway to the top when they were killed by the Indians. It is possible that he had stopped to administer to a wounded soldier when he was killed. He was subsequently scalped in plain view of the other troops. De Wolfe was buried on the slope where he fell; a marble slab presently marks the location.

Disobedience of Orders by Custer at the Battle of the Little Bighorn One of the major controversies that has surrounded the march was the accusation that Custer had willfully disobeyed orders and thereby brought about the loss of his command. The only solid documented evidence remaining that could substantiate or refute this is the written order from Gen. Alfred TERRY to Custer pertaining to the march. The issuance of this order came a day after a June 21, 1876, strategy meeting aboard the steamer *FAR WEST*, attended by Gen. Terry, Custer, Col. John GIBBON, and Maj. James BRISBIN, where verbal orders were in all likelihood provided. It was Terry's intention to have the scouts and guides locate the Indians, then strike with two columns (Custer and Gibbon) within cooperating distance: a "waiting fight" where one would, if possible, give time for the other to come up. The text of Gen. Terry's orders to Custer as dictated to Capt. Smith, the acting assistant adjutant general is as follows:

Camp at Mouth of Rosebud River
Montana Territory

June 22nd, 1876

LIEUT.-COL. CUSTER 7TH CAVALRY
COLONEL:

The Brigadier-General Commanding directs that, as soon as your regiment can be made ready for the march, you will proceed up the Rosebud in pursuit of the Indians whose trail was discovered by Major Reno a few days since. It is, of course, impossible to give you any definite instructions in regard to this movement, and were it not impossible to do so the Department Commander places too much confidence in your zeal, energy, and ability to wish to impose upon you precise orders which might hamper your action when nearly in contact with the enemy. He will, however, indicate to your his views of what your actions should be, and he desires that you should conform to them unless you shall see sufficient reasons for departing from them. He thinks that you should proceed up the Rosebud until you ascertain definitely the direction in which the trail above spoken of leads. Should it be found (as it appears almost certain that it will be found) to turn towards the Little Horn, he thinks that you should still proceed southward, perhaps as far as the headwaters of the Tongue, and then turn toward the Little Horn, feeling constantly, however, to your left, so as to preclude the possibility of the escape of the Indians to the south or southeast by passing around your left flank. The column of Colonel Gibbon is now in motion for the mouth of the Big Horn. As soon as it reaches that point it will cross the Yellowstone and move up at least as far as the forks of the Big and Little Horns. Of its future movements must be controlled by circumstances as they arise, but it is hoped that the Indians, if upon the Little Horn, may be so nearly enclosed by the two columns that their escape will be impossible.

The Department Commander desires that on your way up the Rosebud you should thoroughly examine the upper part of Tulloch's Creek, and that you should endeavor to send a scout through to Colonel Gibbon's column, with information of the result of your examination. The lower part of the creek will be examined by a detachment from Colonel Gibbon's command. The supply steamer will be pushed up the Big Horn as far as the forks if the river is found navigable for that distance, and the Department Commander, who will accompany the column of Colonel Gibbon, desires you to report to him not later than the expiration of the time for which your troops are rationed, unless in the meantime you receive further orders.

Very respectfully your obedient servant
E. W. SMITH
Captain 18th Infantry
Acting Assistant Adjutant General

Some scholars have suggested that Custer was to rendezvous with the Terry-Gibbon Column on June 26, one day after the battle. Perhaps, however, the Terry-Gibbon Column did not arrive until June 27, a day (or two days) late. Custer, in his defense, believed that the presence of the soldiers had been discovered by the SIOUX as evidenced by the episode of the box of hardtack falling from the mules and being surrounded by Indians. That would make it imperative in his mind that he attack immediately due to the Indian custom of fleeing from a large detachment of soldiers. Custer critic Capt. F. W. BENTEEN, whose own compliance with orders can be questioned, wrote to his wife on July 4, 1876: "Had Custer carried out order he got from Genl. Terry the command would have formed a junction exactly at the village—and have captured the whole outfit of tepees, etc. and probably any quantity of squaws, pappooses &c. &c. but Custer disobeyed orders from the fact of not wanting any other command—or body to have a finger in the p ie, and thereby lost his life." Custer's cook, Mary ADAMS, who had accompanied him on the expedition, claimed in an affidavit dated January 16, 1878, that she overheard Gen.

Terry tell Custer: "Use your own judgment and do what you think best if you strike the trail." Gen. Terry told Charles S. Diehl, a reporter for the *Chicago Times* (published September 16, 1876) that Custer, had he survived, would have faced a court-martial for disobeying orders. It should be noted that blame for the failed campaign was initially placed on Terry for incompetence, and at least one newspaper called for *his* court-martial. The ensuing debate has been split—as is the case with any Custer controversy—along loyalty lines. The pro-Custer faction believes that Terry's order was a suggestion, and refers to the opening paragraph (which Custer sent to his wife Libbie as proof of Terry's confidence in his discretion). On the other hand, in military terms, a suggestion by a superior officer becomes a lawful order. *Sources for further study include: Did Custer Disobey Orders at the Battle of the Little Bighorn?* by Charles Kuhlman (Harrisburg, PA: Stackpole, 1957); *"Sufficient Reason?" An Examination of Terry's Celebrated Order to Custer*, by Francis B. Taunton (London: English Westerners' Society, 1977); *Indian Fights and Fighters*, by Cyrus T. Brady (New York: McClure, Phillips, 1904); *The Custer Myth:*

A Source Book of Custeriana, by W. A. Graham (Harrisburg, PA: Stackpole, 1953); and *Custer and the Great Controversy: The Origin and Development of a Legend*, by Robert M. Utley (Pasadena, CA: Westernlore, 1980).

Dog Soldiers *see* CHEYENNE INDIANS

Dorman, Isaiah (Interpreter; Sioux name: Azimpi or "Teat") This *wasicum sapa* or black white man—likely a runaway slave—worked off and on as a courier, guide, scout, and interpreter for the army beginning about 1865. He married a Santee SIOUX girl from Inkpaduta's band, and lived with the Sioux Indians or in a cabin near FORT RICE. It was said that he counted SITTING BULL among his friends, which permitted him to wander through Indian country unmolested. At the Battle of the LITTLE BIGHORN Dorman was attached to Maj. Marcus RENO's battalion, and was killed during RENO'S VALLEY FIGHT after the command left the timber for a retreat across the Little Bighorn River to the bluffs. One story stated that Dorman lay seriously wounded, and was found by Sitting Bull. He asked the chief for a cup of water, which was provided. Other accounts differ, claiming that Dorman was singled out for special torture and mutilation due to his betrayal of the Sioux. Chief Runs-the-Enemy described the death of Dorman in *The Vanishing Race*, by Joseph K. Dixon (Garden City, NY: Doubleday, Page, 1913): "We passed a black man in a soldier's uniform and we had him. He turned on his horse and shot an Indian right through the heart. Then the Indians fired at this one man and riddled his horse with bullets. His horse fell over his back and the black man could not get up. I saw him as I rode by. I afterward saw him lying there dead." Dorman died leaving behind a paycheck (for somewhere between $62.50 and $102.50) from the U.S. government that went unclaimed until 1879, when a man named

Isaac McNutt appeared to present a voucher for the money. McNutt's claim was denied, and the money remains unpaid. *Sources for further study include:* "Isiah Dorman and the Custer Expedition," by Ronald C. McConnell, *Journal of Negro History* 33 (July 1948).

Dull Knife (Northern Cheyenne; ca. 1810–83) Dull Knife fought alongside CRAZY HORSE, GALL, and RAIN-IN-THE-FACE when RED CLOUD waged war against the army over the BOZEMAN TRAIL. He signed the FORT LARAMIE TREATY OF 1868, but did not abide by its provisions and continued to fight, including the battles of the ROSEBUD and the LITTLE BIGHORN. Col. Ranald MACKENSIE attacked Dull Knife's village on November 25, 1876, in the Battle of DULL KNIFE, inflicting many casualties and destroying the Indian possessions and pony herd. In May 1877 Dull Knife and his people surrendered at CAMP ROBINSON, and were sent to the reservation near Fort Reno, I.T., far from their homeland. In September 1878 Dull Knife fled from the reservation, and led his followers northward toward their Tongue River homeland. More than 10,000 soldiers and civilians followed and engaged in minor skirmishes with the refugees. Dull Knife was finally captured and taken to Camp Robinson, from where he subsequently escaped. He hid at Red Cloud's reservation at Pine Ridge, but finally surrendered. He died one year before his people were given a reservation on their Tongue River homeland. *Sources for further study include: Cheyenne Autumn*, by Mari Sandoz (New York: McGraw-Hill, 1953); and "The Northern Cheyennes," by Verne Dusemberry (Helena, MT: *Montana Magazine*, 1955).

Dull Knife, Battle of (November 25, 1876) This battle, fought between the U.S. Army, led by Gen. George CROOK, and CHEYENNE Indians under DULL KNIFE, was part of the GREAT SIOUX WAR OF 1876–77. The Indians lost their village, pony herd, and more than 30 dead; army casualties were 6 dead and 26 wounded. Gen. George Crook with 5 cavalry regiments, 15 companies of infantry, a battery of artillery, and 400 Indian allies—mostly ARAPAHO, Shoshoni, Bannock, and Pawnee—marched from FORT FETTERMAN up the old BOZEMAN TRAIL to a place near the site of his earlier Battle of the ROSEBUD. Scouts brought word of a huge Cheyenne village under chiefs Dull Knife and LITTLE WOLF located in the Bighorn Mountains to the west. At dawn on November 25, 1876, Col. Ranald S. MACKENSIE and 1,100 cavalrymen attacked the 200 lodges. The surprised Indians were quickly routed from their homes. About 400 warriors counterattacked. Many took up position on the rocky hillsides, while others closed in on the soldiers, fighting hand-to-hand combat. It was midafternoon before the soldiers had control of the village. They then burned everything in sight—tepees, clothing, food—and captured 700 ponies. Items belonging to the SEVENTH CAVALRY, that had been recently defeated at the Battle of the LITTLE BIGHORN, were also found. The Cheyenne lost at least 30 dead during the battle; other casualties included a reported 12 babies who froze to death that night. The Cheyenne fled in search of CRAZY HORSE on the upper Tongue River. Crook marched his troops east in search of more Indians, but ended the campaign late in December without another major engagement. *Sources for further study include:* "MacKensie's Last Fight with the Cheyennes: A Winter Campaign in Wyoming and Montana," by John G. Bourke, *Journal of the Institution of the United States* 11 (1890); and *The Fighting Cheyennes*, by George B. GRINNELL (Norman: University of Oklahoma Press, 1956).

E Company, Seventh Cavalry
This company, known as the Gray Horse Troop for the color of their mounts, was commanded during the Battle of the LITTLE BIGHORN by 1st Lt. Algernon E.

SMITH, who was on temporary duty from Company A, with 2nd Lt. James G. STURGIS on temporary duty from Company M as second in command. The company's other officers were elsewhere: 1st Lt. Charles C. DERUDIO was on temporary duty with Company A; and 2nd Lt. William Van W. REILY was on temporary duty with Company F. The company was killed to a man. The bodies of 28 members were buried in DEEP RAVINE but have eluded detection. *Sources for further study include: The Mystery of E Troop* by G. Michno (Missoula, MT: Mountain, 1994).

Edgerly, Winfield Scott (May 29, 1846–September 27, 1927) Second lieutenant, 7th Cavalry. Edgerly, a graduate of West Point, was assigned to the SEVENTH CAVALRY in 1870. He missed the YELLOWSTONE EXPEDITION OF 1873 and the BLACK HILLS EXPEDITION OF 1874 when his company was assigned as the escort and guard for the INTERNATIONAL BOUNDARY SURVEY COMMISSION. He was a frequent social companion of Custer, and accompanied him on an "invitation only" buffalo hunt in April 1874. At the Battle of the LITTLE BIGHORN Edgerly was second in command of Capt. Thomas WEIR's D Company, which was assigned to Capt. F. W. BENTEEN's scout party, while the remainder of the regiment headed toward the Indian village. When Benteen eventually rendezvoused with Maj. Marcus RENO's beaten command on the RENO-BENTEEN DEFENSE SITE, Capt. Weir moved forward of his own accord toward what he perceived to be firing some miles ahead. Edgerly, believing that Weir was under orders (which he wasn't), moved their company to join him. They halted at what is now known as WEIR POINT, and observed Indians some 3 miles away riding around and firing their weapons. (Unknown to them it had been Custer's command being annihilated.) They were soon pushed back by advancing Indians and forced to return to the defensive position on the hilltop. One wounded man was left behind with a promise from Edgerly that they would return for him. Weir, however, refused to allow Edgerly to return and rescue the man, who was subsequently killed by the swarming enemy. Edgerly was of the opinion that the 7th Cavalry would have been victorious had Maj. Marcus RENO charged the Indian village as ordered. Edgerly wrote a letter to Mrs. Libbie Custer on October 10, 1877, to share "some personal recollections of your husband which I wrote at the time after the battle, and which I don't have the heart to send you until I waited so long I was ashamed to write." Edgerly told briefly about the march to the Little Bighorn, then wrote about officer's call the night prior to the final day of Custer's life. Edgerly, a future brigadier general, was promoted to captain and company commander and participated in the 1890 Battle of WOUNDED KNEE. *Sources for further study include:* His own writing, "An Account of the Custer Battle," published in the August 18, 1881, issue of the *Leavenworth Weekly Times.* The letter to Mrs. Custer, in addition to other material pertaining to Edgerly, has been reprinted in *The Custer Myth: A Source Book of Custeriana,* edited by W. A. Graham (Harrisburg, PA: Stackpole, 1953). "Interview with Winfield S. Edgerly" can be found in *Custer in '76: Walter Camp's Notes on the Custer Fight,* edited by Kenneth Hammer (Provo, UT: Brighan Young University Press, 1976).

Elliott, Joel H. (October 27, 1840–November 27, 1868) Major, 7th Cavalry. Elliott began the Civil War as an enlisted man with the 2nd Indiana Cavalry, and fought at such engagements as Shiloh and Perryville. In June 1863 he was commissioned in the 7th Indiana Cavalry, and was wounded twice—once left for dead on the battlefield at White's Station when shot through the lungs—while serving under Col. F. W. BENTEEN. Elliott applied for a commission in the regular army while serving on Custer's staff in Texas after the war. Although field qualified as a captain, he demonstrated excellent intellect and scored well enough on an examination to be appointed—with the assistance of the governor of Indiana—major in the SEVENTH CAVALRY. In late June 1867, during the HANCOCK EXPEDITION, Elliott was selected for a dangerous mission as commander of a detail of 11 men. They traveled over 200 miles through hostile Indian territory—riding at night and hiding during daylight—to deliver dispatches to FORT SEDGWICK and return to Custer's camp near the Republican River. It was on July 7, 1867, that Elliott was involved in an incident that led to charges at Custer's court-martial. The column had halted about noon to rest the horses when 13 troopers, 7 on horseback, deserted in plain view of the command. From Custer's notes: "I directed Major Elliott and Lts. Custer, Cook[e] and Jackson, with a few of the guard, to pursue the deserters who were still visible, tho more than a mile distant, and to bring the dead bodies of as many as could be taken back to camp. Seven of the deserters, being mounted on our best horses, and having two miles' start, made their escape. One, a dangerous character, presented his carbine at Major Elliott, but, before he could fire, was brought down by another of the pursuing party." Three deserters were wounded; one later died. No charges were placed against Elliott or the other shooters since they were simply obeying Custer's orders. (See CUSTER: Court-Martial.) In August 1867, while Custer was under arrest awaiting the court-martial, Elliott assumed command of the 7th Cavalry. He testified at Custer's court-martial on October 5, 1867, and the following day presented a disposition to the court so that he could be released to return to FORT HARKER in order to accompany the peace commissioners. It was at the Battle of WASHITA, however, that Elliott indelibly stamped his name on the history of the 7th Cavalry. As the battle raged, Elliott—without notifying Custer of his actions—called for volunteers to follow him downstream to chase Indians escaping from the village, and 19 troopers chose to follow. Elliott called to fellow officer, Lt. Owen HALE, "Here goes for a brevet or a coffin!" as he galloped past. Later, when the village had been captured, Elliott and his small command were nowhere to be found. Custer ordered Capt. Edward MYERS to scout the area for any sign of Elliott and his men. Myers ventured about 2 miles, and returned without success. By this time, the outnumbered 7th Cavalry was under growing attack by Indians from villages downstream. It was thought that Elliott had simply become lost, and would eventually find his way back. Unfortunately, that was not the case. A later march during the WASHITA CAMPAIGN OF 1868–69 led by Gen. Phil SHERIDAN and Custer returned to the area in early December. They discovered the mutilated bodies of Elliott and his command some miles downstream from the battle site. Evidence showed that the troopers had come under attack and had dismounted to form a small defensive circle in tall grass. The Indians had overwhelmed them within an hour. Capt. F. W. BENTEEN, friend and former Civil War superior, blamed Elliott's tragic death on the fact that Custer had "abandoned" the missing troops. This controversy created dissension among the officers, and continued beyond Custer's death. (See BENTEEN, F. W. for more detail.)

Enlisted Men's Petition This document addressed "To His Excellency the President and the Honorable Representatives of the United States" was dated July 4, 1876—9 days after the Battle of the LITTLE BIGHORN—and was alleged to have been signed by 236 enlisted men of the SEVENTH CAVALRY who participated in the campaign. Its purpose was to gain promotions within the 7th Cavalry for Maj. Marcus RENO and Capt. F. W. BENTEEN. It failed at that time.

However, nearly 80 years later the authenticity of the document was first questioned. The complete text is as follows:

We the enlisted men the survivors of the battle of the Heights of Little Horn River, on the 25th and 26th of June 1876, of the 7th Regiment of Cavalry who subscribe our names to this petition, most earnestly solicit the President and Representatives of our Country, that the vacancies among the Commissioned Officers of our Regiment, made by the slaughter of our brave, heroic, now lamented Lieutenant Colonel George A. Custer, and the other noble dead Commissioned Officers of our Regiment who fell close by him on the bloody field, daring the savage demons to the last, be filled by the Officers of the Regiment only. That Major M. A. Reno, be our Lieutenant Colonel vice Custer, killed; Captain F. W. Benteen our Major vice Reno, promoted. The other vacancies to be filled by officers of the Regiment by seniority. Your petitioners know this to be contrary to the established rule of promotion, but prayerfully solicit a deviation from the usual rule in this case, as it will be conferring a bravely fought for and justly merited promotion on officers who by their bravery, coolness and decision on the 25th and 26th of June 1876, saved the lives of every man now living of the 7th Cavalry who participated in the battle, one of the most bloody on record and one that wold have ended with the loss of life of every officer and enlisted man on the field only for the position taken by Major Reno, which we held with bitter tenacity against fearful odds to the last.

To support this assertion—had our position been taken 100 yards back from the brink of the heights overlooking the river we would have been entirely cut off from water; and from those heights the Indian demons would have swarmed in hundreds picking off our men by detail, and before midday June 25th not an officer or enlisted man of our Regiment would have been left to tell of our dreadful fate as we then would have been completely surrounded.

With prayerful hope that our petitions be granted, we have the honor to forward it through our Commanding Officer.

Very Respectfully,
[236 signatures]

The petition was forwarded through channels until reaching Gen. William SHERMAN, who returned it with his endorsement. It never made it to the White House or Capitol. However, at the time of the RENO COURT OF INQUIRY in 1879 the petition was believed authentic. It was not until 1954 when Maj. E. S. Luce, superintendent of Custer Battlefield, became suspicious of the document. Several of the signees were not on regimental roles at that point in time, and others whose signatures appeared had always signed the payroll with an "X." Luce called in the FBI to investigate. The resulting investigation concluded that at least 76 of the signatures were "probable forgeries." The lack of handwriting specimens from many of the enlisted men prohibited the FBI from determining the authenticity of other alleged signees. Regardless, the evidence clearly showed that the document was certainly a plot by a person or persons within the regiment. Fingers pointed at two men: 1st Sgt. Joseph McCurry of H Company (commanded by Benteen) as the author, and Capt. F. W. BENTEEN as the probable instigator. Many of the signatures were obviously penned by McCurry's hand. As for Benteen, he was well liked by the enlisted men, who might very well have encouraged his promotion had it been proper (Reno would have been another story, but the petition would have been far less credible if Reno had been left off); and McCurry, who would do anything for his commanding officer, likely could not have accomplished the petition without Benteen's knowledge.

F Company, 7th Cavalry This company was commanded during the Battle of the LITTLE BIGHORN by Capt. George W. YATES with 2nd Lt. William Van W. REILY second in command on temporary duty from E Company. F Company was part of Custer's detachment, and likely attempted to charge the Indian village down MEDICINE TAIL COULEE in the initial stages of the battle. It was pushed back to BATTLE RIDGE by heavy fire from the Indians' counterattack. The company was all killed, many of the bodies located on CUSTER HILL, including the two officers.

Far West (Steamship) This steamship, along with the *JOSEPHINE*, both owned by the Coulson Line, was awarded the contract for river transportation for the LITTLE BIGHORN CAMPAIGN (see photo next page). The *Far West*, 190' in length with a beam of 33', had been designed to operate in the shallow and hazardous Western rivers. It had adequate power to pull her through rapids, and could accommodate more than 200 tons of freight. Skippered by Captain Grant MARSH, the *Far West* initially carried a cargo of rations down the Powder River to the Yellowstone River. The steamship was moored at the mouth of the Bighorn River near present-day Hardin, MT, when word came about the fate of Custer's command. About 30 wounded cavalrymen, as well as Capt. Myles KEOGH's horse, COMANCHE, were transported on crude litters from the battlefield and arrived on June 30 at the *Far West*. Shortly after 4 P.M. on July 3, the steamship, its colors at half mast and its decks draped in black mourning cloth, departed for Bismarck, and made the 710-mile trip with 2 brief stops in a record-setting time of 54 hours.

Fetterman Massacre (December 21, 1866) This engagement between the

Steamer *Far West*

U.S. Army under Capt. William J. Fetterman and SIOUX Indian warriors led by CRAZY HORSE was part of RED CLOUD's war over the BOZEMAN TRAIL. All 80 soldiers were killed in a trap. The conflict began when woodcutters from FORT PHIL KEARNY, who were required to range some distance in order to find sufficient wood supplies, alerted the fort of impending trouble with the Sioux. Capt. Fetterman set out with a detail of approximately 80 men to rescue the wagon train. Fetterman had once boasted that he "could ride through the entire hostile nation with 80 good men." Orders from post commander, Col. Henry Carrington, were to merely escort the wagon train back to the fort, but not to cross Lodge Trail Ridge. Fetterman disobeyed orders and crossed Lodge Trail Ridge in order to chase a decoy of fleeing Indians under Crazy Horse. It was the oldest trick in the book of Plains Indian warfare, and Fetterman led his men directly into the trap and was wiped out by Indi-

ans led by HUMP. *Sources for further study include: The Fetterman Massacre,* by D. Brown (Lincoln: University of Nebraska Press, 1971).

Forsyth, George Alexander (1837–1915) Officer, 9th Cavalry. Brother of James W. FORSYTH. "Sandy" Forsyth had been a Civil War cavalry officer under Gen. Phil SHERIDAN, was involved in 86 engagements, and wounded 4 times. He was assigned by Sheridan in 1868 to organize a company of 50 civilian frontiersmen to fight Indians who were raiding west of FORT WALLACE. This unit was attacked by as many as 600 CHEYENNE under ROMAN NOSE at the Arikaree Fork of the Republic River, and for 9 days in the Battle of BEECHER'S ISLAND. Forsyth was wounded 3 times and nearly died. He finished his career as military secretary and later aide-de-camp to Gen. Sheridan. In his autobiography he defended Custer's actions at the LITTLE BIGHORN, and did not believe that Gen.

Alfred TERRY's order had been disobeyed. *Sources for further study include: The Story of a Soldier,* by George A. Forsyth (New York: Appleton, 1909).

Forsyth, James William (1836–1906) Officer, 7th Cavalry. Brother of George A. Forsyth. Like George, he was a favorite of Gen. Phil SHERIDAN. He had served with the general during the Civil War, and from 1869 to 1878 he was a member of his staff. In 1878, however, he was assigned command of the 1st Cavalry at Fort Vancouver, WA, and in 1886 became colonel of the SEVENTH CAVALRY. Forsyth was in charge in December 1890 when his troopers engaged in battle with SIOUX chief Big Foot at WOUNDED KNEE, which resulted in the death of more than 150 Indian, men, women, and children.

Fort Abercrombie This fort, established in 1857, was the first permanent military post in the Dakota Territory. Called the Gateway to the Dakotas for settlers heading for the Northwest, it was located on the Red River about 32 miles south of Fargo (see map on page 71). It had been built with no stockade, and the soldiers commanded by Lt. Col. John J. Abercrombie—for whom the fort was named—were pinned down for 5 weeks during the SIOUX Indian uprising of 1862. The troopers quickly enclosed 10 acres when reinforcements arrived from Fort Snelling. The fort has been partially rebuilt, and is owned by the State Historical Society.

Fort Abraham Lincoln, D.T. This fort was established on June 14, 1872, by Lt. Col. Daniel Huston, 6th U.S. Infantry, at a location 3 miles from Bismarck on the west bank of the Missouri River at the mouth of the Heart River (see map on page 71). Its purpose was to garrison troops whose duty was the protection of surveyors and workers on the NORTHERN PACIFIC RAILROAD. Initially named Fort McKean in honor of Col.

Henry McKean who was killed in the Battle of Cold Harbor on June 3, 1864, it was designated Fort Abraham Lincoln on November 19, 1872, in honor of the assassinated president. Custer and his SEVENTH CAVALRY manned the garrison here on September 23, 1873, upon their return from the YELLOWSTONE EXPEDITION OF 1873. The Custer residence burned to the ground in February 1874 when the insulation in the attic caught fire from the chimney. Ten troops of the 7th Cavalry led by Custer departed from Fort Lincoln on July 2 for the BLACK HILLS EXPEDITION OF 1874, and returned on August 30. On May 17, 1876, Custer and his command left for the Valley of the LITTLE BIGHORN as the regimental band struck up "She Wore a Yellow Ribbon" and "GARRYOWEN." Custer and more than 200 of his officers and men never returned. Fort Lincoln was abandoned on July 22, 1891, 8 years after the completion of the railroad, and has been partially restored in what is now a state park.

Fort Berthold Indian Agency, D.T. This fort originally had been established in 1845 as a trading post for the American Fur Company, and was named in honor of its founder, Bartholomew Berthold. Troops under Gen. SULLY were garrisoned here until Fort Stevenson was built in 1867. The agency became home to Mandan and ARIKARA (REE) Indians. Most of the 39 Indian scouts that participated in the LITTLE BIGHORN CAMPAIGN under the command of 2nd Lt. Charles VARNUM were from here.

Fort Buford, D.T. This remote fort was built in 1866 on the Missouri River across from the mouth of the Yellowstone (map, page 71), and was named for Gen. John Buford, a Civil War hero. It was here that SIOUX chiefs SITTING BULL and GALL surrendered in 1881.

Fort Cobb, I.T. This fort, named for nearby Cobb Creek, was built of pickets

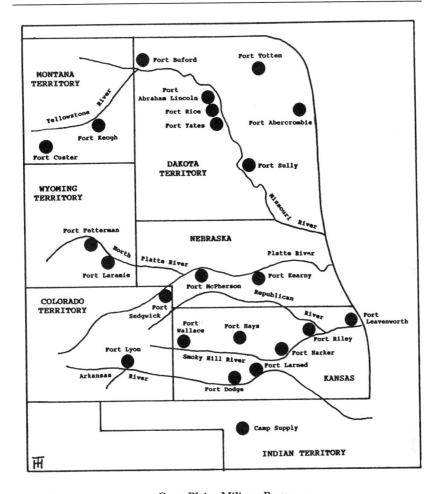

Great Plains Military Posts

and adobe on the Washita River in 1859 for the purpose of stopping COMANCHE and KIOWA Indian raiding parties. Gen. Phil SHERIDAN occupied the fort during the WASHITA CAMPAIGN OF 1868–69 to supervise those Indians who chose to settle on their new reservations as mandated in the MEDICINE LODGE treaties. It was here that Chief BLACK KETTLE came before the Battle of WASHITA and successfully convinced Col. HAZEN that his tribe was friendly. Kiowas under SATANTA and LONE WOLF finally surrendered here in 1869.

Fort Custer, MT This fort, named in honor of Gen. George Armstrong CUSTER, was established July 4, 1877, on a bluff above the confluence of the Bighorn and Little Bighorn rivers, just 11 miles from the famous battlefield (see map above). It was garrisoned until 1898 when the structures were sold at auction and used to build the nearby town of Hardin, MT. Nothing remains on the site except a marker placed by the Daughters of the American Revolution.

Fort Dodge, KA This fort, located on the north bank of the Arkansas River (see map, page 71), was established in 1865 to protect travelers on the SANTA FE TRAIL. It was named for Col. Henry L. Dodge, the uncle of the site founder, Maj. Gen. Grenville M. Dodge. This was the principal base for operations against the ARAPAHO and CHEYENNE, including those by Gen. Alfred SULLY and Gen. Phil SHERIDAN during the WASHITA CAMPAIGN OF 1868–69.

FORT ELLIS, MT Established in 1867 near present-day Bozeman, troops of the 2nd Cavalry under Maj. James BRISBIN stationed here were assigned to Col. John GIBBON's Montana Column during the LITTLE BIGHORN CAMPAIGN.

Fort Fetterman, WY This fort was built in 1867 and used primarily as a supply base for operations against the SIOUX Indians (see map, page 71). It was named in honor of Lt. Col. William J. Fetterman, who was killed by RED CLOUD's Sioux in December 1866. (See FETTERMAN MASSACRE.) Gen. George CROOK marched from this fort with 800 troops on May 29, 1876, as part of the LITTLE BIGHORN CAMPAIGN. See ROSEBUD, BATTLE OF THE.

Fort Harker, KA This fort, located on the north bank of the SMOKY HILL River in central Kansas (see map, page 71), was originally established as Fort Ellsworth in 1864 to protect travelers on the SANTA FE TRAIL. It was moved one mile east and renamed in 1867 in honor of Brig. Gen. C. G. Harker who was killed at the Battle of Kennesaw Mountain in the Civil War. Fort Harker was the base of operations for the HANCOCK EXPEDITION OF 1867. Correspondent Henry M. Stanley ("Dr. Livingstone, I presume") described the fort thus: "in its present naked state it looks like a great wart on the surface of the plain." It was abandoned in 1872 when the railroad to Denver was completed.

Fort Hays, KA This fort, established in 1865 near the mouth of Big Creek in central Kansas, was moved 15 miles upstream in June 1867 because of a flood (see map, page 71). It was originally called Fort Fletcher, but renamed one year later in honor of Brig. Gen. Alexander Hays, who was killed in the Battle of the Wilderness in 1864. Fort Hays saw considerable action during 1867–70, when Custer and the army had the responsibility of protecting workers on the KANSAS PACIFIC RAILROAD. While stationed here in the summers of 1869 and 1870, the Custers, with 2 companies of the SEVENTH CAVALRY, camped at nearby Big Creek where they hunted, fished, and picnicked. The fort was garrisoned until 1889 when it was leveled and the land used as a golf course. Only the blockhouse and guardhouse remain.

Fort Keogh, MT This fort, established by Gen. Nelson MILES in August 1876 on the south bank of the Yellowstone River at the mouth of the Tongue River just west of Miles City, MT (see map, page 71), was named in honor of Capt. Myles W. KEOGH, who perished with Custer at the Battle of the LITTLE BIGHORN. Intended to serve as a base for supplies, it was from here that Gen. Miles forced the final surrender of the SIOUX and CHEYENNE, and from where Miles marched to engage Chief JOSEPH and the NEZ PERCÉ in the crucial Battle of Bear Paw Mountain. Fort Keogh was garrisoned until 1908, when the Interior Department took it over as a Range and Livestock Experiment Station. Several of the original buildings on the officers' row remain in use.

Fort Laramie, WY This fort, initially named fort William, was established by trapper William Sublette and others in 1834 on the west bank of the Laramie River, one mile above its junction with the North Platte River (see map, page 71). It was later used to protect travelers on the Oregon Trail and to

Fort Laramie Treaty of 1868. Commissioner Gen. Alfred Terry, 2nd from right.

monitor the Plains Indians. The FORT LARAMIE TREATY OF 1868 was signed here. It was garrisoned until 1890, and many of the old structures have been preserved as the Fort Laramie National Historic Site.

Fort Laramie Treaty of 1868 This treaty was made between the SIOUX Indian tribe and the U.S. government in order to end hostilities over the BOZEMAN TRAIL in the Powder River country (see photo above). Warrior RED CLOUD demanded that the army abandon forts PHIL KEARNY, Reno, and C. F. Smith, provide the Sioux with a reservation that encompassed nearly all of present-day South Dakota west of the Missouri River (see GREAT SIOUX RESERVATION), grant hunting rights to a wide area on the Republican River and in Wyoming and Nebraska north of the Platte River, and forbid whites to trespass in the Powder River country. Other concessions, such as providing buildings, medical care, education, seeds and agricultural supplies,

and money, were promised by the U.S. government.

This was the first and only occasion in which the United States bowed to Indian demands due to a threat of violence. More than 200 Indian chiefs and subchiefs signed the treaty at FORT RICE on July 2, excluding Red Cloud. Red Cloud waited until the soldiers had abandoned the Bozeman Trail posts in August, then promptly burned them to the ground. The Sioux warrior finally signed the treaty on November 6, 1868. The Fort Laramie Treaty was ratified by the U.S. Congress on February 24, 1869.

Fort Larned, KA This fort, initially known as Camp on Pawnee Fork, and later Camp Alert, was established by 1st Lt. David Bell, 1st U.S. Cavalry, in 1859 at the confluence of Pawnee Creek and the Arkansas River (see map, page 71). It was renamed in 1860 in honor of Gen. Benjamin F. Larned, the paymaster general of the army. The fort was intended as a base to protect travelers on the

SANTA FE TRAIL, and also became a distribution point for CHEYENNE and ARAPAHO Indian annuities. It was abandoned in 1878, and has been preserved by private ownership. During the HANCOCK EXPEDITION OF 1867, southern CHEYENNE and SIOUX Indian chiefs met here with Gen. W. S. HANCOCK. Later, Hancock marched to their nearby village up Pawnee Fork and burned it to the ground.

Fort Leavenworth, KA This fort was established in 1827 on the Missouri River to protect travelers on the SANTA FE TRAIL (see map, page 71). It served mainly as a supply depot for the Rocky Mountain region. Gen. W. S. HANCOCK, commander of the Department of the Missouri, had his headquarters here beginning in 1866. This fort was the site of Custer's court-martial in 1867. While the Custers waited out his suspension from the army, they accepted Gen. Phil SHERIDAN's gracious offer of his quarters here and spent most of the winter of 1867–68 enjoying the social life. The couple returned for the social scene during the winter of 1869–70. It was also here that wife Libbie spent Christmas 1870 alone while Custer returned home to Monroe, MI, perhaps signaling a problem with their marriage that was soon resolved. The fort, which remains operational, is the oldest post west of the Mississippi River.

Fort Lyon, CO This fort, located on the Arkansas River below the mouth of the Purgatoire River, took on its present name on June 25, 1862 (see map, page 71). It had served as Bent's New Fort, then Fort Fauntleroy, and Fort Wise before becoming Fort Lyon in honor of Gen. Nathaniel Lyon, the first Union general to die in the Civil War. It was from here in 1864 that Col. Chivington marched to slaughter CHEYENNE Indians under Chief BLACK KETTLE at what became known as the SAND CREEK MASSACRE. Frontiersman Kit Carson

died here on May 23, 1868. Fort Lyon was one of the posts that came under the responsibility of the SEVENTH CAVALRY during the late 1860s, and one company was usually stationed here. It was abandoned in October 1889 and later became a veterans hospital.

Fort McPherson, NE This fort, established on September 17, 1863, on the south bank of the South Platte River 8 miles from its confluence with the North Platte (see map, page 71), was named in honor of Brig. Gen. James McPherson, who was killed in the Civil War. It was intended as a base to protect travelers on the Oregon Trail as well as to prevent Indians from crossing the South Platte at a traditional ford. Many famous frontiersmen passed through the fort, including Kit Carson, Buffalo Bill CODY, and Grand Duke ALEXIS of Russia. During the HANCOCK EXPEDITION OF 1867, Custer met here with SIOUX Chief PAWNEE KILLER to discuss peace, and later with Gen. William SHERMAN to discuss strategy. It was also near here in early July 1867 that more than 30 men deserted, and created an incident that led to charges at Custer's court-martial. The fort was abandoned in 1880.

Fort Meade, SD This fort, established in honor of Gen. George Meade in 1878, was located on Bear Butte Creek about 14 miles northeast of Deadwood. The location was chosen by Custer during his BLACK HILLS EXPEDITION OF 1874. Its purpose was to protect the mining interests against SIOUX Indian attacks. It became a veterans hospital in 1944.

Fort Morgan, CO This fort, established by Maj. C. A. Morgan on July 1, 1865, was located on the Overland Trail on the South Platte River on the site of present-day Fort Morgan. It was one of the posts that came under the responsibility of the SEVENTH CAVALRY during the late 1860s, and one company was usually stationed here.

Fort Phil Kearny, WY This fort was established by Col. Henry B. Carrington on July 13, 1866, on Big Piney Fork at the foot of the Bighorn Mountains about 15 miles from present-day Buffalo, to protect the BOZEMAN TRAIL. It was near here that the FETTERMAN MASSACRE and the WAGON BOX FIGHT took place. The FORT LARAMIE TREATY OF 1868 provided that the fort be abandoned, and it was quickly burned to the ground by RED CLOUD's SIOUX Indians.

Fort Rice, D.T. This fort, established on July 7, 1864, by Gen. Alfred H. SULLY during his expedition against the SIOUX, and named in honor of Brig. Gen. J. C. Rice who was killed in the Civil War, was located on the west bank of the Missouri River near the mouth of Long Lake Creek (see map, page 71). Custer's SEVENTH CAVALRY assembled here from various posts in March 1873, and on June 20 marched out on the YELLOWSTONE EXPEDITION OF 1873. Fort Rice was abandoned in 1877 when Fort YATES was established downriver.

Fort Riley, KA This fort, named on June 27, 1853, in honor of Col. Bennett Riley, is located on the north bank of the Kansas River at the junction of the Republican and Smoky Hill rivers (see map, page 71). The purpose of the fort was to protect travelers along the SANTA FE TRAIL, as well as the SMOKY HILL TRAIL to Denver. It was here in September 1866 that the 12 companies of the SEVENTH CAVALRY were formed and trained for frontier duty. Custer arrived in late 1866 with his wife Libbie and their cook, Eliza BROWN. The 7th Cavalry departed from Fort Riley on March 1, 1867, on the HANCOCK EXPEDITION OF 1867. Custer returned here to visit his wife without authorization in July, which led to his court-martial. The post is presently operational.

Fort Sedgwick, CO This fort, established on May 17, 1864, in honor of Maj. Gen. John Sedgwick who was killed in the Civil War, was located on the South Platte River, east of Lodgepole Creek near present-day Julesburg (see map, page 71). During the HANCOCK EXPEDITION OF 1867, Custer was ordered to put into Fort Sedgwick for further orders and supplies, but instead sent Maj. Joel ELLIOTT. This caused Lt. Lyman KIDDER to carry Custer's orders on an ill-fated detail. The post was abandoned in 1871.

Fort Sill, I.T. This fort, established on January 7, 1869, by Gen. Phil SHERIDAN in honor of Brig. Gen. Joshua W. Sill who was killed in the Civil War, is located at the confluence of Cache and Medicine Bluff creeks at the eastern edge of the Wichita Mountains. Custer led 2 regiments out of Fort Sill in early 1869, intent on forcing the surrender of CHEYENNE Indians under chief LITTLE ROBE during the WASHITA CAMPAIGN OF 1868–69. Accompanied by the KANSAS VOLUNTEER CAVALRY, Custer completed his mission while skillfully effecting the release of 2 captive white women from the hostile Indian camp without a shot being fired. This was one of the posts where Secretary Belknap and his wife were accused of illegally selling the tradership rights. (See BELKNAP SCANDAL.) The fort is presently operational.

Fort Sully, D.T. This fort, established in 1863 by Brig. Gen. Alfred H. SULLY during his campaign against the SIOUX, was originally located on the west bank of the Missouri River 6 miles below present-day Pierre, but was moved in 1866 some 30 miles north of that city (see map, page 71). It was notable for its involvement in the Ghost Dance of 1890 that led to the Battle of WOUNDED KNEE. The post was abandoned in 1894.

Fort Totten, D.T. This fort, established on July 17, 1867, by Gen. Alfred TERRY and named in honor of Brig. Gen.

Joseph G. Totten—chief engineer of the army who was killed in the Civil War—was located on the south shore of Devils Lake (see map, page 71). Its purpose was to protect travelers enroute from Minnesota to Montana and later became an Indian Agency and industrial school. It has been preserved by the North Dakota Historical Society.

Fort Wallace, KA This fort, the westernmost post in Kansas, was established in 1865 in honor of Brig. Gen. H. L. Wallace, who fell at the Battle of Shiloh. It was located along the SMOKY HILL TRAIL near Pond Creek Station (see map, page 71), and intended to protect settlers from Indians and to provide guards and escorts for stagecoaches, wagon trains, railroad surveyors, and construction crews. Attacks by CHEYENNE and SIOUX were frequent, and the fort was said to be under constant siege. Conditions at Wallace were horrendous: there was no flowing water and the quality of food was so poor that scurvy had become commonplace. To make matters worse, telegraph lines had not reached the fort, and the troops were spread perilously thin. In 1867 Custer's command repelled an assault by several hundred Cheyenne Indians led by Chief ROMAN NOSE. The following year at BEECHER'S ISLAND, Roman Nose pinned down a detail of soldiers for 9 days until troops from this fort rode to the rescue. The post was abandoned in 1881.

Fort Yates, D.T. This fort, established on December 23, 1874, was originally named STANDING ROCK AGENCY but on December 30, 1878, was designated Fort Yates in honor of Capt. George YATES, who perished with Custer at the Battle of the LITTLE BIGHORN. It was at this fort that on December 15, 1890, SITTING BULL was killed by Indian police and initially buried. It was abandoned in 1903, and remains as the headquarters for the Standing Rock Reservation (see map, page 71).

French, Thomas H. Captain, 7th Cavalry. "Tucker" French was considered one of the best marksmen in the unit. On the YELLOWSTONE EXPEDITION OF 1873 Custer and his troops ran into heavy opposition from SIOUX Indians. French was ordered down the valley with 2 companies and successfully thwarted the enemy from crossing the Yellowstone and closing with the main body in what has been called the Battle of the Yellowstone. During the LITTLE BIGHORN CAMPAIGN, he was commander of M Company assigned to Maj. Marcus RENO's battalion. His company participated in RENO's VALLEY FIGHT, and defended the south side of the perimeter on the RENO-BENTEEN DEFENSE SITE where at one point a bullet passed through French's hat without striking him. In June 1880 French wrote a letter to the wife of Dr. A. H. Cooke and, among other interesting items, stated that he would have considered himself fully justified had he shot Reno when the major ordered the disastrous retreat from the timber to the bluffs beyond the Little Bighorn River during RENO's VALLEY FIGHT. (The letter has been reprinted in *The Custer Myth; A Source Book of Custeriana*, edited by W. A. Graham [Harrisburg, Pa: Stackpole, 1953].) French also told a *New York Times* reporter on January 19, 1879, that Reno, presumably drunk, had hidden himself from the rest of the command on the hilltop from the evening of June 25 until noon on June 26. French could not locate Reno, and knew of no one who had. French, however, did not testify at the 1879 RENO COURT OF INQUIRY because he was confined awaiting a court-martial. French retired on February 5, 1880, and died March 27, 1882.

French Creek, D.T. On July 30, 1874, along the upper part of this stream in the BLACK HILLS that ran through a glade that Custer had modestly named "Custer Park" after himself (near the site of present-day Custer, SD), miners

Horatio Nelson Ross and William Mc-
Kay first found gold during the BLACK
HILLS EXPEDITION OF 1874.

G Company, Seventh Cavalry
This company was commanded during
the Battle of the LITTLE BIGHORN by 1st
Lt. Donald MCINTOSH with 2nd Lt.
George D. WALLACE second in com-
mand. G Company was part of Maj.
Marcus RENO's Battalion, and partici-
pated in RENO's VALLEY FIGHT and the
RENO-BENTEEN DEFENSIVE SITE. 1st
Lt. McIntosh was killed during Reno's
Valley Fight. In addition, 13 enlisted men
were killed and 2 were wounded. Pvt.
Theodore GOLDIN was awarded the
MEDAL OF HONOR in 1895 for his ac-
tions.

Galaxy **Magazine** Custer wrote numerous articles for this magazine, beginning with the HANCOCK EXPEDITION OF
1867 and continuing until the time of his
death. In 1874 *Galaxy* published selected
articles in book form entitled *My Life on
the Plains; Or, Personal Experiences with
Indians* (New York: Sheldon, 1874), reprint edited by Edgar I. Stewart (Norman: University of Oklahoma Press,
1962), which established Custer as a respected author.

Gall (HUNKPAPA SIOUX; aka Pizi)
(1840–94) This prominent war chief
possessed great intellect and daring, and
was a physically imposing figure: he
weighed 260 pounds 12 years after the
Battle of the LITTLE BIGHORN (see
photo this page). An orphan, he was
adopted as a younger brother by SITTING
BULL.

Gall's earliest recorded relations with
the white man occurred near FORT
BERTHOLD in the winter of 1865–66
when soldiers came to arrest him for
some unknown offense: probably just because at the time he was notorious and
feared. Many versions of the story exist,
but each includes the fact that this huge

Sioux Chief Gall

man was shot and/or bayoneted numerous times during the encounter but
somehow managed to elude capture. He
took out his vengeance for that attack by
vigorously raiding settlements and stagecoaches.

Gall joined CRAZY HORSE, RAIN-IN-
THE-FACE, and other young men to fight
when OGLALA warrior RED CLOUD waged
war with the U.S. Army over the building of forts on the BOZEMAN TRAIL. He
participated in the FETTERMAN MAS-
SACRE, and probably also the WAGON
BOX FIGHT and HAYFIELD FIGHT. At

the signing of the FORT LARAMIE TREATY OF 1868 that ended hostilities, he refused to "touch the pen," although one biographer of Sitting Bull claimed that he had, and has Sitting Bull stating: "You must not blame Gall. Everyone knows he will do anything for a square meal."

Gall and Crazy Horse were involved in two attacks on Custer's SEVENTH CAVALRY during the YELLOWSTONE EXPEDITION OF 1873, neither causing much damage to either side. The Indians attempted to employ the same decoy tactics that had worked well during the Fetterman Massacre, but Custer had learned from others' mistakes and avoided danger.

Gall played a major role as field commander in the defeat of Custer at the LITTLE BIGHORN. According to Gall, orders were given to move the village as soon as Custer's command was observed down the valley, but troops led by Maj. Marcus RENO came so quickly that the Indians were forced to fight. Gall led a small group of Hunkpapas and BLACK-FEET, who went upstream to engage Reno. Two of his wives and 3 of his children were killed during the initial stages of the fight. (See RENO'S VALLEY FIGHT.)

Gall reported that in the first phase of Custer's attack on the Indian village, the general's men—likely the Gray Horse Troop of 1st Lt. Algernon SMITH attached to Capt. YATES's squadron—were not able to reach the Little Bighorn River but were forced to retreat. Custer was likely with Yates's detachment, and may have been killed or seriously wounded during that action. Warriors rallied by Gall were later mainly responsible for wiping out the commands of Capt. Myles KEOGH and 1st Lt. James CALHOUN on the eastern slope of BATTLE RIDGE. Gall also believed that all of Custer's men had been killed by the time Capt. Thomas WEIR arrived at what is known as WEIR POINT. He credited the soldiers with bravery, and estimated that the entire battle lasted only half an hour. He also revealed that the Indians thought they were fighting Gen. George CROOK not Custer that day.

Gall fled to Canada in 1877 with Sitting Bull, but, after the 2 quarreled he surrendered with about 300 followers in 1881. He lived out his final years near Standing Rock Agency, where he was an influential voice for the good of his people, becoming a judge of the Court of Indian Offenses. He traveled to Washington, D.C., in 1889 as a member of an Indian delegation on treaties. Gall attended a reunion of survivors on the tenth anniversary of the battle and, through an interpreter, captivated the audience with his account. He remained neutral during the Ghost Dance uprising that led to the Battle of WOUNDED KNEE in 1890. His death has been attributed to either falling from a wagon, an overdose of patent medicine, or perhaps his previous bayonet wounds. *Sources for further study include: The Custer Myth: A Source Book of Custeriana*, edited by W. A. Graham (Harrisburg, PA: Stackpole, 1953) contains a chapter, "The Story of [the Little Bighorn Battle by] War Chief Gall of the Uncpapas," which is followed by "General Godfrey's Comment on Gall's Story."

"Garryowen" (Song; composer unknown) This was the jaunty, traditional Irish tune that became synonymous with Custer's SEVENTH CAVALRY. The distinctive theme song was more than likely introduced to Custer by Capt. Myles KEOGH. Evidence of this stems from the fact that Keogh's father served in the 5th Royal Irish Lancers, and that regiment had adopted it as their marching (and drinking) song (see illustration, page 79). Garryowen, Gaelic for Owen's Garden, was a suburb of Limerick, Ireland, where the 5th was stationed. In addition, Capt. Keogh's birthplace, Orchard in Carlow County, is near Limerick on the banks of the River Shannon. Wife Libbie Custer also mentioned that she thought Keogh made her husband aware of the tune.

GARRY OWEN

REGIMENTAL BATTLE SONG OF SEVENTH U. S. CAVALRY

The origin and composer of the tune, quick march or drinking song, entitled "Garry Owen," has been a moot question. After no little research, it has been definitely established that the music is not that of Scottish strain, but without a doubt of Irish origin.

It has been used by several Irish Regiments as their quick march; the Fifth Royal Irish Lancers stationed in the suburb of Limerick called "Garryowen" (the Gaelic word, meaning "Owen's Garden"), used it as their drinking song. The words can hardly be called elevating, but depict the rollicking nature of the Lancers while in town on pay day in search of their peculiar style of "camaraderie." **

Music to "Garryowen"

The Original Lancer Lyrics

1.

Let Bacchus' sons be not dismayed
　But join with me each jovial blade;
Come booze and sing, and lend you aid,
　To help me with the chorus.

Chorus
Instead of Spa we'll drink down ale,
And pay the reck'ning on the nail
No man for debt shall go to gaol
　From Garryowen in glory.

We are the boys that take delight in
　Smashing the Limerick lights when
　　lighting;

Through the streets like sporters fight-
　　ing
　And clearing all before us.

3.

We'll break windows, we'll break doors
　The watch knock down by threes
　　and fours;
Then let doctors work their cures,
　And tinker up our bruises.

4.

We'll beat the bailiffs out of fun
　We'll make the Mayors and Sheriffs
　　run;
We are the boys man dares dun,
　If he regards a whole skin.

5.

Our hearts so stout have got us fame
  For soon 'tis known from whence we
      came;
Where'er we go they dread the name,
  Of Garryowen in glory.

Poetry and Music

Celebrated Irish poet Thomas Moore (1779–1852) employed the tune for his own lyrics and titled the composition "The Daughters of Erin." This can be found in *One Hundred Folksongs of All Nations* (Boston: Oliver Ditson, date unavailable). The tune remained an instrumental for the 7th Cavalry Band until 1905, when Chief Musician J. O. Brockenshire penned three stanzas and a chorus.

The 7th Cavalry Lyrics

1.

We are the pride of the army,
  And a regiment of great renown,
Our name's on the pages of history
  From sixty-six on down.
If you think we stop or falter
  While going into the fray we're goin'
Just watch the steps with our heads
      erect,
When our band plays "Garry Owen."

Chorus

In the fighting Seventh's the place for
      me,
It's the cream of all the cavalry;
No other regiment ever can claim
Its pride, honor, glory and undying
      fame.

2.

We know no fear when stern duty
  Calls us away from home,
Our country's flag shall safely o'er us
      wave,
  No matter where we roam.
'Tis the gallant Seventh Cavalry
  It matters not where we're goin'
Such you'll surely say as we march
      away;
  And our band plays, "Garry Owen."

Then hurrah for our brave commanders!

Who lead us into the fight.
We'll do or die in our country's cause,
  And battle for the right.
And when the war is o'er,
  And to our home we're goin'
Just watch the step, with our heads
      erect,
  When our band plays, "Garry
      Owen."

"Garryowen" was the final song heard by Custer and his men before marching for the Valley of the LITTLE BIGHORN. The regimental band was posted on a knoll overlooking the Powder River, and "Garryowen" was performed to the usual hearty cheers as soon as the troops forded the river and were formed.

Garryowen, MT This landmark is located on the western side of the Little Bighorn River, and marks the southernmost edge of the 3-mile-long allied Indian village in the valley present on June 25, 1876, when Custer approached.

Gatling Guns Some military scholars have suggested that Gatling Guns would have provided Custer the fire superiority necessary to defeat the SIOUX and CHEYENNE at the Battle of the LITTLE BIGHORN. It is true that Gatling Guns would have brought formidable firepower into play; these rapid-fire artillery guns could fire up to 350 rounds in 1 minute. They operated by turning a crank that spun multiple barrels that fed ammunition from a hopper. The offer of 3 Gatling Guns to accompany the SEVENTH CAVALRY into the Valley of the Little Bighorn was made to Custer by Gen. Alfred TERRY. This suggestion was made at the urging of Maj. James BRISBIN, who also desired his 2nd Cavalry to become part of Custer's detachment. Custer respectfully declined both offers, stating that the Gatlings would impede his march. It is possible that these guns could have turned the tide in the army's favor, if they had made it to the battlefield. The Gatlings had major drawbacks, such as frequent jamming due to residue from black powder, and were cumbersome and would cause delays over the route traveled. The guns were drawn by 4 condemned horses, and there were obstacles in such rugged terrain that required their unhitching and the assistance of soldiers to continue. A case in point was Terry's own battery—the one he had offered to Custer—which had a difficult time keeping up with the march of Col. John GIBBON's infantry. Also, the guns were mounted on large wheels, which meant that in order to operate them the gun crew would be standing upright, making them sitting ducks to Indian snipers.

Gerard, Frederic F. (aka Frank Girard; November 14, 1829–?) U.S. Army interpreter. Gerard was a Frenchman born in St. Louis, who married an ARIKARA Indian woman while working as an Indian trader. He had learned to speak Arikara and SIOUX, and knew his way around the upper Missouri country. Gerard was employed as an Arikara interpreter for the LITTLE BIGHORN CAMPAIGN. On the approach to the Valley of the Little Bighorn, Custer paused at a lone tepee that contained the body of a dead Indian. Maj. Marcus RENO and Custer were conferring when Gerard came riding toward them at a furious pace. "Here are your Indians, General, running like devils!" he excitedly yelled, and pointed ahead. Sure enough, they observed clouds of dust from beyond the high bluffs between them and the valley. The SEVENTH CAVALRY then rode off to attack the unseen village. Gerard remained with Reno, and was left behind during RENO'S VALLEY FIGHT, and cut off from the troops on the hilltop. Gerard and scout Billy JACKSON hid together in the timber and along the Little Bighorn River overnight, finally reaching the friendly perimeter on the RENO-BENTEEN DEFENSE SITE the following evening. He remained post interpreter at FORT ABRAHAM LINCOLN until July 1,

1883. *Sources for further study include:* "Interview with Frederic F. Gerard, January 22 and April 3, 1909," in *Custer in '76: Walter Camp's Notes on the Custer Fight,* edited by Kenneth Hammer (Provo, UT: Brigham Young University Press, 1976); and "F. F. Gerard's Story of the Custer Fight," in *The Custer Myth: A Source Book of Custeriana,* edited by W. A. Graham (Harrisburg, PA: Stackpole, 1953).

Ghost Dance War *see* WOUNDED KNEE, BATTLE OF

Gibbon, John (1827–96) Colonel, 7th Infantry, commander of the District of Montana. Gibbon graduated from West Point in 1847 and was highly decorated during the Civil War, winning brevets up to major general. His early service on the frontier was distinguished, but by the time of the LITTLE BIGHORN CAMPAIGN he was well past his prime. Gibbon's Montana Column was part of the 3-pronged attack that was meant to trap and rout the Indians gathered in the vicinity of the Valley of the Little Bighorn. He marched from FORT ELLIS, MT, east down the Yellowstone River on April 3, 1876, with 6 companies of his own regiment and the 2nd Cavalry under Maj. James BRISBIN. His orders were to sweep the north bank of the Yellowstone to prevent the Indians from fleeing to Canada. As early as May 16 Gibbon was aware of the location of the large Indian village that was their target but inexplicably informed no one until June 9, when he met Gen. Alfred TERRY aboard the steamship *FAR WEST.* That set in motion RENO'S POWDER RIVER SCOUT to confirm that information. With the intelligence gathered by Reno, Gen. Terry summoned Gibbon, Custer, and Brisbin to the *Far West* on June 21. Custer would lead the march and strike from the south. Terry would accompany the Gibbon-Montana Column, which would act as a blocking force at the mouth of the Little Bighorn to engage any Indians that fled north. The Terry-Gibbon Column, having heard rumors of Custer's fight, arrived at the LITTLE BIGHORN BATTLEFIELD 2 days after Custer's command had been destroyed. They rescued Reno's command and buried the dead, then transported the wounded to the *Far West* for evacuation. In 1877 Gibbon's command attacked Chief Joseph and his NEZ PERCÉ in the Battle of Big Hole. The Indians' counterattack proved successful, and Gibbon—who was wounded—was forced to withdraw his troops. Gibbon was promoted to brigadier general in 1885 and assigned command of the Department of the Columbia, where he remained until his retirement 6 years later. *Sources for further study include: Gibbon on the Sioux Campaign of 1876*, by John Gibbon (Bellevue, NE: Old Army, 1970); and *On Time for Disaster: The Rescue of Custer's Command*, by Edward J. McClerand (Lincoln: University of Nebraska Press, Bison Book, 1989).

Gibson, Francis M. ("Frank"; December 14, 1847–1919) First lieutenant, 7th Cavalry. Gibson was appointed a second lieutenant on October 5, 1867, and assigned to the SEVENTH CAVALRY, where he participated in every campaign from 1868–77. At the Battle of the LITTLE BIGHORN he was second in command of H Company, which was detailed on a scout while the other battalions headed toward the village. Gibson and a small detachment of troopers rode ahead on 7 occasions to hilltops to reconnoiter the terrain, but found nothing. He then participated in the RENO-BENTEEN DEFENSE SITE. Gibson was of the opinion that his company commander, Capt. F. W. BENTEEN, was "one of the coolest and bravest men I have ever known." Gibson's sister, Mollie, was married to fellow 7th Cavalry officer, Capt. Donald MCINTOSH, who was killed at Little Bighorn. Gibson served during the NEZ PERCÉ Campaign of 1877; and retired on disability in 1890 as a captain. *Sources for further study include:* His daughter,

Katherine Gibson Fougera, wrote an account of her mother's frontier experiences entitled, *With Custer's Cavalry* (Caldwell, ID: Caxton, 1940), reprinted (Lincoln: University of Nebraska Press, 1990); and "Interview with Francis M. Gibson, December 7, 1910," in *Custer in '76: Walter Camp's Notes on the Custer Fight*, edited by Kenneth Hammer (Provo, UT: Brigham Young University Press, 1976).

Godfrey, Edward Settle (October 9, 1843–April 1, 1932) First lieutenant, 7th Cavalry. Godfrey graduated from West Point and was commissioned a second lieutenant in the SEVENTH CAVALRY in 1867. He participated in every regimental expedition with Custer, and was known as a respected and capable officer. However, Col. Samuel D. STURGIS in 1870 recommended that he appear before the "BENZINE BOARD," which was in the process of reducing the officer corps by dismissing undesirables. Sturgis later withdrew Godfrey's name, and the only contemporary who ever offered any serious criticism was the bitter Capt. F. W. BENTEEN in later years, and that was due to the fact that Godfrey was one of the more vocal supporters of Custer after the Battle of the LITTLE BIGHORN. Godfrey commanded K Company at Little Bighorn, accompanying Benteen on his scout to the left and then participating in the RENO-BENTEEN DEFENSE SITE. He fought against the NEZ PERCÉ at the Battle of Bear Paw Mountain in 1877, where he was severely wounded and awarded the Medal of Honor; and he was present at WOUNDED KNEE in 1890. He later served in Cuba and the Philippines, and was promoted to colonel of the 9th Cavalry in 1901. He retired with the rank of brigadier general after President Teddy Roosevelt, who considered Godfrey partially responsible for the killing of women and children at Wounded Knee, finally approved the promotion in 1907. *Sources for further study include:* "Custer's Last Battle," taken from a lecture by Godfrey at West Point, was published in the January 1892 issue of *Century* magazine. Lengthy excerpts of the article as well as other material by and about Godfrey have been published in *The Custer Myth: A Source Book of Custeriana*, edited by W. A. Graham (Harrisburg, PA: Stackpole, 1953); *The Field Diary of Lt. Edward Settle Godfrey, Commanding Co. K, 7th Cavalry Under Lt. Colonel George Armstrong Custer in the Sioux Encounter at the Battle of the Little Bighorn* (Portland, OR: Champoeg, 1957); and "Interview with Edward S. Godfrey," in *Custer in '76: Walter Camp's Notes on the Custer Fight*, edited by Kenneth Hammer (Provo, UT: Brigham Young University Press, 1976).

Goldin, Theodore W. (1858–1935; real name John Stilwell) Private, 7th Cavalry. Goldin enlisted in the regular army in 1875 and was assigned to Troop G, SEVENTH CAVALRY. He was wounded twice at the Battle of the LITTLE BIGHORN in RENO'S VALLEY FIGHT and the RENO-BENTEEN DEFENSE SITE. Goldin was discharged November 13, 1877, as a private of good character because he had concealed a minority enlistment. He became an attorney, and a colonel in the Wisconsin National Guard, as well as chairman of the Republican Central Committee. He applied for and received the congressional MEDAL OF HONOR in 1895 by claiming that he had been among the volunteers who had brought water to the wounded under heavy fire on the Reno-Benteen Defense Site. That, however, is not why he is notable. Between the fall of 1891 and the summer of 1896 Goldin carried on a correspondence with Capt. Frederick BENTEEN that recorded gossip, innuendo, opinion, and memories about the 7th Cavalry, with special emphasis on Custer and the battle. These fascinating accounts bear further witness to the malicious and prejudicial dark side of Benteen. The letters were compiled by historian John M. Carroll, and published as *The Benteen-Goldin Letters on Custer and His Last Battle* (New York: Liveright,

1974). Goldin's Medal of Honor was apparently awarded—19 years after the fact—with the assistance of Benteen, who probably would not have even remembered the enlisted man from the days they served in the same unit.

Grant, Frederick D. (1850–1912) The president's son graduated from West Point in 1871 and was commissioned a second lieutenant in the cavalry. Gen. Phil SHERIDAN, abiding by the wishes of Fred's mother, added the young man to his staff with the rank of lieutenant colonel. Grant accompanied Custer on the YELLOWSTONE EXPEDITION OF 1873, and again as an observer for Sheridan on the BLACK HILLS EXPEDITION OF 1874. Custer wrote to Libbie at the conclusion of the Yellowstone Expedition and asked her to meet Lt. Col. Grant, who would be passing through Monroe, MI, on his way back East, and invite him to dinner. And be sure to "have his father's portrait hung in the parlor." By all accounts, the two men got along famously, although Custer did have occasion to arrest Grant for drunkenness on the Black Hills Expedition. That incident apparently did not exclude Custer and his wife Libbie from attending Grant's wedding in Chicago on October 24, 1874.

Grant, Orvil L. (1835–?) In a blatant case of influence peddling, Orvil, the president's youngest brother, arranged in 1874 with Secretary of the Interior Columbus Delano to revoke all licenses of the Indian traders on the upper Missouri. They would have to deal privately with Orvil and new Secretary of War Belknap in order to gain renewal. Two years later, Custer drew the ire of the president when he testified against Orvil in congressional hearings. See BELKNAP SCANDAL.

Grant, U. S. (1822–85) The eighteenth president of the United States, 1869–77. The general who secured the

Union victory in the Civil War was reportedly a man of unquestioned personal integrity. His administration, however, was plagued with numerous cases of corruption, including that by his own family members. In 1869 Grant appointed Ely Parker as commissioner of Indian affairs, the first Native American to hold the post. When Congress banned military personnel from civil service positions in 1870, he assigned Indian agents from Christian denominations—many of them Quakers—as a part of his peace process of relocating tribes to reservations. He entertained many tribal leaders over the years, and helped raise funds—both public and private—to assist in the assimilation of Indians into white society. Unfortunately, his policies failed to bring an end to Indian hostilities on the Plains. In late 1875, when the public was clamoring over the need to acquire the BLACK HILLS from the SIOUX, Grant lost patience with the peace faction within his administration and turned to the military under generals William SHERMAN and Phil SHERIDAN for a solution. This set in motion events that led to the LITTLE BIGHORN CAMPAIGN of 1876. Grant clashed with Custer in early 1876 when Congress held hearings into the sale of post traderships, and Custer testified against the president's brother, Orvil. He initially refused to permit Custer to accompany the SEVENTH CAVALRY on their march to the Little Bighorn as punishment, but later relented. (See BELKNAP SCANDAL.) In the public debate following the Battle of the LITTLE BIGHORN, Grant's remarks perhaps reflected his malice over the Belknap affair when he said, "I regard Custer's Massacre as a sacrifice of troops brought on by Custer himself, that was wholly unnecessary—wholly unnecessary."

Gray Horse Troop *see* E COMPANY

Greasy Grass, Battle of The SIOUX name for the Battle of the LITTLE BIGHORN.

Greasy Grass River The SIOUX name for the Little Bighorn River.

Great Sioux Reservation The FORT LARAMIE TREATY OF 1868, which ended hostilities over the BOZEMAN TRAIL, set aside all of the state of South Dakota west of the Missouri River for this SIOUX Indian reservation (see map on page 85). RED CLOUD, SPOTTED TAIL, and 15,000 of their tribesmen settled there to live in peace; others, including SITTING BULL, CRAZY HORSE, and GALL refused to submit. The area known as the BLACK HILLS—*Pa Sapa* to the Sioux—was located within this reservation. It was onto this reservation that all freely roaming Sioux Indians were ordered to move by the U.S. government before January 31, 1876, or be considered hostile. Refusal would mean the army would come after them for the purpose of driving them onto the reservation with force. This demand began the GREAT SIOUX WAR OF 1876–77.

Great Sioux War of 1876–77 This conflict was fought from March 1876 to May 1877 between the U.S. Army and the Teton SIOUX, allied with the northern CHEYENNE Indians (see map on page 86). The war for all intents and purposes began when the U.S. government proclaimed that all freely roaming Sioux Indians were required to move onto reservations before January 31, 1876, or be considered hostile. The army would then come after those who refused and force them to submit. The deadline itself would have made it difficult for the Indians to comply, inasmuch as winter travel over long distances was practically impossible. Bands of Sioux and Cheyenne led by such notables as SITTING BULL, CRAZY HORSE, GALL, and TWO MOON ignored the demand and decided to fight for their freedom. During the conflict, nearly 300 soldiers were killed and over 100 wounded, and an estimate from Indian testimony puts their losses at perhaps 100 killed and the same

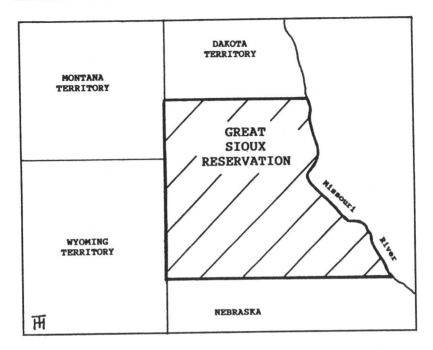

The Great Sioux Reservation

number wounded. By the fall of 1877 most of the dissidents had straggled onto the reservation. Notable battles include: ROSEBUD, LITTLE BIGHORN, LAME DEER, SLIM BUTTES, DULL KNIFE, WOLF MOUNTAIN, and the POWDER RIVER FIGHT. *Sources for further study include: Battles and Skirmishes of the Great Sioux War, 1876–1877: The Military View*, edited by Jerome A. Greene (Norman: University of Oklahoma Press, 1993); *The Great Sioux War of 1876–77*, edited by Paul Hedren (Helena: Montana Historical Society, 1991); *War-Path and Bivouac; Or, The Conquest of the Sioux*, by John T. Finerty (Norman: University of Oklahoma Press, 1961); and *Gibbon on the Sioux Campaign of 1876*, by John Gibbon (Bellevue, NE: Old Army, 1970).

Grinnell, George Bird Grinnell was an assistant paleontologist at Yale University's Peabody Museum of Natural History when he accompanied the BLACK HILLS EXPEDITION OF 1874. His first trip west had come as a college senior on a field trip to fossil beds in Colorado, Kansas, and Nebraska. Grinnell later served as editor of *Field and Stream* magazine, worked for the preservation of Yellowstone and Glacier National parks, and organized the first Audubon Society. He was a notable student of North American ethnology, and the author of *The Fighting Cheyennes*, 2nd edition (Norman: University of Oklahoma Press, 1962); *The Passing of the Great West* (New York: Winchester Press, 1972); and *Two Great Scouts and Their Pawnee Battalion* (Lincoln: University of Nebraska Press, 1973). *Sources for further study include: Custer's Gold: The United States Cavalry Expedition of 1874*, by Donald Jackson (New Haven, CT: Yale University Press, 1966).

Grouard, Frank Army scout (SIOUX names: Standing Bear; The Grabber).

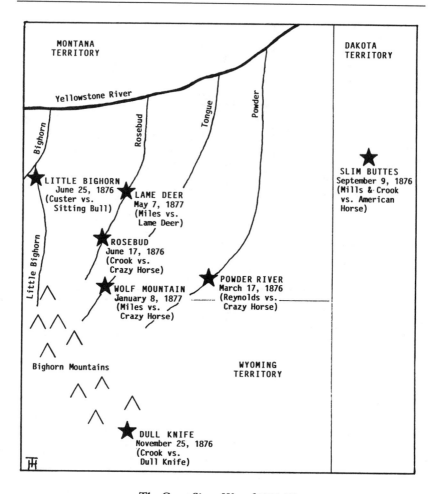

MONTANA
TERRITORY

DAKOTA
TERRITORY

Yellowstone River

Bighorn

Rosebud

Tongue

Powder

★ SLIM BUTTES
September 9, 1876
(Mills & Crook
vs. American
Horse)

★ LITTLE BIGHORN
June 25, 1876
(Custer vs.
Sitting Bull)

★ LAME DEER
May 7, 1877
(Miles vs.
Lame Deer)

Little Bighorn

★ ROSEBUD
June 17, 1876
(Crook vs.
Crazy Horse)

★ WOLF MOUNTAIN
January 8, 1877
(Miles vs.
Crazy Horse)

★ POWDER RIVER
March 17, 1876
(Reynolds vs.
Crazy Horse)

Bighorn Mountains

WYOMING
TERRITORY

★ DULL KNIFE
November 25, 1876
(Crook vs.
Dull Knife)

The Great Sioux War of 1876–77

This frontier character was born about 1850 in the South Seas to a Mormon missionary and a native girl named Nahina. He was raised by a foster family named Pratt in California and Utah. In the mid–1860s he went to work as a teamster in Montana, and ended up wandering around the Dakota Territory consorting with the various Indian tribes. This association reportedly began when he was working as a mail courier between Fort Hall and Fort Peck and was captured by the Sioux under SITTING BULL, who adopted him because of his dark com-

plexion. It was said that Grouard, then known as Standing Bear, fought with the Sioux against Custer on the YELLOW-STONE EXPEDITION OF 1873. He then joined CRAZY HORSE, became known as The Grabber, and continued to fight the whites. In 1875, after a quarrel with Crazy Horse, he appeared at CAMP ROBINSON and was hired as an army scout. Grouard witnessed the Battle of the ROSEBUD as a scout for Gen. George CROOK. At the time of the Battle of the LITTLE BIGHORN he claimed to have read smoke signals while out looking for sign, and later told some officers about the Indian victory but was not believed. Dressed like an Indian, he rode off to investigate, and said he must have passed near the SEVENTH CAVALRY on the RENO-BENTEEN DEFENSE SITE at night but did not notice them. This story, if true, would explain how Crook's scouts apparently knew about the Little Bighorn Battle before the general himself. The Grabber eventually had a treacherous hand in the death of Crazy Horse. Grouard was the interpreter on an occasion in 1877 when Crazy Horse remarked that under certain circumstances he would help fight the NEZ PERCÉ Indians *with* the whites. Later, however, Grouard told Gen. Crook that Crazy Horse was coming to fight *against* the whites. Crook then had Crazy Horse arrested, and he was subsequently killed. Grouard spied on the Sioux for the army during the Ghost Dance episode in 1890–91 that led to the Battle of WOUNDED KNEE. *Sources for further study include:* "An Indian Scout's Recollections of Crazy Horse," by Frank Grouard, *Nebraska History* 12 (January–March 1919); and "Frank Grouard: Kanaka Scout or Mulatto Renegade," by John S. Gray, *Chicago Westerner's Brand Book* 16, no 8 (1959).

H Company, Seventh Cavalry This company was commanded during the Battle of the LITTLE BIGHORN by Capt. Frederick W. BENTEEN, with 1st Lt. Francis GIBSON second in command. H Company was part of Benteen's Battalion, participated in Benteen's scout and the RENO-BENTEEN DEFENSE SITE, losing 1 man killed and 13 wounded. Four members were awarded the MEDAL OF HONOR for their actions. Trumpeter John MARTIN, the bearer of Custer's last message, was assigned as Custer's orderly.

Hale, Owen (July 23, 1843–September 30, 1877) Captain, 7th Cavalry. This descendant of American patriot Nathan Hale was known as "Holy Owen" due to his personification of the ideal army officer. He served in the 1st New York Mounted Rifles during the Civil War as a sergeant major and later as an officer. He was appointed a first lieutenant, regular army, in 1866, assigned to the SEVENTH CAVALRY, and promoted to captain in 1869. Although commander of Troop K at the time of the LITTLE BIGHORN Battle, Hale was on detached service at Jefferson Barracks, MO. He was killed in the first charge on Chief Joseph's NEZ PERCÉ encampment during the 1877 Battle of Bear Paw Mountain.

Hamilton, Louis McLane (July 21, 1844–November 27, 1868) Captain, 7th Cavalry. This paternal grandson of Alexander Hamilton and maternal grandson of Louis McLane, the U.S. senator and member of President Andrew Jackson's cabinet, entered the Civil War with the 3rd Infantry as a second lieutenant at the age of 18 in September 1862. He was cited for bravery in battles at Fredricksburg, Chancellorsville, and Gettysburg. In 1866 he became the youngest captain in the regular army, and was a well-liked and respected troop commander. During the HANCOCK EXPEDITION OF 1867, his leadership skills saved his company from disaster when, in pursuit of hostiles led by SIOUX chief PAWNEE KILLER, he recognized an Indian decoy and halted his men before being lured into an ambush. Hamilton was disappointed when assigned duty as officer of the day at the Battle of WASHITA, which meant he would be detailed to the packtrain in the rear and miss the battle. He arranged to trade places with 1st Lt. E. G. MATHEY, and rejoined his company. As fate would have it, Hamilton was killed by a bullet through the heart in the initial charge on the village. He was buried with full military honors near CAMP SUPPLY on the Beaver River.

Hancock, Winfield Scott (February 14, 1824–February 9, 1886) Major general, U.S. Army. A graduate of West

Point in 1844, Hancock distinguished himself in the Mexican War before serving in primarily quartermaster capacities. He was a bona fide Civil War hero who held the Union center against Pickett's charge at Gettysburg, for which the U.S. Congress formally thanked him. The newspapers referred to him as "Hancock the Superb." General U. S. Grant once wrote: "He commanded a corps longer than any other one, and his name was never mentioned as having committed in battle a blunder for which he was responsible." Custer served as volunteer aide to Hancock on May 5, 1862, in an engagement near Williamsburg, VA, and, leading a charge of infantry, personally captured 6 Confederate soldiers and a large silk battle flag, the first colors ever taken by the Union. In 1867 Hancock commanded the Department of the Missouri, which included the states of Kansas, Colorado, New Mexico, and Indian Territory. His operations against the Plains Indians, however, were a blot on his otherwise notable military career (see HANCOCK EXPEDITION). Custer believed that it was Hancock who ordered his arrest by Col. A. J. SMITH that led to his court-martial in 1867, his being used as a scapegoat for Hancock's own failure on the expedition. Hancock commanded the Department of the Dakota from 1869 until 1872. He was the Democratic nominee for president in 1880 but lost to James A. Garfield and returned to military service in the East.

Hancock Expedition of 1867 (April–July 1867) This expedition led by Maj. Gen. W. S. HANCOCK, commander of the Department of the Missouri, was formed for the purpose of marching into Kansas to demonstrate the might of the military to the Plains Indians. Hancock's orders were to convince the CHEYENNE, SIOUX, KIOWA, COMANCHE, and ARAPAHO tribes to live in peace or suffer severe punishment for the constant menacing of white homesteaders and workers on the KANSAS PACIFIC RAILROAD. The ex-

pedition, Custer's first on the Great Plains, became a series of miscalculations, breakdowns of military discipline, and ended in miserable failure. The Indians easily eluded the army, fighting only when it pleased them, and continued raiding white settlements and travelers at will. The army was also plagued by inadequate forage and rations due to Indian control of the supply lines, and eventually both man and beast suffered from fatigue.

The Hancock Expedition began when more than 1,400 soldiers, including Custer leading 8 companies of the SEVENTH CAVALRY, marched down the SANTA FE TRAIL to the Arkansas River in late March 1867. The army staged aggressive maneuvers and practiced battle tactics during the march, with intentions of intimidating the generally unseen Indian observers.

On the evening of April 12 Hancock addressed several apprehensive Cheyenne and Sioux chiefs, including TALL BULL and PAWNEE KILLER, from a camp near FORT LARNED. He warned them that they must live up to their treaties and, much to their disbelief, stated that he would punish any whites who mistreated Indians. He vowed that his mission was to promote peace, but the tribal leaders grew exceedingly nervous when Hancock decided to march the 21 miles up Pawnee Fork to their village for further talks. The Indians repeatedly requested that Hancock remain a distance from their homes.

Hancock ignored their protestations, marching his command upstream toward the village. The Indians, painted and dressed for war, rode back and forth in front of the column. Hancock ordered his men to prepare for battle, then, accompanied by his officers, rode forward and met the chiefs halfway for a parley. Both sides agreed that they did not desire war. Hancock said he would camp near their village, but would not enter it or allow his men to molest it in any way. The chiefs agreed to meet Hancock for further talks at that time.

Hancock arrived at the village to learn that the warriors had been observed fleeing. Custer was ordered to surround and search the village. He found the nearly 300 lodges abandoned. In fact, the inhabitants had departed in such haste that they had left behind most of their belongings, including 1,000 precious buffalo robes. Hancock concluded that this insulting act signified war, and dispatched Custer's troops to pursue the hostiles. The escaping Sioux and Cheyenne split into numerous fast-traveling small groups, making it impossible for Custer to overtake them.

Meanwhile, back at the Indian encampment Hancock's men disobeyed orders and looted the lodges of weapons, robes, personal items, and any other souvenir they could get their hands on. Hancock received word from Custer that Indians had been attacking stagecoaches and stations along the SMOKY HILL ROAD. Against the advice of others, including Indian agent E. W. WYNKOOP and Col. A. J. SMITH, Hancock ordered the village burned to the ground. This atrocious act, which was quite acceptable by Civil War standards, was a declaration of war to the Indians. It also opened wider an already gaping wound between the military and the Indian Department.

Custer was camped near Old FORT HAYS waiting for supplies, and became bogged down in weeks of rain and mud. Forage had been delayed; large numbers of disgruntled troopers were deserting; wife Libbie's letters hinted of her great loneliness; and Custer, a man of action, became deeply depressed. This mood apparently brought out the worst in him. Capt. Albert BARNITZ, a Custer friend, wrote to his wife: "He is the most complete example of a petty tyrant that I ever have seen. You would be filled with utter amazement, if I were to give you a few instances of his cruelty to the men, and discourtesy to the officers."

At FORT DODGE on April 23 Gen. Hancock met with chiefs from the Kiowa Indians, including KICKING BIRD, and advised them to comply with his requests for peace and the "Great Father" would feed them when the buffalo disappeared. Then on April 28 he held a meeting with Little Raven, an Arapaho chief, who vowed to keep his people away from the Sioux and Cheyenne who were presumably north of the North Platte River. On May 1 Hancock had a parley with SATANTA, head chief of the Kiowas, who professed his peaceful intentions but complained that his tribe had not received their annuity goods. Hancock was so impressed with Satanta's declaration of peace that he gave the Kiowa chief a full major's uniform. A few days later Satanta wore the uniform on a successful raid on the horse herd at Fort Dodge.

Neither Hancock's warnings nor the presence of the military force had much effect on the Indians. The raiding increased to uncontrollable proportions during May and June. No mail station, stagecoach, railroad worker, or traveler of any kind was safe. The SMOKY HILL ROAD was hit the hardest; at times stagecoaches suspended service.

It was June 1 when Custer and 6 companies finally took to the field with orders to clear the area between the Arkansas and Platte rivers of Indians. Custer met with Sioux chief Pawnee Killer near FORT MCPHERSON. The Indians were treated to quantities of coffee, sugar, and other goods. They pledged friendship and promised peace, vowing to bring their families to live near the fort until hostilities between the Cheyenne and the army were resolved. Custer had faith that Pawnee Killer spoke the truth. The chief, however, meant none of it. Instead, his band returned to raiding along the Smoky Hill Road. Custer happened upon Pawnee Killer later in the month when the Indians attempted to stampede and steal cavalry horses from under Custer's nose. Custer and his interpreters held a parley with Pawnee Killer and his band, trying unsuccessfully to learn the location of their village. When they parted, Custer mounted his troops and gave chase. The Indians outmaneuvered the cavalry and attacked, almost trapping Capt. Louis HAMILTON's detachment, but were repulsed and broke contact. Other than a few other sightings and minor skirmishes, Custer and his men found little action but much evidence of the raiding Indians. Custer traversed the 215 miles from Fort Hays to Fort McPherson and arrived on June 15. Gen. William SHERMAN personally met with Custer the following day, and gave the order to advance to FORT SEDGWICK, which had access to the railroad, for supplies.

Custer wrote to his wife Libbie imploring her if possible to travel to FORT WALLACE, the westernmost post in Kansas, and he would send a squadron to fetch her to him. Presumably for that personal reason, Custer did not travel to Fort Sedgwick and resupply. He instead sent Maj. Joel ELLIOTT and a detail there to check on orders. He then ordered a squadron of 48 men led by 1st Lt. W. W. COOKE to travel to Fort Wallace for the purpose of requisitioning supplies. Fort Wallace, which was some distance from the rail and had difficulty provisioning even those stationed there, lay along a route of frequent attacks by the Sioux. The squadron fortunately arrived at Fort Wallace without any problem.

Halfway back on Cooke's return trip from Fort Wallace to Custer's camp on the Republican River the wagon train loaded with supplies came under attack from about 600 to 700 hostile Sioux Indians. Cooke ordered the wagons into 2 parallel columns and had the troopers dismount and surround the wagons in a protective circle. The wagons were kept slowly moving forward. The Indians would ride around and around the wagons in single file at breakneck speed while firing from beneath the neck of their ponies. Each assault, however, was repulsed by the soldiers. The Sioux could not be discouraged. The warriors regrouped after each attack and returned again and again in their classic display of

expert horsemanship. Cooke ordered the soldiers to pace their fire to conserve their diminishing supply of ammunition. The running battle continued for several hours, with the soldiers keeping the Indians at bay. Finally, just as ammunition became critically low, the Indians abruptly broke contact and disappeared. It was not long before Capt. Robert WEST arrived with a detachment of soldiers that had been detailed to relieve the escort. The cavalry had arrived in the nick of time to save 1st Lt. Cooke and the beleaguered wagon train. The supply detail reported that Custer's wife had not been waiting at Fort Wallace, for which he was thankful. Cooke and the other officers had standing orders to shoot any white women to save them from capture should an Indian attack appear overwhelming. Custer learned later that his letter asking Libbie to travel to Fort Wallace had never been delivered.

Maj. Elliott's detachment returned with no new orders; those dispatches had already left Fort Sedgwick in the care of Lt. Lyman S. KIDDER. Kidder and his 10-man detail could not locate Custer, and were discovered by Sioux Indians led by Pawnee Killer. These soldiers had not been as fortunate as the wagon train from Fort Wallace. Custer's scouts later found their mutilated bodies strewn across the Plains where each had fallen in a desperate running battle.

Without new orders, Custer continued to sweep the headwaters of the Republican, his route curiously distant from areas offering evidence of the Indian raiding parties that Gen. Sherman had intended him to locate and fight. The march was difficult, which encouraged mass desertions. More than 60 men had disappeared from the column by early July. On July 7 the column had halted at about noon to rest the horses, during which break 13 troopers, 7 on horseback, deserted in plain view of the command. Custer noted:

> I directed Major Elliott and Lts.
> Custer, Cook[e]and Jackson, with a

few of the guard, to pursue the deserters who were still visible, tho more than a mile distant, and to bring the dead bodies of as many as could be taken back to camp. Seven of the deserters, being mounted on our best horses, and having two miles' start, made their escape. One, a dangerous character, presented his carbine at Major Elliott, but, before he could fire, was brought down by another of the pursuing party. Two others were brought down by pistol shots. The remaining three, by throwing themselves on the ground and feigning death, escaped being shot. Six were brought back to camp. From there to [Fort] Wallace wounds were treated, but did not prove serious. The effect was all that could be desired. There was not another desertion as long as I remained with the command.

Three deserters were wounded, one of whom later died. When the deserters were brought back to camp, Custer boldly proclaimed for all to hear that the wounded were not to be given medical attention but quietly directed the surgeon to do his best.

The command went into a welcome camp near Fort Wallace a week later. Both men and their mounts were worn out and in dire need of rest and supplies. For all intents and purposes the Hancock Expedition had fizzled to an end. Custer visited Fort Wallace to inquire about orders from Gen. Hancock. He was informed that nothing, including mail and dispatches, could get through on the Smoky Hill Road due to the hostile Indian presence.

Custer made the controversial decision to head east to FORT HAYS, a distance of about 200 miles. He assembled 100 men and the best stock available and departed on the morning of July 15. The detail—minus a number of deserters and 2 men killed by Indians near Downer's Station—traversed the difficult 150-mile trip in about 55 hours, an extraordinarily fast time. Custer, along with 1st Lt.

Cooke and Tom CUSTER, went 60 miles farther to FORT HARKER where his wife Libbie resided, arriving at 2 A.M. on July 19. Later that day Custer was placed under arrest and told to report to FORT RILEY pending charges being filed against him. It was perhaps a fitting conclusion to an expedition that required a scapegoat to blame for its counterproductive results.

Custer did indeed face a court-martial in September 1867 for his actions during the Hancock Expedition. The charges ranged from absence without leave to conduct prejudicial to military discipline to unauthorized use of government property. He was subsequently found guilty of all charges, and suspended from rank and command for a year. (See CUSTER: Court-martial.) The Indians were free to terrorize the Smoky Hill, Platte, and Arkansas areas for the remainder of the summer, which caused an outcry from Western governors and an appeal to Washington for action.

Sources for further study include: Custer, Come at Once! The Fort Hays Years of George and Elizabeth Custer, 1867–70, by Blaine Burkey (Hays, KA: Thomas More Prep, 1970); *My Life on the Plains: Or, Personal Experiences with Indians,* by George A. Custer (New York: Sheldon, 1874); *Nomad: George A. Custer in Turf, Field and Farm,* edited by Brian W. Dippie (Austin: University of Texas Press, 1980); *Tenting on the Plains; Or, General Custer in Kansas and Texas,* by Elizabeth Bacon Custer (New York: Harper and Brothers, 1887); *The Court-Martial of General George Armstrong Custer,* by Lawrence A. Frost (Norman: University of Oklahoma Press, 1968); *Life in Custer's Cavalry: Diaries and Letters of Albert and Jennie Barnitz, 1867–68,* edited by Robert M. Utley (New Haven, CT: Yale University Press, 1977; Lincoln: University of Nebraska Press, 1987); "The West Breaks in General Custer," by Minnie Dubbs Millbrook, *Kansas Historical Quarterly* 36 (Summer 1970); "Custer's First Scout in the West," *Kansas Historical*

Quarterly 39 (Spring 1973); and "The Kidder Massacre," by E. A. Brininstool, *Hunter-Trader-Trapper* (December 1932).

Hare, Luther (August 24, 1851–December 22, 1929) Second lieutenant, 7th Cavalry. The son of a Texas lawyer, Hare graduated from West Point and was assigned to the SEVENTH CAVALRY in June 1874. Hare and 2nd Lt. Charles VARNUM were in charge of the Indian scouts at the Battle of the LITTLE BIGHORN, and rode ahead during the advance down Reno Creek, sending back reports of fleeing Indians. He then rejoined his own K company in time for RENO'S VALLEY FIGHT. Hare said of Maj. Marcus RENO's retreat from the timber across the Little Bighorn River during that episode: "The crossing was not covered and no effort was made to hold the Indians back. If the Indians had followed us in force to the hilltop, they would have got us all." As Reno's acting adjutant on the hilltop RENO-BENTEEN DEFENSE SITE, his initial duty was to hurry up the packtrain: fortunately, the Indians had not surrounded the position as of yet. Upon his return, he claimed to have heard firing from Custer's direction and observed some troops advancing that way. Reno then sent Hare to tell Capt. Thomas WEIR of the advance to open communication with Custer if possible. Later, he carried orders to 1st Lt. GODFREY, and decided to remain there with his unit rather than return to Reno. After the Little Bighorn Battle, Hare became second in command to Capt. Henry NOWLAN of I Company. He served in the NEZ PERCÉ Campaign of 1877; the Battle of WOUNDED KNEE in 1890; and in the Philippines during the Spanish-American War. He retired on disability in 1903. *Sources for further study include:* "Interview with Luther Hare, February 7, 1910," in *Custer in '76: Walter Camp's Notes on the Custer Fight,* edited by Kenneth Hammer (Provo, UT: Brigham Young University Press, 1976); and numerous references in *The Custer Myth: A Source Book of Custeriana,* edited

by W. A. Graham (Harrisburg, PA: Stackpole, 1953).

Harrington, Henry Moore (ca. 1850–June 25, 1876) Second lieutenant, 7th Cavalry. Harrington was appointed to West Point from Michigan and upon graduation on June 14, 1872, was commissioned and assigned to Capt. Tom CUSTER's Company C of the SEVENTH CAVALRY. It has been suggested that Capt. Custer served as aide-de-camp to his brother during the Battle of the LITTLE BIGHORN, leaving Harrington in command of the company. Harrington was killed—apparently with the rest of Company C somewhere along BATTLE RIDGE—but his remains have never been located. It has been speculated that his body was so badly mutilated that identification was impossible, or that he was the soldier on the sorrel horse that the Indians claimed had been chased and killed by 2 CHEYENNE and a SIOUX some distance from the battlefield. Harrington had a premonition before the battle, and mailed a sketch to a friend back in the East that depicted himself tied to a tree in the midst of hostile Indians. Harrington's wife mysteriously disappeared after the battle, and was not found until 2 years later in Texas suffering from amnesia. An attack of pneumonia apparently restored her mind, but she recalled nothing about the previous 2 years. Harrington's daughter claimed that the Indians told her about a woman dressed in black who had been seen several times during that 2-year period on the Little Bighorn Battlefield, and she believed this to be her mother.

Hayfield Fight, The (August 1, 1867) This battle was one of a series (FETTERMAN MASSACRE and WAGON BOX FIGHT) waged by RED CLOUD for control of the BOZEMAN TRAIL. SIOUX Indians led by CRAZY HORSE attacked a detachment of soldiers that were guarding haycutters near Fort C. F. Smith. Indian casualties are unknown: the army claimed they killed 8 and wounded 30, which was probably exaggerated. The army lost Lt. Sternberg, 1 private and 1 citizen killed, and 1 sergeant and 2 privates wounded. Capt. Thomas B. Burrowes's official report of the action stated: "On August 1 a part of 19 soldiers and 6 citizens, who were guarding a party cutting hay, were attacked by a force of Indians, variously estimated at from 500 to 800. The troops were partly protected by a brush and log corral and fought heroically for 3 or 4 hours until relieved by troops sent from the post." *Sources for further study include: Indian Fights: New Facts on Seven Encounters*, by J. W. Vaughn (Norman: University of Oklahoma Press, 1966).

Hazen, William B.   (1830–87) Colonel, U.S. Army. Hazen was a Custer rival beginning at West Point, where he was an instructor of infantry tactics and Custer was a student. Officer of the guard Custer was arrested by Hazen for condoning a fist fight between two cadets. The subsequent court-martial would have likely ended Custer's military career had it not been for the outbreak of the Civil War: he received a reprimand rather than dismissal. Hazen served on the frontier, and in 1868 had the unenviable task of determining which Indian tribes were to be considered hostile or peaceful. He was convinced prior to the Battle of WASHITA that Chief BLACK KETTLE was peaceful, but told the chief to make peace with Gen. Phil SHERIDAN to ensure his safety. The chief could not locate the general, and within days was dead at the hands of Custer's troops under Sheridan's orders. Hazen displeased both Sheridan and Custer when he gave safe passage to KIOWA chiefs SATANTA and LONE WOLF, whom the army had trailed toward FORT COBB from the Washita River and were certain had fought in that battle (see WASHITA CAMPAIGN OF 1868–69). Perhaps due to that act and a long-standing disagreement with Sheridan over battle honors

during the Civil War, Hazen was assigned duty as colonel of the 6th Infantry at remote FORT BUFORD in 1872. Hazen and Custer engaged in a literary duel in the early 1870s over the merits of the railroad. Custer was impressed with the agricultural and stock-grazing prospects of the Dakota Plains and the Yellowstone Valley, and made his views known in the national press. This position pleased Jay Cooke, financial agent of the NORTHERN PACIFIC RAILROAD, who desperately needed settlers on the land through which his trains ran to remain solvent. Hazen, however, disagreed with Custer's assessment of the land, and the two traded opinions in the press. Hazen also criticized Custer for the affair with Satanta and the Kiowa, but Custer stood behind his actions. Hazen was also an outspoken critic of Secretary of War Belknap, who was accused of corruption in the awarding of post traderships, an action that placed him in the same unfavorable light as Custer with President GRANT. It was Hazen's list of witnesses (which included Custer), however, that landed Custer in trouble. (See BELKNAP SCANDAL.) He was promoted to brigadier general in 1880, in spite of his combative personality. *Sources for further study include: Great Plains Command: William B. Hazen in the Frontier West*, by Marvin E. Kroeker (Norman: University of Oklahoma Press, 1976).

He Dog (OGLALA SIOUX) He Dog was a member of CRAZY HORSE's decoy party that lured Capt. FETTERMAN and his men into the fatal trap in December 1866 when the SIOUX waged war over the BOZEMAN TRAIL. In March 1876, much to the ire of his good friend CRAZY HORSE, He Dog decided to lead his 10 lodges onto the Red Cloud Agency reservation. They were attacked by Gen. George CROOK along the way but managed to escape. He Dog then joined Crazy Horse and fought at the Battle of the LITTLE BIGHORN. He lived into his 90s, becoming the judge of the Court of Indian Offenses at Pine Ridge Reservation, SD. *Sources for further study include:* "Interview with He Dog, July 13, 1910; William Berger, Interpreter," in *Custer in '76: Walter Camp's Notes on the Custer Fight,* edited by Kenneth Hammer (Provo, UT: Brigham Young University Press, 1976).

Herendeen, George B. (November 28, 1846–June 17, 1918) U.S. Army scout. Herendeen worked as a cowboy in New Mexico and on cattle trails into Montana after the Civil War. He was on the Yellowstone Wagonroad and Prospecting Expedition in 1874, and helped construct Fort Pease. Herendeen reported to Custer's command on June 21, 1876, on loan from Col. John GIBBON, and was detailed to Maj. Marcus RENO's command on June 25. During RENO'S VALLEY FIGHT, he led a detachment of men left stranded in the timber to the RENO-BENTEEN DEFENSE SITE some three hours after Reno's retreat. He later became an outspoken critic of Reno. *Sources for further study include:* "Interview with George Herendeen," in *Custer in '76: Walter Camp's Notes on the Custer Fight,* edited by Kenneth Hammer (Provo, UT: Brigham Young University Press, 1976); and *The Custer Myth: A Source Book of Custeriana,* edited by W. A. Graham (Harrisburg, PA: Stackpole, 1953).

Hickok, William Butler ("Wild Bill"; May 27, 1837–August 2, 1876) This notorious gunfighter and lawman served as an army scout from 1867 until 1869, including the HANCOCK EXPEDITION OF 1867. Custer spent quite a bit of time learning about the Plains Indians from Hickok's extensive knowledge. Capt. Tom CUSTER, the general's brother, got on the wrong side of Wild Bill in Hays City, KA, in 1869, which culminated in Hickok hopping onto a freight train and leaving town. (See CUSTER, THOMAS WARD.) Hickok returned to law enforcement, and was shot to death by Jack McCall while playing poker in Deadwood, D.T.

Hilltop Fight *see* RENO-BENTEEN DEFENSE SITE

Hodgson, Benjamin H. ("Benny"; ca. 1847–June 25, 1876) Second lieutenant, 7th Cavalry. Hodgson was appointed to West Point on July 1, 1865, from Pennsylvania, and commissioned as a second lieutenant in the SEVENTH CAVALRY on June 15, 1870. He had decided to resign his commission in the spring of 1876, but his best friend, 2nd Lt. Charles VARNUM, convinced him to stay for one more campaign—the LITTLE BIGHORN. He was second in command of Capt. T. M. McDOUGALL's B Company, but during the battle was assigned temporary duty as adjutant to his friend Maj. Marcus RENO. On the retreat from the timber during RENO'S VALLEY FIGHT, Hodgson's horse was killed and he was wounded in the leg while crossing the Little Bighorn River. Hodgson had the presence of mind to grab hold of the stirrup from a passing horse, and was being pulled to safety when he was shot and killed. His death greatly affected Maj. Reno. In fact, Reno left Capt. F. W. BENTEEN in charge during the crucial initial stages on the hilltop while he went down to the river on foot to search for Hodgson's body. One report stated that Hodgson was buried where he fell by 2nd Lt. Varnum and a 5-man detail. However, Capt. McDougall testified at the RENO COURT OF INQUIRY as follows: "On the night of the 26th of June, 1876, I took privates Ryan and Moore of my company, and we went and got Liet. Hodgson's body and carried it to the breastworks and kept it until the next morning, the 27th. After sewing him up in a blanket and a poncho, I proceeded with those two men to bury him." Regardless of who buried him, the whereabouts of Hodgson's body remains unknown.

Hump (MINNICONJOU SIOUX) (ca. 1835–1908) Hump, along with CRAZY HORSE, GALL, and other young SIOUX warriors fought for RED CLOUD in his

war against the U.S. Army over the
BOZEMAN TRAIL. He led the charge in
the FETTERMAN MASSACRE that killed
every trooper. Hump participated in the
Battle of the LITTLE BIGHORN, but soon
after settled on the reservation. He
worked briefly as a scout for Gen. Nelson MILES, leading the army to the village of fellow Minniconjou LAME DEER,
who was subsequently killed in a scuffle.
Hump at first embraced the Ghost
Dance ritual in 1890, but lost interest
prior to the Battle of WOUNDED KNEE.
In 1891 he was part of the delegation that
traveled to Washington, D.C., to speak
about the treatment of his people. *Sources
for further study include:* Hump's observations about the Little Bighorn Battle as
well as other references can be found in
*The Custer Myth: A Source Book of Custe-
riana,* edited by W. A. Graham (Harrisburg, PA: Stackpole, 1953).

Hunkpapa Sioux Indians (Also
spelled Unkpapa or Uncpapa) One of
the SIOUX tribes present in the village at
the Little Bighorn River on June 25,
1876, when Custer attacked. Their name
means "They Camp by Themselves," which
was why the Hunkpapa traditionally
camped near the entrance to a village.
SITTING BULL was the most famous
Hunkpapa, followed by RAIN-IN-THE-
FACE, GALL, Black Moon, and CROW
KING.

I Company, Seventh Cavalry This
company was commanded during the
Battle of the LITTLE BIGHORN by Capt.
Myles W. KEOGH, with 1st Lt. James
PORTER second in command. Custer separated his troops into battalions on the
approach to the Little Bighorn Valley at
the head of RENO CREEK. Capt. Keogh
was placed in charge of a battalion consisting of companies C, I, and L, so it is
entirely possible that 1st Lt. Porter actually commanded I Company on the battlefield. Every man from this company,
known as the "Wild I" for its rowdy reputation, was killed. The bodies—exclud-

ing Porter who was never found—were
located on the eastern slope of BATTLE
RIDGE.

Indian Bureau *see* U.S. BUREAU OF
INDIAN AFFAIRS

**Interment of Little Bighorn Ca-
sualties** The soldiers from Maj. Marcus
RENO's command who completed this
gruesome task several days after the battle did not possess proper digging implements, or much time. Therefore, the
more than 200 bodies of Custer's command were buried where they fell only a
few inches under the soil, which was described as resembling sugar. The officers
were identified by a slip of paper stuffed
into a cartridge casing that was then
hammered into a crude wooden marker.
See REINTERMENT.

International Boundary Survey
Two companies of the SEVENTH CAV-
ALRY (KEOGH's I and WEIR's D) with
Maj. Marcus RENO commanding, were
assigned in June 1873 as escort and protection for the American portion of the
International Boundary Survey Team
who, along with the British, were mapping the northern border. This duty,
based at FORT ABERCROMBIE, lasted
until late fall 1874.

Jackson, Robert and William
(Billy) These half-blood Blackfoot brothers served as scouts during the LITTLE
BIGHORN CAMPAIGN. It has been reported that during RENO'S VALLEY
FIGHT, when the troops had taken refuge
in the timber, Billy was asked to carry a
message to Custer but he refused for fear
of losing his life. Billy became separated
from the command and remained in the
timber after the retreat. He, along with
scout Fred GERARD, sneaked out and rejoined their comrades at the RENO-BEN-
TEEN DEFENSE SITE the following evening. *Sources for further study include:*
Billy Jackson's account of the battle is included in *Battles and Skirmishes of the*

Great Sioux War, 1876–1877: The Military View, edited by Jerome A. Greene (Norman: University of Oklahoma Press, 1993); and on William see *William Jackson, Indian Scout*, by James Willard Schultz (Boston: Houghton Mifflin, 1926).

Joseph, Chief *see* NEZ PERCÉ

Josephine One of two steamboats (along with the *FAR WEST*) owned by the Coulson Line that carried supplies up the Yellowstone River during both the YELLOWSTONE EXPEDITION OF 1873 (captained by Grant MARSH), and the LITTLE BIGHORN CAMPAIGN in 1876 (captained by Mart Coulson).

K Company, Seventh Cavalry This company was commanded during the Battle of the LITTLE BIGHORN by 1st Lt. Edward S. GODFREY. Second in command 2nd Lt. Luther HARE split duty between the company and the Indian scouts. The regular commanding officer, Capt. Owen HALE, was on detached service at Jefferson Barracks, MO. Company K was part of Benteen's Battalion, and participated in his scout and the RENO-BENTEEN DEFENSE SITE. It lost 5 killed and 3 wounded. Sgt. Robert H. Hughes had been detailed as Custer's color bearer, and was killed.

Kanipe, Daniel (April 15, 1853– July 18, 1926) Sergeant, C Company, 7th Cavalry. It was Kanipe who carried the first message from Custer (by order of Capt. Tom CUSTER) after the strength of the enemy was known at the Battle of the LITTLE BIGHORN. Kanipe was ordered to tell Capt. MCDOUGALL, who was in the rear with the packtrain of ammunition, to "bring the packtrain straight across to high ground—if packs get loose don't stop to fix them, cut them off. Come quick. Big Indian Camp." As Kanipe rode off, he heard Custer tell the troops to hold their horses, "there are plenty of them down there for us all." Prior to

reaching the packtrain, Kanipe came upon Capt. F. W. BENTEEN and informed him about the impending fight, but apparently the news did not hasten Benteen's leisurely march. Kanipe remained on the RENO-BENTEEN DEFENSE SITE and survived the battle. *Sources for further study include:* "A New Story of Custer's Last Stand, by the Messenger Boy Who Survived," by Will Aiken, *Montana Historical Society Contributions* 4 (1903); "The Story of Sergeant Kanipe, One of Custer's Messengers," by Sgt. Kanipe, in *The Custer Myth: A Source Book of Custeriana*, edited by W. A. Graham (Harrisburg, PA: Stackpole, 1953); "Daniel A. Kanipe's Account of Custer Fight Given to Me on June 16 and 17, 1908," in *Custer in '76: Walter Camp Notes on the Custer Fight*, edited by Kenneth Hammer (Provo, UT: Brigham Young University Press, 1976).

Kansas Pacific Railroad When the SEVENTH CAVALRY was organized at FORT RILEY, KA, in September 1866, one of its duties was to guard the construction workers who toiled on the new railroad that was then called the Union Pacific, Eastern Division, but would soon organize as the Kansas Pacific. By 1870 generals William SHERMAN and Phil SHERIDAN made the protection of this railroad the first responsibility of the army. The Indians occasionally harassed the workers, but for the most part avoided the "Iron Horse."

Kansas Volunteer Cavalry Twelve companies of the 19th Kansas Volunteer Cavalry, commanded by the governor, Col. Samuel J. Crawford, joined the SEVENTH CAVALRY during the WASHITA CAMPAIGN OF 1868–69 in an attempt to force hostile ARAPAHO, CHEYENNE, and KIOWA Indians onto reservations. On March 15, 1869, at Sweetwater Creek, TX, Custer located 2 Cheyenne villages with a combined 260 lodges under chief LITTLE ROBE. The Kansas Volunteer Cavalry believed that those Indians held

2 white women, Miss Sarah C. White and Mrs. Anna Belle Morgan, who had been taken hostage in Kansas. (The brother of Miss White, Daniel Brewster, had accompanied the expedition.) In the company of only 1st Lt. W. W. COOKE, Custer put his life on the line by brazenly entering the Cheyenne village unannounced to parley. The 2 officers managed to leave the village unharmed and with confirmation of the presence of the captives. However, much to the outrage of the Kansas Volunteers—many even branding Custer a coward—he refused to attack the village. He had learned the lesson during the Battle of WASHITA that the Indians would probably kill the captives if attacked. Instead, during another parley under a flag of truce, he managed to seize 3 Indian hostages and threaten to hang them if the white women were not returned unharmed. After 3 days of tense negotiation and near battle, the Cheyenne gave in and gave up their prisoners. The campaign ended when the troops returned to CAMP SUPPLY on March 28. *Sources for further study include: Campaigning with Custer and the Nineteenth Kansas Volunteer Cavalry on the Washita Campaign, 1868–69,* by participant David L. Spotts, edited by E. A. Brininstool (Lincoln: University of Nebraska Press, Bison Book, 1988); and *My Life on the Plains; Or, Personal Experiences with Indians,* by George A. Custer (New York: Sheldon, 1874).

Kellogg, Mark A reporter for the *Bismarck Tribune* who accompanied the LITTLE BIGHORN CAMPAIGN to report Custer's great victory, but instead perished with Custer. As fate would have it, the regular correspondent for the *New York Tribune,* C. A. Lounsbury, was unable to go along so Kellogg was his substitute. Although Gen. Alfred TERRY had discouraged Custer from bringing along reporters, it was probable that the general was aware of Kellogg's presence with the column but did not order him

back to FORT ABRAHAM LINCOLN. Kellogg's body was said to have been found near BATTLE RIDGE or alone some distance from the field of battle: the latter location likely most accurate. *Sources for further study include:* His final dispatch, published in the *New York Herald,* July 11, 1876, can be found in *The Custer Myth: A Source Book of Custeriana,* edited by W. A. Graham (Harrisburg, PA: Stackpole, 1953); and "Custer's 'Mysterious Mr. Kellogg' and the Diary of Mark Kellogg," by John C. Hixon, *North Dakota History* 17, no. 3 (1950).

Keogh, Myles Walter (March 25, 1842, or possible 1839–June 25, 1876) Captain, 7th Cavalry (see photo below). Keogh was one of the more colorful characters in the Little Bighorn saga. He was an Irish soldier of fortune who had fought in 3 wars on 3 continents before joining the SEVENTH CAVALRY in 1866. He was perhaps most notable as the owner of the horse COMANCHE, said to be the only living thing found on the field after the Battle of the LITTLE BIGHORN. He was also alleged to have been the last soldier alive in the battle, and was subsequently

Capt. Myles W. Keogh, 1875

called "the bravest man the SIOUX ever fought." (See LAST SOLDIER TO DIE AT THE BATTLE OF THE LITTLE BIGHORN.)

Keogh stated on his application for a commission in the U.S. Army that he left Carlow College in Ireland at the age of 16 to tour Europe for 6 months, then joined the French Foreign Legion and served briefly in the closing stages of the Algerian Campaign. In 1860 he traveled to Italy where the Papal States were being threatened by Napoleon II and the Piedmontese. Keogh was commissioned a second lieutenant in the Papal Army and assigned to the Battalion of St. Patrick. One month after its inception, the outgunned battalion of about 300 troops was attacked at Spoleto by a superior force of Piedmontese regulars supported by artillery, and repulsed several bayonet charges, driving back the overwhelming numbers of the enemy. For his extraordinary gallantry during this battle, Keogh was decorated by the pope with the coveted *Medaglia de Pro Petri Sede* medal. On September 28 the flag of the Papal States was lowered in defeat, and Keogh sailed for the United States to offer his services to the Union Army, which was engaged in its own Civil War.

Keogh was commissioned a captain in the Army of the Potomac on April 9, 1862. His soldierly qualities quickly came to the attention of the commander, Maj. Gen. George B. McClellan, who had him assigned to his personal staff as aide-de-camp. When President Lincoln decided to visit his army in the field, Keogh with 5 other officers was entrusted with the responsibility of escort and guard of honor on the trip to and from Washington. He was aide-de-camp to a number of generals and participated in such major battles as Cedar Mountain, Kelley's Ford, Gettysburg, 2nd Manassas, South Mountain, Aldie, Beverly Ford, Culpepper, Brandy Station, Kennesaw Mountain, and Sherman's march through Georgia to the sea. During the August 1864 raid on Macon, GA, in an attempt to liberate Andersonville prison, his 700-man unit was captured. The confinement was brief, for on September 30 they were exchanged for Confederate prisoners. He received brevets up to colonel for his Civil War service, and obtained a coveted regular army appointment after the war due to recommendations by several generals.

Keogh joined Custer's SEVENTH CAVALRY on July 28, 1866, as captain and commander of I Company. He was a Custer favorite, and was responsible for introducing Custer to the tune "GARRYOWEN," which became the 7th Cavalry's famous marching song. In November 1866 Keogh was assigned as commander of FORT WALLACE, the westernmost military post in Kansas to provide guards and escorts for stagecoaches, wagon trains, railroad surveyors, and construction crews. Attacks by CHEYENNE and SIOUX Indians were frequent, and the fort was said to be under constant siege. Over the ensuing years Keogh participated in numerous engagements against the Plains Indians, but was on staff duty and missed the November 27, 1868, Battle of WASHITA. He was detailed to the INTERNATIONAL BOUNDARY SURVEY for most of 1873–74, and did not participate in either the YELLOWSTONE EXPEDITION OF 1873 or the BLACK HILLS EXPEDITION OF 1874.

During the Battle of the LITTLE BIGHORN, Keogh commanded a 3-company battalion that maintained one of the few tactical positions on the field. Sioux Indian eyewitnesses stated how Keogh had continuously ridden back and forth along the ridge to deploy his men while exposed to an enemy barrage, once singlehandedly charging and routing a group of warriors. However, his troops were eventually all killed by forces under CRAZY HORSE charging from the north and GALL from the west. His body was found on the eastern slope of BATTLE RIDGE within half a mile of CUSTER HILL. Keogh's actions, according to Indian testimony, have raised speculation that he was the final cavalryman to die that day.

FORT KEOGH was established in his honor on the south bank of the Yellowstone River just west of Miles City, MT, in 1877. Keogh's remains were removed from the battlefield in 1877, and reinterred in the Martin family plot at Auburn, NY.

Sources for further study include: The Honor of Arms, by Charles L. Convis (Tucson: Westernlore, 1990); *Captain Myles Walter Keogh, United States Army, 1840–1876,* by G. A. Hayes-McCoy (Dublin: National University of Ireland, 1965); *Myles Keogh: The Life and Legend of an Irish Dragoon in the Seventh Cavalry,* edited by K. Langellier, H. Cox, and B. C. Pohanka (El Segundo, CA: Upton and Sons, 1991); and *Keogh, Comanche and Custer,* a limited edition of 1,950 copies, by E. S. Luce (Ashland, OR: Lewis Osborne, 1974).

Kicking Bird (KIOWA, 1835–75) Kicking Bird was an advocate of peace among his tribe during the Plains wars to counter the hawkish policy of SATANTA. However, he did participate in a raid into Texas in 1870 in order to disprove a charge of cowardice against him by fellow tribesmen. In 1872 he led a peace delegation to Washington, D.C., and convinced his band to settle on the reservation at FORT SILL in 1875 following what became known as the Red River War of 1874–75. There he had the unenviable task of determining which of his militant tribesmen would be sent into exile. It was said that Kicking Bird died from the power of a medicine man who wanted him dead, but was likely poisoned.

Kidder, Lyman S. Second lieutenant, 2nd Cavalry. During the HANCOCK EXPEDITION OF 1867, Kidder and a 10-man detail were dispatched from FORT SEDGWICK on June 29 to take orders from Gen. SHERMAN to a campaigning Custer, who was believed to be near the forks of the Republican River. Kidder failed to locate Custer in the field, and

was discovered by hostile SIOUX Indians led by PAWNEE KILLER. In a running battle all the soldiers were killed. Their mutilated bodies were later found by scouts of Custer's command some 80 miles from FORT WALLACE when he retraced their route. The 25-year-old Kidder had received his appointment in the army only a few weeks earlier, and had been with his company only a few days before being ordered out on the ill-fated detail. *Sources for further study include:* "The Kidder Massacre," by E. A. Brininstool, *Hunter-Trader-Trapper* (December 1932); and *My Life on the Plains; Or, Personal Experiences with Indians,* by George A. Custer (New York, 1874).

Kiowa and Kiowa-Apache Indians The Kiowa and their kinsman, the Kiowa-Apache, were nomadic people who eventually settled on the southern Plains in present-day Colorado, Kansas, New Mexico, Oklahoma, and Texas. They were a warring people, raiding white settlers and travelers—particularly in Texas and Oklahoma—with their allies the CHEYENNE, COMANCHE, and ARAPAHO for many years before Custer and the SEVENTH CAVALRY met them during the HANCOCK EXPEDITION OF 1867. In late 1867 the Kiowa agreed to suspend hostilities by signing the MEDICINE LODGE treaties, which provided for them a shared reservation with the Comanche and Kiowa-Apache, as well as provisions and educational resources. However, few Kiowa under peace chief KICKING BIRD submitted to the reservation, and the raiding continued. War chief SATANTA and his band were camped downstream from BLACK KETTLE's village during the Battle of WASHITA. The dead bodies of 2 white captives, Clara BLINN and her son, were later found in their abandoned village. Gen. Phil SHERIDAN and Custer tracked down those Kiowas and forced many of them onto their reservation at FORT COBB. (See WASHITA CAMPAIGN OF 1868–69.) The Kiowa fought and were defeated by the army in what was known as the Red River War of 1874–75, initiated to curtail hostilities in Texas. The tribe then settled on the reservation. *Sources for further study include: Bad Medicine and Good: Tales of the Kiowas*, by W. S. Nye (Norman: University of Oklahoma Press, 1962).

L Company, Seventh Cavalry This company was commanded during the Battle of the LITTLE BIGHORN by 1st Lt. James CALHOUN, who was on temporary duty from Company C, and 2nd Lt. John CRITTENDEN, 20th Infantry, was attached as second in command. The company's regular officers were unavailable for duty. Company L was part of Custer's detachment, and were all killed. Most bodies were found around the area of CALHOUN HILL, the extreme southern position of the 7th Cavalry on BATTLE RIDGE. The body of Sgt. James BUTLER—surrounded by numerous cartridge casings—was located farthest from Custer and closest to the RENO-BENTEEN DEFENSE SITE, bringing about speculation that he carried a message that was never delivered.

Lame Deer (MINNICONJOU SIOUX; ca. 1830–May 7, 1877) Lame Deer became a prominent leader of his people when RED CLOUD waged war over the BOZEMAN TRAIL in 1866–68. He was chief of the Minniconjou band under SITTING BULL during the GREAT SIOUX WAR of 1876–77—including the Battle of the LITTLE BIGHORN. He was killed in the battle that bears his name.

Lame Deer, Battle of (May 7, 1877) This battle, part of the GREAT SIOUX WAR OF 1876–77, was fought between SIOUX Indians led by LAME DEER, who was killed, and the U.S. Army commanded by Gen. Nelson MILES. The battle began at dawn when Miles and 4 cavalry troops attacked the Sioux village of 51 lodges camped on Muddy Creek, a tributary of the Rosebud. The surprised Indians fled to the hillsides, while the army secured the village and commandeered the 450-head pony herd. Chiefs Lame Deer and Iron Star were convinced to surrender, and lay down their arms to shake hands with their captors. At this point, a scout rode up and aimed his rifle at the 2 Indians who, in turn, retrieved their weapons. Lame Deer fired at Gen. Miles, the bullet missing him and striking a trooper to the rear. The 2 Indians fled toward the high ground, but were shot down by a barrage of small arms fire.

Last Soldier to Die at the Battle of the Little Bighorn The last man to die, according to SIOUX and CHEYENNE Indian eyewitness testimony, was an officer who wore buckskin. Four SEVENTH CAVALRY officers wore buckskin that day: Custer, Tom CUSTER, W. W. COOKE, and Myles KEOGH. Statements from Red Horse, TWO MOON, Little Soldier, and GALL among others appear to point to Capt. Myles Keogh, the Irish soldier of fortune, as the last man to die. Keogh's position on the field compared to the other three reinforces the idea. The Custers and Cooke were killed behind a breastworks of dead horses on CUSTER HILL, whereas the officer about whom the Indians spoke rallied his troops on horseback some distance to the south. According to the allied Indians, Keogh was notable not merely because he was the last to die but also due to his bravery on the field of battle. His presence of command had been observed during the fray, and Keogh rather than Custer was thought to be the soldier chief. Perhaps he was, if Custer had indeed been killed earlier at MEDICINE TAIL COULEE. It was said that Keogh had continuously ridden back and forth along the ridge to deploy his men while exposing himself to the enemy barrage. When several of his platoons had become separated from the main force, Keogh had single-handedly atop his mount, COMANCHE, brazenly charged into and routed a host of warriors in order to assist his beleaguered troops' return. In 1881 the Sioux chief of the Great Council Lodge, Red Horse, related a personal observation of Keogh: "This officer wore a large brimmed hat and a deerskin coat. This officer saved the lives of many soldiers by turning his horse and covering their retreat. The Sioux for a long time fought many brave men of different people, but the Sioux say that this officer was the bravest man they ever fought." *Sources for further study include: Keogh, Comanche and Custer*, a limited edition of 1,950 copies, by E. S. Luce (Ashland, OR: Lewis Osborne, 1974); and *Legend into History: The Custer Mystery*, by Charles Kuhlman (Harrisburg, PA: Stackpole, 1951).

Little Bighorn Associates (P.O. Box 640286, El Paso, TX 79904) This interest group founded in 1967 "is an organization dedicated to seeking the truth about the famous battle and all aspects of the settlement of the west."

Little Bighorn, Battle of the (June 25, 1876) (For events preceding and following this battle please see LITTLE BIGHORN CAMPAIGN) This battle, part of the GREAT SIOUX WAR OF 1876–77, was fought in south-central Montana near the Little Bighorn River between the U.S. SEVENTH CAVALRY commanded by Lt. Col. George Armstrong CUSTER and allied forces of Teton SIOUX and northern CHEYENNE Indians under SITTING BULL (see map, page 102). Custer and 5 companies—approximately 225 men—were annihilated by the superior force. Another 7th Cavalry detachment commanded by Maj. Marcus RENO was pinned down for 2 days before reinforcements arrived. (See RENO-BENTEEN DEFENSE SITE.) Indian casualties are unknown.

The Approach of the 7th Cavalry

The SEVENTH CAVALRY passed in review for Gen. Alfred TERRY at noon on June 21, 1876, as they departed the base camp on the Yellowstone River at the mouth of the Rosebud in search of hostile Indians. The column consisted of nearly 600 officers and enlisted men, 35 Indian scouts, and about 12 civilian packers, foragers, and guides. The command covered over 70 miles in the next 3 days; after the second day they followed the Indian trail that Maj. Marcus Reno had discovered a week earlier on RENO'S POWDER RIVER SCOUT. Early in the morning of June 24 they had passed the limits of Reno's scout and located a large abandoned village site. The Sioux had staged a Sun Dance there just a few days before, which made the Indian scouts extremely nervous. The trail leading away from the site was fresh. Custer sent his scouts under 2nd Lt. Charles VARNUM ahead to gather information while the cavalry halted for their noon meal. The regiment continued on, and camped at dusk on Mud Creek, after traveling about 28 miles. While the troops finished supper and settled down to rest, the scouts returned and reported to Custer. Their information indicated that the Indians were on the lower Little Bighorn River. Officers call was sounded, and Custer informed them that the regiment would march at 11:00 P.M. At about 2:00 A.M. on June 25 they paused for coffee and a brief rest, then it was back into the saddle.

It was 8:00 A.M. when Custer was summoned by 2nd Lt. Varnum to a place called CROW'S NEST. This was a promontory that, because of its topographical location rather than height, afforded a fair view of the Valley of the Little Bighorn, although neither the river nor the bordering trees were visible from this vantage point (the Indian village they were seeking also was not visible). Varnum had led a party of scouts that included "Lonesome Charley" REYNOLDS, Mitch BOUYER, and a number of CROW and ARIKARA Indians to this traditional Plains Indian lookout, which, unknown to them, was located some 15 miles distant from SITTING BULL's village. The scouts had observed smoke and what they believed to be a sizable pony herd grazing

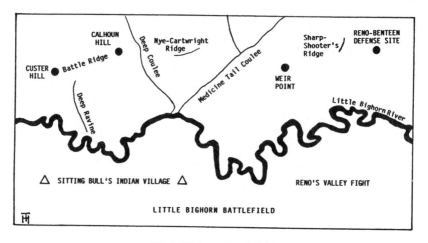

CALHOUN HILL

Nye-Cartwright Ridge

Deep Coulee

Sharp-Shooter's Ridge

RENO-BENTEEN DEFENSE SITE

CUSTER HILL   Battle Ridge

Medicine Tail Coulee

WEIR POINT

Deep Ravine

Little Bighorn River

△ SITTING BULL'S INDIAN VILLAGE △

RENO'S VALLEY FIGHT

LITTLE BIGHORN BATTLEFIELD

Little Bighorn Battlefield

in the valley. Reynolds claimed it was "the largest pony herd any white man ever laid eyes on." Custer arrived at Crow's Nest about 9 A.M., but by that time a haze had settled over the hilly terrain that made it impossible for him—even with the expensive European field glasses borrowed from 1st Lt. Charles DeRudio (ones he never returned)—to recognize anything that far away. He did, however, accept Varnum's assessment and that of the other scouts that a huge Indian village lay ahead (see map, page 103).

Custer returned to camp, and was informed by his brother Tom Custer that Capt. Myles Keogh, who had been detailed with the packtrain, had reported that Indians had been observed on their back trail. Sgt. Curtis of F Company and 2 others had been sent back to retrieve a missing box of hardtack that had fallen off a mule during the night. The sergeant located the box, which was surrounded by several Indians sampling the contents. Curtis chased them off, and galloped back to report his discovery. Custer was convinced that the presence and location of the 7th Cavalry was certainly now known by the Sioux. His worst fears would be realized: the village would scatter in all directions before he could attack.

Time was now of the essence: the column would march at once in the direction of the hostile Indian village. Custer would formulate his plan of attack as events warranted.

Custer Separates His Command

It was a little after noon when the 7th Cavalry paused at the head of Reno Creek. Custer ordered adjutant 1st Lt. W. W. Cooke to separate the regiment into battalions. Maj. Marcus Reno would command one battalion consisting of companies A, G, and M: about 140 men; Capt. F. W. Benteen was assigned companies D, H, and K: about 125 men; Capt. Keogh would take C, I, and L; and Capt. George Yates, E and F—about 225 men—under Custer's direct control. Capt. Thomas McDougall with Company B and the civilian packers—a total of about 85 men—would be packtrain escort (see map, page 104).

Custer detailed Capt. Benteen's battalion on a reconnaissance to the left, along the top of a series of ridges until one was found that overlooked the Little Bighorn Valley. He would then catch up with the command farther down Reno Creek and report his findings. Benteen would be permitted, if necessary, to engage any enemy he might locate.

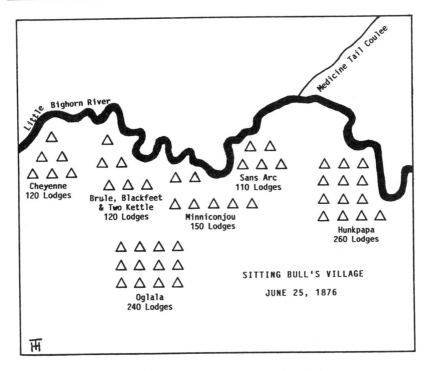

Cheyenne
120 Lodges

Brule, Blackfeet
& Two Kettle
120 Lodges

Minniconjou
150 Lodges

Sans Arc
110 Lodges

Hunkpapa
260 Lodges

Oglala
240 Lodges

SITTING BULL'S VILLAGE

JUNE 25, 1876

Sitting Bull's Village on the Little Bighorn River

The remainder of the regiment then marched down Reno Creek: Custer's troops on the east side, Reno's on the west side. McDougall's packtrain could not keep up, and quickly fell to the rear. About 8 miles and 2 hours later, the regiment reached an abandoned village site. Only a lone tepee remained standing. Inside was the body of a dead warrior, which the REE scouts set on fire. Reno had crossed the creek to confer with Custer when a shout alerted them. Scout Fred GERARD rode in, and excitedly called, "Here are your Indians, General, running like devils!" Sure enough, dust could be seen rising from beyond the distant hills. Custer realized that he must decide on an immediate strategy, otherwise the Indians would escape. The entire regiment trotted for a distance of about 3 miles before halting on a fork of Reno Creek.

The Attack of the 7th Cavalry

Adjutant Cooke, accompanied by Capt. Keogh, crossed the tributary to convey Custer's orders to Reno. It was thought that the Indians were running away. Custer wanted Reno to move rapidly forward toward the village, "and charge afterward, and you will be supported by the whole outfit." Another version of the order replaced "charge afterward" with "charge after crossing the river."

Please note that there are countless versions that speculate about Custer's actions from this point on, far too numerous to document in detail here. Many of those have been listed under sources following this entry. This interpretation has been re-created from eyewitness testimony of Indian and white observers and participants; archaeological evidence; theory based on Custer's known tendencies in battle; military strategies applied in prior engagements

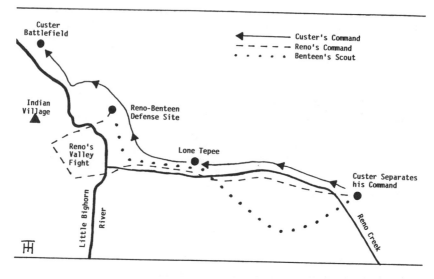

7th Cavalry Battlefield approach

between the Plains Indians and the U.S. Cavalry; and, of course, the influence of those scholars who have previously presented their credible accounts. For simultaneous action see RENO'S VALLEY FIGHT.

It was about 3:00 P.M. Reno's troops were in the process of charging the village on the west side of the Little Bighorn River, an action that began the disastrous Reno's Valley Fight. Custer had led his command of 5 companies downstream on the opposite side of the river. It is likely that he moved along the ridge in order to observe the commencement of Reno's charge, but more importantly, to have his first view of the Indian village (see map on page 105). He could then assess the terrain and formulate his plan to attack. When a portion of the immense village came into sight, he immediately had his brother, Capt. Tom CUSTER, dispatch courier Sgt. Daniel KANIPE with orders to tell Capt. McDougall with the packtrain to "bring the pack train straight across to high ground—if packs get loose don't stop to fix them, cut them off. Come quick. Big Indian camp." Reno charged across the valley below just as Kanipe wheeled his

mount, and a spontaneous loud cheer erupted from Custer's troops, which caused the excited horses to become uneasy and difficult to manage. Kanipe heard Custer say, "Hold your horses in, boys; there are plenty of them down there for all of us."

A steep bluff blocked Custer's route to the river on the flank of the village. He may have noticed at this point that the village was not being quickly disassembled as expected, which likely meant that the Indians intended to fight. Custer headed north at a trot, parallel to the village, and studied the terrain. At about the time Custer would have traveled one-half mile and approached Cedar Coulee, Reno had inexplicably halted his charge and deployed a skirmisher line. Custer then moved his command down the coulee a short distance. Perhaps Custer waited on the ridge to determine Reno's fate, because at about 3:30 P.M. there was another possible sighting of Custer by Reno's men. Custer then likely visited WEIR POINT, alone or in the company of other officers, where he could have observed the entire village, and realized that it was larger than first thought. He might

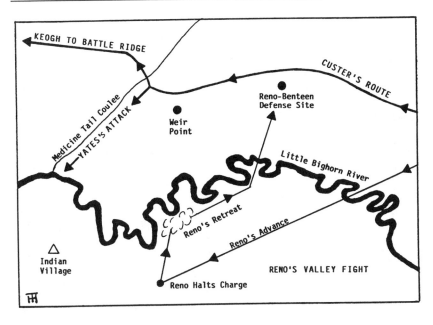

The Battle of the Little Bighorn (known troop movement)

have also noticed from there that Reno was in trouble. The Indians were flanking his skirmisher line, forcing a retreat to a stand of timber. Orderly Pvt. John MARTIN was then dispatched to locate Capt. Benteen in the rear with what became Custer's last known order (see illustration, page 106). It had been hastily scribbled on a piece of notepaper by 1st Lt. Cooke because Martin was a recent immigrant and spoke only broken English. "Benteen. Come on. Big village. Be quick. Bring packs. P. Bring packs. W. W. Cooke."

Reno, by aborting his charge and halting short of the village, had apparently second-guessed a strategy of which he did not have complete knowledge. It is likely that Custer's intention for the 5 companies under his personal command was to flank the village on the eastern side of the river. When Reno's troops penetrated the village, which would cause mass confusion within, individual companies could then be sent down coulees at intervals to cross and attack. The re-maining detachment could ride for the northern end of the village to head off the escaping warriors. It had always been the custom of the Indians to scatter and run when their village was attacked. Flight was Custer's greatest fear, and he had no reason to believe that they would react otherwise in this instance. With that being the case, Reno's command on a charge into the village would have most likely suffered at least moderate casualties, but would have routed the disorganized Indians into the hands of Custer's five companies.

But the retreat by Reno placed Custer, whether he knew it or not, in an extremely vulnerable position. Instead of charging into a village in chaos to rendezvous with Reno's troops according to plan, he was now on his own.

Had Custer known about Reno's fate, he could have chosen to retrace his route in order to assist that beleaguered command. Or he could have attacked the village from the flank while the Indians were occupied with Reno's troops.

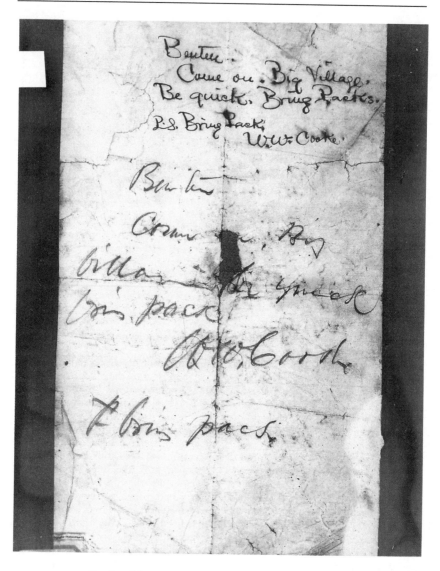

Battle of the Little Bighorn: "Custer's Last Message"

Perhaps he was unaware that Reno was fleeing across the river to dig in on the bluffs, an action which would soon free the entire force of Indians. Regardless, he chose to strike the village.

The main obstacle now was locating a likely place to cross the Little Bighorn River and strike the village. Custer moved his command down Cedar Coulee to upper MEDICINE TAIL COULEE. It would be likely that Custer halted his troops here to adjust equipment in preparation for battle as well as to wait for the possible arrival of Benteen's reinforcements. It was now about 4 P.M., and time to deploy the troops.

Custer Engages the Indians

Orderly John Martin claimed to have looked back, and his last sight of Custer was watching the Gray Horse Troop—Capt. George Yates' battalion of companies E and F—galloping down Medicine Tail Coulee toward the center of the sprawling village. Capt. Myles Keogh's 3-company battalion—C, I, and L—would then have ascended the slope to higher ground. Sioux eyewitnesses related that Yates ran into a stubborn and furious barrage from Indians along the river, and took enough casualties to force him to pull back. Many warriors had arrived from tending the pony herd, as well as those who had routed Reno onto the RENO-BENTEEN DEFENSE SITE, and could now concentrate on Custer's threat to their village (see map, page 108). Regardless, there is little doubt that the cavalrymen were repulsed and sent retreating up the bluffs behind them. By then, Sioux Chief GALL had assembled a force of warriors and moved across the river. Yates would have deployed dismounted skirmishers to cover his pullback. Another theory has been presented concerning Yates's charge. This action may have been intended as merely a feint or decoy to distract the Indians' attention while the other battalion struck elsewhere to rout the village. It must be remembered that it had been the custom of the Plains Indians to scatter rather than fight when attacked in this manner.

There has been speculation based on Sioux and Cheyenne eyewitness testimony and oral tradition that Custer was struck down in this initial assault down Medicine Tail Coulee. Custer's body was found (on CUSTER HILL) with 2 wounds: a bullet hole in the left breast at or near the heart and one in the left temple. It is conceivable that he was severely wounded or killed on the charge down Medicine Tail Coulee, a presumption based in part on his Civil War habit of personally leading charges. Dead or alive, Custer would have been carried from the river to the

high bluffs by his troopers (see illustration, page 109). However, had he been killed, it would be assumed that Capt. Keogh as senior captain should have taken command. Given the position of Keogh's body, which was found some distance from adjutant Cooke or the command center on Custer Hill, it could be assumed that had Custer been hit he was still alive when taken to Custer Hill. (The regimental adjutant—Cooke—would have been at the commander's side, whether Custer or Keogh. Of course, considering the chaos on the field, it is entirely possible that Keogh was unaware of Custer's death, or he or Cooke simply could not or chose not to rendezvous. Testimony from the allied Indians later stated that Keogh's actions made them believe that he was indeed the soldier chief at that point in time.

Keogh, with companies I and F, had taken position on the high ridge between Medicine Tail and Deep Coulee, which has become known as BATTLE RIDGE (see illustrations on page 110). Keogh had ordered his men to dismount and form a skirmisher line. Company L under 1st Lt. James CALHOUN was farthest south on this line on what became known as CALHOUN HILL, likely acting as a rear guard waiting for Benteen's and the packtrain's expected approach.

It is entirely possible that Custer's command continued on beyond Custer Hill: farther to the north—near or past the end of the Indian village—than first thought, as evidenced by a recent find of archeological artifacts. From there they might have pulled back to Custer Hill while engaged with the enemy.

The Indians at this point in time would not have charged Custer's troops en masse. Rather, they would have remained a safe distance away—hidden by tall grass, bushes and the rugged terrain features—and fired from long range. An endless stream of arcing arrows would take a heavy toll on pinned-down troops. The Indians would have also sneaked up

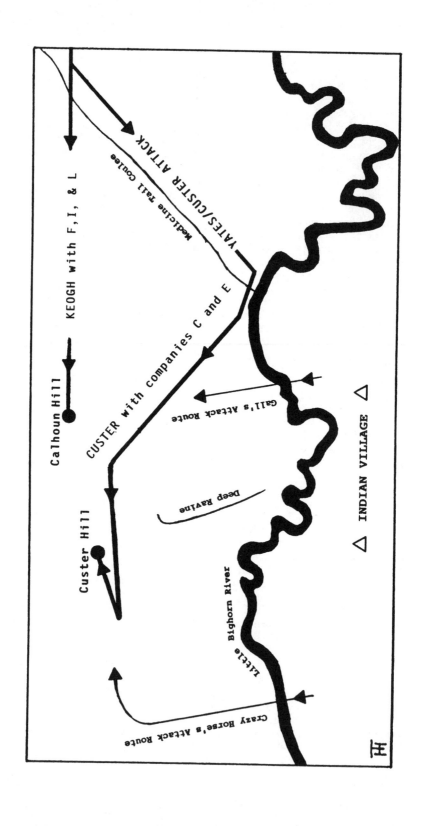

Custer kin killed in Battle of the Little Bighorn. Custer, center. Clockwise: Capt. T. W. Custer; Boston Custer; Harry "Autie" Reed; 1st Lt. James Calhoun.

to wave blankets and take particular aim at horseholders (every fourth man) in an attempt to stampede the cavalry horses that carried precious ammunition in their saddlebags. The herds of cavalry horses would then be captured by the Indian women and boys from the village and later stampeded through the soldiers' positions. Eventually, the Indians would become more brave and rush vulnerable

Opposite: **The Battle of the Little Bighorn (Custer's probable route)**

Little Bighorn Battlefield. *Top:* View looking northwest toward Custer Hill from the position of I Company; *bottom:* View looking south from Medicine Tail Coulee.

defenses as each became depleted of troops to count coup. It should be noted that tactics employed by the Indians on the battlefield sometimes make it difficult to piece together one consistent story of events from the various eyewitness accounts. Unlike the U.S. Army, the Indians for the most part *did not* fight as a unit. Certain respected warriors, such as CRAZY HORSE or GALL, might occasionally rally a group of braves to accompany them to attack some objective. However, once the battle began, each individual warrior was free to do whatever he pleased. If he decided to close with the enemy and fight hand-to-hand that was his privilege. If he wanted to lie behind a bush 200 yards away and lob arrows into a group of the enemy that also was his right. Individual Indians generally had no idea regarding time frames or an overall perspective of exactly how the battle unfolded. For this reason, certain testimony may at first glance appear contradictory, when actually it is the view of the actions of a particular warrior who had little knowledge of the movements of his comrades.

Fighting escalated all along Battle Ridge as additional warriors entered the fray. Custer, if he had remained in command, ordered either Company C or E down the slope a short distance, where they dismounted and fought on foot. Keogh and Calhoun held the vicinity of Calhoun Hill. The troopers had shot their horses for breastworks as they fought a desperate struggle against the superior force. One by one they fell, until each pocket of resistance was thoroughly weakened by loss of manpower. Incidents of bravery by the soldiers were commonplace. Numerous Indians later spoke of the incidents of courage: a trait of great importance and a matter of respect in their eyes. However, the Indian long-distance fire was withering, and created an enormous number of casualties. The Indians had yet to close with the cavalrymen, and they realized that it would only be a matter of time. In addition they knew something Custer's command did

not know. There would be no blue-clad reinforcements to dramatically arrive in the nick of time to save them. The beaten command of Reno and Benteen with the packtrain were presently digging in as best they could some 4 miles to the south and they themselves wondering why Custer did not appear to save *them*. (See RENO-BENTEEN DEFENSE SITE.)

The end probably came within an hour's time. By now, the Indians had become more brave and wanted to count coup on their enemy: to close with them and fight man to man. Incidents of hand-to-hand combat became commonplace as the Sioux and Cheyenne came forward with hatchets, clubs, and coup sticks. The fatal tactical blow was administered by Crazy Horse, who led a large force of warriors down the valley above the village, crossed the Little Bighorn River, and from the north attacked those left alive on Custer Hill (see illustration, page 112). Then, continuing south down the ravine, he swept the eastern slope, crushing what remained of Keogh and Calhoun's troops against Gall's warriors who had attacked from the direction of the Little Bighorn River. The Battle of the Little Bighorn had come to an end for Custer and five companies of the 7th Cavalry.

Immediately following the battle, Indian women, old men, and children rushed to the battlefield to strip, loot, and mutilate the bodies. On Custer Hill they found Custer surrounded by his brothers, Tom and Boston; his nephew Autie REED; Capt. Yates; and lieutenants Cooke, Smith, and REILY. The body of Dr. Lord was found about 20 feet southwest of Custer (see illustration, page 112). Capt. Keogh fell to the south on the eastern slope; lieutenants Calhoun and Crittenden on Calhoun Hill (see map, page 113). Three bodies were never found: lieutenants HARRINGTON; PORTER; and STURGIS. See also AMMUNITION RESOURCES OF THE CAVALRYMEN; CUSTER'S LAST STAND; DISOBEDIENCE OF ORDERS BY CUSTER; GATLING GUNS;

Little Bighorn Battlefield. *Top:* Custer Hill; *bottom:* Custer Hill looking toward the Little Bighorn River. Black marker denotes position of Custer's body.

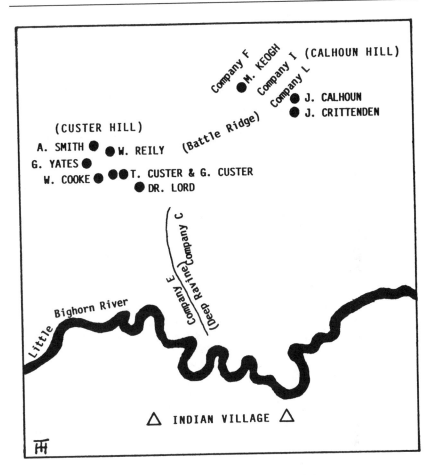

Company F
M. KEOGH
Company I   (CALHOUN HILL)
Company L
J. CALHOUN
J. CRITTENDEN
(CUSTER HILL)
(Battle Ridge)
A. SMITH ● ● W. REILY
G. YATES ●
W. COOKE ● ● ● T. CUSTER & G. CUSTER
● DR. LORD
Company C
Company E
(Deep Ravine)
Little Bighorn River
△ INDIAN VILLAGE △

Location of 7th Cavalry Officers' Bodies

LAST SOLDIER TO DIE; MALFUNCTION OF THE SPRINGFIELD CARBINES; MEDALS OF HONOR FOR BRAVERY AT THE BATTLE OF THE LITTLE BIGHORN; MUTILATION OF CAVALRYMEN; PRESIDENTIAL ASPIRATIONS OF CUSTER; READINESS OF THE CAVALRYMEN; RESPONSIBILITY FOR CUSTER'S DEFEAT; SABERS; SEPARATION OF COMMAND BY CUSTER; STRENGTH OF ALLIED INDIANS; SUICIDE ALLEGATIONS; SURVIVORS OF THE BATTLE; WEAPONS OF THE ALLIED INDIANS; WEAPONS OF THE CAVALRYMEN.

Sources for further study include:

Troopers with Custer: Historic Incidents of the Battle of the Little Bighorn, by E. A. Brininstool (Harrisburg, PA: Stackpole, 1952); *General Custer and the Battle of the Little Bighorn: The Federal View,* official government documents edited by John M. Carroll (New Brunswick, NJ: Garry Owen, 1976); *Custer's Last Stand: The Anatomy of an American Myth,* by Brian W. Dippie (Missoula: University of Montana Publications in History, 1976); *The Vanishing Race,* by Joseph K. Dixon (Garden City, NY: Doubleday, Page, 1913); *War-Path and Bivouac: Or, The Conquest of the Sioux,* by John Finerty

(Norman: University of Oklahoma Press, 1961); *Archaeology, History, and Custer's Last Battle: The Little Bighorn Reexamined,* by Richard Allan Fox, Jr. (Norman: University of Oklahoma Press, 1993); *The Custer Myth: A Source Book of Custeriana,* edited by W. A. Graham (Harrisburg, PA: Stackpole, 1953); *Abstract of the Official Record of Proceedings of the Reno Court of Inquiry,* by W. A. Graham (Harrisburg, PA: Stackpole, 1954); *Centennial Campaign: The Sioux War of 1876,* by John S. Gray (Fort Collins, CO: Old Army, 1976); *Custer's Last Campaign: Mitch Bouyer and the Little Bighorn Reconstructed,* by John S. Gray (Lincoln: University of Nebraska Press, 1991); *Evidence and the Custer Enigma: A Reconstruction of Indian-Military History,* by Jerome A. Greene (Kansas City, KA: Kansas City Posse of Westerners, 1973); *The Fighting Cheyennes,* by George Bird Grinnell (Norman: University of Oklahoma Press, 1956); *Custer in '76: Walter Camp's Notes on the Custer Fight,* edited by Kenneth Hammer (Provo, UT: Brigham Young University Press, 1976); *Markers, Artifacts and Indian Testimony: Preliminary Findings on the Custer Battle,* by Richard G. Hardorff (Short Hill, NJ: W. Donald Horn, 1985); *Legend into History,* by Charles Kuhlman (Harrisburg, PA: Old Army, 1951); *Soldiers Falling into Camp: The Battles at the Rosebud and the Little Bighorn,* by Frederick Lefthand, Robert Kammen, and Joseph Marshall (Encampment, WY: Affiliated Writers of America, 1991); *My Friend the Indian,* by James McLaughlin (Lincoln: University of Nebraska Press, Bison Book, 1989); *Wooden Leg: A Warrior Who Fought Custer,* by Thomas B. Marquis (Lincoln: University of Nebraska Press, 1931); *Custer on the Little Bighorn,* by Thomas B. Marquis (Lodi, CA: Kain, 1969); *Custer's Fall: The Indian Side of the Story,* by David Humphreys Miller (New York: Duell, Sloan and Pearce, 1957), reprinted (Lincoln: University of Nebraska Press, Bison Book, 1985); *Black Elk Speaks,* by John G. Neihardt (New York: William Morrow, 1932); *The Little Bighorn 1876: The Official Communications, Documents, and Reports,* compiled by Loyd J. Overfield II (Glendale, CA: Arthur H. Clark, 1971); *The Battle of the Little Bighorn,* by Mari Sandoz (Philadelphia: J. B. Lippincott, 1966); *The Little Bighorn Campaign,* by Wayne Michael Sarf (Conshohocken, PA: Combined Books, 1993); *Custer's Luck,* by Edgar I. Stewart (Norman: University of Oklahoma Press, 1955); *Warpath: The True Story of the Fighting Sioux Told in a Biography of Chief White Bull,* by Stanley Vestal (Boston: Houghton Mifflin, 1934), reprinted (Lincoln: University of Nebraska Press, Bison Book, 1985); and *Little Bighorn Diary: Chronicle of the 1876 Indian War,* by James Willert (La Mirada, CA: James Willert, 1977).

Little Bighorn Battlefield National Monument (Formerly "Custer Battlefield National Monument"; P.O. Box 39, Crow Agency, MT 59022) Plans for a memorial to Custer and his men were discussed within weeks after the battle. Newspapers created the initial interest by publishing sensational stories about half-buried bodies strewn across the field, which was true. This caused an outcry from the public and high-ranking army officers, who began to lobby Congress to allocate funds for a cemetery. One year after the battle, troopers from Company I of the SEVENTH CAVALRY visited the battlefield for the purpose of exhuming the bodies of the officers for burial elsewhere and the proper burial of the enlisted where they had fallen. Then, on August 1, 1879, General Order no. 78 established Custer Battlefield National Cemetery. On Custer Hill, a log memorial was erected and each individual grave was marked with a wooden stake. This memorial was replaced in 1881 with one of white granite bearing the names of each trooper, and at the same time the collective remains were reburied in a common grave surrounding this monument (see illustration, page 115). In 1930 the RENO-BENTEEN DEFENSE SITE was added, making the battlefield two disconnected parcels of land with a right-of-way road between them. Responsibility for the battlefield came under the War Department until 1940, when it was transferred to the National Park Service. In 1946 it was renamed Custer Battlefield National Monument; and renamed once more in 1991 to Little Bighorn Battlefield National Monument by an act of Congress in order to recognize the participation of the Indian in the famous battle. A visitor center and historical museum (see photo, page 116) features military and Indian artifacts, dioramas, an array of artwork, maps, photographs, and an impressive document collection of interest to the serious researcher (see illustrations, page 116 and 117). Custer's widow Libbie donated nearly 50,000 letters and

Little Bighorn Battlefield: Granite Memorial at crest of Custer Hill. Bodies of enlisted cavalrymen were buried in a mass grave beneath.

papers to the museum. Little Bighorn Battlefield National Monument is located 15 miles south of Hardin, MT, via exit 510 off Interstate 90. Park personnel provide tour information and a schedule of lectures in season to familiarize the visitor with the famous battle (see illustrations, pages 117 and 118). *Sources for further study include:* "Myth to Monument: The Establishment of Custer Battlefield National Monument," by Don Rickey, Jr. *Journal of the West* 7 (April 1969); and "Whose Shrine Is It? The Ideological Struggle for Custer Battle-

field," by Robert M. Utley *Montana: the Magazine of Western History* 42 (Winter 1992).

Little Bighorn Campaign, The

(February 1, 1876–September 13, 1876) This campaign was a series of battles and skirmishes waged between troops of the U.S. Army against what the U.S. government had determined were hostile warriors of the Teton SIOUX and northern CHEYENNE Indian tribes. It was part of the GREAT SIOUX WAR OF 1876–77.

Little Bighorn Battlefield. *Top:* View looking northwest from Custer Hill toward museum building; *bottom:* Standard marker, "U.S. Soldier 7th Cavalry Fell Here, June 25, 1876."

Little Bighorn Battlefield. *Top:* Marker: "Calhoun Hill"; *bottom:* Grave of Major Marcus Reno in National Cemetery.

The Cause of the Conflict

The campaign came as a direct result of Custer's BLACK HILLS EXPEDITION OF 1874, the published purpose of which was to explore the BLACK HILLS region of Dakota Territory in order to identify suitable sites for military posts. The Sioux, who had received the Black Hills as part of their reservation by the provisions of the FORT LARAMIE TREATY OF 1868, considered the intrusion a broken promise and a grave injustice. Normally, this one expedition would not have escalated hostilities and, indeed, no direct opposition was encountered by the troops at that time. However, another factor became more alluring to the public: the discovery of gold deposits. This factor, which would have naturally provoked a gold rush, was coupled with an economic depression brought about by the Panic of 1873. By the summer of 1875 more than 800 miners had defied the U.S. government and ignored the treaty to invade the Sioux Reservation to search for gold. The army was dispatched under Gen. George CROOK to chase the miners from the hills. This half-hearted effort was in vain. The prospectors continued their work, calling for the U.S. government to protect *them* from Indian attacks. Newspapers jumped on the bandwagon, especially those from nearby Dakota towns promoting themselves as the ideal place from which to enter the Black Hills in order to profit from outfitting the prospectors.

The U.S. government authorized another expedition into the Black Hills in the summer of 1875 to confirm Custer's conclusions from the previous year. This expedition, headed by geologist Walter P. Jenny, incensed the Indians. Once more, troops—under Lt. Col. Richard I. Dodge—had violated the Black Hills Sioux Reservation. And, when Jenny reported that the Black Hills did indeed hold rich mineral deposits, the gold rush began in earnest. Nothing could stop the increased migration now. Therefore, speculation began about how to relieve the Sioux of the land that they had been promised by treaty.

The U.S. government began making overtures toward the Sioux to sell the Black Hills. RED CLOUD, SPOTTED TAIL, and other chiefs were invited to Washington, D.C., in June 1875, the reason for which—to their surprise (they considered this their chance to complain about agency business)—was to sign over title to the Black Hills. They refused, citing a lack of authority.

The Sioux were split over the proposal. Most reservation Indians liked the idea, believing that they would be paid handsomely for land they would rarely or never use. Another faction—led by SITTING BULL and CRAZY HORSE—vowed to sell only over their dead bodies. Spotted Tail visited the hills soon after his return from Washington and decided they were worth somewhere between 7 and 40 million dollars, along with enough provisions for 7 generations of Sioux to live well.

The Allison Commission, chaired by Iowa senator William B. Allison, met in September 1875 with the Sioux near Red Cloud Agency, and ineptly handled the hostility over the issue of the Black Hills. Younger warriors from Sitting Bull's bands arrived from the hills to disrupt proceedings and to threaten severe reprisal against any Sioux chief who accepted the proposals and signed a treaty. The commissioners were clearly intimidated, the chiefs apprehensive, and nothing could be settled. The commission finally recommended that Congress offer fair value for the Black Hills. If the Sioux refused to sell, rations would be cut off.

The young men of the Sioux tribes remained adamant in their opposition to the sale. The Black Hills had been given to them fair and square, and no white man was permitted within its boundary. Yet, the area was infested with miners— some 15,000 had now entered the Sioux domain—which meant for all intents and purposes the area was in white possession. In protest, the warriors began to raid in the unceded territory, attack nearby friendly Indian tribes, interfere with the railroad, and disrupt day-to-day life on the reservation.

The frustration over the Black Hills and the raiding warriors in the unceded territory finally came to a head when President U. S. GRANT held a meeting in Washington, D.C., in November with Secretary of War Belknap, Secretary of the Interior Zachariah Chandler, Commissioner of Indian Affairs Smith, and

his military commanders: generals SHER-
MAN and SHERIDAN. It was decided that
measures should be taken to put a halt to
the warring factions of the Sioux tribe
known to be led by Chief Sitting Bull.
On December 6 an edict was issued stating that all Indians must peacefully report to reservations by January 31, 1876,
or suffer the consequences. At that time,
should they not comply, the Interior Department would assign the disposition of
those Indians to the War Department.

The U.S. government ultimatum was
carried by runners to those Indians
known to be camped along the Yellowstone River and thereabouts. It should be
noted that had the Indians decided to
comply, it would have been extremely
difficult for them to travel at that time of
the year. However, it was evident that
they had intended all along to defy the
order and remain at a distance from the
reservation.

The Commencement of the Campaign

On February 1, 1876, those Indians remaining off the reservation were deemed
hostile. Gen. Sherman set in motion
plans for an immediate campaign in order
to catch the Indians in their vulnerable
winter camps. Gen. Sheridan assigned
the responsibility of organizing military
operations to Gen. George Crook, commander of the Department of the Platte,
and Gen. Alfred TERRY, commander of
the Department of the Dakota. The
strategy was to have 3 columns approach
the Indians—whose specific location was
not known—and catch them in a pincer
movement. The prospects for a swift
march by the Dakota Column, which included the SEVENTH CAVALRY from
FORT ABRAHAM LINCOLN, however,
were prevented by poor weather that delayed receipt of vital supplies as well as
other organizational preparations. Gen.
Crook, meanwhile, was able to march
with 800 men from FORT FETTERMAN
by the beginning of March, but encountered a savage adversary in the Wyoming
winter. However, on March 17, the first

blow was struck when 6 companies under
Col. Joseph J. Reynolds attacked an Indian village on the Powder River. The Indians were quickly routed, but organized
such a fierce counterattack that Reynolds
abandoned the field and retreated. (See
POWDER RIVER FIGHT.) The timid action by his subordinate infuriated Crook,
who returned his command to Fort Fetterman and drew up charges against
Reynolds. It was early April when the
second of the 3 columns—the Montana
Column—marched from FORT ELLIS
with 450 troops under Col. John GIB-
BON. The Dakota Column, including the
7th Cavalry, would be personally led by
Gen. Terry. Custer, whom Terry had
been counting on to lead his regiment,
had been delayed by politics in Washington, D.C. Custer had offered some
inflammatory testimony against President Grant's brother regarding the sale of
post traderships (see BELKNAP SCAN-
DAL). Grant intended to punish Custer
by not permitting him to accompany the
expedition. Only after some intense lob-
bying by generals Sheridan and Terry did
the president relent and reinstate Custer
to duty. Finally, on May 17 the Dakota
Column—nearly 1,000 strong and with
Custer and his 7th Cavalry—marched
out of Fort Lincoln (see map on page
120). The Indians in the Powder River
Valley were aware that the U.S. Army—
as evidenced by Col. Reynolds's attack—
were preparing to wage war. The various
bands began to assemble under Sitting
Bull. They believed there was strength in
numbers, and by early June had accumu-
lated more than 400 lodges—some 3,000
people—and steadily moved toward the
Rosebud River Valley. The three army
columns were on the march in search of
Indians: Gibbon's scouts actually found
them but failed to inform Terry's command. Terry detailed Maj. Marcus RENO
and 6 companies of the 7th Cavalry to
scout the Powder and Tongue River valleys and rejoin the command at the
mouth of the Tongue, where a supply
depot had been established. (See RENO'S

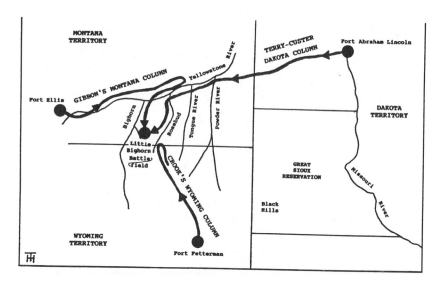

The Three-Pronged Column "Pincer" Battlefield Approach

POWDER RIVER SCOUT.) On June 17, while Reno was on his scout, Gen. Crook's column had halted some 40 miles away for a midmorning coffee break on upper Rosebud Creek. The soldiers were suddenly attacked by a large force of Indians under Crazy Horse. The Battle of the ROSEBUD was waged for perhaps 6 hours until the Indians finally broke contact. Crook proclaimed victory since he held the field at the end, but in truth he had been severely bloodied. Rather than pursue the hostiles, he immediately fell back to his camp on Goose Creek without informing anyone about the engagement.

Custer Marches for the Little Bighorn Valley

Maj. Reno returned from his scout, and it was determined that he had disobeyed orders by venturing to the Rosebud. Terry was furious. However, Reno's information was valuable. He had located an abandoned Indian village, which told them where the Indians were not and in which direction they had gone. Terry could now assume that his quarry was

somewhere around the Valley of the Little Bighorn River. On June 21 Terry detailed his orders to Col. Gibbon and Custer aboard the steamer *FAR WEST*, which was moored on the Yellowstone River at the mouth of the Rosebud. His plan was simple: Gibbon's column would maintain a blocking position at the mouth of the Little Bighorn; Custer would follow the Indian trail. The following day Custer and 12 companies of the 7th Cavalry marched for the purpose of locating and engaging hostile Sioux and Cheyenne Indians. Custer pushed up the Rosebud and eventually struck the Indian trail discovered by Maj. Reno. In the meantime the Indians had moved their village to the valley of the Little Bighorn River. The village had grown from 400 lodges to nearly 1,000—bolstered by those Indians who had left the reservations for a summer of freedom—some 7,000 people including perhaps 2,000 or more warriors. On Sunday June 25 Custer came upon this village and attacked. The Battle of the LITTLE BIGHORN had commenced.

The battle began with orders for Maj.

Reno and his 3 companies to storm the village on the west side of the Little Bighorn River. He inexplicably balked during the charge. The surprised Indians rallied to defend their village. This began RENO'S VALLEY FIGHT, a series of disastrous decisions by the commander that resulted in many casualties to the cavalry. The beaten troops eventually retreated across the river to the high bluffs on what is known as the RENO-BENTEEN DEFENSE SITE.

Custer and his 5 companies had remained on the eastern side along the ridge, and so were the recipients of the full force of warriors who broke contact with Reno to attack this column threatening their village from the east. Within an hour, Custer and approximately 225 cavalrymen were all killed.

The soldiers pinned down on the Reno-Benteen Defense Site were assaulted by small groups of warriors and were the victim of Indian sharpshooters. That night, terror came in the form of the Indians' celebration emanating from the village. The darkness reverberated with the rhythmic pounding of tomtoms, the bouncing flames of huge bonfires, and the terrifying wails of the women singing songs for their dead.

The battle resumed at daybreak. The hilltop was surrounded by hundreds, perhaps thousands of Indians who sustained a withering fire. Occasionally, a group of warriors would charge on foot or horseback, only to be repulsed by a volley of fire from the line. There was nowhere to hide on the hilltop, and the troops were spread thinly in spots, but they persevered.

At about noon on June 26 the firing was less intense. By late afternoon a column of Indian men, women, and children some 2–3 miles long could be observed moving southward toward the Bighorn Mountains. On the morning of June 27 Gen. Terry, with Col. Gibbon's command, arrived and found the bodies of Custer's men and the remnants of Reno's command some 4 miles to the south. On June 28 a detail buried over 200 troops where they fell on the battlefield. Preparations began to move Reno's wounded to the *Far West* for transportation to Fort Lincoln for medical care.

The United States was in the midst of celebrating the July 4 centennial by the time word reached the East coast from the frontier about the disaster. The country was shocked and outraged. Congress readily authorized 2 new forts on the Yellowstone, and an additional 2,500 men were recruited for duty. Fresh troops were dispatched for duty on the frontier. More than 600 recruits calling themselves "Custer's Avengers" joined the 7th Cavalry. The Indians, well aware that there would be retaliation, broke up into smaller bands and scattered.

The Campaign Continues

The first battle following the Little Bighorn was July 17 at Warbonnet Creek, an embarrassing skirmish in which legendary Buffalo Bill CODY shot, killed, and scalped a Cheyenne subchief in what was later called a duel. The scout then held up the hair and proclaimed it the "first scalp for Custer." The episode became a favorite part of his Wild West Show. The remainder of the battle consisted of Gen. Crook's men chasing a handful of warriors back to their reservation.

On August 5 Gen. Crook and nearly 2,300 men headed down the Tongue River on an Indian trail, eventually turning west. Gen. Terry headed down the Yellowstone to the mouth of the Rosebud and followed Custer's route. To the surprise of both columns, they met on August 10 in the Rosebud valley. The reinforced column—now nearly 4,000 strong—marched together on a month-old Indian trail through mud and rain. The going was arduous: sickness and fatigue factors were high and morale was low. On August 17 they arrived at the mouth of the Yellowstone River, never having come within 100 miles of their prey. Sitting Bull had escaped to the lower Missouri, while Crazy Horse and his people were headed toward the Black Hills.

On September 5 Gen. Terry disbanded his portion of the expedition. Gibbon returned to Fort Ellis, and the 7th Cavalry returned to Fort Lincoln. Crook decided to break away from Terry and quick march to the Black Hills. He wanted to catch up with those Indians who had embarrassed him on the Rosebud. However, the weather and supply problems plagued Crook's column. He believed that he would locate the Indians quickly, and ordered all wagons, tents, and extra clothing to be abandoned. The march became exceedingly difficult; scores of exhausted animals died, and the men were in almost as bad a shape. Rations were soon expended, and mule and horse meat became the only food. Near the town of Deadwood, Crook dispatched a detail to buy rations.

On September 9 the food-procuring detail of 150 cavalrymen under Capt. Anson MILLS happened upon a Sioux camp of 37 lodges near SLIM BUTTES, a landmark rock formation. Mills charged and occupied the village, withstanding heavy fire from the Indians in the hills until Crook and reinforcements arrived. Casualties were light on both sides. Chief AMERICAN HORSE, however, was killed. Various cavalry items that had been taken from Custer's command were discovered in the village.

On September 13 a herd of cattle and wagons laden with supplies finally reached Crook's beleaguered column. The Little Bighorn Campaign had finally come to an inauspicious end.

Little Wolf (Northern Cheyenne; ca. 1820–1904) Little Wolf fought beside CRAZY HORSE when RED CLOUD waged war on the army over the BOZEMAN TRAIL. He signed the FORT LARAMIE TREATY OF 1868 pledging peace, but continued to fight. He participated in several battles during the GREAT SIOUX WAR OF 1876–77, including the Battle of the LITTLE BIGHORN and the Battle of DULL KNIFE, where he was shot numerous times but survived. In 1879 TWO MOON convinced Little Wolf to scout for Gen. MILES. A year later he killed a fellow Cheyenne and was exiled from the reservation until his death. *Sources for further study include: Cheyenne Autumn* by Mari Sandoz (New York: McGraw-Hill, 1953).

Lone Wolf (KIOWA; ca. 1820–79) Lone Wolf visited President Abraham Lincoln in 1863 as part of a delegation of tribal leaders. He signed the MEDICINE LODGE TREATY OF 1867, but refused to submit to the reservation. During the WASHITA CAMPAIGN OF 1868–69, Lone Wolf along with another Kiowa chief, SATANTA, were taken hostage by Gen. Phil SHERIDAN and Custer when the Indians refused to submit to the reservation policy. The soldiers threatened to hang the two chiefs unless the tribe complied with their demand to surrender to the reservation near FORT COBB. The Kiowa people grudgingly straggled in, and Lone Wolf and Satanta were freed. Lone Wolf visited Washington, D.C., for a second time in 1872, and promised peace. However, following the death of his son, he waged war once more. He fought the army in what was known as the Red River War of 1874–75, initiated to curtail Indian raiding parties in Texas. He and his people were pursued by Gen. Nelson MILES and Col. Ranald MACKENSIE until finally surrendering at FORT SILL in 1875. Lone Wolf was subsequently exiled to Fort Marion, FL, where he contracted malaria and, returning home in 1878, died a year later of the disease.

Lord, Dr. George Edwin Assistant surgeon, 7th Cavalry. Dr. Lord joined the SEVENTH CAVALRY at FORT ABRAHAM LINCOLN, D.T., almost one year to the day prior to the Battle of the LITTLE BIGHORN: he had been commissioned a first lieutenant on June 26, 1875. During the march up the Rosebud on the approach to the LITTLE BIGHORN, Lord had become ill and had stopped some distance behind the main column to rest. He arrived at the bivouac the night before the battle several hours after the others, and was too weary and sick to eat. Custer suggested that he remain behind with the packtrain, but Lord refused. He was attached to Custer's command and was killed on CUSTER HILL. There was the usual presence of officers and men from different companies at that location during the battle—as evidenced by their bodies—and it has been speculated that they had been brought there for medical attention from Dr. Lord. His body was found on Custer Hill about 20 feet southwest of Custer. The doctor's surgical case was discovered 2 days later in the abandoned Indian village.

M Company, 7th Cavalry This company was commanded during the Battle of the LITTLE BIGHORN by Capt. Thomas H. FRENCH. The company's other officers were on temporary duty: 1st Lt. Edward G. MATHEY commanding the packtrain detail, and 2nd Lt. James G. STURGIS as second in command of E Company. M Company was part of Maj. Marcus RENO's Battalion, and participated in RENO'S VALLEY FIGHT and the RENO-BENTEEN DEFENSE SITE. It lost 10 killed and 9 wounded, 2 of whom later died.

McDougall, Thomas Mower (May 21, 1845–July 3, 1909) Captain, 7th Cavalry. McDougall joined the service over the protests of his father who was an army surgeon. He served during the Civil War as a second lieutenant in the 10th Louisiana Volunteers. He was commissioned as a first lieutenant and assigned to the SEVENTH CAVALRY in December 1870, and was promoted to captain in late 1875. McDougall's B Company was detailed as packtrain escort at the LITTLE BIGHORN. The pesky mules caused them

to lag well behind the main column, but they eventually arrived safely at the RENO-BENTEEN DEFENSE SITE, where McDougall was subsequently slightly wounded in action. McDougall, who had previously commanded E Company, was detailed to bury the members of that company in DEEP RAVINE after the battle because of his ability to identify many of the remains. A bloody photograph of McDougall's sister, that had inexplicably been carried out by Capt. Myles KEOGH, was found in the CHEYENNE village of DULL KNIFE on November 25, 1876. McDougall retired on disability from the army in 1890. *Sources for further study include:* "An Interview with Thomas M. McDougall," in *Custer in '76: Walter Camp's Notes on the Custer Fight*, edited by Kenneth Hammer (Provo, UT: Brigham Young University Press, 1976); and numerous references in *The Custer Myth: A Source Book of Custeriana*, edited by W. A. Graham (Harrisburg, PA: Stackpole, 1953).

McIntosh, Donald ("Tosh"; ?–June 25, 1876) First lieutenant, 7th Cavalry. This native of Canada, said to be a half-breed (Canadian father and Mohawk or "Six Nations" mother), was commissioned a second lieutenant in the SEVENTH CAVALRY on August 17, 1867, and promoted to first lieutenant on March 22, 1870. During RENO'S VALLEY FIGHT, McIntosh, the commander of G Company, was directing his men out of the timber toward the bluffs when he was shot off his horse. A trooper provided him with another mount, but he was last seen surrounded by an overwhelming number of Indians. Capt. F. W. BENTEEN wrote: "I am inclined to think that had McIntosh divested himself of that slow poking way which was his peculiar characteristic, he might have been left in the land of the living." Tosh, called "a gentleman of culture" in his obituary, was married to Mollie, the sister of 1st Lt. Francis GIBSON of H Company and the best friend of Libbie Custer. Gibson identified McIntosh's body from sleeve buttons his sister had given him at FORT ABRAHAM LINCOLN. His remains were reinterred at FORT LEAVENWORTH, KA, on August 3, 1877, then moved to Arlington National Cemetery in 1909. McIntosh's diary—damaged by a bullet hole and valued at $120,000—was stolen in 1993 from the museum at the LITTLE BIGHORN BATTLEFIELD NATIONAL MONUMENT, and allegedly destroyed by the admitted thief.

MacKensie, Ranald Slidell (1840–89) Colonel, 4th Cavalry. MacKensie graduated first in his class at West Point in 1862, and distinguished himself in the Civil War with brevets to major general. He commanded the 4th Cavalry in Texas in 1871 and fought Plains and Apache Indians. Gen. Phil SHERIDAN transferred him to the Plains, where on November 25, 1876, his troops attacked and destroyed the village of CHEYENNE chief DULL KNIFE. The following year he returned to Texas, and later he was sent to fight Apaches in New Mexico and Arizona. He was promoted to brigadier general in 1882, but then developed a mental illness and was institutionalized until his death.

Malfunction of Springfield Carbines at the Battle of the Little Bighorn Scholars have for years debated the issue of whether or not the Model 1873 Springfield carbine carried by the cavalrymen malfunctioned during the battle and was one reason for the defeat. The controversy results from the known failure of the carbine to extract the spent .45/55 caliber cartridge. The cartridge cases were made of copper, which expands when hot. That—coupled with a faulty extractor mechanism and common dirt—could cause the head of the cartridge to be torn away when the block was opened, and the cartridge cylinder would then be left inside the chamber. Thus a jam was created and led to a malfunction. The casing would have to be

removed manually with a pocketknife before firing again. This defect was noted by the board of officers (which included Maj. Marcus RENO) that selected the weapon in 1872, but was not considered particularly serious at that time. This leads to the question: How often did this defect occur and cause the weapon to malfunction on June 25, 1876? According to Dr. Richard Fox in his *Archaeology, History, and Custer's Last Battle* (Norman: University of Oklahoma Press, 1993), there were very few .45/55 caliber cartridge casings found during digs on the battlefield that showed any evidence of pry or scratch marks. Only 3 of the 88 found on the Custer portion of the battlefield could possibly have been involved in an extraction jam. On the RENO-BENTEEN DEFENSE SITE, 7 out of 257 fit this category. If this was a representative number it would appear that malfunction from that source was minimal. But eyewitnesses—both white and Indian—are contradictory. Both sides apparently believed that some weapons malfunctioned. Indian testimony, including SIOUX chief GALL, reported that some soldiers threw down their long guns and fought with their short guns. Could this indicate a malfunctioning weapon that was discarded and therefore could not have left its marked casings on the field? Or were the troopers simply bringing into play their Colt revolvers that would have been more effective at short range than the carbines? No definitive conclusion can be drawn about the possible malfunction of the Springfield carbine as being a significant cause of Custer's defeat. Writers of both pro– and anti–Custer material over the years (beginning with Maj. Reno, who needed an alternate excuse) have incorporated the theory into their works, and it does make for an acceptable cause for some. One final note: the Springfield carbine remained the official cavalry firearm until the early 1890s. *Sources for further study include: The Springfield Carbine on the Western Frontier*, by Kenneth Hammer (Fort Collins, CO: Old Army, 1971).

Marsh, Grant Price (1834–1916) Captain of the steamboat, *FAR WEST.* Marsh was known as the premier navigator on the Missouri River, so expert that he could "navigate a steamer on a light dew." The *Far West,* owned by the Coulson Company, along with Capt. Marsh were contracted by Gen. Alfred TERRY to haul supplies during the LITTLE BIGHORN Campaign. On the night of June 21—the night before the SEVENTH CAVALRY marched into the Valley of the Little Bighorn—Marsh and Maj. RENO, captains Tom CUSTER and KEOGH, 1st Lt. CALHOUN, and a couple of infantry officers stayed up all night playing poker and drinking on board the *Far West.* The steamship was moored at the mouth of the Little Bighorn River when word came about the fate of Custer's command. The wounded cavalrymen, as well as Capt. Keogh's horse, COMANCHE, were transported on crude litters from the battlefield and arrived on June 30 at the *Far West.* Shortly after 4 P.M. on July 3 the steamship, its colors at half-mast and its decks draped in black mourning cloth, departed for Bismarck. Marsh courageously navigated his craft through uncharted water, and made the 710-mile trip with 2 brief stops in a record-setting time of 54 hours. Custer's widow, Libbie, sent her carriage and a note asking Capt. Marsh to visit her, but he refused in the name of pressing duties elsewhere. *Sources for further study include: Conquest of the Missouri: Being the Story of the Life and Exploits of Captain Grant Marsh,* by J. M. Hanson (New York: Murray Hill Books, 1946).

Martin, John (Giovanni Martini; 1853–1922) Private, 7th Cavalry, trumpeter, H Company. Martin, detailed as an orderly at the Battle of the LITTLE BIGHORN, carried Custer's last known order to Capt. F. W. BENTEEN, thereby making him the last man to see Custer alive. The message was hastily scribbled on notepaper by Adjutant 1st Lt. W. W. COOKE due to the fact that Martin, an emigrant from Italy, spoke little English. The order read as follows: "Benteen. Come on. Big Village. Be Quick. Bring Packs. W. W. Cooke. P. bring pacs." Some scholars theorize that had Benteen immediately acted on the order he and his command could have reached the battlefield in time to assist Custer. In his defense, Benteen may have received the impression from Martin's confident words that Custer had the Indians on the run. Martin was overheard telling Benteen's men that the Indian village was the largest he had ever seen, and that Maj. RENO had charged and was killing everybody, which was not true. (See RENO'S VALLEY FIGHT.) Martin claimed that his last view of Custer's men was of the Gray Horse Troop (Company E) heading down Medicine Tail Coulee at the gallop. Benteen later referred to Martin as a "thick-headed, dull-witted Italian, just as much cut out for a cavalryman as he was for a king." Martin remained with Benteen's Battalion, and participated in the RENO-BENTEEN DEFENSE SITE. Following the battle, he remained in the army, retiring as a sergeant in 1904. See also BATES, COL. CHARLES. *Sources for further study include:* "Interview with John Martin, October 24, 1908," and "Interview with John Martin, May 4, 1910," in *Custer in '76: Walter Camp's Notes on the Custer Fight,* edited by Kenneth Hammer (Provo, UT: Brigham Young University Press, 1976); chapter 9 of *The Custer Myth: A Source Book of Custeriana,* edited by W. A. Graham (Harrisburg, PA: Stackpole, 1953); and "John A. Martin—Custer's Last Courier," by Raymond J. Ross, *The West* (April 1967).

Mathey, Edward Gustave (October 27, 1837–July 19, 1915) First lieutenant, 7th Cavalry. Known as "Bible-Thumper" due to his blasphemous language. This native of France enlisted in the Indiana Volunteer Infantry in June 1861, and was appointed second lieutenant in the 81st Volunteer Infantry in May 1862. He fought Civil War battles at Stones River, Chickamauga, Atlanta, and Nashville. Mathey was commissioned a second lieutenant in the SEVENTH CAVALRY in 1867 and promoted to first lieutenant 3 years later. He suffered from snow blindness at the Battle of WASHITA, which allowed Capt. Louis HAMILTON, who was anxious to take part in the fight, to trade places. Mathey was detailed to the supply train. Hamilton was killed in the initial charge. In 1870, when the War Department had held board hearings to reduce the number of officers, Mathey was recommended for discharge by Col. Samuel STURGIS, apparently due to a personal dislike of the French immigrant. However, Mathey successfully convinced the board that he was not undesirable or incompetent and should be retained. At the Battle of the LITTLE BIGHORN he was on temporary duty in charge of a detachment of troops from each of the companies as packtrain guard for escort Capt. Thomas MC-DOUGALL and B Company. He participated in the RENO-BENTEEN DEFENSE SITE, testifying at the RENO COURT OF INQUIRY that he had observed the major with a flask of whiskey that first night but did not consider him drunk. Mathey fought the following year against the NEZ PERCÉ. He was retired on disability as a major in 1896. *Sources for further study include:* "Interview with Edward G. Mathey, October 19, 1910," in *Custer in '76: Walter Camp's Notes on the Custer Fight*, edited by Kenneth Hammer (Provo, UT: Brigham Young University Press, 1976).

Medals of Honor for Bravery at the Battle of the Little Bighorn There were 26 SEVENTH CAVALRY troopers who were awarded the Congressional Medal of Honor during the battle: the highest number cited in any one engagement in U.S. history. Most of these men were cited for bravery under fire as volunteer water carriers who descended the ravine from the RENO-BENTEEN DEFENSE SITE to the river to resupply the

parched troops; others were volunteer sharpshooters who covered the detail. Company A: Neil Bancroft, David W. Harris, Stanislaus Roy; Company B: Thomas Callan (in 1891), Benjamin Criswell, Charles Cunningham, Rufus Hutchinson, Thomas Murray, James Pym; Company C: Richard Hanley, Peter Thompson; Company D: Abram Brant, Frederick Deitline, William Harris, Henry Holden, George Scott, Thomas Stivers, Frank Tolan, Charles Welch; Company G: Theodore GOLDIN (in 1895), T. Stevenson; Company H: George Geiger, Henry Mechlin, Otto Voit, Charles WINDOLPH; and Company M: W Slaper.

Medicine Lodge, Treaties of These 1867–68 treaties were signed by representatives of the U.S. government and the chiefs of Plains Indian tribes, including the KIOWA, KIOWA-APACHE, COMANCHE, and CHEYENNE. Provisions of the treaties called for the United States to provide 2 large reservations in western Indian Territory; one for the Kiowas, Kiowa-Apaches, and Comanches, and the other for the Cheyenne and ARAPAHO. Whites, other than teachers, doctors, instructors, or other authorized personnel, would not be permitted within the reservation limits; agricultural equipment and seed would be provided; and for the next 30 years the United States would issue clothing and other essential supplies. The Indians, on the other hand, would relinquish all territory beyond the specified reservations, and would promise not to attack the railroad, military posts, and in general not harm white people outside of the reservation. In late October 1867, some 7,000 Indians gathered at Medicine Lodge Creek, KA, about 70 miles from FORT LARNED, at a traditional Sun Dance location for the signing festivities. These Indians, who had never been anything but hunters and warriors, were about to become farmers. *Sources for further study include: The Treaty of Medicine Lodge: The Story of the*

Great Treaty Council as Told by Eyewitnesses, by Douglas C. Jones (Norman: University of Oklahoma Press, 1966).

Medicine Tail Coulee This landmark on LITTLE BIGHORN Battlefield sloped from north of WEIR POINT on BATTLE RIDGE to the Little Bighorn River at about the center of the Indian village on the opposite bank. It has been theorized that in the early moments of Custer's engagement, the battalion that included the Gray Horse Troop—the nickname of Company E commanded by 1st Lt. Algernon E. SMITH—descended this ravine either as a feint or a real attack and were met with fierce opposition. It is also speculated that Custer was killed or wounded at this location during that initial assault. See LITTLE BIGHORN, BATTLE OF THE.

Merritt, Wesley (1834–1910) Colonel, 5th Cavalry. Merritt graduated from West Point in 1860, and served as a brigadier general of cavalry along with Custer under Gen. Phil SHERIDAN. Following the Battle of the LITTLE BIGHORN, Merritt was transferred from the 9th Cavalry in Texas to join Gen. George CROOK and he participated in the Battle of Warbonnet Creek. He subsequently fought against the NEZ PERCÉ in 1877; commanded the 5th Cavalry in the Ute War of 1879; was promoted to brigadier general and served as superintendent of West Point; and was promoted to major general and led the assault on and received the surrender of Manila during the Spanish-American War of 1898. Merritt also participated in the Paris peace negotiations that followed the war.

Miles, Nelson Appleton (1839–1925) Colonel, 5th Infantry. Miles rose quickly in rank during the Civil War. He was wounded three times and received the Congressional Medal of Honor. Following the war, he commanded the 5th Infantry and battled southern Plains Indians in the vicinity of Texas. After the

Battle of the LITTLE BIGHORN he came north to fight the Plains Indians. He defeated CRAZY HORSE in the Battle of WOLF MOUNTAIN, and LAME DEER soon after. In 1877 he subdued Chief Joseph and the NEZ PERCÉ in the Bear Paw Mountains. Miles pursued SITTING BULL into Canada in 1879, but failed to capture the HUNKPAPA medicine man. Promoted to brigadier general, he was able to force Geronimo to surrender in 1886. During the Ghost Dance fascination of 1890, Miles arrested Sitting Bull (who had surrendered and was living on the reservation) whom Miles believed was responsible for the uprising. Sitting Bull was subsequently killed, and Miles ordered a massive force of troops to the Pine Ridge Reservation. This led to the Battle of WOUNDED KNEE on December 29, 1890, and a blot on Miles's otherwise respectable record of Indian fighting. He participated in the Spanish-American War, and retired with the rank of lieutenant general in 1903. He became a writer of military events, and was quickly embroiled in the debate over the Battle of the Little Bighorn. He supported Custer's strategy, and placed the blame for the defeat squarely on the shoulders of Maj. Marcus RENO for his retreat and Capt. F. W. BENTEEN for failing to ride to the sound of gunfire. He created a controversy by claiming to have in his possession an affidavit that would refute any charge that Custer had disobeyed Gen. Alfred TERRY's orders for the battle. (See also ADAMS, MARY.) In 1892 he petitioned Congress to allocate ample funds for a memorial building at the LITTLE BIGHORN BATTLEFIELD NATIONAL MONUMENT. *Sources for further study include: Personal Recollections and Observations of General Nelson A. Miles* (New York: Da Capo, 1969); and *Nelson A. Miles: A Documentary Biography of His Military Career, 1861–1903,* edited by Brian Pohanka (Glendale, CA: Arthur H. Clark, 1985).

Mills, Anson (1834–1924) Captain, 3rd Cavalry. Mills, who served in the

18th Infantry during the Civil War, commanded a battalion under Gen. George CROOK during the LITTLE BIGHORN CAMPAIGN. He fought in the POWDER RIVER FIGHT under Col. J. Reynolds, and the Battle of the ROSEBUD. At the latter engagement Mills was dispatched to seek out the Indian village that Crook surmised was close by. During his march, Mills recognized a trap set by SIOUX warrior CRAZY HORSE and safely retreated from a canyon ambush. It was a 150-man detachment commanded by Mills that, while on a mission to reach Deadwood, SD, for supplies during Crook's "Starvation March" in fall 1876, attacked a 37-lodge Sioux village near SLIM BUTTES on September 9. The cavalrymen routed the Indians and killed their chief, AMERICAN HORSE. Crazy Horse and about 200 warriors counterattacked, but Mills held them off until Crook arrived with reinforcements. Mills retired as a brigadier general, and wrote *My Story* (Washington, D.C.: Press of Byron S. Adams, 1921).

Milner, Moses Embree (California Joe) (May 8, 1829–October 29, 1876) Trapper; mountain man; Indian fighter; army scout and guide. Joe departed Kentucky at the age of 14 to head west and become a mountain man. He first scouted for the army during the Mexican War. After successfully prospecting for gold in California as a Forty-niner, he established a cattle ranch in Oregon until leaving to fight in the Civil War. Milner served briefly as chief scout for Custer during the HANCOCK EXPEDITION OF 1867, but a bout with the bottle resulted in his demotion to regular scout. He scouted for Custer during the WASHITA CAMPAIGN OF 1868–69. Following the Battle of WASHITA, he and another scout traveled 100 miles in 2 days through the severe winter and hostile Indian country to report about Custer's engagement to Gen. Phil SHERIDAN at CAMP SUPPLY. He scouted for the Jenny Expedition into the BLACK HILLS in 1875 and remained

to prospect for gold. Milner was a scout for Gen. George CROOK's 5th Cavalry when he was murdered at CAMP ROBINSON over a disagreement. He was considered a good friend of Custer and his wife Libbie, and had frequently corresponded with them. *Sources for further study include: California Joe: Noted Scout and Indian Fighter*, by Joe E. Milner (his grandson) and Earle R. Forrest (Lincoln: University of Nebraska Press, Bison Book, 1987).

Minniconjou Sioux One of the SIOUX tribes camped in the large village along the Little Bighorn River on June 25, 1876, when Custer attacked. Prominent members include HUMP, Fast Bull, and Black Shield.

Monahsetah (*Me-o-tzi*: translated meaning "The young grass that shoots in the spring") This CHEYENNE Indian girl was the source of gossip during Custer's life, and subsequently the subject of much controversy. She was one of the 53 captives taken by the SEVENTH CAVALRY following the Battle of WASHITA. Her father was Chief Little Rock, who was killed during the battle. Monahsetah first came to Custer's attention when another captive Cheyenne woman, the sister of Chief BLACK KETTLE, Mahwisa, attempted to marry Custer to the girl. Custer had assembled the captive women to assure them of kind treatment. Mahwisa asked to speak on behalf of the women, and when finished received hearty approval for her words. Mahwisa then brought Monahsetah, a divorced teenager who was about 7 months pregnant, to where Custer was standing. She proceeded to administer a ceremony that Custer patiently endured. Finally, he asked his scout, Raphael Romero, the purpose of the ritual. Custer was informed that he was being married to the girl. The ceremony abruptly ended. Custer then explained to the Cheyenne women through his interpreter that he was already spoken for. His repudiation of the ceremony satisfied him. Evidently, it did not satisfy the Cheyenne, whose oral tradition documents a marriage between Custer and Monahsetah. The Cheyenne girl gave birth on January 14, 1869. It has been speculated over the years that this was Custer's child. This was clearly not possible, given the fact that Custer only met the girl on November 27, 1868. No less of an authority than Custer critic Capt. F. W. BENTEEN wrote to Theodore GOLDIN on February 19, 1896: "Of course you have heard of an informal invitation from Custer for officers desiring to avail themselves of the services of a captured squaw, to come to the squaw round-up corral and select one![?] Custer took first choice, and lived with her during the winter and spring of 1868 and '69. To crown the marriage[?] the squaw "calved" at site of the present FORT SILL. The issue was, however, a simon-pure Cheyenne baby, the seed having been sown before we came down on their fold at Washita." However, to add fuel to the fires of gossip, Monahsetah along with Mahwisa and another woman were chosen to accompany Custer for the remainder of the WASHITA CAMPAIGN OF 1868–69 and act as liaisons between the whites and Cheyenne. Custer clearly thought highly of Monahsetah, and described her as "an exceedingly comely squaw, possessing a bright, cheery face, a countenance beaming with intelligence, and a disposition more inclined to be merry than one usually finds among Indians." Whether their "marriage" was consummated remains a matter of speculation. Cheyenne oral tradition, as reported by a number of historians, contends that another child was born, this one in the summer or fall of 1869, and that Custer was the father. Regardless, the relationship between Custer and Monahsetah ended that spring when the Cheyenne returned to their reservation and she and the rest of the captives from Black Kettle's village were released to join them. *Sources for further study include: My Life on the Plains; Or, Personal*

Experiences with Indians, by George A. Custer, edited by Edgar I. Stewart (Norman: University of Oklahoma Press, 1962).

Montana Column *see* GIBBON, JOHN

Motion Pictures and Videos Relating to Custer and the Little Bighorn The first depictions were early silent features. It began with the one-reeler *Custer's Last Stand (on the Little Bighorn),* by William Selig in 1909, which featured a reenactment on the actual battle site by the Montana National Guard. That was followed by the 1912 three-reeler *Custer's Last Raid,* from Thomas Ince, which portrayed savage Sioux warrior RAIN-IN-THE-FACE as Custer's nemesis. This film—which portrayed SITTING BULL as a coward—was directed by Francis Ford, the brother of famed John Ford (see below). Then came *The Massacre,* from D. W. Griffith in 1912, which furthered the myth of a heroic Custer sacrificing himself for the good of western progress. Thomas Ince returned with *Campaigning with Custer* in 1913 and *Custer's Last Scout* in 1915; *Britton of the Seventh,* from Vitagraph in 1916; and *Bob Hampton of Place,* from Marshall Neilan in 1921. *The Scarlet West,* a nine-reeler by J. G. Adolfi came in 1925 to coincide with the fiftieth anniversary of the battle. The next year Anthony J. Xydias and Sunset Pictures released *With General Custer at the Little Big Horn.* Cowboy hero Hoot Gibson played Custer's scout in the 1926 *The Flaming Frontier* (Gen. E. S. GODFREY attended the New York premier). Then came the talkies, beginning with a remake of the *Last Frontier* in 1932, and in 1937 Cecil B. De Mille's epic *The Plainsman,* starring Gary Cooper. In 1940 there were the forgettable *Wyoming* from MGM, starring Wallace Beery, who helped Custer run the bad guys out of town; and the entertaining if not historically accurate *Santa Fe Trail* from Warner Bros. and director Michael Curtiz, with Custer played by

Ronald Reagan and Errol Flynn as Jeb Stuart. Universal released Alfred Green's *Badlands of Dakota* in 1941, but more popular was *They Died with Their Boots On* (1941) from Warner Bros., directed by Raoul Walsh and starring Errol Flynn as Custer and Olivia de Havilland as his wife Libbie. The film attempted to portray historical events as well as the relationship between Custer and his wife. Although it is an entertaining film and does bring forth events previously ignored, it struggles with fact as well as the portrayal of Custer, which at times is laughable. John Ford claimed that his *Fort Apache* in 1948, starring Henry Fonda, John Wayne, and Shirley Temple, was a fictionalized account of the Custer story set in the Southwest. Evidently, Ford failed to study both Custer or the Little Bighorn Battle before plunging ahead with this project. *She Wore a Yellow Ribbon* (1949) began a series of films that make use of Custer or the battle, but are not necessarily Custer films: *Warpath* (1951); *Little Big Horn* (1951); *Bugles in the Afternoon* (1952); *Sitting Bull* (1954); *Chief Crazy Horse* (1955); *Seventh Cavalry* (1956); *Tonka* (1958); *The Canadians* (1961); *The Great Sioux Massacre* (1965); *The Glory Guys* (1965); and *Red Tomahawk* (1967). *Custer of the West* (1968) starring Robert Shaw is notable inasmuch as a grandnephew of Maj. Marcus RENO sued the producers. He claimed Reno was slandered; the New York Supreme Court dismissed the case. Then came the appearance of anti–Custer films, beginning with *Little Big Man* in 1970, starring Dustin Hoffman, which depicted a pompous Custer who became a raving maniac at his last stand. A French film, *Touchez pas la femme blanche* (1974), starred Marcello Mastroianni and a host of Vietnamese refugees who portrayed Sioux Indians. The made-for-television NBC "Hallmark Hall of Fame" teleplay "The Court-Martial of George Armstrong Custer," based on the excellent novel of the same name by Douglas C. Jones (New York: Warner Books,

1977), examined the premise that Custer alone survived the battle to stand trial. The most recent portrayal was "Son of the Morning Star," an ABC teleplay loosely based on Evan Connell's bestseller of the same name (San Francisco: North Point, 1984).

VHS video tapes include the aforementioned *Custer's Last Raid* from 1912, 45 minutes in length with an 8-page reproduction of the original promotional pamphlet. Part of the the "Saga of Western Man" series from 1966 includes *Custer: The American Surge Westward. Red Sunday* (1975), narrated by television personality John McIntyre, relates the story with drawings, artwork, photographs, reenactments, and aerial photography. Excellent reenactments at such interesting locations as the CROW'S NEST, Reno's river crossing, the Indian village, and CUSTER HILL—along with computer graphics—highlight *A Good Day to Die* (no date). *Contrasts* (no date) examines the battle and contrasts between cavalrymen and Plains Indian warriors, including an explanation of their weapons, dress, and gear. *Custer's Last Trooper* (1990) features an archeological dig at the battlefield that discovered partial remains of a cavalryman subsequently named "Trooper Mike." A 1992 production called *Custer at Little Bighorn* documents the peace commissions, military expeditions, and the conflict itself with reenactments. "How the West Was Lost, Vol. 3: A Good Day to Die; Kill the Indians, Save the Man" (1993), a Discovery Channel production that portrays the Native American perspective of the battle. Arts and Entertainment Network included Custer in their recent "Biography" series. "Touring the Little Bighorn Battlefield" takes you on a 30-minute tour of the Indian village site, the museum, National Cemetery, RENO'S VALLEY FIGHT, the RENO-BENTEEN DEFENSE SITE, WEIR POINT, and, of course, Custer Hill. *Sources for further study include: Western Films: A Complete Guide* by Brian Garfield (New York: Rawson Associates,

1982); *The BFI Companion to the Western*, edited by Edward Buscombe (New York: Atheneum, 1988); *The Video Resource Book* (Detroit: Gale Research, 1995); and *The Custer Reader*, edited by Paul Andrew Hutton (Lincoln: University of Nebraska Press, 1992).

Moylan, Myles (December 17, 1838–December 11, 1909) Captain, 7th Cavalry. Moylan enlisted in the army in 1857, and fought the first two years of the Civil War, including battles at Fort Donelson and Shiloh, as a sergeant. He was commissioned a second lieutenant in the 5th Cavalry—with 1st Lt. George A. Custer—in February 1863, and saw action at such places as Beverly Ford and Gettysburg. His commission did not last long. In October 1863 he faced a court-martial for an unauthorized visit to Washington, D.C. He was found guilty and dismissed from the service. He immediately enlisted in the 4th Massachusetts Cavalry under the name "Charles E. Thomas." In January 1864 he was commissioned a first lieutenant and promoted to captain in December 1864, while serving on the staff of Maj. Gen. John GIBBON. After the war Moylan enlisted under his real name as a private in the SEVENTH CAVALRY. He caught the eye of his commander, Lt. Col. Custer, who appointed Moylan sergeant major of the regiment. Custer encouraged Moylan to seek a commission, and submitted a glowing recommendation, endorsed by other 7th Cavalry officers including Col. A. J. SMITH. Moylan, however, failed the examination. With Custer's tutelage, he passed a subsequent test and was commissioned a second lieutenant in the 7th Cavalry. Moylan was ostracized by some of the junior officers, denying him such privileges as an invitation to join the bachelor officers' mess. The prejudice toward Moylan was allegedly not based on the fact that he had been an enlisted man but rather from the fact that he was simply too vulgar and unpolished when in the company of men. Custer invited Moylan to dine with him, and promoted him to captain in 1872 over other eligible first lieutenants. Moylan became an even closer member of the Custer clan when he married Charlotte Calhoun, sister of 1st Lt. James CALHOUN, who had married Custer's half sister, Maggie. At the Battle of the Little Bighorn, Moylan commanded Company A, and participated in RENO'S VALLEY FIGHT, where he attempted to provide protection for Company G in the rear on the retreat from the timber; and the RENO-BENTEEN DEFENSE SITE, where his company was entrenched on the eastern line. Moylan was seriously wounded at the 1877 Battle of Bear Paw Mountain, and received the Congressional Medal of Honor for his "distinguished gallantry" against the NEZ PERCÉ. He also was involved in the 1890 Battle of WOUNDED KNEE. He was assigned to the 10th Cavalry as major in 1892, and retired in 1893. *Sources for further study include:* numerous references in *The Custer Myth: A Source Book of Custeriana* edited by W. A. Graham (Harrisburg, PA: Stackpole, 1953).

Mutilation of Cavalrymen at the Battle of the Little Bighorn Many of the dead from Custer's command were mutilated by the SIOUX and CHEYENNE Indians. This mutilation included dismemberment, crushed skulls, decapitation, slashes, entrails emerging, brains exposed, multiple bullet holes, multiple arrows, or scalped. Custer, however, was apparently unmarked. He was found naked in a sitting position leaning against and between two troopers, his face wearing the expression of a man who "had fallen asleep and enjoyed peaceful dreams." Cheyenne Kate Bighead testified that two women recognized Custer's dead body on the battlefield, and prevented his mutilation out of respect for their tribal sister, MONAHSETAH, whom they thought had gained Custer's affection while working as his translator. Kate said the women pushed the sharp point of a sewing awl into each of Custer's ears to "improve his hearing," as it seemed he had not heard the chiefs when he smoked the pipe with them at the Treaty of MEDICINE LODGE. Custer's brother, Tom, was singled out for possibly the worst treatment. He could be identified only from a fancy tattoo on his arm. This has fueled speculation that Sioux warrior RAIN-IN-THE-FACE had made good on his vow to cut out Tom CUSTER's heart and eat it, due to an earlier incident between the two. That was highly unlikely, even though Rain-in-the-Face was on the field at some point during the day, because Custer's heart had not been removed. See CUSTER, THOMAS WARD.

Nez Percé Indians This tribe from present-day Idaho, led by legendary strategic genius Chief Joseph, waged war in 1877 with the U.S. government over continuing land disputes. The tribe had eluded Col. John GIBBON in early August at Big Hole Valley, with both sides suffering serious losses. The Nez Percé decided to make an attempt to cross the Canadian border and take refuge with SITTING BULL and the SIOUX. Three hundred fifty troopers from the SEVENTH CAVALRY under Col. Samuel D. STURGIS intercepted the tribe at Canyon Creek. In a running battle the Nez Percé successfully fought off the army.

In late September Gen. Nelson MILES and 600 additional soldiers joined the chase. On September 30 Miles's troops attacked the Nez Percé camp at Snake Creek near the Bear Paw Mountains. The Indians inflicted heavy casualties on the soldiers: Capt. Owen HALE was killed and Capt. Myles MOYLAN and 1st Lt. Edward GODFREY were severely wounded. The Nez Percé, who had traveled nearly 1,700 miles on their flight, held out until October 5. On that morning Chief Joseph eloquently surrendered the remainder of his people. *Sources for further study include: The Flight of the Nez Percé: A History of the Nez Percé War*, by Mark H. Brown (New York: Putnam, 1967).

Nineteenth Kansas Cavalry *see* KANSAS VOLUNTEER CAVALRY

Northern Cheyenne Indians *see* CHEYENNE INDIANS

Northern Pacific Railroad The iron horse was one of the primary purposes for the army's presence in the West. It was the Northern Pacific Railroad's intention to connect Duluth, MN, with the Pacific Northwest. That route would take them directly through the Yellowstone River Valley, territory coveted by the SIOUX and northern CHEYENNE Indians. The Indians realized the disastrous ramifications of the railroad: the influx of settlers and hunters, the elimination of the buffalo, and eventually a forced existence on the reservation. In order to lay track, the route had to first be surveyed, and this was where the army entered the picture. In 1872 Gen. William SHERMAN wrote to Gen. Phil SHERIDAN: "The Indians will be hostile in an extreme degree, yet I think our interest is to favor the undertaking of the Road, as it will help to bring the Indian problem to a final solution." Throughout the West the army provided security for survey and construction crews on their advance. The YELLOWSTONE EXPEDITION OF 1873 — a major survey involving Custer's SEVENTH CAVALRY — included battles with the Sioux under CRAZY HORSE and SITTING BULL. Custer, in his position as respected Indian fighter, was the darling of the Northern Pacific Railroad hierarchy. The railroad, however, fell on hard times and filed for bankruptcy in 1873, which helped create the Panic of 1873. Only one thing could save them: the sale of company-owned land in the West. Sherman, and especially Custer, were high on the agricultural and stock-grazing prospects of the Dakota Plains and the Yellowstone Valley, and made their views known in the national press. This position and promotion by such respected men greatly pleased Jay Cooke, financial agent of the Northern Pacific Railroad. One detractor, however, was former Custer nemesis, Col. William B. HAZEN. The colonel disagreed with Custer's assessment of the land, and the two engaged in a literary duel in the press. Custer stood behind his opinion, and in what could be construed as a conflict of interest, accepted certain favors from the railroad. His wall tent had NPRR stenciled on its side, and his and Libbie's passage on the railroad was gratis and usually in a private car. In Custer's defense, the military mind-set at that point in time was that what was good for the railroad was good for America. Following the BLACK HILLS EXPEDITION OF 1874, the railroad brought to Bismarck droves of gold seekers, regardless of the fact that Eastern newspapers called the discovery of gold simply a ploy by the railroad to promote its land. The continued advance of the rails incited the Indians to increase raiding parties on white interests. This activity resulted in the informal declaration of war by the army against the SIOUX and CHEYENNE that led to the GREAT SIOUX WAR OF 1876–77. In summary, the introduction of the railroad to the West, perhaps more than any other reason, brought about the defeat of the Indian. *Sources for further study include: Penny-an-Acre Empire in the West,* edited by Edgar I. Stewart (Norman: University of Oklahoma Press, 1968).

Nowlan, Henry J. (June 17, 1837–November 10, 1898) First lieutenant, 7th Cavalry. This Irishman, a graduate of Sandhurst—the British equivalent of West Point—fought for the British Army in the Crimean War, then emigrated to the United States in 1862. He was commissioned a first lieutenant in January 1863 and assigned to the 14th New York Cavalry. He was captured by the Confederate Army in June 1863 and spent two years as a prisoner in the notorious Andersonville and Charleston prisons. He escaped in February 1865 and joined Gen. William SHERMAN's division. After the Civil War he was appointed a second

lieutenant in the SEVENTH CAVALRY, and promoted to first lieutenant in December 1866. He served as regimental commissary of substance from 1867 until 1870, regimental quartermaster from 1872 until 1876, and was known as the best marksman in the unit. At the LITTLE BIGHORN he was on detached service with Gen. TERRY. It was likely that he was the one who recognized COMANCHE, his best friend Capt. Myles KEOGH's horse on the battlefield, and vowed to save him. Nowlan had been given Keogh's last will and testament just days before, with instructions to deliver it to Keogh's sister should anything happen to the captain. Nowlan was promoted to captain in 1876, and assumed command of Keogh's I Company. He participated in the Nez Percé Campaign of 1877, as well as the June 1877 reburial detail at Little Bighorn Battlefield. Nowlan was present at the Battle of WOUNDED KNEE, and promoted to major in 1895.

Nye-Cartwright Ridge This ridge on LITTLE BIGHORN Battlefield between MEDICINE TAIL COULEE and Deep Coulee was named for two students of the battle who located firing positions in the vicinity. It is not known whether cavalrymen who took up position there were deployed to guard Custer's right flank, to cover the anticipated approach of the packtrain, or had simply become separated from the command.

Oglala Sioux Indians One of the SIOUX tribes present in the large village on the Little Bighorn River on June 25, 1876, when Custer attacked. Their name means scattered or divided, perhaps because of ostracization at some point in time due to their contemptuous notion to raise crops. The most notable Oglala warriors are CRAZY HORSE, RED CLOUD, PAWNEE KILLER, BLACK ELK, One Stab, and Low Dog. It was the Oglala Sioux who sent a delegation to Nevada in 1889 to investigate the Ghost Dance being performed by Wovoka in

Nevada. Their adoption of the ceremony led to the Battle of WOUNDED KNEE in 1890.

Order of Indian Wars, The (P.O. Box 7401, Little Rock, AR 72216) This interest group keeps members informed about events and information related to the Indian wars.

Osage Indians This peaceful southeastern Plains tribe regularly served as army scouts and guides. Thirteen Osage Indians assisted Custer on the WASHITA CAMPAIGN OF 1868–69.

Pawnee Killer (OGLALA SIOUX) This war chief received his name due to his actions against the Pawnees, who were traditional Sioux enemies. He became a thorn in Custer's side during the HANCOCK EXPEDITION OF 1867, participating in a number of skirmishes with the SEVENTH CAVALRY. Pawnee Killer and his warriors were responsible for the killing of Lt. Lyman KIDDER and his 10-man detachment, who were carrying orders to Custer in the field. The Sioux chief fought the next year at the Battle of BEECHER ISLAND and the Battle of SUMMIT SPRINGS. In January 1872 Pawnee Killer joined the entourage—including his former enemy Custer—that had assembled for a special buffalo hunt in honor of visiting Russian Grand Duke ALEXIS. The Sioux chief's band eventually surrendered to Red Cloud Agency, but Pawnee Killer was not with them. His fate remains a mystery. *Sources for further study include: My Life on the Plains; Or, Personal Experiences with Indians,* by George A. Custer (New York: Sheldon, 1874).

Porter, Dr. Henry Renaldo (February 3, 1848–March 3, 1903) Porter graduated from Georgetown University School of Medicine in 1872, and had served with the 5th Cavalry in Arizona before joining the SEVENTH CAVALRY. He had resigned his commission in 1875

and opened a drugstore in Bismarck, D.T. However, he was under contract as acting assistant surgeon attached to Maj. Marcus RENO's command at the Battle of the LITTLE BIGHORN. He participated in RENO'S POWDER RIVER SCOUT, RENO'S VALLEY FIGHT, and the RENO-BENTEEN DEFENSE SITE. Following Reno's disastrous retreat from the valley to the bluffs across the river, Porter approached Maj. Reno to notify him that the troops were quite demoralized by the bloody retreat. An irritated Reno replied, "That was a cavalry charge, sir!" Porter established a makeshift hospital in the shallow area on the hilltop and cared as best he could for the wounded, amputating limbs and rationing out the diminishing water supply. When the Terry-Gibbon Column arrived two days later to save them, he supervised the transportation of the wounded to the steamer *FAR WEST.* Porter also visited the battlefield where Custer's men fell, and removed locks of hair from all the dead officers. Following the battle he returned to his business in Bismarck, and upon occasion served as acting assistant surgeon for the army. He died in Agra, India. *Sources for further study include:* Porter's "The Terrible Sioux Doctor Porter's Account of the Battle," was published in the *New York Herald,* July 11, 1876.

Porter, James Ezekiel (ca. 1846–June 25, 1876) First lieutenant, 7th Cavalry. Porter was appointed in 1864 to West Point from the state of Maine, and commissioned a second lieutenant in the SEVENTH CAVALRY June 15, 1869. He was promoted to first lieutenant March 1, 1872, and assigned second in command of Capt. Myles KEOGH's I Company in July 1872 when Myles MOYLAN was promoted to captain and given command of A Company. He missed the YELLOW-STONE EXPEDITION OF 1873 and the BLACK HILLS EXPEDITION OF 1874 due to being detailed with his company on the INTERNATIONAL BOUNDARY SURVEY. At the Battle of the LITTLE

BIGHORN Porter was apparently killed with Keogh and their troops on the eastern slope of BATTLE RIDGE. His body, however, was either too badly mutilated to be recognized or had disappeared from the field. His bloody coat with two bullet holes in it was discovered in the abandoned Indian village site two days after the battle.

Powder River Fight (March 17, 1876) This engagement between the SIOUX and CHEYENNE Indians and a detachment of Gen. George CROOK's Wyoming Column was the first battle of the LITTLE BIGHORN CAMPAIGN and the GREAT SIOUX WAR OF 1876–77. The army captured an allied Sioux-Cheyenne village on the Powder River with minimal casualties on either side, but retreated when CRAZY HORSE counterattacked later in the day.

On March 16 U.S. Army scouts located a Sioux-Cheyenne village, consisting of about 100 lodges with perhaps 250 warriors on the Powder River. Col. Joseph Reynolds with 6 companies of the 3rd Cavalry—about 300 men—attacked on the morning of March 17. The surprised Indians were routed, and the cavalrymen began destroying everything of value, including a large quantity of meat that could have been used by the poorly supplied army. Casualties were minimal: 4 soldiers killed, 6 wounded; the Indians claimed 1 killed, 1 wounded, but their great loss was in provisions and homes. By early afternoon the Indians had regrouped under Crazy Horse and counterattacked from the bluffs. Instead of holding his ground, Reynolds ordered a withdrawal, leaving behind the bodies of several dead soldiers, and 1 who had been wounded. Further, the Indians had easily recaptured many of their horses from the unguarded herd. Gen. Crook was furious with Reynolds for failing to aggressively attack and hold the village. When the command returned to FORT FETTERMAN on March 26, Crook filed court-martial charges against Reynolds.

The colonel was subsequently found guilty of neglect of duty. He was punished with a one-year suspension, which was eventually commuted by his former West Point classmate President U. S. Grant. Col. Reynolds quietly retired on disability the following year. See ROSEBUD, BATTLE OF THE for subsequent action.

Presidential Aspirations of Custer There has been conjecture that Custer intended to use his victory at the Battle of the LITTLE BIGHORN to launch himself into the presidency of the United States at the upcoming 1876 election. There is no question that he would have made an attractive candidate at some future date, and military commanders traditionally attained the presidency when they won major wars. However, there is little to confirm that this was an aspiration of his at that time. The theory has been based on an alleged conversation prior to the battle between Custer and his ARIKARA scouts. A scout named Red Star stated that Custer told them he would become the "Great Father" in Washington with a victory over the SIOUX. One problem would have been timing. Word of a victory—much less Custer in person—could not have reached the Democratic Convention in St. Louis in time to have any impact on the party's choice. And, taking into consideration Custer's prior embarrassing forays into politics while campaigning for President Andrew Johnson and later the BELKNAP SCANDAL, he probably realized that he was best suited to be a soldier rather than a politician. The statement made by Custer to the REE scout could likely be dismissed as playful banter. *Sources for further study include:* "The Arikara Narrative of the Campaign Against the Hostile Dakotas," edited by Orin G. Libby, *North Dakota Historical Collections* 6 (Bismarck, 1920).

Rain-in-the-Face (HUNKPAPA SIOUX; ca. 1835–1905) This warrior terrorized the BOZEMAN TRAIL under RED CLOUD in the late 1860s, and also was present at the Battle of the LITTLE BIGHORN. However, his claim to fame came from an incident with Capt. Tom CUSTER that produced a controversy that has yet to be settled. In 1874 Rain-in-the-Face promised to someday cut out Tom Custer's heart and eat it as revenge for his arrest for the murder of 3 men during the YELLOWSTONE EXPEDITION OF 1874. In spite of the absence of any solid evidence that he made good on his threat, the story about Rain-in-the-Face and Tom Custer has been romanced to this day. The most popular poet of that age, Henry Wadsworth Longfellow, took it upon himself to perpetrate the myth with his poem, "The Revenge of Rain-in-the-Face." (See CUSTER, THOMAS WARD for more.) Rain-in-the-Face submitted to the reservation in 1880 (see illustration, p. 137). Ten years later, he was stabbed by his wife in a fit of jealousy. He survived, and requested that he be punished for the act rather than his wife. Rain-in-the-Face, by the way, had 7 wives during his life. In 1893 he was a featured attraction at the World's Fair, billed as the most famous survivor of the Battle of the Little Bighorn now that SITTING BULL had been killed. Rain-in-the-Face had learned how to write his name, and in later years cashed in on his fame by selling autographs at Coney Island, NY. He retired to the reservation and was a frequent source of material—much of it contradictory or far-fetched—for any researcher who wanted to discuss the battle. Incidentally, Rain-in-the-Face has also been credited—along with a host of others— with killing George Armstrong Custer, a deed he admitted on his death bed. (See CUSTER'S LAST STAND.) Thomas Ince's three-reel 1912 film, *Custer's Last Fight*, which starred Francis Ford, the brother of director John Ford, and depicted Rain-in-the-Face as stalking Custer at Little Bighorn to avenge his earlier arrest. He died in 1905. *Sources for further study include:* "The Personal Story of Rain-in-

Sioux warrior **Rain-in-the-Face,** 1881

the Face," in *Indian Fights and Fighters*, by Cyrus T. Brady (Lincoln: University of Nebraska Press, 1904).

Readiness of Cavalrymen at the Battle of the Little Bighorn Two major questions regarding the readiness to fight of the SEVENTH CAVALRY troopers have been a matter of controversy. The first pertains to the number of poorly trained recruits in the regiment. This theory has long been used to excuse what some judge as a poor showing by the troops. It had been a matter of discussion after the battle, but was first brought to the forefront in testimony at RENO'S COURT OF INQUIRY in 1879. In October 1875, 150 recruits had joined the 7th Cavalry, with about 60 of them having prior service. Then 62 more recruits joined the regiment in April 1876. These men were admittedly undertrained, their time consumed by guard duty, fatigue duty, and daily post activities. Maj. Marcus RENO, who commanded the 7th Cavalry in Custer's absence during preparation for the campaign, had neglected to schedule training in even the basics of using their firearms: no target practice was held. This fact, given in testimony at Reno's Inquiry, would tend to support the theory of poorly trained troops. There is no question that such troops are more vulnerable under combat conditions. The ability to fight is dependent upon learning the skills necessary to have both proficiency and confidence. However, 2nd Lt. Charles VARNUM—a battle participant—in "Varnum, Reno and the Little Bighorn," by W. J. Ghent, *Winners of the West* (April 30, 1936), stated that the number of recruits at Reno's Inquiry was exaggerated in order to aid Reno's case. Further, he claimed that most of the recruits had been left at the Powder River base camp, and companies had no more than 2 recruits each in action at the battle. Another likely problem would have been "green" horses taken into combat for the first time. It has been estimated that 50 percent of the cavalry mounts were newly acquired. Their reactions to the sounds, smells, and chaos of battle would certainly affect their riders, who were perhaps not the best horsemen themselves. Training in horsemanship—other than feeding and cleaning stalls—had been lacking as well. Was training, if not raw recruits, a factor in Custer's defeat? Probably. However, to what degree would be a matter of supposition only.

The second allegation charges that the cavalrymen were too fatigued to fight. The 7th Cavalry had marched long and hard with little sleep or nourishment before engaging in battle with the Sioux and Cheyenne. The regiment had traveled approximately 113 miles between June 22 and June 25. History has shown that soldiers—just as any other human—in a state of tiredness do not function at peak performance. Testimony of officers from Reno's command, in particular 1st Lt. Edward GODFREY, believed that the troops were worn out when they entered the battle. Field rations during the previous month consisted of hardtack and bacon, occasionally supplemented by wild game, and these were not much of a diet. Fatigue and malnourishment un-

questionably sap the spirit and could cause a breakdown in discipline and morale. Whether this was a major factor in Custer's defeat is unknown. Soldiers have traditionally gone into battle under less than ideal circumstances. These cavalrymen were proud professionals in an elite unit, expected to hold their own under most adverse conditions. Some of them had braved freezing temperatures and a blizzard to successfully attack the southern CHEYENNE Indians at WASHITA 8 years earlier. However, it is doubtful that they could have fared much better at the Little Bighorn with a full belly and a good night's sleep, considering the overwhelming odds against them.

Red Cloud (OGLALA SIOUX; 1822–1909) This prominent warrior became in 1868 the only Indian to ever force the U.S. government to grant his treaty demands due to acts of violence in what became known as "Red Cloud's War."

The conflict was waged over his people's opposition to the BOZEMAN TRAIL, a route to the Montana gold fields that passed through prime SIOUX buffalo hunting ranges. In 1865 the U.S. government began to build a road along the trail and a new fort to protect it. The Sioux, led by Red Cloud and SPOTTED TAIL, began to frequently attack miners, wagon trains, and army patrols along the road. The army chased them to no avail, and in June 1866 attempted to negotiate a treaty to stop the bloodshed. Red Cloud stated that he would sign if he was promised no forts would be built along the Bozeman Trail. The army refused, and set about building 3 new forts: PHIL KEARNY, C. F. SMITH, and later Reno.

Red Cloud was incensed, and retaliated by keeping Fort Phil Kearny under a constant state of siege by his 2,000 warriors. He masterminded hit-and-run tactics utilizing the bravery of his young warriors, among them CRAZY HORSE, GALL and RAIN-IN-THE-FACE. Crazy Horse, in particular, was adept at using a group of Indians as decoys for the army to chase while others lay in ambush. Their greatest victory came on December 21, 1866, when Crazy Horse lured 80 troopers into a trap. The detachment from Fort Phil Kearny was all killed in what became known as the FETTERMAN MASSACRE. The next meaningful engagements came the following August when Crazy Horse twice ambushed work details from the fort. The warriors suffered serious casualties during the WAGON BOX FIGHT and the HAYFIELD FIGHT, but succeeded in curtailing activities at the fort as well as along the Bozeman Trail. The soldiers were virtual prisoners, and safe travel along the trail was impossible.

Red Cloud's constant harassment finally became successful: the government yielded to his demands. The FORT LARAMIE TREATY OF 1868 was drawn up to end the conflict. Red Cloud and the Sioux would promise to suspend hostilities against the whites. In return the Indians would receive the following: the army would abandon forts Phil Kearny, Reno, and C. F. Smith; provide the Sioux a reservation that encompassed nearly all of present-day South Dakota west of the Missouri River, including the BLACK HILLS (see GREAT SIOUX RESERVATION); grant hunting rights to a wide area of the Republican River and in Wyoming and Nebraska north of the Platte River; and forbid whites to trespass in the Powder River country. Other concessions, such as providing buildings, medical care, education, seeds and agricultural supplies, and money, were also guaranteed to the Sioux. More than 200 Indians chiefs and subchiefs signed the treaty at FORT RICE on July 2. Red Cloud, however, refused to sign until the soldiers were completely gone. The army finally abandoned the Bozeman Trail posts in August. Red Cloud promptly ordered them burned to the ground, and signed the treaty on November 6, 1868.

Red Cloud made the first of a number of trips to Washington, D.C., in 1870 to meet with President U. S. GRANT and other dignitaries. The young warriors of the tribe continued their raiding ways, but were for the most part under control until 1874. It was then that Custer led the BLACK HILLS EXPEDITION OF 1874 onto Sioux land, in violation of the 1868 treaty. Worse yet, Custer had discovered gold deposits, and soon hundreds of gold miners flooded into the Black Hills to seek their fortune.

Red Cloud, SPOTTED TAIL, and other chiefs were invited to Washington in the summer of 1875 for a meeting that they thought was concerning agency business. Instead, much to their surprise, they were pressured to sign over title to the Black Hills. The chiefs refused, saying they lacked authority. The government told them to consider the offer; the "Great Father" would be very generous.

Red Cloud returned to the reservation and continued to advocate peace with the whites. His words went unheeded by SITTING BULL, Crazy Horse, and the others who once regarded him as a great warrior. They vowed that the Black Hills would be sold only over their dead bodies. Most of the reservation Indians, however, were in favor of selling the Black Hills. Spotted Tail was chosen to look over the land in question and set a price while negotiations continued.

The dispute over the Black Hills caused the army to declare war in 1876 on the nonreservation Sioux who were spoiling negotiations over the proposed sale. The Sioux under Sitting Bull decided to fight. Red Cloud continued to encourage peace, but could no longer control his people. However, following Custer's defeat at the Battle of the LITTLE BIGHORN, Red Cloud was accused of secretly aiding the hostiles. He was grievously insulted when the Indian Bureau demoted him from principal chief at the Indian agency bearing his name in favor of Spotted Tail.

Red Cloud and his people moved to Pine Ridge Reservation in 1878. He once more advocated peace with the whites during the Ghost Dance ritual that led to the 1890 Battle of WOUNDED KNEE, and he was again ignored. His health slowly declined and he became blind. Prior to his death he accepted baptism in the Roman Catholic Church.

Sources for further study include: Red Cloud's Folk: A History of the Oglala Sioux Indians, by George E. Hyde (Norman: University of Oklahoma Press, 1937); *Red Cloud and the Indian Problem,* by James C. Olson (Lincoln: University of Nebraska Press, 1965); and *The Bozeman Trail,* by G. R. Hebard and E. A. Brininstool, (Cleveland: Arthur H. Clark, 1922).

Ree Indians *see* ARIKARA INDIANS

Reed, Lydia Ann Kirkpatrick (Mrs. David Reed) (Custer's maternal half sister) Ann, who was 14 years old when Custer was born, held a special place in Custer's life as his second mother. At the age of 10, he was sent to live with her and her husband David Reed, a drayman and real estate investor, in Monroe, MI, where he was treated like a son. Ann was the recipient of countless letters from Custer during the Civil War. He would tell her about his current duties, details of battles, personalities of those with whom he served, and general chatter about social events both at home and in Washington, D.C. An incident occurred while Custer was on sick leave from the army in 1862 that wife Libbie would in later years call "that awful day." Custer met several friends for a few drinks at a downtown Monroe tavern. He imbibed to excess, and while staggering home happened to pass the Bacon residence and was observed by a horrified Libbie. Once home, Ann—with Bible in hand—took Custer into her bedroom and made him pledge before God that he would never drink even one more drop of an intoxicating beverage. It worked, because from that day on Custer, who possessed remarkable self-discipline, never again touched alcoholic beverages, not

even wine at formal dinner parties. Ann was deeply religious, and she made sure that Custer faithfully attended Sunday school. She tried in vain to convince him that church membership was the only way he could get to heaven. The combined influence of Libbie and Ann, however, was successful in converting Custer to Christianity. He wrote a letter from army headquarters in Virginia to Rev. D. C. Mattoon dated February 19, 1865, that read in part: "It was about this very hour two weeks ago tonight that I knelt with you and your family circle in Monroe. ... In your presence I accepted Christ as my Savior." Ann's prayers had been answered. Husband David Reed departed for FORT ABRAHAM LINCOLN the moment he heard about the disaster at the LITTLE BIGHORN, and escorted the Monroe ladies back home.

Reed, Henry (Harry) Armstrong "Autie" (April 27, 1858–June 25, 1876) Autie REED—nicknamed after his uncle, Custer—was born to half sister Lydia Ann REED and her husband in Monroe, MI, just after Custer had entered West Point. Autie was 18 when he headed west to accompany his famous uncle on the LITTLE BIGHORN CAMPAIGN. He had been hired as a herder for the SEVENTH CAVALRY beef herd. Reed wrote to his parents on June 21: "Uncle Autie is now in full command. ... Everybody is sure of success for the Indians are moving very slowly, not over 4 or 5 miles a day. At that rate we can soon catch them." He died with his 3 uncles on CUSTER HILL. His name was incorrectly inscribed as Arthur Reed on the granite monument at LITTLE BIGHORN BATTLEFIELD NATIONAL MONUMENT.

Reily, William Van W. (ca. 1855– June 26, 1876) Second lieutenant, 7th Cavalry. This District of Columbia native, whose father was a naval officer lost at sea in 1855, was transferred to the SEVENTH CAVALRY from the 10th Cavalry on January 26, 1876, just months before the Battle of the LITTLE BIGHORN. He was on temporary duty from Company E as second in command of Capt. YATES's F Company during the battle. Reily perished on CUSTER HILL, and was reinterred in 1877 in Washington, D.C.

Reinterments of Dead from the Battle of the Little Bighorn On June 25, 1877—one year to the day following the battle—Capt. Henry NOWLAN and the newly recruited I Company of the SEVENTH CAVALRY arrived at Little Bighorn Battlefield for the purpose of removing the bodies of the 7th Cavalry officers. Custer was reinterred at West Point; Myles KEOGH in Auburn, NY; Tom CUSTER, George YATES, Algernon SMITH, Donald McINTOSH, and James CALHOUN at FORT LEAVENWORTH; William COOKE at Hamilton, Ontario; John CRITTENDEN on the field where he fell, later in Battlefield Cemetery; and William REILY in Washington, D.C. The bodies of Henry HARRINGTON, Benjamin HODGSON, James PORTER, and James STURGIS were never found. The dead enlisted men were buried in a mass grave on CUSTER HILL over which the granite monument was erected. See INTERMENT.

Reno, Marcus A. (November 15, 1834–March 29, 1889) Major, 7th Cavalry. The charge of cowardice and incompetence at the Battle of the LITTLE BIGHORN will forever haunt Reno's name. Many scholars of the battle theorize that his failure to carry out orders and charge the southern end of the Indian village led to Custer's devastating defeat. (See RENO'S VALLEY FIGHT.) Later, on the hilltop where the remnants of Reno's beaten command had taken refuge, he was accused of cowardice and drunkenness by a number of officers and men. (See RENO-BENTEEN DEFENSE SITE.)

Reno was a graduate of the U.S. Military Academy at West Point—barely. He was scheduled to graduate with the class

of 1855 but due to excessive demerits (he set the record for demerits with 1,031) finally graduated in 1857 as twentieth in a class of 38.

Reno earned an exemplary record in the Civil War, serving in both combat and staff positions. On November 12, 1861, he was commissioned as a captain in the 1st Cavalry. He was cited for bravery and breveted major for his actions at Kelley's Ford when he led a charge against the Rebels and his horse went down, pinning him beneath. At Cedar Creek he was breveted lieutenant colonel for his actions. He also fought in other battles, including Gaines Mill, Beverly Ford, Upperville, and on the Peninsula.

At the end of the war Reno received brevets up to brigadier general of the U.S. Volunteers. He was assigned as an infantry tactics instructor at West Point, but soon requested to be relieved of that duty and assigned to the cavalry. He was sent to New Orleans as provost marshal, which displeased him, so he enlisted the aid of a senator and was sent to Washington Territory as the assistant inspector general.

In 1869 he was promoted to major and got his wish: assignment to the SEVENTH CAVALRY (see illustration, page 141). Reno's attitude toward Custer has been described as less than complimentary. Reno had watched as a younger Custer had reaped glory during the Civil War, glory that Reno considered himself more deserving. And, although Reno was not outwardly antagonistic toward Custer in the vein of Capt. F. W. BENTEEN, he was clearly not friendly. Reno was detailed as commander of the INTERNATIONAL BOUNDARY SURVEY, which was mapping the northern border of the United States, and did not accompany the regiment on the YELLOWSTONE EXPEDITION OF 1873 or the BLACK HILLS EXPEDITION OF 1874. He took two long leaves of absence during the years 1873 to 1875, but the one he was denied in 1874 likely affected him most. His wife, the former Mary Hannah Ross, daughter of a Pennsylvania banker and industrialist, unexpectedly passed away. Reno requested permission from headquarters to attend her funeral, and received the reply: "While fully sympathizing with your affliction, the Department Commander feels it is imperative to decline to grant you leave." His wife's family dealt him another blow by denying him any of the family fortune.

Reno was not liked and even was despised by many of his contemporaries. General Hugh Scott, then a young second lieutenant, "disliked him intensely." Lt. F. M. GIBSON was "wary of Reno and considered him to be arrogant and vicious." Future general E. S. GODFREY wrote in his journal, "Reno's self important rudeness makes him unbearable." Even Capt. Benteen once slapped Reno in public, called him an "S.O.B." and challenged him to a fight. Reno declined the invitation.

In early 1876, with Custer involved with the BELKNAP SCANDAL in Washington, D.C., Gen. Alfred TERRY appointed Reno temporary commander of the 7th Cavalry for the LITTLE BIGHORN Campaign. Reno requested that his position be permanent. Terry, however, delayed his decision, pending a determination of Custer's fate. Further resentment of Custer must have festered within the major when Custer returned in time to assume command. Reno's conduct at the Battle of the LITTLE BIGHORN can only be described as disgraceful. In addition to disobeying Terry's orders (see RENO'S POWDER RIVER SCOUT), he disobeyed Custer's orders to charge the village (see RENO'S VALLEY FIGHT), and apparently lost control of his command. (See RENO-BENTEEN DEFENSE SITE.)

Reno's actions as commander of a battalion during the battle came under immediate and intense criticism from numerous directions. In addition to the private opinions of those officers and men who witnessed his actions, there was a furious public condemnation. One example was an exchange of letters in the *New York Herald* between Reno and Cus-

Major Marcus A. Reno, 1875

ter's old West Point roommate, Tom Rosser, the former Confederate major general, who questioned Reno's conduct. (The Reno-Rosser letters can be found in *The Custer Myth: A Source Book of Custeriana*, edited by W. A. Graham [Harrisburg, PA: Stackpole, 1953].) Another public attack came from Custer's first biographer, Frederick Whittaker. The military establishment apparently was not too pleased with Reno either, and assigned him to FORT ABERCROMBIE, known as the armpit of the Dakotas.

Shortly after arriving at his new duty station, Reno was accused of cavorting with Mrs. Emeline Bell, a fellow officer's wife. He was ordered to St. Paul, MN, on March 8, 1877, to face a general court-martial on the charge of "conduct unbecoming an officer and gentleman." Not only was he charged with improper advances toward Mrs. Bell but the accusation of being drunk on duty was tacked on as well. The charges apparently developed from "post politics," in that Reno engaged in a losing feud with the local preacher to whom he refused permission to hold services at the fort. Reno pleaded not guilty to the charges, but was readily found guilty. The sentence handed down was dismissal from the service. However, President Rutherford B. Hayes, citing Reno's exemplary record, commuted Reno's sentence to two years suspension, effective May 1, 1877.

The public and the major himself welcomed the RENO COURT OF INQUIRY, an "investigation" into Reno's questionable conduct at the Little Bighorn, that convened in Chicago in 1879. The song-and-dance performance was actually little more than a display of officers desiring not to bring disgrace upon their unit: they closed ranks around the elite 7th Cavalry. Stories were conveniently altered, testimony was evasive, and certain key witnesses were not called or were not available. The inquiry, which "cleared" Reno's name, was more farcical than credible.

Reno was restored to active duty, and assigned to FORT MEADE, D.T. However, he soon found himself in more trouble. He was charged a second time with conduct unbecoming of an officer not long after his arrival. This one stemmed from his one-sided interest in Ella, the 20-year-old daughter of Col. Samuel STURGIS, whose son had perished with Custer. Reno had made a habit out of being drunk and rowdy at the billiard room of the Officer's Club. Col. Sturgis finally confined Reno to his quarters after a brawl in which Reno hit a fellow officer over the head with a pool cue after losing money gambling. While strolling around the parade ground on the night of November 10, 1879, Reno inexplicably peeped into the window of Col Sturgis's parlor. As if that was not enough, he spied young Ella Sturgis and tapped on the window. She screamed loudly and Mrs. Sturgis summoned her husband, who left his bed to chase Reno with a cane. Reno wrote a note the following morning to Mrs. Sturgis, which read in part: "I write this that you may appreciate what motives actuated me when I stopped to look through your window. It

has been my habit since in arrest to walk on favorable nights on the pathway in front of the officers' quarters two or three times for exercise. On the evening in question I saw your daughter in complete toilet through the window, and it was such a picture that I said to myself. Can there be any harm in looking upon it?"

Reno's court martial convened on November 28. He pleaded not guilty, but once more was found guilty. The peeping Tom incident was the straw that broke the camel's back. His sentence was once more dismissal from the service. In spite of a petition for clemency from generals TERRY and SHERMAN, President Hayes refused to commute the sentence this time. Reno was dishonorably discharged on April 1, 1880, after 23 years in the army.

Reno fell on hard times in civilian life. He had been married for only a few months when his second wife left him; his accounts of the famous battle were rejected by most newspaper and magazine editors; and he was unable to attend his son's wedding for want of travel expenses. He finally landed a job as an examiner for the Bureau of Pensions, but apparently that did not last long. Reno developed cancer of the tongue and, complicated by erysipelas and pneumonia, passed away on March 29, 1889, at Providence Hospital in Washington, D.C. His brief obituary in the *Washington Evening Star* read: "Reno—In this city died, Marcus A. Reno, late major and Brevet Lt. Col., U.S. Army."

In 1926 Libbie Custer added her name to those believing Reno responsible for her husband's defeat. Upon the occasion of the unveiling of a memorial to Reno at the fiftieth anniversary ceremonies, she implored that no memorial "to so great a coward as Major Reno" be dedicated on the ground where her husband died. She would have been even more dismayed to know that on September 9, 1967, Reno was reinterred with full military honors in the cemetery at LITTLE BIGHORN BATTLEFIELD NATIONAL

Reno-Benteen Defense Site: View from bluffs showing the ravine soldiers descended to replenish water supplies from the Little Bighorn River

MONUMENT. This came about when Reno's great-nephew convinced the judge advocate general's office that Reno had been improperly dismissed from the service; thus making him the only Little Bighorn battle participant honored with such pomp and circumstance. *Sources for further study include:* A biography, *Faint the Trumpet Sounds,* by John Upton Terrell and George Walton (New York: David McKay, 1966); *Court-Martial of Major M. A. Reno Resulting in His Dismissal from the Service,* Senate Report no. 926, 47th Congress, 2nd Session, 1883; *The Reno Court of Inquiry: The* Chicago Times *Account* (Fort Collins, CO: Old Army, 1972); *Abstract of the Official Record of Proceedings of the Reno Court of Inquiry,* by W. A. Graham (Harrisburg, PA: Stackpole, 1954); and "Major Marcus A. Reno at the Little Bighorn," by Lee Noyes *North Dakota History* 28, no. 1 (1961).

Reno-Benteen Defense Site (aka the Hilltop Fight; June 25–27, 1876) At the Battle of the LITTLE BIGHORN, 7 companies of the SEVENTH CAVALRY under the command of Maj. Marcus RENO took up a defensive position on a bluff on the eastern side of the Little Bighorn River after retreating from the valley (see illustration above). The detachment endured 2 days pinned down by SIOUX and CHEYENNE Indians until the Indians departed when Gen. Alfred TERRY and reinforcements approached. (See RENO'S POWDER RIVER SCOUT and RENO'S VALLEY FIGHT first if chronological order is desired, and LITTLE BIGHORN, BATTLE OF THE, for simultaneous action, and LITTLE BIGHORN CAMPAIGN for an overall perspective of events.)

The remnants of Maj. Reno's beaten command took refuge on the high bluffs above the Little Bighorn River some 4 miles south of CUSTER HILL following the disastrous Reno's Valley Fight. Meanwhile, the 125-man battalion commanded by Capt. F. W. BENTEEN had been patrolling the ridges and ravines of the broken terrain to the left. After 6 grueling miles, Benteen had observed little but empty landscape and considered his march a wild goose chase. The village ahead was obscured by the winding nature of the Little Bighorn River and high promontories, and no Indians had been observed. Benteen had been on the scout for about 10 miles when he decided to follow orders—to use his own judgment—and return to the main trail followed by Custer, Reno, and the packtrain.

Benteen called a halt of perhaps 20 minutes to water the horses in a spring hole that one trooper described as "alkali and would take the hide off your tongue but it was wet." It was here that the sound of firing was first heard by Benteen's command: probably Reno's men engaged in the valley fight. Some of the officers, Capt. Thomas WEIR in particular, wanted to move out immediately. Benteen ignored the request for some time before finally mounting the battalion and riding out at a slow trot. Three miles later they passed the site of the abandoned Indian village with the smoldering lone tepee that Custer's REE scouts had earlier set on fire. Moments later, they met Sgt. Daniel KANIPE, who was taking orders from Custer requesting that Capt. Thomas McDOUGALL quickly bring up the packtrain of ammunition. Kanipe called, "We've got them, boys!" as he rode past. Although most of Benteen's battalion took that to mean that Custer had engaged the enemy, Benteen continued patiently along. About a mile farther, which brought them to within a mile or so of Reno's men on the bluff, Benteen again halted to water the horses. Custer's orderly, trumpeter Pvt. John MARTIN (Giovanni Martini), riding a wounded horse, came from the north to meet Benteen. Martin handed Benteen Custer's last known order. It had been hastily scribbled on notepaper by adjutant 1st Lt. W. W. COOKE, and read: "Benteen. Come on. Big village. Be Quick. Bring packs. W. W. Cooke. P. bring pacs." Benteen noted that the message had not been dated before reportedly showing it to Capt. Weir and 2nd Lt. EDGERLY. Martin, who spoke little English, made some sort of remark that the Indians had escaped, which was interpreted to mean that Custer had charged the village. Benteen claimed to not understand Custer's last message; the reactions of Weir and Edgerly are unknown. Boston CUSTER, who had been behind with the lagging packtrain, waved as he rode past heading north toward his brother's position.

Benteen's battalion now heard the unmistakable sound of firing. The order was given to move out, and moments later they began to gallop. The battalion topped the ridge for their first view of the valley below. The final moments of Reno's Valley Fight and the beginning of the fight on the bluffs was in progress. Benteen estimated that at least 1,500 Indians could be seen in the river bottom and farther downstream. Instead of charging down the valley, Benteen turned his battalion and rode for the bluffs on the eastern side of the Little Bighorn River. They were 200 yards from the place where Reno's men were gathering when Maj. Reno rode out to meet them. "For God's sake, Benteen," Reno implored, "halt your command and help me! I've lost half my men!" The 2 officers reportedly exchanged respective orders from Custer: Reno set in the belief that he would be supported by Custer's command once he had charged; Benteen offering Cooke's note to "Come on." Benteen asked about Custer's whereabouts. Reno could only inform him that Custer had started downstream with 5 companies. Neither man speculated at that time as to the reason why the Indians had suddenly broken contact with Reno's troops and had headed in Custer's direction; nor did Reno accept the fact that Benteen's order from 1st Lt. Cooke had now become his to obey. Benteen decided to join his command with Reno's 3 companies, which drew no protests from Reno.

Considerable firing continued to be heard from downstream by many of the men and officers with Reno and Benteen, who must have realized that it could involve none other than Custer's men. Neither Reno nor Benteen, however, could hear any firing from that direction other than a few sporadic shots, but 2nd Lt. VARNUM heard it; Dr. PORTER said it was heavy and sharp; Capt. MOYLAN described it as very faint; and Scout Muggins TAYLOR could hear it. When some officers and men suggested to Reno that they should ride to Custer's support, the major replied that they could not leave due to the short supply of ammunition, to which 2nd Lt. WALLACE replied that there was an open box from which the men could simply take what ammo they needed, and 1st Lt. (later Gen.) GODFREY also did not believe that they were short of ammo. He later wrote in *Century* magazine that the officers thought Custer was engaged and they should ride to his support, and that "the command ought to do something or Custer would be after Reno with a sharp stick." The Reno-Benteen command had procrastinated for more than 30 minutes without taking steps to establish contact with Custer. One age-old adage of military science dictated that, in the absence of orders, a command should march to the sound of firing. Reno, however, was more concerned about locating the body of his friend, 2nd Lt. Benny HODGSON. He took 10–12 troopers with him to the river below to search for Hodgson's remains.

Capt. Thomas Weir, commander of D Company, lost patience with Reno's timidity. Weir thought Reno's entire command should seek out Custer. He asked Reno to order such a move, or at least permit Weir and a detail to scout downstream. Permission for both requests was denied, and a heated exchange ensued. Weir then disobeyed orders and rode off on his own to the north. His second in command, 2nd Lt. Edgerly, believing that Weir had obtained permission, moved Company D down the ravine to the north. Weir rode forward about a mile or so to a promontory now known as WEIR POINT. There he could observe CUSTER HILL. His vision was obscured by dust and smoke, but nevertheless he could recognize Indians riding around shooting at objects on the ground. Weir then saw another group of Indians advancing toward Edgerly and the troopers in the ravine so he ordered them to high ground. Capt. McDougall had by this time brought his packtrain up to the bluff on which Reno's men had retreated. The captain had heard heavy firing from what he thought to be perhaps 3 miles away. When McDougall mentioned this to Reno, the major absently replied, "Captain, you have lost your lieutenant [Hodgson]. He has been killed down there." Then 2nd Lt. Luther HARE, who had assumed duty as Reno's adjutant, was ordered by the major to inform Weir that the rest of the command would soon join him and he directed Weir to attempt to open communication with Custer. This order had possibly been given at the urging of Benteen. Regardless, it was too late. The firing downstream had ceased.

Onto the Reno-Benteen Defense Site

An estimated 1,500 Sioux Indians, with possibly more hidden in the coulees, began advancing with great zeal from the north. Unknowingly, Company D, followed by Benteen and companies H, K, and M, and then the rest of the command straggling behind moved toward Weir's position. Most of the troops halted at Weir Point; some may have gone slightly farther. The soldiers then observed the large force of onrushing Indians, and an impromptu retreat ensued as the troops hurried back to the more defensible position where they had initially arrived on the bluffs. At some point the withdrawal became nominally organized in military fashion. Covering fire was supplied by one company as the others pulled back as a unit.

It was about 7 P.M. when a perimeter consisting of 7 companies had been established on the hilltop. The Indians were right on their rear guard and, fresh from the defeat of Reno and annihilation of Custer, were a formidable enemy. A ferocious barrage of Indian rifle fire from the surrounding bluffs and ravines pinned down the cavalrymen. The defensive position itself, about 100 feet above the Little Bighorn River, was formed by 2 parallel ridges running east and west with a depression, or swale, between, resembling a horseshoe or a saucer with an edge broken off. The troops ringed the crests of the ridges; with deployment of companies K, D, A, H, M, and B clockwise from the north. The horses, mules, and a field hospital for the wounded men were placed in the low-lying portion (see map on page 147).

The position on the bluff, however, was in the line of sight from several nearby ridges that were somewhat higher in elevation, making it extremely vulnerable. In the hours before darkness, snipers further punished the soldiers with their devastating fire.

The Indians, other than a number of well-positioned snipers, broke contact with the coming of darkness and returned to the village for a night of feasting, dancing, and recounting their individual exploits of daring and counting coup from the day's victories.

Meanwhile, the exhausted, desperate men trapped on the hilltop spent their time fortifying their position. An attempt was made to dig rifle pits, but the soil was too porous and there were few shovels. They resorted to fashioning breastworks with whatever was available to them: packs, saddles, hardtack boxes, and a picket line of dead horses and mules.

There was much debate on the Reno-Benteen Defense Site during the course of the night regarding the whereabouts of Custer and the other five companies of the 7th Cavalry. The Benteen faction swore that he had abandoned them; the Custer faction refuted that and stated that Custer would be there if at all humanly possible. Apparently no one seriously speculated that Custer had been defeated and killed by the Indians. One effort was made during the night to make contact with Custer or Gen. TERRY when several Indian scouts were sent outside the lines. However, they were fired upon and quickly returned.

The night, with its shadows and noises combined with the horror of the day, played havoc with the imaginations of the frightened, fatigued troopers. The worst fears were provoked by the clamorous celebration emanating from the village. The night reverberated with the rhythmic pounding of tom-toms, the exultant war cries of the men, and the terrifying wails of the women singing songs for their dead: all set in eerie shadows from the bouncing flames of huge bonfires. At one point it was thought that columns of cavalry could be recognized in the distance, which caused the trumpeters to be summoned to alert the soldiers to the hilltop position. However, hopes were quickly dashed when it was determined that the "cavalry" was probably Indians wearing army uniforms and riding cavalry mounts.

The conduct of Maj. Reno during that night has been the subject of controversy, with some testimony painting him as a drunken coward who hid in a protected position: one officer, 1st Lt. Godfrey, recalled that "it was evident that Reno carried no vigor or decision and his personal behavior gave us no confidence in him." In addition, Godfrey reported that he had not seen Reno during that night, nor had he received any orders from him. Capt. FRENCH swore that Reno had hidden himself from the evening of June 25 until about noon the next day. Another officer, 2nd Lt. Edgerly, testified that he had observed Reno apparently sleeping. Dr. Porter saw Reno during the night, as did Benteen, who claimed to have been with Reno most of that time. Reno was reportedly

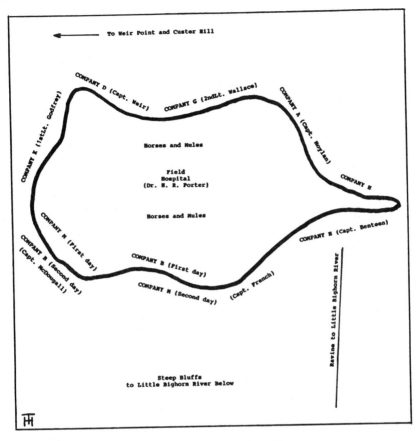

Field
Hospital
(Dr. H. R. Porter)

The Reno-Benteen Defense Site

seen by a civilian mule packer named John Frett who ran into him at the pack-train sometime between 9 and 10 P.M. Reno asked Frett a question that the packer did not understand. Reno became angry, and allegedly slapped Frett. The action caused a flask in Reno's other hand to spill whiskey on the packer. Other witnesses claimed that Reno gave the appearance of being under the influence of alcohol. Reno later admitted to having had a drink that night, but declared that he was perfectly sober. Another controversy that arose during that terrible night was created when Reno suggested to Benteen that they mount the command and make a forced march back to the base

camp on the Powder River. The wounded who could travel would accompany them; the wounded who could not be moved would be left behind. Benteen—to his credit—rejected the idea. However, the rumor spread to the wounded, which was only one of the horrible visions with which they and the other soldiers had to contend that night.

Capt. Benteen, it should be noted, displayed great courage—constantly exposing himself to fire throughout the ordeal—as he assumed de facto command of the unit.

The battle resumed at daybreak. The hilltop was surrounded by hundreds, perhaps thousands of Indians who sustained a withering fire, particularly from the ridges to the east and southeast. One sharpshooter on a hill 500 yards north gained the grudging respect of the troops for his accurate fire. Warriors had crept close to the lines during the night, which required immediate action or the defense would be overrun. Benteen assembled a detail of troops that counterattacked and pushed the surprised Indians back. From time to time warriors alone or in a group would charge on foot or horseback, only to be repulsed by a volley of fire from the line. There was nowhere to hide on the hilltop, and the troops were spread thinly in spots, particularly in H Company's sector. The number of Indians involved in the attack can not be accurately substantiated. Indian testimony later boasted that there were so many of them that not everyone could even take part in the attack. Reno estimated 2,500 or more, while others placed the number at no more than 500. Regardless, it clearly would have been possible for them to mount one concerted attack and overwhelm the hilltop defenders. Chief GALL, however, later explained that the medicine men did not consider the medicine right for such an attack. Besides, the sun and lack of water on the hill would soon become allies for the Indians, for the soldiers had been without water for quite some time.

Trooper Edwin Pickard's account reads: "Our throats were parched, the smoke stung our nostrils, it seemed as if our tongues had swollen so we couldn't close our mouths, and the heat of the sun seemed fairly to cook the blood in our veins." The wounded, in particular, needed water badly. The Little Bighorn River flowed about 600 yards away down a ravine in front of Benteen's line. The Indians, however, presently occupied this pathway to the water. Benteen assembled a number of his men and led a charge down the ravine and drove the surprised Indians away, killing several. Every pot, pan, canteen, and suitable container was then collected. Volunteers were requested. Sharpshooters were positioned to provide covering fire, and many successful trips were made with only 2 fatalities. MEDALS OF HONOR were awarded in 1878 to those water carriers, sharpshooters, and others who participated.

The Siege Ends

The heaviest of the Indians' fire slackened about noon on June 26. Some officers and men considered it a trick to lure them out of their position, where they could be easily picked off. It has been theorized that this was the point in time that the Terry-Gibbon Column had entered the valley. One pocket of Indian snipers, however, continued to rain devastation upon Capt. McDougall's B Company. A group of troopers from companies B and D were formed, and another charge on foot was executed to rout the hostiles. The officer in charge of this action has been a matter of dispute. Either Benteen or Reno, depending on who was asked, accompanied the soldiers. Nonetheless, the firing began to wane as the day wore on. In late afternoon the Indians attempted to fire the grass and could be seen packing up their village. Eventually, a column, perhaps 2–3 miles long, of Sioux and Cheyenne men, women, and children could be observed marching southward toward the Bighorn Mountains. Benteen stated: "It started about sunset and was in sight till darkness came. It was in a straight line about three miles long, and I think a half mile wide, as densely packed as animals could be. They had an advance guard and platoons formed, and were in as regular order as a corps or division." Edgerly stated that the estimated 20,000 ponies resembled "a great brown carpet being dragged over the ground." Reno, not knowing whether it was a trap or not—a few snipers had remained to pester them—decided to remain in that position for the time being. The surviving horses and mules were taken to the river to drink and then put out to graze. The cooks prepared supper, and the men on the lines relaxed, but were prepared to occupy their pits at a moment's notice. Scouts "Billy" JACKSON, George HERENDEEN and Fred GERARD, who had been trapped in the timber below, appeared on the bluff that evening, and 1st Lt. DERUDIO and Pvt. O'Neil soon followed. Each had his tale of harrowing experiences after being abandoned near the Indian village during Reno's Valley Fight the day before.

On the morning of June 27, there was much speculation on the hilltop as to the identity of the winding column of blue that could be viewed approaching from the south. Some thought it would be Custer; others guessed Gen. George CROOK. The rescuers were the Terry-Gibbon Column, following rumors that Custer had met the Indians. After contact was made, the entire outfit—the Montana Column, the survivors of the 7th Cavalry, the civilian packers, and other personnel—then moved to a more defensible position in the valley near the site of the abandoned Indian village.

The next morning, June 28, Reno and his survivors rode over to Custer Hill for the grisly task of burying their dead 7th Cavalry comrades. The bodies were placed in shallow graves—some in only a few inches of dirt and covered with brush—because of the scarcity of digging implements. (See INTERMENT.) The only living thing found on the battlefield was Capt. KEOGH's horse, COMANCHE, who was saved. Litters were prepared for the evacuation march of Reno's 60 wounded men to the steamer FAR WEST waiting on the Yellowstone River. The Battle of the Little Bighorn had come to a conclusion for the 7th Cavalry. *Sources for further study:* Follow LITTLE BIGHORN, BATTLE OF THE.

Reno Court of Inquiry The public as well as Maj. Marcus RENO himself welcomed this "investigation" into Reno's conduct during the Battle of the LITTLE BIGHORN. This court convened at the Palmer House in Chicago on January 13,

1879. However, the "inquiry" was little more than a song-and-dance performance. Reno was defended by civilian counsel, and was aided by the testimony of fellow officers desiring not to bring disgrace upon their unit. In other words, they closed ranks around the elite SEVENTH CAVALRY. Stories were carefully altered and were often evasive, and certain key witnesses were not called or were not available. The finding of the court was as follows: "While subordinates in some instances did more for the safety of the command by brilliant displays of courage than did Major Reno, there was nothing in his conduct which requires animadversion from this Court." The inquiry, which supposedly "cleared" Reno's name, was more farcical than credible and simply furthered the debate over his conduct.

Sources for further study include: The Reno Court of Inquiry: The Chicago Times *Account* (Fort Collins, CO: Old Army, 1972); *Abstract of the Official Record of Proceedings of the Reno Court of Inquiry,* by W. A. Graham (Harrisburg, PA: Stackpole, 1954).

Reno Creek The name the white man gave to a tributary of the Little Bighorn River that the SIOUX Indians called Ash Creek or Sundance Creek.

Reno's Hilltop Fight *see* RENO-BENTEEN DEFENSE SITE

Reno's Powder River Scout (June 7–19, 1876) As a prelude to the Battle of the LITTLE BIGHORN, Col. John GIBBON, commanding the Montana Column, arrived at the mouth of the Powder River and reported to Gen. Alfred TERRY aboard the steamer FAR WEST. Gibbon was of the opinion that the location of the hostile Indians was west of the Powder River and south of the Yellowstone River. Terry decided that a reconnaissance would be in order and, ignoring the protest of Custer who wanted to lead the command, chose Maj. Marcus

RENO for the scouting expedition. Had Terry thought that the scouting expedition would encounter Indians, Custer certainly would have been his choice to lead. He simply wanted to make certain that the specific area of the scout was free of hostiles. Custer, however, did not like Terry's plan, believing that the entire force should move forward and locate and attack the enemy. On June 13 Reno's command was camped on upper Mizpah Creek, a waterway that Terry had ordered him to scout. The major decided that he could see far enough in that direction from a promontory on the western divide that a scout was not necessary. Instead, he deviated from the assigned route and marched westward. On June 16 Reno discovered an abandoned Indian village estimated at 400 lodges and perhaps 1,000 warriors. Reno, in direct disobedience of Terry's orders, followed the trail of this village down the ROSEBUD. Reno came within 40 miles of Gen. George CROOK, who was engaged with the Indians at the Battle of the Rosebud on June 17. On June 19 Reno was camped upriver from Col. Gibbon at the mouth of the Rosebud, and notified Terry of his position. Reno's march, of which the original itinerary had called for about 175 miles, had traversed more than 240. Reno informed the general that he had not only scouted the Powder and Tongue valleys but had entered the Rosebud Valley following a fresh Indian trail. Both Terry and Custer were furious at Reno for exceeding his orders, and dressed him down. Terry had verbally warned Reno not to go to the Rosebud, and feared that the action had jeopardized his pincers movement with the three columns. The commanding general would perhaps have ordered a court-martial had Reno not been the only major in Custer's command. Custer's anger apparently stemmed from his belief that Reno should have pursued and attacked the hostiles he trailed. Reno, however, had provided vital information: he had identified where the Indians were not. Terry could

not assume that the Indians were heading toward the Valley of the Little Bighorn River, and could make plans accordingly.

Reno's Valley Fight (June 25, 1876) This action began the Battle of the LITTLE BIGHORN when Maj. Marcus RENO with 3 companies of the SEVENTH CAVALRY were ordered by Custer to charge the allied SIOUX and CHEYENNE Indian village. Inexplicably, Reno halted his charge, which led to disastrous results. The command retreated, and was then routed by the Indians. The cavalry suffered many casualties until taking refuge on a bluff across the Little Bighorn River. (See RENO-BENTEEN DEFENSE SITE; for chronological order see RENO'S POWDER RIVER SCOUT, RENO'S VALLEY FIGHT, RENO-BENTEEN DEFENSE SITE in that order; see LITTLE BIGHORN, BATTLE OF THE, for events preceding and simultaneous to Reno's Valley Fight; see LITTLE BIGHORN CAMPAIGN for an overall perspective.)

At the fork of Reno Creek, Adjutant 1st Lt. W. W. COOKE, accompanied by Capt. Myles KEOGH, relayed Custer's orders to Maj. Reno. Believing the Indians to be running away, Custer wanted Reno to move rapidly forward toward the village, "and charge afterward, and you will be supported by the whole outfit." Another version of the order replaced "charge afterward" with "charge after crossing the river." Reno's 3 companies— M, commanded by Capt. Myles MOYLAN; A, commanded by Capt. Thomas FRENCH; and G, commanded by 1st Lt. Donald MCINTOSH—about 140 men strong, moved out in that order and crossed Reno Creek a short distance upstream from where it flows into the Little Bighorn River. Cooke and Keogh, who had ridden along this far engaging in friendly banter, now departed and returned to Custer's position thought to be across the river on the high bluffs to the east.

Reno had traveled this far in columns

Reno's Valley Fight: View from bluffs showing position of the first skirmish line.

of fours, but now as he commenced his charge, he sent Company A and Company M forward in a line and held Company G in reserve.

The Charge

It was just after 3 P.M. The village was about 2 miles directly ahead, and the valley began significantly widening (see illustration this page). Reno ordered his command to accelerate from a trot to a gallop. The ground was level but ragged, having been reduced to loose dirt from the hooves and recent heavy grazing of the Indian pony herd. To their front, the troopers could see great swirls of dust and the flight of a number—perhaps 40–50—Indians driving ponies away. These Indians set fire to the grass in an effort to disguise their retreat. The surprised village was now aware that danger was approaching the southern end. The cavalrymen had the field to themselves; their enemy had yet to make an appearance.

Reno brought G company up on line with the other two, and across the prairie they galloped on a collision course with the village. The troopers, fueled by adrenaline and the anticipation of a fight, began to wildly cheer. Reno ordered them to be quiet.

The village was in bedlam. The women had been tending to their tasks, while the men were sleeping, fishing, racing ponies, or repairing weapons and equipment. Sioux Chief GALL said when word reached them that the soldiers were attacking, the order to strike camp was immediately given. He and a few other warriors then set out on their ponies to meet Reno and attempt to delay the entry of the soldiers into the village in order to allow enough time for their families to escape. Just outside the village, the Indians began racing their ponies back and forth to give them their second wind and to cover the retreat of the village. The soldiers steadily advanced toward their objective. An odd occurrence, however, was about to change the complexion of the entire battle.

The village lay straight ahead, there had been little opposition to this point, and he had not lost a man. Reno, however, in his first meaningful encounter with Plains Indians, inexplicably and abruptly aborted the charge and halted his battalion about a quarter of a mile before reaching the village. Perhaps the blinding dust swirls and smoke, or the uncertainty about Custer's whereabouts, or simply the pressure of command caused this decision. Reno later claimed that he had observed a ditch up ahead that held hundreds of warriors in ambush, a version of events that most eyewitnesses contradicted. In all fairness, a couple of his officers later stated that had the command continued forward they would have faced certain disaster; others disagreed.

We now know that there were more than 1,000 lodges in the village, which would mean at least 1,500 to 2,000 warriors. Reno, however, did not have that information at his disposal. Up to that moment, there had been no casualties, no direct contact with the enemy, and he should have known that the village would have been in a panicked state and packing to move. Chief Gall stated that only the fast approach of Reno deprived the Indians from all running away; there had been no time. It is probable that an officer more loyal to Custer would have carried out orders and charged that Indian village. Reno, on the other hand, appeared to have second-guessed a strategy on which he did not have complete knowledge, rather than execute his portion of it. There is no indication that Custer specifically stated that his other 5 companies would be coming in *behind* Reno's men as some, including Reno, seemed to interpret. It is evident that Custer's intentions for the other 5 companies was to flank the village on the eastern side of the river. Individual companies could then be sent down coulees

at intervals to cross and attack. The remaining detachment could ride for the northern end of the village to head off the escaping warriors. It had always been the custom of the Indians to scatter and run when their village was attacked. Flight was Custer's greatest fear, and he had no reason to believe that they would react otherwise in this instance. With that being the case, Reno's command on a charge into the village would have most likely suffered at least moderate casualties, but would have routed the Indians into the hands of Custer's 5 companies. And if Benteen and his men had arrived in timely fashion on the field the entire battle scenario would have dramatically improved for the U.S. Army.

Meanwhile, back on the prairie, Reno's halted troopers had dismounted and formed a skirmisher line a few hundred yards across. Some used a convenient prairie dog colony for breastworks. Several horses bolted: trooper G. F. Smith was carried into the village, never to be seen again. A detail was sent to reconnoiter the underbrush by the riverbank 50 yards to the east, and reported it clear. The horse holders (every fourth man) then led the mounts there for protection.

About 90 cavalrymen lay on the skirmisher line. Several observed Custer's command far away on the high bluffs a mile to the east at this point in time. The troopers now could see Indians gathering in growing numbers and, in spite of their being far out of range, began firing in earnest at them. Apparently, no attempt was made to control this heavy rate of fire. Ammunition supplies rapidly became exhausted. Every other trooper was sent to his horse down by the river to retrieve ammo from his saddlebags. When one returned the alternate man would then go. Intervals along the line were ignored; the men bunched together and became easier targets. Nevertheless, the troopers poured a barrage into the village: Gall reported that he lost 2 wives and 3 children in this onslaught.

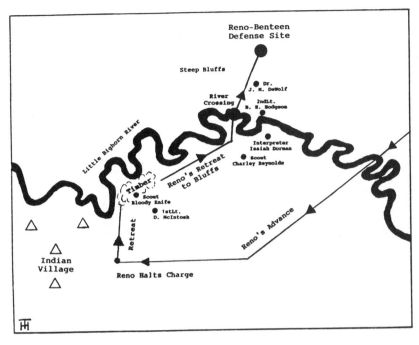

Reno's Valley Fight

The Retreat

A group of Indians was noticed maneuvering down the gully toward the horses, which caused Reno to order G Company off the line and to the river. That left the skirmisher line spread out much too thinly. Reno, who was now becoming flustered and uncertain of what course of action to undertake, either ordered a retreat to a stand of timber along the river or the battalion simply executed it of their own accord (see illustration on page 154). Regardless, no tactical covering fire was employed for the movement, and the soldiers' firing almost ceased as they fled. This permitted their mounted enemy to press forward more vigorously. It was now about 3:30 P.M. Reno's troops found protection in a stand of trees near a cut bank formed by the river's changing course. By this time, the gathering Indians had endeavored to surround Reno's command. However, the crescent-shaped

stand of timber—some 25 yards wide—was an excellent site to defend because of its density and thick underbrush. Additionally, it was lower in elevation and posed no direct threat to the village. The Indians were now free to pack up and move if they so desired. Reno's command had lost only several men killed and wounded up to this point. The troopers had been deployed, and set up a base of fire to keep the Indians at bay. Reno, in his wisdom, was planning too far ahead rather than devising a temporary strategy. It was evident that his command could not hold the timber indefinitely. They were short on ammo, had no rations, and no tools with which to use for digging in. Eventually, the Indians would creep through the high grass and overrun them. However, that would take 3, 4, perhaps many more hours. Custer could arrive before then, or at least Benteen.

Rather than simply holding the timber until it became necessary to move or

Reno's Valley Fight: View from bluffs, dotted line shows Reno's retreat route

waiting until reinforcements arrived, Reno reasoned that the high bluffs across the Little Bighorn River to the east afforded the best possible defensive position. There was one major problem: getting there. The river itself was one-half to one mile of open terrain away. Reno issued an oral order—ignoring a trumpet call that could have been heard above the din—for the command to mount in a small clearing and prepare to move out. Most men of companies A and M mounted, but Company G was scattered and was not formed by the time the others were ready to ride. In fact, many men had not heard the order to retreat. Others had problems controlling or catching their excited horses.

While the command was being formed, no provisions had been made for covering the move, and the soldiers' firing had almost completely ceased. This permitted a sizable party of Indians to approach within 30 yards of the gathered troops and fire their weapons point-blank. The volley was deadly; many troopers dropped. One casualty was BLOODY KNIFE, Custer's favorite ARIKARA scout. His death was notable because he had been conferring with Reno when a bullet struck him between the eyes, sending his blood and brains splattering onto the major's face. Reno panicked. He ordered the troops to dismount. Then he ordered them to remount. Then, without regard for the wounded in the timber, Reno put the spurs to his horse and tore off for the river. His disorganized command obediently trailed along behind.

No effort had been made by Reno to cover the retreat with a base of fire, and the fleeing soldiers could offer little resistance. The Indians initially thought the soldiers were attacking, and scattered. But to their surprise, it was quickly realized that the soldiers were actually running away. The warriors seized the opportunity, and rode to within about 50 feet away on the flanks of the loose formation and opened fire. It could be likened to a buffalo hunt for the Indians, as they easily picked off the exposed troopers one by one. The loss of life would have been even more devastating had the warriors ridden in closer. It is likely that the battalion would have been wiped out had that been the case. Scout Charley REYNOLDS left the timber a little late and had his horse shot out from under him. His dead body was found behind the horse with a pile of shell casings beside him indicating that he held out for some time. Interpreter Isaiah DORMAN also made a desperate last stand. The Indian army scouts suffered the worst of it. The soldiers could not distinguish them from the enemy, and the enemy had a special hatred for their brethren who worked for the white man.

When Reno's panicked command reached the Little Bighorn River, they found more obstacles in their way. The water itself slowed them up, but waiting on the far side was an 8-feet-high riverbank. The bank was steep and slippery, which caused the horses to balk, lose their footing, or become an easy target for a sniper's bullet. A few of the braver warriors closed with the bunched-up command and clubbed soldiers off their mounts. Those troopers who successfully reached the eastern shore and scrambled up the bluff offered no assistance to the others. No one organized them to provide covering fire for their comrades who were being blistered from both banks by the Indians. Military discipline had completely broken down. It was truly every man for himself. The route that Reno had taken from the timber to the river was easily identifiable by the dead bodies of both man and horse strewn along the way.

Company G commander, 1st Lt. Donald McINTOSH, was one of the last to leave the timber. He had 2 horses shot out from under him, and never made it to the river. He was last seen surrounded

by 20 or 30 determined Indians. Another group with 1st Lt. Charles DERUDIO, perhaps up to a dozen troopers, and scouts Billy JACKSON, George HERENDEEN and Fred GERARD, found themselves cut off from their retreating comrades. They remained secreted in the timber for the time being.

Meanwhile, that part of the command who had made it safely across the Little Bighorn straggled up to the top of the bluff, with Reno reportedly among the first to arrive. The Indians had for the most part broken contact. Only a token number of sharpshooters remained to harass the troops. The main body of Indians, released from the worry that their village was threatened by Reno's men, had been noticed riding toward the north on another pressing mission. The troops on the bluff thought nothing about the sudden disappearance of the enemy. They were too immersed in their own preservation to care. And that fact would soon become bad news for Gen. George Armstrong Custer, because it was his command that the Indians now targeted. It was about 4:10 P.M. About 40 of Reno's men had been killed and 13 wounded in the action. Acting assistant surgeon Dr. Henry PORTER approached Reno after their arrival on the bluff to notify him that the troops were quite demoralized by the bloody retreat. An irritated Reno replied, "That was a cavalry charge, sir!" (See RENO-BENTEEN DEFENSE SITE.)

Sources for further study: Follow LITTLE BIGHORN, BATTLE OF THE.

Responsibility for Custer's Defeat at the Battle of the Little Bighorn

Blame has been alternately, and at times collectively, placed on Custer, Maj. Marcus RENO, Capt. F. W. BENTEEN, Gen. Alfred TERRY, Gen. Phil SHERIDAN, Gen. George CROOK, the War Department, the Bureau of Indian Affairs, and even President U. S. GRANT. Perhaps each shares some responsibility. What if Custer had not underestimated his enemy? What if Reno had charged the

Indian village? What if Benteen had galloped to the rescue? What if Terry had formulated a more effective campaign strategy? What if Crook had pursued the SIOUX following the Battle of the ROSE-BUD? However, the most plausible reason for Custer's defeat is that the Sioux and CHEYENNE Indians had simply become sufficiently provoked and infuriated enough about their treatment to stand and fight. And, taking into consideration their overwhelming numbers on the field, even the best military strategy likely would have failed that day. The Indians fought for a cause in which they believed: indeed, their very existence. The troopers fought for $13 a month.

Reynolds, Charles Alexander ("Lonesome Charley"; March 20, 1842–June 25, 1876) Custer's chief white scout and friend, a quiet and introverted man, hence the nickname (see illustration on this page). Reynolds, who was well educated, shared many interests with Custer, including geology, zoology, and reading, and also neither smoked nor drank. He roamed the frontier at an early age, and served in a Kansas regiment during the Civil War. He worked as a trapper, supplier of firewood to steamships, buffalo hunter, and trader. In 1870 he supplied meat for FORT RICE, D.T., and was known to the local Indians as "White Hunter Who Never Goes Out for Nothing." He was a scout for the SEVENTH CAVALRY on the YELLOWSTONE EXPEDITION OF 1873 as well as the BLACK HILLS EXPEDITION OF 1874. On the latter Reynolds was entrusted with a message, dated August 2, 1874, that told about the discovery of gold. He traveled alone 100 miles in 4 nights to FORT LARAMIE through hostile country to deliver it. Custer had provided Charley with a canvas mail bag that had been inscribed: "Black Hills Express. Charley Reynolds, Manager. Connecting with All Points East, West, North, South. Cheap rates; Quick Transit; Safe Passage. We are protected by the Seventh Cavalry." In

"Lonesome Charley" Reynolds, 1874

December 1874 Reynolds happened to be visiting the Standing Rock Indian Agency when he overheard SIOUX warrior RAIN-IN-THE-FACE bragging about killing 3 men of Custer's command in the Yellowstone in 1873. Charley informed Custer, who dispatched Capt. YATES and Tom CUSTER to arrest Rain-in-the-Face. This led to the famous controversy about whether or not the warrior made good on a vow to eat Tom Custer's heart at the LITTLE BIGHORN Battle. (See CUSTER, THOMAS WARD for more detail.) Prior to that battle, Reynolds was suffering from an infected hand. It was suggested he remain behind, but he refused. On the morning of June 25, 1876—the day of the battle—Reynolds had a premonition that he was about to die and gave away all of his possessions. He was one of the scouts who visited the promontory known as CROW'S NEST with Custer that morning, and pointed out the distant Indian village. He was attached to Maj. Marcus RENO's command, and was later killed in RENO'S VALLEY FIGHT. Reynolds was late to leave the timber on Reno's retreat to the bluffs. His horse was shot out from under him, and he made a gallant last stand using the dead mount for breastworks. Many expended cartridges were found near his body. *Sources for further study include:* His diary, with entries from May 17–June 22, 1876, can be found in the archives of the Minnesota Historical Society; "Last Rites for Lonesome Charley Reynolds," by John S. Gray, *Montana* 13, no. 3 (1963); "On the Trail of Lonesome Charley Reynolds," by John S. Gray, *Chicago Westerner's Brand Book* 16, no. 8 (1959); and *Charley Reynolds,* by John E. and George J. Remsburg (Kansas City, MO 1931).

Roman Nose (Southern Cheyenne; 1830–68) This warrior became so famous in the 1860s that he was accused of nearly every Indian raid on the Plains. He became a terror along the BOZEMAN TRAIL, but agreed to meet with Gen. Winfield S. HANCOCK at FORT LARNED in the spring of 1867 during the HANCOCK EXPEDITION OF 1867. Roman Nose came away unimpressed, believing that Hancock wanted war. He returned to raiding wagon trains and railroad workers in Kansas. During this time, Custer and the SEVENTH CAVALRY chased him without success. However, Roman Nose's luck ran out on September 16, 1868, at the Battle of BEECHER'S ISLAND. He fully expected to die that day: the power was removed from his warbonnet the night before when a woman touched it. Indeed, he was shot through the spine that afternoon and died that night.

Rosebud, Battle of the (June 17, 1876) This battle was the first major engagement of the LITTLE BIGHORN CAMPAIGN and the GREAT SIOUX WAR OF 1876–77. It was fought near Rosebud Creek between a detachment of the U.S. Army commanded by Gen. George CROOK and a force of allied CHEYENNE and SIOUX Indians under CRAZY HORSE.

The fight was for all intents and purposes a stalemate. However, Crook proclaimed victory when the Indians broke contact and he was left holding the field of battle. That fact, however, did not prevent Crook from falling back to his camp on Goose Creek rather than pursuing his enemy.

In early June 1876 a Sioux and Cheyenne Indian village of about 400 lodges camped in the Valley of the Rosebud Creek, and held a sacred Sun Dance and prepared for war. In the meantime, Gen. Crook's column of more than 1,000 men had departed from Fort FETTERMAN on May 29 on a march toward the north as part of a 3-pronged net (the others being Col. John GIBBON from FORT ELLIS, MT; and Gen. Alfred TERRY with Custer from FORT ABRAHAM LINCOLN, D.T.), designed to close around allied Indians and force them onto reservations. On June 9 Crook's column reached the head of the Tongue River near the Wyoming-Montana border, and established a base camp there on Goose Creek to wait for the arrival from the reservations of 260 Shoshoni and CROW allies who desired to be part of the fight against their traditional enemies. Unknown to Crook, SITTING BULL's village lay directly in the path of the planned march, and the army had been under constant surveillance by Cheyenne scouts. When Crook finally broke camp on June 16 and headed down Rosebud Creek, the Indians became greatly concerned about the well-being of their families. They held a council, and it was decided that instead of waiting for Crook to approach, Crazy Horse would strike the army with around 500-1,000 warriors—perhaps half the total number available—while the others remained behind to protect the village. Crook and Crazy Horse and their respective men were on the move during the early morning hours of June 17.

Crook called a halt at midmorning for coffee and to graze the horses in a valley of broken terrain dotted with trees, bushes, and rocks. Crazy Horse appeared and spotted the army at about the same time that Crook's Crow Indian scouts spotted the hostile Indians. The scouts hightailed it for Crook, shouting out the warning as they rode for their lives. Crazy Horse departed from the customary tactics of circling around prey from a distance, and instead led a headlong charge into the surprised troopers. Due to the terrain, the fighting was fragmented: every man for himself in a battle of small, disorganized units. At one point Crook ordered the cavalry under Capt. Anson MILLS to head downstream to search for and attack the Indian village that he correctly surmised was located there. Mills became apprehensive when the valley became narrower with abundant ambush sites. Crazy Horse, the master of the decoy, had indeed deployed warriors in ambush. Perhaps the trick had been overused; Mills turned back and escaped disaster. After an undetermined period—possibly as long as three hours—of fierce fighting, the Indians massed for one final concentrated attack. Crook noticed this, and ordered Mills to regroup his cavalry and maneuver behind the Indians. This caused the Indians to break contact and leave the field to the army, effectively ending the Battle of the Rosebud.

The casualty figures have become a matter of controversy. Crook's official report claimed 10 dead and 21 wounded. Chief scout Frank GROUARD, however, set the figure at 28 killed and 56 wounded. Crazy Horse later said the Indians lost 36 warriors killed and 63 wounded.

Crook proclaimed victory because his men held the field at the end, but in truth he had fought to a stalemate at best. Some reports indicate that it might have been worse had not the army's Crow and Shoshoni allies saved the day on more than one occasion with bold feats of bravery. Crook, perhaps admitting defeat by his action, countermarched and returned to his camp back on Goose Creek. While the other army columns headed for a rendezvous with the Indians in the Valley of the Little Bighorn, Crook decided to re-

main safe and secure in camp: fishing, hunting, and licking his wounded pride. The general the Indians called "Three Stars" had of his own accord taken his command out of action, and failed to inform the other columns or anyone else about that decision. Meanwhile, Sitting Bull, Crazy Horse, and the others who had felt the taste of victory, struck the camp on the Rosebud and headed for a new site in the Valley of the Little Bighorn on a tributary called ASH CREEK. The village had more than doubled in size to over 1,000 lodges in one week, bolstered by the arrival of brethren who had left the reservations for a summer of freedom. The Indians' high spirits brought on by their success had them believing that they could whip the whole U.S. Army. They would get another chance to prove that belief about a week later at the Battle of the LITTLE BIG-HORN.

Sources for further study include: Campaigning with Crook, by Capt. Charles King (Norman: University of Oklahoma Press, 1961); With Crook at the Rosebud, by J. W. Vaughn (Harrisburg, PA: Stackpole, 1956); Battle of the Rosebud: Prelude to the Little Bighorn, by Neil C. Mangum (El Segundo, CA: Upton and Sons, 1987); Soldiers Falling into Camp: The Battles of the Rosebud and the Little Bighorn, by Frederick Lefthand, Joseph Marshall, and Robert Kammen (Encampment, WY: Affiliated Writers of America, 1991); and The Reynolds Campaign on Powder River, by J. W. Vaughn (Norman: University of Oklahoma Press, 1961).

Sabers Carried by Custer's Command at the Battle of the Little Bighorn Contrary to renderings by countless artists over the years in their depiction of the battle as well as the testimony from some allied Indian eyewitnesses, sabers were not carried on June 25, 1876, by the SEVENTH CAVALRY officers. They had been purposely left behind at the Powder River base camp.

Possible exceptions were the Italian count 1st Lt. Charles C. DeRUDIO and the Frenchman 1st Lt. Edward G. MATHEY. It has been said that European soldiers do not consider themselves fully dressed without wearing a saber. However, Mathey stated that his saber had been left with the packtrain, and DeRudio's was apparently missing after the battle.

Sand Creek, Massacre at (November 29, 1864) Almost 150 CHEYENNE people, in what had been designated a peaceful camp, were slaughtered by a troop of the Colorado militia. In the fall of 1864 the governor of Colorado had invited all Plains Indians in the area to prove their peaceful intentions by moving near the forts where they could be protected by the army. One such band of Cheyenne under Chief BLACK KETTLE presented themselves to FORT LYON. They were treated to supplies by the commandant, and directed to spend a peaceful and safe winter at a place about 40 miles northeast called Sand Creek. At dawn on November 29, a troop of Colorado militia under diabolic Methodist preacher, Col. John Chivington, attacked the unsuspecting village on Sand Creek. Chivington believed that it was honorable under God's law to kill Indians by any means. He ordered: "Kill and scalp all, big and little. Nits make lice." The Indians put up a fight, but within several hours nearly 200 Cheyenne men, women, and children had been killed, many scalped and mutilated. Chief Black Kettle escaped, but was killed almost 4 years later at the Battle of WASHITA. *Sources for further study include: The Fighting Cheyennes,* by George Bird Grinnell (Norman: University of Oklahoma Press, 1955); and *The Sand Creek Massacre,* by Stan Hoig (Norman: University of Oklahoma Press, 1961).

Sans Arc Sioux Indians (Those without bows; or No Bows) One of the Sioux Indian tribes present in the village at the Little Bighorn River on June 25, 1876, when Custer attacked. They were named as a result of setting aside their weapons at the behest of a hermaphrodite (bisexual) prophet, then being attacked by an enemy war party. Prominent Sans Arc warriors at Little Bighorn included Old Eagle, Two Eagles, and Black Eagle.

Santa Fe Trail The primary trade route from western Missouri to Santa Fe, New Mexico Territory, in use from about 1820 until replaced by the railroad about 1880.

Santee Sioux Indians (aka Minnesota Sioux) One of the Sioux tribes present in the village at the Little Bighorn River on June 25, 1876, when Custer attacked. Inkpaduta, who fled with SITTING BULL to Canada, was the most prominent member of his tribe.

Satanta (KIOWA; 1830–October 11, 1878) This Kiowa chief, known as the "Orator of the Plains," was a highly respected warrior and thorn in the side of the white man. He so impressed Gen. W. S. HANCOCK with his declarations of peace at an April meeting during the HANCOCK EXPEDITION OF 1867 that the general presented Satanta with a major general's dress uniform. Satanta later wore the uniform on a successful raid on the horse herd at FORT DODGE. In late 1867 he signed the Treaty of MEDICINE LODGE, but continued raiding on the southern Plains. Satanta was camped downstream from BLACK KETTLE's village during the Battle of WASHITA. The dead bodies of 2 white captives, Clara BLINN and her son, were later found in Satanta's abandoned village. Gen. Phil SHERIDAN and Custer tracked him down, but by then Satanta had secured a document from Col. William HAZEN that proclaimed him a peaceful Indian. The military men could do little more than order the Kiowa to move onto their reservation at FORT COBB. When the chief wavered, he was taken hostage and scheduled to hang should his followers fail to appear. Within 48 hours, enough Kiowas had straggled in to save their chief. (See WASHITA CAMPAIGN OF 1868–69.) Satanta was later imprisoned for murder and released in 1873. He fought the army in what was known as the Red River War of 1874–75—initiated to curtail hostilities in Texas—and was again imprisoned. On March 11, 1878, he committed suicide in the penitentiary by jumping out of a window in the hospital. *Sources for further study include: Satanta and the Kiowas*, by F. Stanley (Borger, TX: Jim Hess Printers, 1968); and *My Life on the Plains; Or, Personal Experiences with Indians*, by George A. Custer (New York: Sheldon, 1874).

Separation of Command by Custer Prior to the Battle of the Little Bighorn

Some scholars speculate that Custer was wrong to separate his command into 3 battalions at the mouth of Reno Creek prior to his advance toward the Little Bighorn Battlefield. Custer had, however, separated his command into 4 detachments at the Battle of WASHITA with great success. The actual effect this tactic would have had on the outcome of the Battle of the LITTLE BIGHORN will never be known, due to the fact that neither Maj. Marcus RENO nor Capt. F. W. BENTEEN had executed their orders to the letter. It had been the custom of the Plains Indians to flee when their village was attacked. It is entirely possible that, had Reno and his detachment of about 140 men continued the charge into the SIOUX and CHEYENNE village as ordered, the Indians would have been in such a panicked state that no organized defense and certainly no effective offense could have been established. In that case, Custer could have struck the village from his position on the east with his 225 men and caused further confusion. It would then have been a matter of securing the village and deploying the men for the expected counterattack.

However, by then Benteen and his 125 men would have arrived as ordered to reinforce the unit in a defensive position. Capt. Thomas McDOUGALL was on his way with the packtrain of ammunition and about 85 men. Custer would have had a force of over 500 cavalrymen, depending on prior casualties. The captured Indian women and children could have been held as hostages with which to bargain. Messengers could have been dispatched to hurry the Terry-Gibbon Column, which upon arrival would have afforded enough firepower to repel any counterattack. Considering the estimated number of warriors (1,500–2,000), and those being scattered about the area, the odds with 500 soldiers and more on the way would have been much more favorable. Therefore, it could be concluded that Custer's downfall was not caused solely by his separation of the command.

Seventh U.S. Cavalry (July 28, 1866–   )

The legendary army regiment never commanded by Custer but clearly associated with him.

Formation

The 7th Cavalry Regiment was one of four new regiments authorized by an act of Congress on July 28, 1866 (illustration, page 161). It was assigned to FORT RILEY, KS, with the primary mission of protecting surveyors and workers on the KANSAS PACIFIC RAILROAD from hostile Indians. Recruits arrived at the fort throughout the summer and fall, and by the end of the year most officers had reported. Lt. Col. Custer, second in command to Col. A. J. SMITH, who spent much of the time on detached duty, made his first appearance on the evening of November 3, 1866. He was accompanied by his wife Libbie, her friend, and their cook, Eliza BROWN. The regiment immediately began the work of turning raw recruits into soldiers. Regimental headquarters of the 7th Cavalry remained at Fort Riley, KS, while individual companies were assigned to garrison various posts on the

Seventh Cavalry, regimental standard

SANTA FE and SMOKY HILL TRAILS, including: FORT DODGE, KS; FORT HARKER, KS; FORT HAYS, KS; FORT LYON, Colorado Territory; FORT MORGAN, Colorado Territory; and FORT WALLACE, KS.

The Cavalryman

The enlisted cavalryman of Custer's era was a volunteer: a great number of immigrants from Ireland, Germany, Italy, and England; and many were Civil War veterans, who earned $13 a month and keep. He was taught to ride and care for his horse, and how to fight on horseback or dismounted. However, most of his day in garrison was spent fulfilling routine tasks such as stable call, guard duty, construction details, preparing for dress reviews or inspections, and participating in drill. He wore a dark blue blouse, sky blue trousers, a gray shirt, black boots, and a wide-brimmed hat of either army-issue blue or white straw during the hot summers. He was issued a .45 caliber Springfield Model 1873 single-shot, breech-loading carbine (see illustration on page 162), a 6-shot .45 caliber Colt single-action pistol, and a rarely used saber. His campaign outfit would consist of his weapons and cartridge belt, shelter half, blanket, canteen, mess kit, several days' rations (usually greasy salt pork and hardtack washed down with bitter coffee), haversack, poncho, extra clothing, extra ammunition, a feedbag, 15 pounds of grain, picket pin and lariat, and other personal items. He endured months of isolation, monotony, and rigid discipline, interrupted only by the occasional brief action against his enemy, the Plains Indian. *Sources for further study include: The Troopers: An Informal History of the Plains Cavalry,* by S. E. Whitman (New York: Hastings House, 1962); and *Forty Miles a Day on Beans and Hay:*

Model 1873 Springfield .45 caliber, single-shot, breech-loading carbine

The Enlisted Soldier Fighting the Indian Wars, by Don Rickey (Norman: University of Oklahoma Press, 1966).

Field Duty

Custer and the 7th Cavalry joined the HANCOCK EXPEDITION OF 1867 in early March in what became a futile search for hostile Indians. Custer's actions concerning personal business led to charges against him at a court-martial in September, which resulted in a year's suspension. The regiment remained mostly in garrison throughout the winter of 1867–68 when cold weather kept the Indians idle. The peace commissioners worked to make treaties with the Plains tribes. However, when spring arrived the hostilities commenced. Following a summer of war waged by the Indians, Gen. Phil SHERIDAN knew he must take drastic action. On September 1, 1868, Brig. Gen. Alfred SULLY marched out of FORT DODGE with 11 companies of the 7th Cavalry under acting commander Maj. Joel ELLIOTT for the purpose of punishing the Indians. Sully soon returned to Fort Dodge, his expedition an embarrassing failure. Sheridan called on Custer to rejoin the regiment early, and the 7th Cavalry marched again in October 1868, this time with a leader who had the en-

ergy and desire to fight Indians. Thus commenced the WASHITA CAMPAIGN OF 1868–69, which included the Battle of WASHITA and other encounters with Plains tribes. The expedition concluded in March 1869, a temporary success. In 1871 the 7th was assigned in small detachments around the south—Kentucky, Tennessee, and South Carolina—with orders to control the activities of the Ku Klux Klan and moonshiners. In the spring of 1873 the regiment reassembled in Memphis, TN, for the journey to FORT RICE, D.T. From there they marched in June on the YELLOWSTONE EXPEDITION OF 1873 to provide security for the NORTHERN PACIFIC RAILROAD survey team. This provided Custer with his initial encounter with SIOUX warrior CRAZY HORSE. The regiment returned from the expedition on September 23 to their new home, FORT ABRAHAM LINCOLN, near Bismarck, D.T. THE BLACK HILLS EXPEDITION OF 1874 marched out of Fort Lincoln July 2, 1874, with Custer commanding 10 companies of the 7th Cavalry. Their mission was to explore the wilderness region known as the BLACK HILLS, which had been given to the Sioux by treaty. The expedition found gold deposits on the Sioux reservation, which began a gold rush. The cavalry returned to Fort Lincoln on August 30 and settled in for the harsh Dakota winter. The year 1875 was spent with garrison duty, routine drills, and dress parades. In the spring of 1876 Custer and the 7th Cavalry marched out of Fort Lincoln on May 17 on the LITTLE BIGHORN CAMPAIGN as the band played the regimental battle song "GARRYOWEN." On June 25 Custer and more than 200 of his troopers were killed by Sioux and CHEYENNE Indians at the BATTLE OF THE LITTLE BIGHORN. The newly manned 7th Cavalry fought the following year in the NEZ PERCÉ CAMPAIGN, and in 1890 at WOUNDED KNEE to bring the Indian wars to an inglorious conclusion. The regiment answered the call in ensuing wars and conflicts, and continues to proudly serve its country.

Notable 7th Cavalry officers during the Custer years include (those with an [*] were present at the Battle of the Little Bighorn; those names italicized were killed at the Battle of the Little Bighorn): Albert BARNITZ, James M. BELL; *F. W. BENTEEN; *James *CALHOUN*; *W. W. *COOKE*; *John J. *CRITTENDEN* (attached); *George Armstrong *CUSTER*; *Thomas W. *CUSTER*; *Charles C. DERUDIO; *Winfield S. EDGERLY; Joel ELLIOTT; *Thomas H. FRENCH; *Francis M. GIBSON; *Edward S. GODFREY; Owen HALE; Louis M. HAMILTON; *Luther R. HARE; *Henry M. *HARRINGTON*; *Benjamin H. *HODGSON*; *Myles W. *KEOGH*; *Thomas M. MC-DOUGALL; *Donald *MCINTOSH*; *Edward G. MATHEY; *Myles MOYLAN; Henry J. NOWLAN; *James E. *PORTER*; *William Van W. *REILY*; *Marcus A. RENO; *Algernon E. *SMITH*; Andrew J. SMITH; *James G. *STURGIS*; Samuel D. STURGIS; Joseph TILFORD; *Charles A. VARNUM; *George D. WALLACE; *Thomas B. WEIR; and *George W. YATES.

Notable scouts, guides, and interpreters for the regiment during the Custer years include: *BLOODY KNIFE; *Mitch *BOUYER*; Buffalo Bill CODY; *CURLY; *Isaiah *DORMAN*; *Fred GERARD; Frank GROUARD; *George HEREN-DEEN; Wild Bill HICKOK; *Billy JACKSON; Moses (California Joe) MILNER; *Charley *REYNOLDS*.

Sources for further study include: *They Rode with Custer: A Biographical Directory of the Men That Rode with General George A. Custer,* edited by John M. Carroll (Bryan, TX: J. M. Carroll, 1987); *Of Garryowen in Glory: The History of the 7th U.S. Cavalry* by Melborne C. Chandler (Annadale, VA: Turnpike, 1960); the three personal recollections written by Elizabeth Bacon Custer: *"Boots and Saddles"; Or, Life in Dakota with General Custer* (Harper and Brothers, 1885), *Tenting on the Plains: Or, General Custer in Kansas and Texas* (New York: Harper and Brothers, 1887), and *Following the Guidon* (New York: Harper and Brothers, 1890); *My Life on the Plains; Or, Personal Experiences with Indians,* by George A. Custer (New York: Sheldon, 1874); *Rosters from Seventh U.S. Cavalry Campaigns, 1866–1896,* by Charles K. Mills (Bryan, TX: J. M. Carroll, 1983); *Custer's 7th Cavalry: From Fort Riley to the Little Bighorn,* by E. Lisle Reedstrom (New York: Sterling Publishing, 1992); and *Frontier Regulars: The United States Army and the Indian, 1866–1891,* by Robert M. Utley (New York: Macmillan, 1973.

Sharpshooter's Ridge This hill, 500 yards north of the RENO-BENTEEN DEFENSE SITE, was where an Indian sharpshooter gained the grudging respect of the cavalrymen for his effective marksmanship on June 26, 1876. He killed and wounded a number of the pinned-down troopers before either being killed himself or run off by concentrated fire from the perimeter.

Sheridan, Phillip H. ("Little Phil"; 1831–August 5, 1888) Sheridan graduated from West Point in 1853, a year late due to a suspension after threatening an upperclassman with a bayonet. He was subsequently assigned to the Northwest where he distinguished himself in the Yakima War of 1855. He entered the

Civil War a captain, and was promoted to brigadier general in 1862 and major general soon after. Sheridan became commander of the Army of the Potomac's cavalry in March 1864, thus inheriting Brig. Gen. Custer who proved himself a dependable division commander. Sheridan became famous for what was called "Sheridan's Ride," when he raced from Winchester to rally his troops—including Custer—at Cedar Creek. Sheridan, along with Gen. William SHERMAN, believed in the total war policy (a rein of terror on the civilian populace as well as the enemy army) that he perfected in the Shenandoah Valley and was eventually implemented successfully against the Plains Indians. He helped bring the Civil War to an end by cutting off the Confederate line of retreat from Appomattox. After the war he served as commander of the Department of Missouri with a mission of reconstruction. In 1869 Sheridan succeeded Sherman as commander of the Military Division of the Missouri—which included the departments of the Platte, Dakota, and Texas—extending from the Mississippi River west to the Rocky Mountains, and north and south from border to border. He continued to favor Custer, offering him the use of his private quarters at FORT LEAVENWORTH in 1867 after Custer's court-martial and suspension from the army; and calling Custer back to service early in order to lead the WASHITA CAMPAIGN OF 1868–69. It was on Sheridan's watch that the GREAT SIOUX WAR OF 1876–77 was fought—including the Battle of the LITTLE BIGHORN—and the Plains Indians were finally subdued by the military. He received his fourth star and succeeded Gen. Sherman as general in chief of the army in 1883. *Sources for further study include: Personal memoirs of P. H. Sheridan, General, United States Army*, by P. H. Sheridan, 2 vols. (New York: Charles Webster, 1888); and *Phil Sheridan and His Army*, by Paul A. Hutton (Lincoln: University of Nebraska Press, 1985).

Sherman, William Tecumseh (February 18, 1820–February 14, 1891) General, U.S. Army. "Cump" Sherman graduated from West Point in 1840, but resigned his commission in 1853 to go into business. He was failing in banking and other commercial endeavors when the Civil War came along and rescued him. Sherman became a prominent Union commander during the war, second only in importance to U. S. Grant. He fought at Bull Run, Shiloh, Vicksburg, Chattanooga, and was famous (or infamous) for his bloody and destructive march through Georgia to the sea. After the war he was commanding general of the Division of the Missouri that included the Great Plains, where most of the Indians' conflicts of Custer's time took place. He received a fourth star and became general in chief of the army in 1869. Sherman, along with Gen. SHERIDAN, believed in the total war policy (a rein of terror on the civilian populace as well as the enemy army) that he perfected on his march to the sea and was eventually implemented successfully against the Plains Indians. *Sources for further study include: William Tecumseh Sherman and the Settlement of the West*, by Robert G. Athearn (Norman: University of Oklahoma Press, 1956).

Sioux Indians (aka Dakota, Nakota; Lakota) This nomadic Indian tribe originated in Minnesota. In about 1775 they moved west to the Great Plains to follow herds of buffalo, becoming the final major group of Indians to arrive in that part of the country. The Sioux became the most resolute tribe in opposition to white incursions into their vast territory, and fought continuously against the U.S. Army until subdued in 1890.

The Sioux Warrior

Warfare was fundamental to the way of life for young males. Sioux warriors gained status within the tribe by brave deeds performed in battle with their enemies. Warfare was both sport and ceremony, and closely related to the supernatural. Young men would journey alone, usually to a mountaintop, and meditate without food or rest until a vision appeared. This image would become an important part of the warrior's protection and preparation for battle for the remainder of their lives. CRAZY HORSE, for example, never entered battle without painting his body with white hail spots, a streak of lightning on one cheek, and a brown pebble tied behind his ear. Horses were the Sioux medium of exchange. An individual's wealth was measured by the number of horses he possessed. Therefore, stealing horses from other tribes became the primary target of raids; war was generally waged only to defend their village or hunting ground. Counting coup was the act that brought the most glory upon a warrior. This meant closing with an enemy, and with a sacred stick or simply hand to hand, striking the first blow or wound. A coup could also be awarded for saving a life or stealing a horse. The reward for each coup was an eagle feather, worn in a warbonnet on subsequent raids.

A History of Warfare

It was during mid-nineteenth century that the white advance encroached upon Sioux land. A treaty was made at FORT LARAMIE in 1851 in hopes of forestalling trouble. However, as more and more whites came west—particularly during the Gold Rush of 1849—trouble was inevitable. The first major Sioux offensive came when warrior RED CLOUD rallied his people to fight the U.S. Army over the BOZEMAN TRAIL (illustration on page 166). The army built three forts with which to protect this travel route. Red Cloud waged war—the FETTERMAN FIGHT, the WAGON BOX FIGHT, and the HAYFIELD FIGHT—until the U.S. government relented and signed the FORT LARAMIE TREATY OF 1868. The Sioux were given a reservation—the GREAT SIOUX RESERVATION—which was composed of most of present-day South Dakota west of the Missouri River, including the BLACK HILLS. Red Cloud and others retired to this reservation. The younger warriors, however, refused to submit and continued raiding in an expanded territory.

The Sioux continued to fight western settlement by the whites. Crazy Horse led warriors against Custer during the YELLOWSTONE EXPEDITION OF 1873: an army operation with the mission of protecting surveyors for the NORTHERN PACIFIC RAILROAD. However, it was the following year when Custer led the BLACK HILLS EXPEDITION OF 1874 that the Sioux were most threatened. Custer's route, which the Sioux called the Thieves Road, intruded on their reservation. Worse yet, gold deposits had been discovered, and a hoard of prospectors followed. The U.S. government made entreaties toward the Indians to sell the Black Hills. Most reservation Indians were willing, but dissidents under SITTING BULL refused. Negotiations began but failed, and hostilities escalated.

The U.S. government lost patience with the Sioux over their refusal to sell the Black Hills as well as the continued raids on white wagon trains, mail routes, and settlements. Late in 1875 runners were sent with a message from Washington, D.C., to Sioux and their northern CHEYENNE allies camped in the area of the Yellowstone. All nonreservation Indians must report to the reservation by January 31, 1876, or the army would force them to submit. Had the band under Sitting Bull desired to comply—which they did not—it would have been difficult due to the limited ability to travel in winter. This led to the GREAT SIOUX WAR OF 1876–77, a series of skirmishes and battles between the Sioux and the U.S. Army.

The U.S. Army was determined to enforce its government's edict on the Sioux. First blood was drawn in March on the Powder River when a detachment of Gen. George CROOK's command destroyed a Sioux-Cheyenne village. In

From left: Sioux American Horse, "Buffalo Bill" Cody, Sioux warrior Red Cloud

early June at a sacred Sun Dance, Sitting Bull told of a vision: a vision of dead soldiers falling from the sky into their camp. This was interpreted by his people to mean that they would be victorious in battle against the army. On June 17 the Indians fought to a stalemate against Crook's forces at the Battle of the ROSE-BUD. Eight days later they annihilated 5 companies of the SEVENTH CAVALRY under Custer at the Battle of the LITTLE BIGHORN. Further battles ensued: SLIM BUTTES, DULL KNIFE, and WOLF MOUNTAINS. The U.S. Army bolstered by additional recruits, was relentless in its pursuit (illustration, page 167) of the Sioux.

Bands of Sioux, weary of battle, eventually straggled onto reservations during the following year. Crazy Horse surrendered in 1877, and was subsequently killed. Sitting Bull, after fleeing to Canada, finally submitted in 1881. However, Sioux resistance was not for all intents and purposes ended until 1890 when a new religion—called the Ghost Dance—led to the murder of Sitting Bull and the killing of nearly 150 men, women, and children at WOUNDED KNEE. See also AMERICAN HORSE; GALL; HE DOG; HUMP; PAWNEE KILLER; RAIN-IN-THE-FACE; SPOTTED TAIL; BLACKFEET; BRULÉ; HUNKPAPA; MINNICONJOU; OGLALA; SANS ARC; SANTEE; and TWO KETTLE. *Sources for further study include: A History of the Dakota or Sioux Indians,* by Doane Robinson (Minneapolis: Ross and Haines, 1904); *The Sioux: Life and Customs of a Warrior Society,* by Royal B. Hassrick (Norman: University of Oklahoma Press, 1964); and *The Last Days of the Sioux Nation,* by Robert M. Utley (New Haven, CT: Yale University Press, 1963).

Sitting Bull (Hunkpapa Sioux; 1831–90) Revered warrior, medicine

Sioux Indian camp on the Tongue River, 1879

man, and principle chief of the SIOUX Indians (see illustration, page 169).

Sitting Bull was born near present-day Bullhead, SD, the son of a chief named Jumping Bull. He was called "Slow," and was thought to be simply an ordinary boy. He killed his first buffalo at age 10, and touched a CROW Indian with his coup stick at age 14. It was that act of bravery that prompted his father to bestow upon him the name Sitting Bull. He was a member of the Strong Hearts warrior society, and became their chief in his early twenties. Sitting Bull was a fierce warrior, gaining the respect of his peers. He led raids against traditional Sioux enemies, such as the Crow, Blackfeet (including Piegan), Shoshoni, and ARAPAHO. It eventually became widely known that he was special, that his medicine was good, although he was not raised as a mystic. He was one of the few warriors who practiced the Sash Dance, where in the face of the enemy the participant pinned himself to the ground with a sash to show that he would never retreat.

Sitting Bull did not "touch the pen" to the Fort Laramie Treaty of 1851 that was to guarantee safe passage for white travelers along the Oregon Trail. However, he chose not to participate in the battles against Gratten in 1854 or the Battle of Ash Hollow the following year. His active opposition to white intrusion onto Sioux land came in the early 1860s when he began skirmishing with small army units and took part in the Battle of Killdeer Mountain in the summer of 1864. While RED CLOUD fought his war over the BOZEMAN TRAIL in 1866–68, Sitting Bull was raiding in the vicinity of FORT BUFORD in northern Montana Territory and Dakota. Red Cloud's FORT LARAMIE TREATY OF 1868 caused many Sioux to submit to the reservation. Sitting Bull, however, refused, and continued to follow the traditional nomadic way of life. He and his people would occasionally visit the reservation and obtain supplies from the Indian agent, while spreading discontent among their brethren. It was wandering bands under Sitting Bull that harassed Custer and his

SEVENTH CAVALRY on the YELLOW-STONE EXPEDITION OF 1873.

Although Sitting Bull had not signed the Fort Laramie Treaty, he was protective of what he considered Sioux land. He was angered to learn that Custer had violated the treaty by entering the BLACK HILLS on his BLACK HILLS EXPEDITION OF 1874. Worse yet, the discovery of gold deposits began an intrusion by hundreds of prospectors seeking their fortune. To a proud warrior like Sitting Bull, this was a declaration of war.

Sitting Bull became head of the war council, and gathered around him bands of Sioux and northern CHEYENNE. The U.S. government in late 1875 had dispatched runners to inform the Indians in the area of the Yellowstone that they must report to the reservation by January 31, 1876, or be considered hostile. In the case of their refusal, the army would come and force them to submit to the reservation. Sitting Bull, with his trusted warriors CRAZY HORSE, GALL, RAIN-IN-THE-FACE, and Cheyenne allies under TWO MOON, defied the edict. The first indication that the military meant business came in mid–March when troops under Gen. George CROOK attacked and destroyed a Sioux-Cheyenne village on the POWDER RIVER. Crazy Horse came to their rescue that night and recaptured the pony herd. However, the gauntlet had been thrown; the army must be fought.

In early June Sitting Bull and his followers camped in the Rosebud Valley and held a Sun Dance. The Indians arranged buffalo skulls and other tribal items and constructed an arbor with a pole in the middle. Strips of rawhide dangled to the ground from this center pole. Warriors would then have the skin of their chest slashed by a medicine man. A stick would be inserted inside the flesh, then attached to one strip of rawhide. The warrior would be lifted off the ground, and prove his fortitude by being supported solely by the strip of rawhide. He could not cry out or would he would be branded a squaw. Sitting Bull did not participate in this particular Sun Dance. Instead, he directed his adopted brother to slice strips of flesh from his arms. Sitting Bull then commenced dancing until he passed out. Once revived, he told of a vision: a vision of dead soldiers falling from the sky into their camp. This was interpreted by his people to mean that they would be victorious in battle against the enemy.

The first opportunity to verify Sitting Bull's vision came on June 17 when Crazy Horse led his warriors against Gen. George Crook's troops at the Battle of the ROSEBUD: a battle in which Sitting Bull did not participate. Although all the soldiers were not killed as was foretold in the vision, the results were sufficient enough to encourage the Indians that they could not be defeated by the government's army.

Two days later Sitting Bull moved his village into the Valley of the Little Bighorn River. During the previous week the village had more than doubled in size—from 400 lodges to nearly 1,000—including as many as 2,000 warriors. The population had been bolstered by brethren who had left the reservation to enjoy a summer of freedom. Six Sioux tribal circles and their northern Cheyenne allies filled the narrow valley. On June 25, 1876, Custer and the 7th Cavalry attacked this village. It began with RENO'S VALLEY FIGHT, an aborted charge of the village by Maj. Marcus RENO, who then retreated across the river to a bluff and dug in at the RENO-BENTEEN DEFENSE SITE. Custer with 5 companies struck the village from the eastern flank, and they were all killed. Sitting Bull did not actively participate in the battle; that was the responsibility of the young warriors. His place as an older chief and counselor was to protect the women and children. However, he did ride onto the field to rally his warriors when they counterattacked Reno's troops during RENO'S VALLEY FIGHT. Sitting Bull then rode near Custer's position to encourage his people and observe that engagement for a short time before returning to his duties in the village. His vision of soldiers falling into camp had come true.

Sitting Bull's village departed the day following the battle, and split up into smaller bands. Sitting Bull and his followers headed southwest—into the protection of the Bighorn Mountains—where they celebrated their victory with dances and feasts. However, the army remained on the trail as evidenced by the Battle of SLIM BUTTES and Crazy Horse's skirmish at DULL KNIFE village. In May 1877 Sitting Bull decided to take refuge in Canada. However, life was hard north of the border, and the Canadian government refused to provide supplies. On July 19, 1881, Sitting Bull and nearly 200 followers surrendered at Fort Buford, D.T. He was held prisoner at Fort Randall for two years before being permitted to settle on the Standing Rock Indian Agency. His protests about government neglect of Indian needs were ignored.

Sioux Medicine Man Sitting Bull, 1881

In 1885 he went on tour for one year as a featured attraction with Buffalo Bill CODY's Wild West Show. His reception by Eastern audiences was disrespectful, which caused him to leave the tour in disgust. He did profit from his notoriety, however, by learning to sign his name and selling autographs.

In late October 1890 the Sioux had embraced a new religion called the Ghost Dance. Sitting Bull did not participate in this ritual, but clearly enjoyed and encouraged the turmoil it provoked among his reservation brethren. The Indian agent believed that Sitting Bull was inciting Indians to defy the U.S. government, and ordered his arrest. A confrontation ensued outside Sitting Bull's cabin between more than 40 Indian po-lice, 100 soldiers, and the militant Ghost Dancers. In the resultant melee, Sitting Bull was shot and killed, not by a white man but by one of his own. *Sources for further study include: The Lance and the Shield: The Life and Times of Sitting Bull,* by Robert M. Utley (Henry Holt, 1993); *Sitting Bull: Champion of the Sioux,* by Stanley Vestal (Norman: University of Oklahoma Press, 1957); *Sitting Bull,* by Alexander B. Adams (New York: Putnam and Sons, 1973); "The True Story of the Death of Sitting Bull," by E. G. Fechet, *Proceedings and Collections of the Nebraska State Historical Society,* 2nd ser., 2 (1898); and "Surrender of Sitting Bull," by E. H. Allison, *South Dakota Historical Quarterly* 6 (1912).

Slim Buttes, Battle of (September 9, 1876) The U.S. Army, after the devastating defeat at the Battle of the LITTLE BIGHORN, continued its search for the hostile Indians who were responsible for the massacre. On September 9, 1876, Capt. Anson MILLS and about 150 cavalrymen from Gen. George CROOK's command located and attacked a SIOUX village consisting of 37 lodges. The Indians were routed from their homes, and took up a defensive position in a forested gulch, killing 3 and wounding 12 soldiers before eventually surrendering. The Indians lost several men and women as well as their chief AMERICAN HORSE, who died from a stomach wound. An inspection of the village turned up a gauntlet belonging to Cap. Myles KEOGH of the SEVENTH CAVALRY, who was killed at LITTLE BIGHORN; a guidon; various articles of cavalry clothing; and cavalry horses and saddles. While Capt. Mills and his men rested and ate captured buffalo meat, CRAZY HORSE and about 200 warriors attacked at about noon. The battle raged without a decision until Gen. Crook and his sizable command arrived in the late afternoon and the Indians broke contact. *Sources for further study include: Slim Buttes, 1876: An Episode of the Great Sioux War,* by Jerome A. Greene (Norman: University of Oklahoma Press, 1982); and *Campaigning with Crook,* by Charles King (Norman: University of Oklahoma Press, 1964).

Smith, Algernon E. (September 17, 1842–June 25, 1876) First lieutenant, 7th Cavalry. "Fresh" Smith began his Civil War career August 20, 1862, as a second lieutenant with the 117th New York Infantry. He was promoted to first lieutenant on April 25, 1864, and captain on October 12. He served primarily as a staff officer, but saw action during the siege of Petersburg, the Battle of Cold Harbor, and Drury's Farm. At Fort Fisher, NC, Smith was severely wounded in the shoulder and had limited use of his arm for the remainder of his life: he could not put on his coat without assistance. Smith was commissioned a second lieutenant in the SEVENTH CAVALRY on August 9, 1867, and promoted to first lieutenant on December 5, 1868. He served as regi-

mental quartermaster from March 31 until July 7, 1869. He applied in 1870 for disability retirement due to the arm injury, but withdrew the request. Col. Samuel STURGIS recommended Smith for discharge under the "BENZINE BOARDS" criteria that same year, calling him "wanting in integrity." The board, however, did not agree with Sturgis and returned Smith to duty as second in command of A company. Smith's wife, Nettie, was one of Libbie Custer's closest friends. In fact, during 1872 the Smiths and the Custers shared a house, with the two wives alternating housekeeping chores each week. In the spring of 1876 Smith was given command of E Company, the Gray Horse Troop: so named for the color of their mounts. It has been speculated that in the opening stages of the LITTLE BIGHORN Battle this company was deployed down MEDICINE TAIL COULEE to probe the flank of the Indian village. Company E was annihilated, and most of the bodies were said to have been located in DEEP RAVINE. Smith's body, however, was the only one of his company found on CUSTER HILL. He was reinterred on August 3, 1877, at FORT LEAVENWORTH, KS.

Smith, Andrew Jackson (April 28, 1815–January 30, 1897) Colonel, 7th Cavalry, commanding. Smith graduated from West Point, and served in the Mexican War and frontier posts prior to the Civil War. At the outbreak of war he was corps commander in the Army of the Tennessee with the brevet of major general. He distinguished himself at Vicksburg and Nashville, and had the distinction of defeating Confederate Gen. Nathan Bedford Forrest on July 14, 1864, at Tupelo, MS. He was appointed on July 28, 1866, as the first commanding officer of the SEVENTH CAVALRY. Smith preferred administrative duty as opposed to field duty, which permitted Custer to become de facto commander of the regiment in the field. In 1867 he filed the charges that led to Custer's court-martial, probably at the insistence of Gen. W. S. HANCOCK. Smith commanded the 7th Cavalry until May 6, 1869, when he resigned his commission to become postmaster of St. Louis, MO.

Smoky Hill Road or Trail This was one of the east–west routes through Kansas that was popular with those people migrating west following the Civil War. Along this trail were forts RILEY, HARKER, HAYS, and WALLACE, which were garrisoned by the SEVENTH CAVALRY. The trail was located within traditional CHEYENNE and ARAPAHO Indian hunting grounds, a location that caused hostilities between those tribes, their allies, and the whites. See the HANCOCK EXPEDITION OF 1867.

Spotted Tail (BRULÉ SIOUX; ca. 1833–81) This uncle of CRAZY HORSE became a proponent of peace after waging war against the whites in the 1860s under RED CLOUD. He signed the FORT LARAMIE TREATY OF 1868, and traveled many times to Washington, DC, for negotiations. Spotted Tail was not opposed to selling the BLACK HILLS to the U.S. government, and he was given the task by his tribe of attempting to set the price; which did not make him popular with certain hostile factions. He was appointed agency chief of the Sioux Indians—over Red Cloud—in 1876, and helped convince militant bands to surrender. However, many Sioux believed that Spotted Tail was irresponsible in his actions, and plotted to remove him from power. In 1881 he was shot to death by Crow Dog in a dispute over a woman. Crow Dog was tried, convicted, and imprisoned for the murder, but later freed when the U.S. Supreme Court handed down a landmark decision stating that federal courts had no jurisdiction on Indian reservations. *Sources for further study include: Spotted Tail's Folk: A History of the Brulé Sioux*, by George E. Hyde (Norman: University of Oklahoma Press, 1961).

Stanley, David Sloane (1828–1902) Colonel, U.S. Army. Stanley graduated from West Point in 1852, and was assigned to duty on the frontier. At the outbreak of the Civil War he refused a commission in the Confederate Army and joined Union forces in Missouri. In November 1862 Brig. Gen. Stanley became chief of cavalry of the Army of the Cumberland, and later returned west as a corps commander. Following the war he served in Texas and various frontier posts. Stanley, colonel of the 22nd Infantry, was chosen to lead the YELLOWSTONE EXPEDITION OF 1873, and was immediately at odds with Custer. The problem stemmed from Stanley's drinking problem and Custer's desire to be free of Stanley's supervision. Stanley was promoted to brigadier general in 1884; he retired from the service in 1892. *Sources for further study include: The Personal Memoirs of Major General David S. Stanley* (Cambridge, MA: Harvard University Press, 1917).

Strength of Allied Indians at the Battle of the Little Bighorn The question of how many SIOUX and CHEYENNE warriors were present at the battle was bandied about even before the smoke on the field had cleared. Estimates of anywhere between 1,000 and 9,000 fighting men—and even more—have been given by eyewitness testimony from both Indians and whites. Each version of the battle offers its own estimate, calculated by either the logical number of warriors per lodge in the village or by establishing credibility to one or more eyewitnesses—usually military observers. Capt. F. W. BENTEEN, for example, at first set the number at 1,500, then in later years changed it to 8,000–9,000 warriors. A safe estimate would be a minimum of 1,500 to 2,000; in any case, a superior number to the approximately 225 men of the 5 companies of Custer's command or the combined 12 companies of the SEVENTH CAVALRY—over 500 troops—that rode into battle that day.

Sturgis, James Garland (1854–76) Second lieutenant, 7th Cavalry. The son of Col. Samuel D. STURGIS, commander of the SEVENTH CAVALRY, was just a few months out of West Point when he marched for the Valley of the Little Bighorn. "Jack" was the youngest and final regular officer to be assigned to the regiment prior to the campaign: an assignment he requested due to his father's presence. Sturgis assumed third in command of M Company, and was said to be very popular with the troops. In the spring of 1876 he was transferred to E Company where he became second in command. At the Battle of the LITTLE BIGHORN he was killed with Custer's command, possibly in DEEP RAVINE where many Company E troopers' bodies were said to have been found. Sturgis's remains, however, were never found. His blood-soaked undergarments were found in the abandoned Indian village by the Terry-Gibbon column two days after the battle. His sister, Ella, who later became the subject of a peeping Tom incident by Maj. Marcus RENO, visited the battlefield but could not identify her brother's remains. A photograph of a primitive monument of stones with a board lettered "Lt. STURGIS 7th CAV JUNE, '76" is in the U.S. Signal Corps archives. This photo, however, was the result of a ruse perpetrated on Sturgis's mother when she visited the battlefield in 1881. She had not been informed that her son's remains had not been recovered. In late summer after the battle a temporary military post was established at BEAR BUTTE on the edge of the BLACK HILLS and named Camp Sturgis in his honor.

Sturgis, Samuel Davis (1822–89) Colonel, 7th Cavalry. Sturgis graduated from West Point in 1846 and served in the Mexican War, where he was captured and held prisoner for eight days. During the Civil War, he served as a cavalry division and corps commander. He fought in such battles as Second Bull Run, South Mountain, Antietam, and Fredericks-burg, and won brevets to brigadier general. His failure to contain Confederate cavalryman Nathan Bedford Forrest in eastern Tennessee, however, led to his being relieved of duty. He faced an inquiry, and spent the remainder of the war awaiting assignment. Sturgis became commanding officer of the SEVENTH CAVALRY in the spring of 1869. He remained in an administrative role, however, and did not participate in any of the regiment's expeditions or battles. His son, 2nd Lt. James G. STURGIS, was with Custer at the Battle of the LITTLE BIGHORN and was killed, his body never found. In the fall of 1877 Sturgis took field command of his regiment to successfully pursue the NEZ PERCÉ Indians. In April 1878 he issued a general order that honored and retired the cavalry horse COMANCHE, the only living thing found on the battlefield following the Battle of the Little Bighorn. In 1879, when Sturgis was headquartered at FORT MEADE, D.T., he had occasion to court-martial Maj. Marcus RENO. Sturgis retired as a colonel in 1888.

Suicide Allegations Relative to Custer's Command at the Battle of the Little Bighorn The theory that Custer's command committed mass suicide at the Battle of the LITTLE BIGHORN was advanced by Dr. Thomas B. Marquis, a government physician who lived and worked on the northern CHEYENNE Reservation in 1922–23, and thereafter had a private practice at Lodge Grass, MT. He gained the trust of the Cheyenne, and spent many years researching and writing about the battle. Marquis's primary informants were the Cheyenne warrior WOODEN LEG, and Kate Bighead, who was on the field shortly after the battle. This contention is likely to be incorrect. It is certainly conceivable that some soldiers might have committed suicide when all hope was lost. They would have known about or had possibly witnessed the results of the torture that would have faced them had they been taken alive. However, a mass suicide, with all due respect to Dr. Marquis, is doubtful. Wooden Leg in later years recanted his story; and nothing can be found in SIOUX oral history to support the Cheyenne contention. Custer, by the way, had no powder burns on his temple surrounding the bullet hole and would have had to awkwardly execute the deed lefthanded. Dr. Marquis presents his case in *Keep the Last Bullet for Yourself: The True Story of Custer's Last Stand* (New York: Reference Publications, 1976).

Sully, Alfred (1821–79) General, U.S. Army. This son of famed artist Thomas Sully graduated from West Point in 1841 and was commissioned a second lieutenant in the 2nd Infantry. He fought in the Seminole War and Mexican War before being appointed as colonel of the 1st Minnesota Infantry in 1862. In September 1862 he was commissioned a brigadier general and sent to the upper Missouri to fight not the Confederacy but SIOUX Indians. For the next three years Sully pursued the Indians around Dakota. After the Civil War he remained in the West and gained the reputation as an "ambulance" general: preferring to ride rather than seek action. This caused him to be removed by Gen. Phil SHERIDAN from field command in the WASHITA CAMPAIGN OF 1868–69 in favor of Custer. He later became superintendent of Indian Affairs for Montana, and was embroiled in a controversy over the massacre of 170 Piegans of the Blackfeet Confederacy in January 1870. Over the years he painted many Western landscapes, specializing in views of forts. *Sources for further study include: No Tears for the General: The Life of Alfred Sully, 1821–1879*, edited by Langdon Sully (Palo Alto, CA: American West, 1974).

Summit Springs, Battle of (July 11, 1869) This battle, waged between the 5th Cavalry under Maj. Eugene Carr and CHEYENNE Indians led by TALL BULL,

was an army victory that virtually ended Cheyenne hostilities on the Great Plains. Following the close of the WASHITA CAMPAIGN OF 1868–69, many Cheyenne Indians procrastinated about submitting to the reservation. Fearing that there would be another summer of Indian raids, the Republican River Expedition was formed by the U.S. Army for the purpose of rounding up Cheyenne renegades. While Custer and his command remained in garrison at FORT HAYS, the 5th Cavalry under Maj. Carr, accompanied by a battalion of Frank North's Pawnee Indian scouts and Buffalo Bill CODY, marched from FORT McPHERSON on June 9. On July 11 the soldiers attacked an Indian village of 84 lodges at Summit Springs, about 60 miles upstream from FORT SEDGWICK on the South Platte River. The surprised Indians fled, but not before losing 52 killed, including Chief Tall Bull, and 17 women and children were taken prisoner. Army losses were 1 wounded. There were 2 white captives in the village: Mrs. Susanna Alderice who was killed, and Mrs. Maria Weichell who was critically wounded but survived. This engagement effectively disorganized the Cheyenne, and they began to straggle onto their reservation.

Sundance Creek This was the name, along with Ash Creek, that the SIOUX called the waterway the whites named Reno Creek, which flowed into the Little Bighorn River.

Survivors Reputedly from Custer's Command Following the Battle of the Little Bighorn Many people came forward in the ensuing years claiming to have been the sole survivor of the famous battle. Some even squeezed a living from their story by fleecing gullible tourists or ambitious Eastern writers. The first sole survivor was reputed to be Custer's CROW Indian scout, CURLY. Over the years he encouraged researchers with several tantalizing tales of daring escapes.

They were all untrue. Curly was confronted by SIOUX Chief GALL at the tenth reunion of the battle. Gall told the Crow scout that had he been there that day he would now be dead. Curly declined to answer. There was perhaps only one remotely credible claimant as the last survivor: his name was Frank Finkel (aka Frank Hall), a resident of Dayton, WA, whose story appeared as a feature in the *Walla Walla Bulletin* on March 20, 1921. He claimed that he had been a member of C Company under Capt. Tom CUSTER on the battlefield that day. He further stated that he had been wounded several times, and escaped when his horse bolted. He had been found the next morning by a man, possibly a trapper, at a cabin some miles away, and nursed back to health. Finkel said he had then reported to Fort Benton and told his story to a disbelieving officer in charge. Soon thereafter he deserted, and became a farmer in St. Louis and later in Dayton, WA. His description of the terrain was near perfect, and his body showed scars from bullet wounds. The one problem with Finkel's story that has prevented historians from accurately gauging its credibility has been the lack of the alias he used to enlist in the army, the practice of which was common at that time. He died in 1930 from a malignancy caused by a bullet in his side that had been received decades before, perhaps from an Indian rifle during the Battle of the Little Bighorn.

Tall Bull (Southern CHEYENNE, ca. 1815–1869) Tall Bull was one of the leaders of the warrior society known as the Dog Soldiers during the 1850s and 1860s. He signed the MEDICINE LODGE TREATY in 1867, but ignored its provision and encouraged hostilities against the whites. He met with Gen. W. S. HANCOCK at FORT LARNED during the HANCOCK EXPEDITION OF 1867, and Custer described him as "a fine, warlike–looking chieftain." Tall Bull claimed at the time that he liked white people and that he

would be pleased to accept presents. He participated in the 1868 Battle of BEECHER'S ISLAND, and was killed July 11, 1869, at the Battle of SUMMIT SPRINGS.

Taylor, H. M. "Muggins" This U.S. Army scout carried the first news of the Battle of the LITTLE BIGHORN to the outside world. Col. John GIBBON wrote the message, dated June 28, 1876, on pages torn from his notebook: "General Custer's command met with terrible disaster here on the 25th. Custer, with five companies, were so for as we can ascertain, completely annihilated." Taylor was instructed to deliver the message to Capt. D. W. Benham at FORT ELLIS, MT. He left camp on June 28, but by July 2 he arrived exhausted in Stillwater (present-day Columbus), MT, where he spent the night. Taylor and local resident Horace Countryman departed the next morning, and arrived at Fort Ellis by mid-afternoon. Muggins delivered the message, but for some inexplicable reason it was not transmitted over the telegraph until after the July 4 Centennial celebrations were completed. Countryman, on the other hand, paid a visit to E. S. Wilkinson, editor of the *Bozeman Times*, who published an "Extra" at 7 P.M. that evening, thus scooping every other newspaper in the land by publishing the first story of Custer's defeat. *Sources for further study include:* "Montana Editors and the Custer Battle," by Rex C. Myers, *Montana: The Magazine of Western History* 26 (Spring 1976), reprinted as a chapter in *The Great Sioux War 1876–77: The Best from* Montana: The Magazine of Western History, edited by Paul L. Hedren (Helena: Montana Historical Society, 1991).

Terry, Alfred Howe (1827–90) Brigadier general U.S. Army, commander of the Department of Dakota, which included the state of Minnesota and the territories of Dakota and Montana. Terry had succeeded Gen. W. S. HANCOCK in the spring of 1873 prior to the YELLOW-STONE EXPEDITION OF 1873. He had been a lawyer before the Civil War, and his successes in that conflict had gained him a regular army commission. He served on the commission that condemned the SAND CREEK MASSACRE, and as a member of the 1867–68 peace commission appointed by Congress to negotiate the MEDICINE LODGE treaties with the Plains tribes. Terry was a strong advocate of Indian rights, and a proponent of arming the Indians with the latest weapons for hunting purposes. He opposed white intrusion into the BLACK HILLS, but supervised the expedition of 1874 and 1875 and served on the commission that negotiated their sale. In the spring of 1876, when Custer found himself bogged down in Washington politics (see BELKNAP SCANDAL), Terry was grudgingly obliged to command the Dakota Column on the LITTLE BIGHORN CAMPAIGN.

Custer was so devastated by President GRANT's refusal to allow him to accompany the SEVENTH CAVALRY that he sought out Terry at his headquarters in St. Paul on May 6 and, as Terry later related, "with tears in his eyes, begged my aid." Terry, who was known as a kindly man, had never fought Indians and had no particular interest in doing so without Custer. He sent a message to Grant and, without questioning the president's prior order, made it clear that Custer's services would be quite useful to ensure a successful campaign. Grant relented, and Custer was free to report for the march. One of the many controversies that has surrounded the march was the accusation that Custer had willfully disobeyed orders and thereby brought abut the loss of his command. The only documented evidence that remains to substantiate or refute this accusation is the written order from Gen. Terry to Custer pertaining to the march. The issuance of this order came a day after a June 21, 1876, strategy meeting on board the steamer FAR WEST, attended by Gen.

Terry, Custer, Col. John GIBBON, and Maj. James BRISBIN, where verbal orders in all likelihood were provided. It was Terry's strategy to have the scouts and guides locate the Indians, then strike with two columns (Custer and Gibbon) within cooperating distance: a "waiting fight" where one would, if possible, give time for the other to come up. Regardless of the debate about orders, the Terry-Gibbon Column arrived on the LITTLE BIGHORN Battlefield on June 27, 1876, to discover the grisly scene of Custer's annihilated command. (See DISOBEDIENCE OF ORDERS BY CUSTER AT LITTLE BIGHORN for more, including the text of Gen. Terry's order.) In the fall of 1877 Terry met with SITTING BULL in Canada and offered amnesty but was refused. In 1886 he became commander of the Division of the Missouri, and then retired in 1888. His death came the day after Sitting Bull was shot and killed. *Sources for further study include: The Field Diary of General Alfred H. Terry: The Yellowstone Expedition—1876* (Bellevue, NE: Old Army, 1970); and *Pacifying the Plains: General Alfred Terry and the Decline of the Sioux, 1866–1890*, by John W. Bailey (Westport, CT: Greenwood, 1979).

Teton Sioux Indians *see* SIOUX INDIANS.

Thieves Road   This was the name given by the SIOUX Indians to Custer's route into the BLACK HILLS during the BLACK HILLS EXPEDITION OF 1874.

Tilford, Joseph G. Major, 7th Cavalry. Tilford was a reluctant battalion commander during the BLACK HILLS EXPEDITION OF 1874. He had chosen to remain at FORT RICE, but was pressed into duty when no other officer could be found. He was described as being in ill health—he had missed the YELLOWSTONE EXPEDITION for this reason—and of ill temperament, and was known as a Custer antagonist. At the time of the LITTLE BIGHORN CAMPAIGN Tilford was on a leave of absence. He did enter Custer's life (death?) once more when in July 1877 he wrote to widow Libbie Custer. The out of character yet magnanimous letter certainly soothed Libbie's worry over the identification of her husband's remains. The text is from *General Custer's Libbie*, by Lawrence A. Frost (Seattle: Superior Publishing , 1976.)

On yesterday ... I shipped by U.S. Express via Chicago, the remains of your heroic husband Genl. Custer to West Point, N.Y., care of the Commanding Officer of that Post. Those were my instructions from Genl. Sheridan. I presume an officer will accompany the remains from Chicago on. It may be some consolation for you to know that I personally superintended the transfer of the remains from the box in which they came from the battlefield to the casket which conveys them to West Point. I enclose you a lock of hair taken from the remains which are so precious to you. I also kept a few hairs for myself as having been worn by a man who was my beau ideal of a soldier and honorable Gentleman.

Turf, Field and Farm **Magazine** This sportsman's weekly began publishing in 1865 and, until it was absorbed by *Sports of the Times* in 1903, was one of the country's leading publications. Custer, under the pseudonym Nomad, published 15 letters between 1867 and 1876 that described his adventures with horses, hounds, and hunting. The letters have been compiled into a book, *Nomad—George A. Custer in Turf, Field and Farm*, edited by Brian W. Dippie (Austin: University of Texas Press, 1980).

Two Kettle(s) One of the tribes of SIOUX Indians present in the village on the Little Bighorn River on June 25, 1876, when Custer attacked. Their name apparently was derived from "Two Cookings," for the fact that their hunters claimed they could provide meat enough for two meals on one hunt.

Two Moon(s) (Northern CHEYENNE; 1847–1917) Two Moon's uncle, Two Moon, was one of the chiefs who pleaded with the army in 1866 to discontinue construction of FORT PHIL KEARNY on the BOZEMAN TRAIL in the Powder River country, accurately predicting that it would mean war. (See RED CLOUD.) On March 17, 1876, Two Moon's village was attacked and destroyed by Col. J. J. Reynolds of General George CROOK's command in the POWDER RIVER FIGHT. Although there were few casualties, the army burned tepees, clothing, and the meat supply. The angry Cheyenne fled to SITTING BULL's village, and prepared for war. Two Moon participated in the Battle of the LITTLE BIGHORN, and has been credited—with a host of others—with killing or counting first coup on Custer. In 1877 he surrendered to Gen. MILES, and served as an army scout in the NEZ PERCÉ War. In the ensuing years, he was a source of much information regarding the Little Bighorn Battle. Two Moon was the model for the "buffalo" or Indian Head nickel that was circulated in 1913 (see illustration, page 177*). Sources for further study include:* "General Custer's Fight as Seen by Two Moon," by Hamlin Garland, *McClure's Magazine* 11 (May–October 1898); "Last Summer's Expedition against the Sioux," by John Gibbon, *American Catholic Quarterly Review* 2 (April 1877); and *The Custer Myth: A Source Book of Custeriana*, edited by W. A. Graham (Harrisburg, PA: Stackpole, 1953).

Unceded Indian Territory This area, which was roughly east of the Bighorn Mountains and north of the North Platte River (known as the Powder River Basin Country) was reserved by treaty for Indian use only: no whites could trespass without Indian consent. The exact boundaries became an issue of debate, especially with the Indian who considered traditional buffalo hunting grounds, such as the Yellowstone Basin, to be included. This territory became a haven for those Indians who refused to sign treaties and report to reservations, among them SITTING BULL, GALL, and CRAZY HORSE. In the summer months other Indians would leave the reservation to join bands of their "free" kinsmen in the unceded territory to live in the old way of life.

Union Pacific Railroad, Eastern Division This railroad reorganized in the late 1860s as the KANSAS PACIFIC RAILROAD.

Unkpapa *see* HUNKPAPA

U.S. Bureau of Indian Affairs This government agency was created in 1824 to oversee the welfare of American Indians. It was responsible for supervising reservations and providing goods and services, such as education, to the Indian. For a description of operations at the time of the Battle of the LITTLE BIGHORN see GRANT, U. S.

Varnum, Charles Albert (June 21, 1849–February 26, 1936) Second Lieutenant, 7th Cavalry. Varnum graduated from West Point in 1872 (a classmate of 2nd Lt. George D. WALLACE), and was assigned to Company A of the SEVENTH CAVALRY. He participated in the YELLOWSTONE EXPEDITION OF 1873 and the BLACK HILLS EXPEDITION OF 1874. He was on temporary duty as chief of scouts at the Battle of the LITTLE BIGHORN. Varnum was on advance guard ahead of Custer's column on the march up the Rosebud, following the Indian trail into Little Bighorn Valley. Early in the morning on the day of the battle, June 25, Varnum led a party of scouts that included Charley REYNOLDS, Mitch BOUYER, and a number of CROW and REE Indians to a traditional Indian lookout called CROW'S NEST which, unknown to them, was located some 15 miles from SITTING BULL's village. The village itself could not be observed, but the scouts recognized smoke and what they believed to

Cheyenne Chief Two Moon

be a sizable pony herd grazing in the valley. Reynolds claimed it was "the largest pony herd any white man ever laid eyes on." Varnum summoned Custer, but by the time he arrived at Crow's Nest about 9 A.M. a haze had settled over the hilly terrain that made it impossible to recognize anything that far away. Custer did, however, accept his scouts' assessment that a huge Indian village lay ahead. Varnum remained with the scouts attached to the command of Maj. Marcus RENO, and participated in RENO'S VALLEY FIGHT and the RENO-BENTEEN DEFENSE SITE. Varnum fought in the NEZ PERCÉ Campaign of 1877; the Battle of WOUNDED KNEE (where he had his pipe shot out of his mouth); and one day later at White Clay Creek where he was awarded the Medal of Honor for most distinguished gallantry. He was retired on disability in 1907, and became the final surviving officer of the Battle of Little Bighorn. *Sources for further study include:* His unfinished memoir was published as *Custer's Chief of Scouts: The Reminiscences of Charles A. Varnum*, edited by John M. Carroll (Lincoln: University of Nebraska Press, 1987); "Interview with Charles A. Varnum, May 1909," in *Custer in '76: Walter Camp's Notes on the Custer Fight*, edited by Kenneth Hammer (Provo, UT: Brigham Young University Press, 1976); and numerous references in *The Custer Myth: A Source Book of*

Custeriana, edited by W. A. Graham (Harrisburg, PA: Stackpole, 1953.

Wagon Box Fight (August 2, 1867) This battle was one in a series waged by SIOUX warrior RED CLOUD against the U.S. Army in protest over military posts on the BOZEMAN TRAIL. Company C of the 27th Infantry was attacked by an overwhelming number of SIOUX Indians led by CRAZY HORSE—estimates range up to 3,000—while guarding a woodcutting detail about 6 miles from FORT PHIL KEARNY. The army lost 1 officer and 5 enlisted killed and 2 wounded. Indian losses were estimated by the army at 60 killed and 120 wounded; the Indians set that figure at only 6 killed and 6 wounded. Some of the detail made it back to the fort during the initial attack; other men—2 officers, 26 soldiers, and 4 civilians—took shelter in a corral constructed from wagon beds. The Indians alternated sniping and charging the position, but were discouraged by the superior firepower from the soldiers. About 4½ hours later, a detachment arrived from the fort. The Indians quickly broke contact, taking with them captured horses and mules. *Sources for further study include: Fort Phil Kearny: An American Saga,* by Dee Brown (New York: Putnam and Sons, 1962); and *Red Cloud's Folk: A History of the Oglala Sioux Indians,* by George E. Hyde (Norman: University of Oklahoma Press, 1937).

Wallace, George D. (1851–90) Second lieutenant, 7th Cavalry. Wallace hailed from South Carolina, the son of a man who had supported the Union in the Civil War. This caused the family to be ostracized and their farm was destroyed by vindictive neighbors. The elder Wallace worked to restore his name and property, and was eventually elected to Congress. Wallace joined the SEVENTH CAVALRY in 1872 after graduating from West Point (a classmate of 2nd Lt. Charles VARNUM), and his first assignment was reconstruction duty in Spartanburg, SC,

a few miles from home. On the LITTLE BIGHORN CAMPAIGN he was second in command of Capt. Donald MCINTOSH's G Company. Custer had assembled his officers the evening before the battle and, in addition to issuing orders, lectured them on morale. Afterward, Wallace remarked to 1st Lt. Edward GODFREY that he believed Custer was going to be killed. In answer to Godfrey's inquiry as to why, Wallace opined that he had never before heard Custer talk in such a disheartening manner. Wallace with Company G was involved in RENO'S VALLEY FIGHT, and assumed command of the company when Capt. McIntosh was killed on Reno's retreat from the timber to the bluffs. He claimed that from WEIR POINT thousands of Indians could be observed riding around on CUSTER HILL. Wallace kept a daybook during the campaign that has been studied with great interest. He had been promoted to captain when he was killed in 1890 at the Battle of WOUNDED KNEE. *Sources for further study include: March of the Seventh Cavalry June 22 to June 25, 1876,* Report of Chief of Engineers for Fiscal year Ending June 30, 1877, Appendix PP.

Warbonnet Creek, Battle of *see* CODY, WILLIAM F.

Washita, Battle of (November 27, 1868) This engagement, a part of the WASHITA CAMPAIGN OF 1868–69, was fought on the Washita River in present-day Oklahoma between Custer's SEVENTH CAVALRY and southern CHEYENNE Indians under Chief BLACK KETTLE. The cavalry destroyed the village, killed over 100 Cheyenne (Indian estimates are 60 killed), and captured a large group of women and children. (For events preceding and following this battle see WASHITA CAMPAIGN OF 1868–69.)

Custer and 11 companies—800 men— of the SEVENTH CAVALRY had marched on November 23 from CAMP SUPPLY on the North Canadian river, heading south through a blizzard. Several days later they had arrived in the Washita River Valley, where a reported 6,000 Indians were camped for the winter. Maj. Joel ELLIOTT located a fresh trail on November 26 that was presumed to be Indians returning from raiding in Kansas. Custer's men followed, and eventually halted on a ridge above the Washita River. Below on the south side they observed an Indian village of 51 lodges. According to the OSAGE Indian scouts, the village was occupied by a band of mostly Cheyenne under Chief Black Kettle. Unknown to Custer, the chief had just returned from a meeting with Col. William B. HAZEN, who had the unenviable task of determining which Indian tribes were to be considered hostile or peaceful. Hazen had been convinced during their meeting that Black Kettle was peaceful, but told the chief to personally make peace with Gen. Phil SHERIDAN to ensure his safety. The general could not be located, so Black Kettle had returned home and was asleep in his lodge.

While the Indians slept, Custer held officer's call to detail his plans for a dawn attack. The regiment would be separated into 4 detachments. Maj. Elliott with companies G, H, and M would approach from the northeast; Capt. William Thompson with companies B and F from the south; Capt. Edward Myers with companies E and I from the west; and Custer with his 4 companies broken into 2 squadrons commanded by capts. Louis HAMILTON and Robert West would strike the village from the north.

At dawn a rifle shot rang out in the village. Custer ordered the regimental band to strike up "GARRYOWEN," the buglers sounded the charge, and the Battle of Washita commenced. The music soon ceased on account of frozen instruments, but the echoing bugle calls could be heard surrounding the village. The cavalrymen—720 strong; 80 had remained with the wagon train—swept into the village of unsuspecting Indians, shooting,

slashing with sabers, and running down those who fled. Capt. Hamilton was shot through the heart in the first moments, and 1st Lt. Tom CUSTER, who suffered a wounded hand, took over this command. Thompson's attack from the south came a little late creating a gap between that detachment and Elliott's, thus permitting a number of Indians to escape. Most of the Indians, however, took refuge in nearby ravines and timber or in the river, and fired back at the soldiers. When 2nd Lt. GODFREY and a platoon captured the pony herd south of the village, they noticed that the valley to the east was teeming with tepees and Indians heading for the battle. Godfrey reported the discovery to an apparently surprised Custer, who learned through his interpreter that villages of hostile ARAPAHO, KIOWA, COMANCHE, and KIOWA-APACHE containing a large number of warriors were located from 2 to 10 miles away in that direction.

Without Custer's knowledge, Maj. Elliott and a 19-man detachment chased after a group of fleeing Indians to the east. As he passed 1st Lt. Owen HALE, Elliott had shouted, "Here goes for a brevet or a coffin!" He and his men were not seen alive again. (See WASHITA CAMPAIGN OF 1868–69.)

In the village itself some troopers watched aghast as an Indian woman disemboweled a small white boy before their eyes. Another captive had been killed earlier, probably at the first alarm. Chief Black Kettle and his wife tried to flee on his pony, but were shot down at the river. The feeble defense of Black Kettle's village quickly wilted; Custer's men had control in about 10 minutes. The remainder of the morning was spent eliminating small pockets of resistance.

The 7th Cavalry had lost 2 officers and 19 enlisted killed, and 3 officers and 11 enlisted were wounded. The wounded included Capt. Albert BARNITZ, who was in critical condition after being shot in the abdomen. Indian fatalities were reported by the army at 103. Indian estimates differ, claiming that 60 were lost: two-thirds of them women and children.

The overzealous command of Capt. Myers was observed firing into a large group of Indian women and children. Custer sent scout Ben Clark over to order Myers to stop shooting and instead capture and detain the noncombatants. In all 53 women and children were captured, and would accompany the soldiers back to CAMP SUPPLY. One captive, a Cheyenne Indian girl named MONAHSETAH, became an interpreter and guide for the remainder of the expedition, and the subject of controversy in Custer's personal life.

The troopers set about the task of destroying everything within sight. Bonfires blazed as clothing—including an estimated 100 buffalo robes—weapons, saddles, food, even 700 pounds of tobacco, as well as every tepee was burned. The pony herd, numbering 875, was also destroyed by slitting their throats or shooting them. Among the contents of the village, Custer's men found mail, daguerreotypes, bedding, and other goods taken from white settlements. A military dispatch carried by one of Gen. Phil SHERIDAN's couriers who had been killed was also recovered.

About noon Indians from the villages downstream began firing from the surrounding bluffs. Custer formed a defensive perimeter, and established a field hospital for Dr. Morris Asch in a large tepee. Ammunition supplies had been replenished through the brave efforts of the quartermaster, 1st Lt. James BELL, who had fought his way through and Indian attack to bring forward an ammunition wagon. However, the wagon train with overcoats and rations was in danger. As dusk approached, Custer realized that they must quickly depart. Warriors now completely surrounded the cavalrymen. Custer called it an "immensely superior force." However, Maj. Elliott and his men had not returned. Custer ordered Capt. Myers to scout down the valley. He returned after 2 miles without finding

any sign of the missing men. Custer's situation was becoming precarious with the threat from the large gathering of Indians, estimated at 1,500. Therefore, in a bold tactical move, he mounted the regiment, ordered the band to play "Ain't I Glad to Get Out of the Wilderness," and marched down the valley toward the villages. This caused the surprised warriors to fall back to defend their families. Under the cover of darkness, Custer then had the command execute a countermarch, and hastily moved out in the direction of the supply train. The men were fatigued from 2 nights without sleep, had no overcoats in the freezing weather, but still marched until 2:00 A.M. when Custer finally called a halt and allowed them to rest and build fires for warmth. They met the wagon train later that day, and triumphantly returned to Camp Supply on December 2. *Sources for further study* have been listed following the WASHITA CAMPAIGN OF 1868–69 entry.

Washita Campaign of 1868–69

This campaign was staged from October 1868–March 1969 by the U. S. Army against Indians primarily from the CHEYENNE, ARAPAHO, and KIOWA tribes who had been raiding on the Great Plains. The purpose was to force the hostiles onto reservations and punish those responsible for the atrocities.

Cheyenne and Arapaho Indian attacks against settlers, soldiers, and stage lines in Kansas became so numerous in the summer and fall of 1868 that the government was forced to decide on a solution to the Indian problem. Government policy had vacillated for a decade between those in the East who lobbied the Indian Bureau for kindness and tolerance toward the Indians and Westerners who believed that only with military control could a solution be found. Peace commission councils (see MEDICINE LODGE TREATY) had failed in their mission to persuade the Indians to forsake the area between the Platte and Arkansas rivers and move to reservations north or south.

Hostile acts by the Indians reached the limit of patience with the BEECHER'S ISLAND battle on September 17. The tough decision was finally made. The secretary of war and the president directed Gen. Phil SHERIDAN to take whatever measures were necessary to drive the hostiles onto reservations and deliver up for punishment the perpetrators of the acts. War against the Indians had been declared.

Col. Alfred SULLY and his 3rd Infantry, bolstered by Maj. Joel ELLIOTT commanding 8 companies of the SEVENTH CAVALRY, was sent after the Cheyennes, who had been raiding south of the Arkansas river. Sully, who had successfully fought Indians in the Dakota Territory years earlier had grown timid with age, returned empty-handed after a week's march.

Custer was residing in Monroe, MI, serving out the one-year suspension from the army that had been determined as punishment at his court-marital the previous year when the campaign commenced. Sheridan, disgusted with Sully's inaction, knew Custer had the ability to execute his policy, if only his suspension could be lifted early. Custer received the following telegram from headquarters, Department of the Missouri, in the field at FORT HAYS on September 24, 1868: "Generals Sherman, Sully, and myself and nearly all the officers of your regiment, have asked for you, and I hope the applications (for reinstatement) will be successful. Can you come at once? Eleven companies of your regiment will move about the first of October against the hostile Indians, from Medicine Lodge Creek toward the Wichita Mountains, [signed] P. H. Sheridan, Major General Commanding." Custer was on board a train the following day, steaming toward the Plains as quickly as possible.

Custer reported for duty at Fort Hays on September 30 with intentions of preparing for a winter campaign. The army, however, debated the practicality of such an operation that unquestionably would present many dangers. In addition to the obvious misery and potential health dangers to the troops, keeping open an adequate supply line would become the biggest obstacle. No less of an authority than guide, scout, and mountain man Jim Bridger arrived from St. Louis for the purpose of discouraging Gen. Sheridan from undertaking such a hazardous campaign. Custer, however, disagreed with Bridger and set out to convince Sheridan that a winter campaign was the only way to have a chance at locating and engaging the Indians. They were immobile this time of year, whereas in the summer months they could hit and run at their discretion. Custer's arguments prevailed.

On October 11 Custer rode into the 7th Cavalry's camp on Cavalry Creek, 40 miles south of FORT DODGE, and was greeted with great enthusiasm (see illustration below). The campaign, however, was delayed due to the tardiness of supplies, and was forced to return to camp near Fort Dodge for nearly a month. It was November 12 when finally Custer and 11 companies of the 7th cavalry under the command of Col. Sully and his 5 companies of infantry marched south.

Lt. Col. George Armstrong Custer during the Washita Campaign, 1869

They arrived at the North Canadian River a week later and began the construction of a supply base appropriately named CAMP SUPPLY. While camped waiting for the KANSAS VOLUNTEER CAVALRY, who were to join the campaign, Custer came upon fresh Indian signs and decided to follow. Sully, however, as commander refused permission until the Kansas Cavalry had arrived. Custer was dismayed with Sully's typical passivity, and complained about it when Gen. Sheridan arrived on November 21. Sheridan, having earlier witnessed Sully's sorry Indian fighting prowess, resolved the problem by sending Sully back to FORT HARKER. Custer was now free to pursue the Indians.

On November 23, with the regimental band playing *The Girl I Left Behind Me*, Custer and the 7th Cavalry marched to the south toward the Washita River Valley where an estimated 6,000 Indians were camped for the winter. It was at Antelope Hills on November 26 that Maj. Joel ELLIOTT located a fresh Indian trail leading south toward the village of Cheyenne chief BLACK KETTLE.

At dawn on November 27, 1868, Custer and 720 cavalrymen surprised Black Kettle's village of 51 lodges on the south side of the Washita River. The engagement was brief and highly successful for the soldiers. According to the army, over 100 Indians, including Black Kettle and his wife, were killed. The Indian count was somewhat lower, and included mostly women and children. But 53 women and children were taken prisoner, a pony herd of 875 was killed, and the entire village—tepees, weapons, food, and clothing—was burned to the ground. Custer and the 7th Cavalry managed to escape before a superior number of warriors from villages downstream could inflict much damage. (See WASHITA, BATTLE OF for a complete account.)

Generals Sherman and Sheridan as well as the military establishment were immensely pleased with the victory. Two days after the battle Gen. Sheridan dispatched General Field order no. 6 to Custer in the care of scout Moses MILNER (California Joe). It read in part: "The energy and rapidity shown during one of the heaviest snowstorms that has visited this section of the country, with the temperature below freezing point, and the gallantry and bravery displayed, resulting in such signal success, reflect the highest credit upon both the officers and men of the 7th Cavalry." Eastern humanitarians, however, called it a massacre, accusing Custer of slaughtering innocent women and children. Indian agent Edward W. WYNKOOP resigned his post to protest the attack and, in particular, the killing of Black Kettle, who was known as a proponent of peace among his people. Peace commission member, Maj. Gen. W. S. Harney, wrote: "I have worn the uniform of my country 55 years, and I know Black Kettle was as good a friend of the U.S. as I am." Black Kettle most likely was a peaceful Indian. However, he could not control the actions of the hot-tempered young warriors of this tribe, and eventually paid for that with his life. Division Commander Gen. William T. SHERMAN defended the action in a December 23, 1868, letter to Gen. Sheridan: "This you know is a free country, and people have the lawful right to misrepresent as much as they please—and to print them—but the great mass of our people cannot be humbugged into the belief that Black Kettle's camp was friendly with its captive women and children, its herds of stolen horses and its stolen mail, arms, powder, etc.—trophies of war."

The continuance of the campaign led Custer and Gen. Sheridan, now reinforced by the Kansas Volunteer Cavalry, to return to the Washita battlefield. The fate of the missing Maj. Joel Elliott who, with a 19-man detachment, had taken off on his own chasing after fleeing Indians, was a burning question within the regiment. It had been thought that Elliott had simply become lost, and would eventually find his way back. Unfortunately, that was not the case. On December 10 they discovered the mutilated bodies of Elliott and his command some miles downstream. Evidence showed that the troopers had come under attack and had dismounted to form a small defensive circle in tall grass. The Indians had overwhelmed them within an hour. Elliott's tragic death provided his former Civil War superior, Capt. F. W. BENTEEN—already a notorious Custer critic—with fodder to create a controversy based around the accusation that Elliott was abandoned. The debate over Eliott lasted well beyond Custer's death.

The troopers continued on to inspect the abandoned villages downstream. In one, reportedly belonging to the Kiowa of Chief SATANTA, they discovered the bodies of white captives Mrs. Clara BLINN and her son, who had been taken in October. Sheridan decided that the 700-man force would follow an Indian trail that led down the Washita River toward FORT COBB.

On December 17, after a cold and miserable 75-mile march, they came upon a large contingent of Indians. The soldiers were advancing slowly, when a chief rode out to meet them. He told them his name was Satanta, and he was friendly. To further his argument, a courier arrived from Fort Cobb with a message from Col. W. B. HAZEN, whose duty it was to decide which Indians were peaceful and which were not. Hazen's message stated that Satanta and another chief present, LONE WOLF, and their people were peaceful and should not be molested. The news did not sit well with Sheridan and Custer. They had just trailed this band from the Washita where white captives and Maj. Elliott had been killed, not to mention the evidence found from past raiding parties. Sheridan demanded that the "friendly" Indians accompany them to Fort Cobb and settle on the reservation. Satanta hesitated. In an attempt to ensure compliance, Sheridan seized Satanta and Lone Wolf as hostages. When the column arrived at

Fort Cobb the following day, the village of Kiowas had not followed to comply with the submission to the reservation. Sheridan set an ultimatum: Satanta and Lone Wolf would be hanged in 48 hours if the tribe failed to appear. It worked; most of the Kiowas grudgingly moved onto the reservation.

In January 1869 Sheridan began construction of a new post named FORT SILL, at the eastern foot of the Wichita Mountains some 30 miles south of Fort Cobb. The 7th Cavalry moved to the new site, but had problems receiving rations and forage, which drastically curtailed operations. Custer, however, set out in early January with a detail of 40 sharpshooters led by 1st Lt. W. W. COOKE. They soon located an Arapaho village in the Wichita Mountains with 65 lodges under Chief Little Raven, and convinced them to surrender.

It was the Cheyenne Indians, however, that became Custer's main focus. He intended to either fight them or make them peacefully surrender. On March 15 at Sweetwater Creek, TX, Custer located 2 Cheyenne villages with a combined 260 lodges under chiefs Medicine Arrow and Little Robe. The Kansas Volunteer Cavalry, which was part of the column, believed that those Indians held 2 white women, Miss Sarah C. White and Mrs. Anna Belle Morgan, who had been taken hostage in Kansas. The brother of Miss White, Daniel A. Brewster, had accompanied the expedition. In the company of only 1st Lt. Cooke, Custer put his life on the line by brazenly entering the Cheyenne village unannounced to parley. In the chief's lodge Custer was introduced to ceremonies and rituals by a holy man that were designed to intimidate him with warnings that if he acted treacherously toward Indians he and his command would be killed. The 2 officers managed to leave the village unharmed and with confirmation of the presence of the captives. Much to the outrage of the Kansas Volunteers—many even branding Custer a coward—he refused to attack the village. He had learned the lesson during the Battle of Washita that the Indians, if attacked, likely would kill the captives. Instead, during another parley under a flag of truce, Custer managed to seize 3 Indian chiefs, used them as hostages, and threatened to hang them if the white women were not returned unharmed. After 3 days of tense negotiation and near battle, the Cheyenne gave in and gave up their prisoners. As for the Indians, they promised to report to Camp Supply as soon as their ponies grew strong enough. Custer had little choice but to agree. He did, however, keep the hostages in custody, and promised to free them in addition to the women and children captured at Washita when the Cheyenne surrendered.

The Washita Campaign quietly came to an end on March 28, 1869, when Custer and his exhausted men returned to Camp Supply. The Cheyenne never did surrender as promised, but were defeated severely enough by Maj. E. A. Carr at the Battle of SUMMIT SPRINGS on July 11 to cause them to straggle onto their reservation by fall. In one sense the Washita Campaign had been successful. The original mission of clearing all hostile Indians from the Plains between the Platte and Arkansas rivers had been accomplished.

Sources for further study include: Custer's own detailed account of the campaign can be found in his own *My Life on the Plains; Or Personal Experiences with Indians* (New York: Sheldon, 1874), and *Nomad: George A. Custer in Turf, Field, and Farm,* edited by Brian W. Dippie (Austin: University of Texas Press, 1980). The official documents are printed in *General Custer and the Battle of the Washita: The Federal View,* edited by John M. Carroll (Bryan, TX: Guidon, 1978). Other sources include: *The Battle of the Washita: The Sheridan-Custer Indian Campaign of 1867–68,* by Stan Hoig (Garden City, NY: Doubleday, 1976); *Campaigning with Custer and the Nineteenth Kansas Volunteer Cavalry on the*

Washita Campaign, 1868–69, by participant David L. Spotts, edited by E. A. Brininstool (Lincoln: University of Nebraska Press, Bison Book, 1988); *Life in Custer's Cavalry: Diaries and Letters of Albert and Jennie Barnitz, 1867–68,* edited by Robert M. Utley (New Haven, CT: Yale University Press, 1977); *The Fighting Cheyennes,* by George Bird GRINNELL (Norman: University of Oklahoma Press, 1955); *Sheridan's Troopers on the Borders: A Winter Campaign on the Plains,* by De B. Randolph Keim (Philadelphia: Clayton, Remsen and Habbelfinger, 1870); and *Following the Guidon* by Elizabeth B. Custer (New York: Harper and Brothers, 1890).

Weapons of Allied Indians at the Battle of the Little Bighorn SIOUX and CHEYENNE weapons included everything from primitive clubs, bows and arrows, lances, and hatchets to an array of new and old firearms: muzzleloaders, Spencers, Sharps, Henry and Winchester repeating rifles, and, of course, Springfield carbines taken from Reno's dead cavalrymen. It has been estimated that perhaps 200 repeating rifles were possessed by the Indians: nearly one for each enemy soldier. However, Indian tactics differ from the U.S. military in that Indians were more concerned about counting coup in order to reap battle honors: which must be accomplished at close range and usually with primitive weapons such as a coup stick. The question has been debated about whether the Sioux and Cheyenne were better armed than the cavalrymen, a possible reason for the devastating defeat. The answer comes down to the fact that, rather than dwell on armament as a cause for the army defeat (because there does not appear to be a wide disparity) a more plausible theory is that sheer numbers alone dictated superiority—and the numbers lay with the Indians. It could be argued that bows and arrows alone from such a large force could have resulted in the identical outcome.

Weapons of the Cavalry at the Battle of the Little Bighorn Troopers of the SEVENTH CAVALRY were armed with Model 1873 Springfield .45/55 caliber, single-shot, breech-loading carbines, and a Colt revolver of the same year and caliber. Each man carried into battle 100 .45/55 caliber cartridges: 50 in his cartridge belt and 50 in his saddlebags. That afforded Custer's command more than 20,000 available shots. The soldiers did not carry a saber. (See also MALFUNCTION OF SPRINGFIELD CARBINES AT THE BATTLE OF THE LITTLE BIGHORN.)

Weir, Thomas B. (November 28, 1838–December 9, 1876) Captain, 7th Cavalry. Weir was one of Custer's most loyal supporters, and also the subject of controversy in Custer's personal life.

His military career began in August 1861 when he left the University of Michigan during his third year to enlist in the 3rd Michigan Cavalry to fight in the Civil War. He served as both enlisted man and officer in the western theater, and was held prisoner for six months in 1862. As a major, Weir served in 1865 on the staff of Custer in Texas. He was appointed a first lieutenant in the SEVENTH CAVALRY in 1866, and promoted to captain the following year.

Weir's relationship with Custer's wife Libbie came under scrutiny at FORT HAYS, KA, while Custer was away on the HANCOCK EXPEDITION OF 1867. It began one evening when Weir escorted Libbie and another woman outside the post. Upon their return, the sentries mistook them for Indians and opened fire. Weir began crawling toward the closed gates in order to identify himself. Meanwhile, bugles inside the fort sounded at 10 P.M. to signal that Weir and the two women had not returned. Suddenly, panicked sentries blindly opened fire. It was some time before Weir succeeded in gaining entry. The episode was the cause of great embarrassment for the three.

Another incident—one that may have

been a factor leading to one of the charges at Custer's court-martial—occurred when Custer left his command without permission and made an exhaustive mad dash across nearly 200 miles of Kansas in order to be at Libbie's side. Custer explained that the forced march was necessary to obtain supplies for this troops at FORT WALLACE and to receive fresh orders. Custer nemesis Capt. F. W. BENTEEN claimed that an anonymous letter warned Custer that he had better return home and "look after his wife a little closer." Rumor had it that his wife Libbie and Capt. Weir were becoming an item. (See CUSTER: Court-Martial for more detail.) More than a year later, on January 8, 1869, Custer wrote to Libbie from Fort DODGE: "Weir I reprimanded sharply in writing and as you prophesied when speaking to him, he has been huffy ever since. ... The more I see of him, Little One, the more I am surprised that a woman of your perceptive faculties and moral training could have entertained the opinion of him you have." Weir, it should be noted, was a heavy drinker.

At the Battle of the LITTLE BIGHORN Weir's D Company was attached to Capt. Benteen's battalion that had been sent on a scout while the others approached the village. When Benteen's battalion arrived at the bluff where the beaten command of Maj. Marcus RENO had taken refuge (see RENO-BENTEEN DEFENSE SITE), Weir was the officer who wanted to march toward the sound of firing: that unknown to them was Custer under attack. Reno refused Weir permission to move out, and Weir, by some reports, engaged in a shouting match with his commanding officer. Weir then disobeyed orders and advanced forward, followed by his company, to a promontory now called WEIR POINT. He was eventually pushed back to the bluff defensive position by onrushing warriors.

Following the Little Bighorn Battle, Weir and other officers were asked by Frederick Whittaker, who was writing a biography of Custer, to provide statements derogatory to Reno's conduct. Weir was the only officer who did not refuse to answer, but never actually did. Instead, he wrote to Libbie Custer: "I have so much to tell you that I will tell you nothing now," except that he was coming to visit her in Monroe, MI, and would then present "life business to vindicate my friends of that day." Weir did not make the trip to Monroe at that time, instead writing; "I know if we were all of us [Libbie, Maggie CALHOUN, and Annie (Mrs. George) YATES] alone in the parlor, at night, the curtains all down and everybody else asleep, one or the other of you would make me tell you everything I know." At Monroe he could "say something to you that would make you feel glad for a little while at least." Exactly what Weir wanted to relate to Libbie, a woman whom he probably loved, was never revealed.

He was in the advanced stages of alcoholism when on December 9, 1876—less than 6 months after the battle—he died of "congestion of the brain" while on recruiting detail in New York City. *Sources for further study include: The Custer Story: The Life and Intimate Letters of General George H. Custer and His Wife Elizabeth*, by Marguerite Merington (New York: Devin-Adair, 1950); and *Elizabeth Bacon Custer and the Making of a Myth*, by Shirley A. Leckie (Norman: University of Oklahoma Press, 1993).

Weir Point This promontory that rises south and above MEDICINE TAIL COULEE was the location during the Battle of the LITTLE BIGHORN where Capt. Thomas WEIR had advanced forward and observed Indians in the distance shooting at objects on the ground on CUSTER HILL. Weir had approached this position on his own after being denied permission to do so by Maj. Marcus RENO. (See RENO-BENTEEN DEFENSE SITE.)

White Bull, Joseph (Minniconjou Sioux; nephew of SITTING BULL) He was credited during the LITTLE BIGHORN Battle with 2 kills, 7 coups, and 12 captured horses. His pony was killed and he was shot in the ankle. He later drew pictures of the conflict and helped assemble a tribal history. *Sources for further study include: The True Story of the Fighting Sioux Told in a Biography of Chief White Bull*, by Stanley Vestal (Boston: Houghton Mifflin, 1934); and *The Warrior Who Killed Custer: The Personal Narrative of Chief White Bull*, translated and edited by James H. Howard (Lincoln: University of Nebraska Press, 1968).

Windolph, Charles Private H Company, 7th Cavalry. Windolph participated in the Battle of the LITTLE BIGHORN, and received the MEDAL OF HONOR for his sharpshooter duty covering water carriers on the RENO-BENTEEN DEFENSE SITE. He is notable for being the last living survivor of that battle. *Sources for further study include: I Fought with Custer: The Story of Sergeant Windolph*, by F. and R. Hunt (New York: Charles Scribner's Sons, 1947).

Wolf Mountain, Battle of (January 8, 1877) This battle, part of the GREAT SIOUX WAR OF 1876–77, was fought between the U.S. Army commanded by Gen. Nelson MILES and allied SIOUX and CHEYENNE Indians under CRAZY HORSE near the Tongue River. Neither side claimed victory; casualties were minimal. The Cheyenne had been severely beaten two months earlier in the Battle of DULL KNIFE and had sought refuge with the Sioux under Crazy Horse. Many of these people were prepared to surrender, and the chiefs opened talks with Gen. Miles to discuss terms. However, as the Cheyenne approached the Tongue River Cantonment, some of Miles's CROW Indian scouts attacked them, killing five. The Indians fled, and hostilities continued. In early January, Miles with about 350 troops were searching the Tongue River Valley when the Indians attempted to lure them into a trap. The ambush was sprung too early, and Miles was able to capture a number of Cheyenne women and children. Then 500 warriors under Crazy Horse attacked at dawn on January 8 with intentions of freeing the captives. Miles was well prepared, and bombarded them with artillery and skillfully deployed marksmen. The battle ended around noon when a blizzard obscured visibility and the Indians withdrew. Neither side sustained many casualties. *Sources for further study include:* "The Battle of Wolf Mountain," by Don Rickey, Jr., *Montana: The Magazine of Western History* 13 (Spring 1963).

Wooden Leg (Northern CHEYENNE 1858–1940) This warrior fought against a detachment of Gen. George CROOK's Wyoming column led by Col. J. J. Reynolds in the POWDER RIVER FIGHT, and helped defeat Custer at the Battle of the LITTLE BIGHORN. He surrendered the following year, and was sent to a reservation in Indian Territory where he refused to join DULL KNIFE in an escape attempt. Wooden Leg scouted for the army in the 1880s; participated in the Ghost Dance episode in 1890; and in 1908 became a Christian. *Sources for further study include:* His eyewitness testimony abut the Little Bighorn Battle became the basis of a book by Thomas B. Marquis, *Wooden Leg: A Warrior Who Fought Custer* (Lincoln: University of Nebraska Press, 1931); and excerpts can be found in *The Custer Myth: A Source Book of Custeriana,* edited by W. A. Graham (Harrisburg, PA: Stackpole, 1953).

Wounded Knee, Battle of (aka Ghost Dance War and Big Foot Massacre; December 29, 1890) This engagement, the last of the Plains Indian wars, between SIOUX Indians under Chief Big Foot and elements of the SEVENTH CAVALRY commanded by Col. James FORSYTH was fought near Wounded Knee Creek. In what many consider an excessive use of force by the army, more than

150 Indian men, women, and children were killed.

In 1889 a Paiute Indian named Jack Wilson, who called himself Wovoka, allegedly had a spiritual experience that prompted him to create the messianic Ghost Dance, a religion based on the premise that the white man would disappear and the buffalo would return to Western lands. The religion was quickly embraced by Indians of many tribes, including the Sioux. Most tribes accepted the peaceful doctrine of the Ghost Dance. The Sioux, however, converted the ceremony to conform to their hostility. The OGLALAS at Pine Ridge and the BRULÉS at Rosebud began to defy their agents to the extent that the outbreak of an Indian war was feared by the army. The military responded with additional troops at the two reservations. This action incited the Indians. Sitting Bull embraced the turmoil caused by the Ghost Dance, as did MINNICONJOU Chief Big Foot. Gen. Nelson MILES ordered the arrest of two chiefs. SITTING BULL resisted, and was killed by his own people acting as policemen. This murder caused further unrest. Big Foot's arrest was a matter of procrastination by the post commander, who feared the act would provoke violence. Meanwhile, Big Foot—known as a peacemaker—with 350 Minniconjous and HUNKPAPAS slipped away with intentions of visiting the Pine Ridge Agency. That idea did not please Gen. Miles. He ordered troops to stop Big Foot from reaching Pine Ridge. The Minniconjou chief, who lay in a wagon suffering from pneumonia, eluded those troops. The 7th Cavalry, brought to Dakota from FORT RILEY due to the Indian trouble, was then dispatched to catch Big Foot's people, and did so some 20 miles from Pine Ridge in the valley of Wounded Knee Creek. The Indians accepted the military escort, and camped for the night. The next morning the Indians found themselves surrounded by 500 troops and 4 cannon. The 7th Cavalry commander, Col. James W. Forsyth, ordered the Indians to give up their firearms. The Indians refused and a search was then ordered. Yellow Bird called for them to resist. Meanwhile, an Indian and a soldier began to struggle, and a rifle went off. The young men of the tribe then began firing into the nearest soldiers. The soldiers fired back, and the battle commenced, supported by artillery that destroyed the village. When the firing stopped more than 150 Indians—including Big Foot and Yellow Bird—lay dead. The number of bodies later found on the field included 84 men and boys, 44 women, and 18 children. In addition, 51 Indians were treated at the hospital for wounds, 7 later dying. The 7th Cavalry lost 1 officer and 18 enlisted killed and 33 wounded. Participants included the remaining veteran 7th Cavalry officers who had fought at the LITTLE BIGHORN: Capts. EDGERLY, GODFREY, MOYLAN, NOWLAN, VARNUM, and WALLACE, the latter being the officer who was killed. *Sources for further study include: Eyewitness at Wounded Knee*, by Richard Jensen, R. Eli Paul, and John E. Carter (Lincoln: University of Nebraska Press, 1991); *Wovoka and the Ghost Dance*, edited by Don Lynch (Carson City, NV: Grace Foundation, 1990; and *The Ghost Dance Religion and Wounded Knee*, by James Mooney (New York: Dover, 1973).

Wynkoop, Edward W. (June 19, 1836–September 11, 1891) Wynkoop came to Colorado from Kansas during the Pikes Peak gold rush of 1858, and was one of the founders of Denver. In 1862 he was commissioned a major in the 1st Colorado Volunteers, and fought the Confederates at the battles of Apache Canyon and Glorieta Pass. He was commander of FORT LYON during the time his superior Col. Chivington attacked Chief BLACK KETTLE's village at nearby SAND CREEK and massacred and mutilated 500 Cheyenne men, women, and children. Wynkoop did not share Chivington's philosophy concerning the In-

dian, believing that hostilities could be prevented. He became an Indian agent to the CHEYENNE and ARAPAHO in 1866, but could not prevent the army—of which the officers and men had little respect for Wynkoop—from waging war against what they considered hostiles. He accompanied the HANCOCK EXPEDITION OF 1867, and was dismayed at Gen. W. S. HANCOCK's actions, especially the destruction of the Cheyenne village on Pawnee Fork. Finally, following the Battle of WASHITA and the killing of Black Kettle, he resigned in protest. He then participated in the BLACK HILLS gold rush (where he fought Indians under Capt. Jack Crawford), became adjutant general of New Mexico, and warden of the New Mexico Penitentiary.

Yates, George Wilhelmus Mancius (February 26, 1843–June 25, 1876) Captain, 7th Cavalry. Yates began his military career by enlisting in the 4th Michigan Infantry in 1861 at the age of 18. He was commissioned a first lieutenant on September 26, 1862, and made captain with the 13th Missouri Cavalry on September 22, 1864. He fought at Bull Run, Antietam, Beverly Ford, Chancellorsville, Gettysburg, and Fredericksburg, where he was wounded when a Confederate shell exploded beneath his horse. Yates and Custer became friends when their paths crossed while Yates was in Monroe, MI, recuperating from his wounding January 1863. He was briefly married to Lucretia Beaumont Irwin while on duty in St. Louis in 1865. "Lilly" as she was known, abandoned him, and a divorce was granted in January 1867. Yates was appointed a second lieutenant in the 2nd Cavalry in May 1866 and stationed at FORT MCPHERSON, NE. With Custer's assistance, he was transferred to the SEVENTH CAVALRY as captain in June 1867. He commanded Company F, known as the "Bandbox" troop for its smart appearance, and participated in every regimental campaign until June 1876. Yates married Annie Gibson

Roberts Yates in New York City in 1872; they had three children, two boys and a girl. Yates commanded the detail that in December 1874 arrested Sioux warrior RAIN-IN-THE-FACE for three murders during the YELLOWSTONE EXPEDITION OF 1873. During the LITTLE BIGHORN CAMPAIGN, his company was part of Maj. Marcus Reno's nine-day POWDER RIVER SCOUT. With Custer's command in the opening stages of the Battle of the LITTLE BIGHORN, it is believed that Yate's two-company battalion probed the Indian village down MEDICINE TAIL COULEE, but was repulsed by heavy fire. Yates was killed beside his friend Custer on CUSTER HILL. On August 3, 1877, his remains were reinterred at Fort Leavenworth, KA.

Yellowstone Expedition of 1873 (aka the Stanley Expedition) (June 20– September 23, 1873) This expedition, commanded by Col. David S. STANLEY, had the mission of protecting surveyors and workers on the NORTHERN PACIFIC RAILROAD from hostile Indians: primarily SIOUX under SITTING BULL. Track was being laid east of the Missouri River, but to the west there remained the work of staking the route to be followed.

The SEVENTH CAVALRY regiment had been spread out mainly across the Southern United States on various duties, and now assembled in Memphis, TN, the last week of March 1873. On June 10 after a steamboat ride, railroad trip, and a march of 350 miles, they arrived at FORT RICE in the Dakota Territory.

The column departed from Fort Rice on June 20, 1873, with 1,500 soldiers, the 17th and 22nd infantries, and 10 troops of the 7th Cavalry commanded by Lt. Col. George Armstrong Custer (2 companies—Capt. Thomas WEIR's D and Capt. Myles KEOGH's I—under Maj. Marcus RENO had been assigned temporary duty escorting surveyors on the INTERNATIONAL BOUNDARY SURVEY and did not accompany the expedition), 450 civilians, a train of 275 wagons, plus 2 chartered steamboats—the FAR WEST and the JOSEPHINE—to haul supplies. The column headed west across Dakota Territory toward Montana. The initial portion of the trek was little more than an extended party, both hunting and socializing.

Custer led hunting details each day, and bagged deer, elk, pronghorn antelope, buffalo, geese, ducks, prairie chickens, and sage hens, all of which kept the messes in fresh meat. He also shot two white wolves and one red fox. Custer wrote to wife Libby on June 26 from their camp on the Heart River: "Our march has been delightful. Such hunting I never have seen." Other animals, such as a porcupine and a wildcat, were brought in alive with intentions of donating them to the CENTRAL PARK ZOO in New York City. C. W. Bennett, a taxidermist, had accompanied the column, and his craft became an obsession for Custer. Late into the night Custer would work on mounting his various trophies under the watchful eye of Bennett. He mounted many specimens, including a complete elk, which he donated to the Detroit Audubon Club.

The social aspect of camp was not quite as agreeable to Custer. He watched as some members of his "royal family" let their vices get the better of them. Capt. George YATES went on a binge and stayed drunk for days; brother-in-law 1st Lt. James CALHOUN lost all his money playing high-stakes poker; and Col. Frederick GRANT, the president's son along as an observer, also allowed the bottle to get the best of him, although Custer readily admitted to enjoying his company immensely. Custer wrote to Libbie abut the gambling on June 26: "The officers have been sitting day and night, playing, since we left Fort Rice. They are now in Dr. Honsinger's tent, next to mine. I carry [his brother] Tom's funds now. Mr. Calhoun began playing as soon as we left Rice, and only stopped, night before last, from lack of funds. He borrowed $20 from me, but cannot get any more from me, nor any from Tom, since Tom has to borrow in order to play. I hope Calhoun will lose every time he sits down. Otherwise he will return to winter quarters with nothing to go on with."

One member whose company Custer particularly enjoyed was his West Point roommate, former Confederate Gen. Thomas Rosser, who was chief engineer on the Northern Pacific Railroad's Dakota Division survey team. Rosser and Custer would spend most nights swapping war stories; Rosser admitted that his worst Civil War defeat came at the hands of Custer on October 9, 1864, at the Battle of Tom's Brook, VA.

Custer, however, had problems with Col. Stanley. It was perhaps inevitable that they would clash. Neither man had much respect for the other. Stanley wrote to his wife on June 28: "I have had no trouble with Custer, and will try to avoid having any; but I have seen enough of him to convince me that he is a cold-blooded, untruthful and unprincipled man. He is universally despised by all the officers of his regiment excepting his relatives and one or two sycophants." Custer wrote to his wife Libbie in June: "General Stanley is acting very badly, drinking, and I anticipate official trouble with him. Our officers are terribly down on him. One day, after leaving [Fort] Rice, he abused Mr. Baliran (the sutler) in such coarse terms, calling him foul names ... and threatening to hang him, should he seek to come into camp at any time. Mr. Baliran, who is a great favorite with our officers, asked me what he should do. I bade him come into camp with me ... and no one has been hanged as yet." Custer did indeed have official trouble with Col. Stanley. It seemed that Custer's detachment marched off ahead of the main column, which displeased Stanley. The Colonel wrote to his wife, on July 1: "Without consulting me, [Custer] marched off 15 miles, coolly sending me a note to send him forage and rations. I

sent after him, ordered him to halt where he was, to unload his wagons and send for his own rations and forage, and never presume to make another movement without orders. ... He was just gradually assuming command, and now he knows he has a Commanding Officer who will not tolerate his arrogance." Custer was placed under arrest, and the 7th Cavalry was exiled to march at the rear of the column. Tom Rosser became the voice of reason with Gen. Stanley, insinuating that the Northern Pacific believed that the 7th Cavalry's presence was the only way the survey would get done on time and that common-sense safety precautions predicated the cavalry at the head of the column. A sober Col. Stanley rescinded the arrest, asked Custer's forgiveness, and promised to reform. Stanley reportedly also resented the popularity of Custer's mess with the other officers. Custer had brought along a cast-iron stove—a habit he learned from Gen. Phil SHERIDAN who disliked army food—and his cook, Mary ADAMS. Her preparation of wild game created a nightly feast that was extremely popular. The stove—nonmilitary equipment—survived several attempts by Stanley to have it abandoned.

Stanley, regardless of promises, remained in a constant state of drunkenness, which in effect made Custer the one to whom leadership of the expedition fell. Custer led two companies on a treacherous march through the Badlands to reach Glendive Creek, where the steamer *Far West* waited with provisions and mail. They constructed a supply depot, "Stanley's Stockade," and left Capt. F. W. BENTEEN and two companies behind as guard. It was here that Lt. Col. Grant learned that his grandfather had died, and left the expedition to head home. Custer now moved the expedition into the Yellowstone Valley, an area known to be populated by Sitting Bull's Sioux. The order of march was Custer's cavalry, then the surveyors with their transits and maps, and the infantry bringing up the rear. Custer, his favorite scout BLOODY KNIFE, and a small detachment normally rode in advance of the column.

On August 4 Custer, Capt. Myles MOYLAN, Tom CUSTER, and about 90 men had halted at noon near the mouth of the Tongue River (the site of present-day Miles City, MT). The horses had been turned out to graze, the men were lazing around, and Custer was taking a nap. Little did they know it, but they were under surveillance by CRAZY HORSE and a group Sioux and Cheyenne. Crazy Horse, the master of the decoy and ambush, sent—or was perhaps part of— a handful of mounted warriors who, whooping shrilly, brazenly charged the cavalry horses with intentions of stampeding them. The horse guards began firing and sounding the alarm, and the Indians tore off down the valley toward a stand of timber. The cavalrymen immediately gave chase, the two Custers, Calhoun, and about 20 troopers in the lead. Moylan and the remaining troopers advanced more slowly. Custer in his official report stated:

Following the Indians at a brisk gait, my suspicions became excited by the confident bearing exhibited by the six Sioux in our front, whose course seemed to lead us near a heavy growth of timber which stood along the river bank above us. When almost within rifle range of this timber, I directed the squadron to halt, while I with two orderlies, all being well mounted, continued after the Sioux in order to develop their intentions. Proceeding a few hundred yards in advance of the squadron, and keeping a watchful eye on the timber to my left, I halted. The six Indians in my front also halted, as if to tempt further pursuit.

Custer had recognized Crazy Horse's plans for an ambush and knew he should not advance any further.

Suddenly, 300 mounted warriors burst from the timber and charged. Custer wheeled around his mount, Dandy, and the thoroughbred easily outdistanced the Indian ponies. Custer arrived back where he had left his brother and 20 men, and quickly formed them in a skirmisher line. The cavalrymen rose from the tall grass and fired 3 point-blank volleys into the onrushing mass of warriors. The effective barrages discouraged any further mounted attacks. The Indians dismounted, and began to creep through the grass toward the soldiers. Custer, greatly outnumbered, wisely deployed his troopers downstream into a stand of timber. They spent the remainder of the afternoon defending their position. The Sioux tried to set fire to the grass but it burned out without covering any ground. Ammunition became dangerously low for the soldiers, but just like the script of an old-time western movie, late in the afternoon the rest of the cavalry came riding to the rescue in the nick of time. Custer then ordered his detachment to mount, and they joined the others to charge the Sioux. The Indians broke and ran in the face of the well-armed cavalrymen. Custer lost only 1 man and 2 horses in the battle. There were 3 other casualties, however, because the regimental veterinarian and ardent card player, Dr. John Honsinger, the controversial sutler, Augustus Baliran, and a trooper, Private John H. Ball, wandered off before the fight and were killed. Sioux warrior RAIN-IN-THE-FACE was arrested the following year for killings when he openly boasted about committing the murders. (See CUSTER, THOMAS WARD for more detail.)

On August 8 the expedition happened upon the site of a recently abandoned village of an estimated 500 lodges, which would account for as many as 1,000 warriors. Custer received Stanley's permission to pursue the hot trail, and departed immediately on a night march with 8 companies. Almost 36 hours later the command arrived near the mouth of the Bighorn River to discover that the Indians had crossed to the south bank of the Yellowstone. The river at this point, however, was too deep and swift for his men to easily cross. Meanwhile, the Indians realized that they had been followed, and prepared to attack the bogged-down soldiers in what has been called the Battle of the Yellowstone.

Custer's men continued their attempt to cross at daybreak on August 11. They were met by withering fire from warriors hidden in the cottonwoods 300 yards away on the opposite bank. The Indian women and children had gathered on the bluffs behind their men to watch the show and to cheer for their side. Crazy Horse and about 200 warriors swam the river above and below Custer's position and began to close in. Custer reacted quickly to the threat. He deployed sharpshooters to return fire across the river and others to cover the bluffs on his side. Two companies commanded by Capt. Thomas FRENCH were sent down the valley, 2 companies commanded by Capt. Verlin Hart headed up the valley, and 20 men under Lt. Charles Braden dropped off to defend a benchland position. This latter position was hit first, and the unit barely fought off 4 Indian charges consisting of 100 warriors each. Braden was seriously wounded when a bullet struck his thigh. The other detachments successfully defended their positions against aggressive Indian attacks. Custer—who had his horse shot out from under him but commandeered another—mounted the entire 450-man command, signaled the regimental band to strike up "GARRYOWEN," and ordered a charge. The surprise action routed the Indians, who scattered in all directions. Custer chased them for 9 miles before he lost them when they recrossed the Yellowstone.

The army lost 3 men killed, 4 wounded and 8 horses lost. Indian casualties were unknown: Custer estimated that abut 40 were killed in the engagements of August 4 and August 11 combined.

The survey moved up the Yellowstone only another 30 miles before halting at Pompey's Pillar, a lone landmark some 380 miles west of Fort Rice. It was here that the final Indian battle was fought when a small group of warriors appeared on the opposite riverbank and fired into a group of swimming soldiers, scaring and scattering them but causing no casualties. The return march was uneventful: overland to the Musselshell River and down the Missouri to FORT ABRAHAM LINCOLN, the 7th Cavalry's new post under construction.

The Yellowstone Expedition rewarded Custer with further career accolades as the country's premier Indian fighter. He also strengthened his relationship and gained great regard from the Northern Pacific Railroad ownership. His articles in *Galaxy* magazine, such as "Battling with the Sioux on the Yellowstone" (*Galaxy* 22 [July 1876]), were complemented by his official report that was published in its entirety by the *New York Tribune* and the *Army and Navy Journal*.

Sources for further study include: Custer's Seventh Cavalry and the Campaign of 1873, by Lawrence A. Frost (El Segundo, CA: Upton and Sons, 1986): "The Yellowstone Expedition of 1873," by Charles Braden, *Journal of the U. S. Cavalry Association* 16 (1905); "Expedition to the Yellowstone River in 1873: Letters of a Young Cavalry Officer," edited by George F. Howe, *Mississippi Valley Historical Review* 39 (December 1952); *The Custer Story: The Life and Intimate Letters of General George A. Custer and His Wife Elizabeth*, edited by Marguerite Merington (New York: Devin-Adair, 1950); and *Personal Memoirs of Major General David S. Stanley*, by David S. Stanley (Cambridge, MA. Harvard University Press, 1917).

Appendix:
Custer Civil War Chronology
and Battle Summary

April 12, 1861   Confederate soldiers fired on Fort Sumter, SC; the war began.

June 24, 1861   Custer graduated from the U.S. Military Academy at West Point, NY.

July 21, 1861   First Battle of Bull Run or Manassas. Three days out of West Point, 2nd Lt. Custer was assigned to G Company, 2nd Cavalry, under Gen. David Hunter, which was at the head of the Union Column and one of the last to leave the field that day. The Union believed that they had won the battle when a force of fresh rebel troops surprised the Federal soldiers and routed them for a Southern victory. Custer, in his only action of the day, was cited for bravery under fire when he stepped forward to turn an every man for himself retreat at a blocked bridge across Cub Run into an orderly formation.

May 1862   The Siege of Yorktown, VA. In the spring of 1862 Lt. Custer was assigned duty as a military observer from a hot-air balloon. Custer usually ascended at night to a height of 1,000 feet for his reconnaissance with field glasses. With map and compass he would note gun emplacements, count enemy campfires, and plot the number of white tents, sketching their locations in his notebook.

In the middle of the night of May 4 he noticed the city in darkness and speculated that the Confederates had departed. He reported his findings to Gen. W. F. (Baldy) Smith, who called for volunteers to investigate; Custer and another officer confirmed the pullout.

May 5, 1862   The Battle of Williamsburg. Lt. Custer was serving as an aide on the staff of Gen. Winfield Scott HANCOCK, whom he would later accompany on the HANCOCK EXPEDITION OF 1867. Hancock had attacked the enemy, but had been driven off the field by Confederate reinforcements. Hancock deployed the Union soldiers on a skirmisher line and, when the Rebels were within striking distance, ordered a bayonet charge. The anxious Union troops hesitated. Custer impatiently spurred his horse and burst from their midst to lead them. The men obediently followed. The Rebel advance faltered and broke into a retreat. Custer returned later to friendly lines with a captured officer, five enlisted men, and—the real trophy—a Confederate battle flag: the first one taken in the war by the Army of the Potomac.

May 23, 1862   Custer reconnoitered the Chickahominy River where his actions came to the attention of Gen. George McClellan, commander of the

Army of the Potomac. An impressed Mc-Clellan appointed Custer aide-de-camp on his staff with the brevet rank of captain effective June 5.

May 31–June 1, 1862   The Battle of Fair Oaks, VA. This indecisive engagement, also known as Seven Pines, was the one in a series of the Seven Days Battles or Campaign. Capt. Custer, aide-de-camp to Gen. George McClellan, was assigned the duty of observer as army engineers struggled to build a bridge over the rising waters of the Chickahominy River.

June 27, 1862   The Battle of Gaines Mill, VA. The third in a series of the Seven Days Battles or Campaign. Capt. Custer, aide-de-camp to Gen. George McClellan, was assigned the duty of marking out the positions for the Union forces. He remained in the rear while the 5th Cavalry regiment executed a saber charge to protect their artillery from enemy infantry. More that 300 horsemen struck at Gen. James Longstreet's corps. 56 Union troopers were hit; Rebel losses were minimal.

August 3, 1862   Custer, in a brief engagement, killed a Confederate cavalry officer and claimed his sword as a trophy. The blade was inscribed: "Draw me not without provocation. Sheathe me not without honor."

September 17, 1862   The battle of Antietam. This 12-hour battle was the bloodiest single day of the Civil War: 4,710 dead, 18,440 wounded, 3,043 missing. The Union Army under Gen. George McClellan, with staff aide-de-camp Custer seeing little action, halted Lee's attack in Washington.

May 6, 1863   Custer was assigned as aide-de-camp to Gen. Alfred Pleasanton.

June 9, 1863   The Battle of Brandy Station, VA. (aka Fleetwood Hill or Bev-erly Ford) this was the first and largest true cavalry engagement of the Civil War. Although Rebel Maj. Gen. J. E. B. Stuart's men held the field, it has been said that this battle *made* the Federal cavalry. It also helped to create the Custer legend. When Col. Benjamin Davis was killed, Custer took command of 3 brigades, and brazenly charged the enemy, which was estimated at 5,000 strong. He was outnumbered and surrounded, but still captured Confederate artillery pieces as well as Stuart's headquarters before leaving the field. Custer had 2 horses shot out from under him during the engagement; a bullet tore through his boot. This bravery led to Custer's brevet promotion to brigadier general later in the month.

June 17, 1863   The Battle of Aldie, VA. Custer, serving as aide-de-camp to Gen. Alfred Pleasanton, has been credited by some with a daring charge during this skirmish with Confederate troops. Actually, he wrote home stating that while carrying a message his horse, Black Harry, bolted and carried him into enemy territory. He was mistaken for a Rebel officer on account of his tattered straw hat, and quickly returned safely to friendly lines.

June 26, 1863   Custer was notified of his promotion to brigadier general, U.S. Volunteers.

June 29, 1863   Brevet Brig. Gen. Custer was placed in command of the Michigan Cavalry Brigade, which consisted of the 1st, 5th, 6th, and 7th Michigan Cavalry in addition to the 1st Vermont (August 20–April, 1864)

July 2, 1863   The Battle of Hunterstown, PA. In a prelude to the Battle of Gettysburg, Brig. Gen. Custer commanding the Michigan Brigade, approached Hunterstown and noticed a solid mass of Confederate cavalry under Gen. Wade Hampton in the fields ahead. He deployed most of this brigade and, with sword at the ready, personally led a charge of one squadron down the road directly into the midst of the enemy. The attack was a complete failure, and would have been worse had not Custer's artillery covered a hasty retreat. Custer had his horse shot out from under him, and was later cited for bravery under fire by Gen. Kilpatrick.

July 3, 1863   The Battle of Gettysburg, PA. Custer's participation in the Battle of Gettysburg launched his reputation as a Civil War hero, at least in his own time. His extraordinary bravery and significance in this particular battle has been all but ignored by modern historians and filmmakers, but nonetheless is worthy of a prominent place in the history of the Civil War as well as that of cavalry warfare.

It was July 3, 1863, the third day of the bloody battle. Confederate troopers numbering 12,000 under the command of Maj. Gen. George E. Pickett were poised to charge the Union center at Cemetery Ridge. Maj. Gen. James Ewell Brown Stuart—the famed "Jeb" Stuart— had maneuvered his "Invincibles" into position 3 miles behind the Union center. Stuart's Confederate cavalry had, without exception, whipped the Union horsemen in every encounter for the past 2 years, and there was no reason to believe that today would offer a different outcome.

Stuart's dismounted cavalrymen began the battle entrenched, and it became Custer's job to dig them out and push them backward. Custer's 5th Michigan advanced steadily toward the rebel lines, but had to fall back when ammunition ran low. The rebels quickly pursued the fleeing 5th, and Union Gen. David M. Gregg ordered the 7th Michigan to relieve the pressure with a mounted charge.

Custer, his saber drawn, galloped to the head of the column and shouted, "Come on, you Wolverines!" Explosions ripped the earth around them and bullets filled the air, but the 7th Michigan,

cheering loudly never wavered as they responded with a fury and followed their new young general with the golden curls and scarlet necktie. The initial charge drove the Rebels into a disorganized retreat. The 7th, however, was trapped by a stone wall and were obliged to engage in hand-to-hand combat in order to hold their ground. They finally broke through the wall for two more furious assaults, each of which was repelled. As they regrouped, a large force of Confederates struck at their flank, causing Custer to order his troops back to safety.

Gen. Stuart, always the strategic opportunist, seized the moment and ordered his 8 Confederate cavalry regiments led by Gen. Wade Hampton to the attack. One lieutenant remarked about the awesome sight: "In close columns of squadrons, advancing as if in review, with sabers drawn and glistening like silver in the bright sunlight, the spectacle called forth a murmur of admiration." Only the 1st Michigan stood between the onrushing Rebels and the vulnerable Union rear. There was no question that this would be the deciding engagement of the battle.

Once more, Custer—brandishing his saber—galloped to the head of the ranks and shouted, "Come on, you Wolverines!" And the second charge began. An eyewitness recounted his impressions: "The two columns drew nearer and nearer, the Confederates outnumbering their opponents as three or four to one. The gait increased—first the trot, then the gallop. As the charge was ordered the speed increased, every horse on the jump, every man yelling like a demon. As the opposing columns drew nearer and nearer, each with perfect alignment, every man gathered his horse well under him and gripped his weapon the tighter," With Custer four lengths ahead, the two opposing cavalries struck so violently that countless horses were toppled, crushing their riders. Capt. W. E. Miller observed, "The clashing of sabers, the firing of pistols, the demands for surrender and the cries of the combatants now "filled the air." Custer reported as follows: "For a moment, but only for a moment, that long, heavy column stood its ground; then, unable to withstand the impetuosity of our attack, it gave way in a disorderly rout, leaving vast numbers of dead in our possession. I challenge the annals of warfare to produce a more brilliant or successful charge of cavalry."

The legendary Jeb Stuart was soundly beaten at the same moment that Gen. Pickett's division was pouring across the battlefield in a prelude to disaster. Had Custer not handed the famous Southern general his first defeat, Stuart's forces would likely have arrived on the field in time to support Pickett's charge and change the course of the Battle of Gettysburg, if not history. Capt. S. H. Ballard of the 6th Michigan spoke for officer and enlisted alike when he said, "The Michigan Brigade adorned its Brigadier, and all felt as if he weighed about a ton." Indeed, Custer—in spite of his tender age—had earned the respect of his men. One trooper wrote after the battle: "He is a glorious fellow, full of energy, quick to plan and bold to execute, and with us he has never failed in any attempt he has yet made." The troops immediately began to emulate their leader by securing scarlet neckties, a Custer trademark, for themselves. James E. Taylor, artist for *Frank Leslie's Illustrated Newspaper*, described Custer's necktie as "An emblem of bravado and challenge to combat—with the Motion of the Toreador flouting the Crimson cloth to infuriate and lure the Bull to doom." Thus began the legend of the "Boy General." Just 23 years old, a general less than a week, and he had humiliated one of the greatest cavalry generals in history. The press had a fresh story, and a star was born.

July 14, 1863 The Battle of Falling Waters, VA. Custer's 5th Michigan Brigade had been fighting Gen. Lee's rear guard for two days when word was received that the Rebels had forded the Potomac near Williamsport and had marched another 4 miles to Falling Waters. Custer galloped to that point and ordered a charge that pushed back the enemy. Custer then had half his men dismount and advance on foot while the other half executed a mounted charge. At this point, Maj. Gen. H. J. Kilpatrick—Custer's superior and nemesis—arrived and changed part of the order, which caused excessive casualties as the men charged a Confederate force 10 times their size. The remainder of the division arrived on the field and captured 1,500 of Lee's men while the general escaped across the Potomac. This battle brought to a close the Gettysburg Campaign. Kilpatrick wrote in his official report, "To General Custer all praise is due."

July 23, 1863 Custer's command penetrated 50 miles into enemy-held territory in an attempt to create a wedge between Confederate troops under generals James Longstreet and A. P. Hill. He soon realized that he would require reinforcements in order to continue forward. Gen. George G. Meade refused the request, and Custer was forced to retreat.

September 13, 1863 The Battle of Culpepper Courthouse. Entrenched Confederates began shelling the attacking Union forces in order to protect the headquarters of Gen. J. E. B. Stuart. Custer's Brigade was deployed on the extreme left of a semicircle on the Union front line and had been delayed in a swamp. Custer, however, refused to wait for the remainder of his command, and with just over 100 men charged the artillery battery. A cannonball was fired directly at Custer, killing his white stallion, ripping through his boot and striking him on the inside of his thigh—his lone war wound—and also hitting 2 others. Custer quickly remounted, and resumed his charge. The Confederates hastily retreated, including Stuart who had abandoned his dinner to flee. Custer was deemed unfit for active duty due to the wound, and returned home to Monroe, MI.

October 3, 1863 *Harper's Weekly* featured a picture of a classic Custer charge.

October 11, 1863 Custer, only 3 days back to duty, liberated almost 250 New York Infantrymen who had been captured on the previous day by Gen. J. E. B. Stuart near Culpepper Courthouse. Stuart, however, pressed his attack, and Gen. Alfred Pleasanton found his command surrounded. Pleasanton could either surrender or fight his way out. Custer suggested a charge; the request was granted. Custer and his Michigan Wolverines brazenly attacked the enemy fortifications. An unexpected ditch along the way delayed the advance, but Custer—who had 2 horses shot out from under him—managed to maneuver his troops around the obstacle and through enemy lines to rendezvous with Gen. Meade's infantry on the Union side of the Rappahannock River.

February 9, 1864 Custer and Elizabeth Clift (Libbie) Bacon were married in Monroe, MI.

May 6, 1864 The Battle of Wilderness. In a place of dense Virginia second-growth timber appropriately named the Wilderness, Confederate troops under Gen. Robert E. Lee, supported by cavalry under Gen. J. E. B. Stuart—including Custer's West Point roommate, Gen. Tom Rosser—engaged the Union's 2nd and 3rd Cavalry divisions. Custer's Michigan Brigade marched off at 2 A.M. toward the front where fighting had raged since the previous day. Once there, they met exhausted Union soldiers who had been taking a beating from Stuart's cavalry. Custer deployed his troops across an open field 500 yards wide, and braced for an attack. At 5 A.M. they came—Confederate infantry followed by cavalry—charging across the clearing, their Rebel yells splitting the predawn stillness. Custer rode to the front of his troops, saber in hand, and signaled the band to

play his customary song for the charge, "Yankee Doodle." On his order, two Union regiments exploded across the field toward the enemy. The Rebels were somewhat startled by the bold move, but kept coming and the battle intensified. Reinforcements arrived to assist Custer's men, and the Rebels were finally driven back into the timber in retreat. Custer requested orders to pursue the fleeing Confederate soldiers, but was denied permission. He then deployed his troops in order to maintain control of the field and began the task of counting the prisoners.

May 9, 1864 The Battle of Beaverdam Station. The Union cavalry—10,000 strong—was headed for the Confederate capital of Richmond, VA, with Custer's command in the lead, when firing could be heard from the rearguard. While that skirmish raged, Custer was ordered to continue his march, which brought him into the small community of Beaverdam Station. Once there, he came upon 2 trains. One train had recently arrived from Richmond and was loaded with vital supplies for the Confederate army. The other train was boarding a large contingent of Union prisoners, obviously under Rebel supervision. Custer swiftly made his presence known and, in a matter of minutes, had captured both trains and liberated the prisoners. He ordered his troops and nearly 400 appreciative former prisoners to take all the booty they could carry—bacon, flour, sugar, meal, medical items, and anything else of use—from the supply train. He then burned the depot and excess supplies, and fired artillery shells through the boilers of the trains. The troops then tore up the railroad tracks in either direction and cut the telegraph line for a distance of 10 miles.

May 11, 1864 The Battle of Yellow Tavern. Gen. Phil SHERIDAN's Union cavalry—10,000 strong—had broken away from Gen. George Meade's infantry and were headed for Richmond, VA. The huge column, which included Custer's Michigan Brigade, was strung out for 13 miles. Sheridan understood that somewhere up ahead they would encounter Confederate Gen. J. E. B. Stuart's elite cavalry, and the only way into Richmond would be over his dead body. At a crossroads called Yellow Tavern some 6 miles from Richmond, Stuart began lobbing shells from the battery at the south end of his line. The constant barrage was taking its toll on the 1st and 7th Michigan as well as the brigade's held horses. Custer volunteered to charge the battery. He formed the 1st Michigan Cavalry, his veteran saber regiment, in a column of squadrons in the timber and ordered the 5th and 6th to advance on foot. A member of Gen. Wesley Merritt's staff watched with admiration as Custer's cavalry fearlessly dashed away with sabers at the ready to charge the cannon's mouth: "His headquarters flag—of the grayest colors—was flying in advance of the moving mass of glittering blades. ... [The] brave men of the Michigan Brigade rode boot to boot into what seemed the very jaws of death." Gen. Sheridan later wrote: "Custer's charge was brilliantly executed. Beginning at a walk, he increased his gait to a trot, and then at full speed rushed at the enemy." The Union cavalry encountered heavy fire from the entrenched Rebels, but pressed forward to overwhelm and rout the Confederate cavalry. At least 200 Rebels were killed, wounded, or captured along with the capture of 2 guns. The remainder of Stuart's confused force was driven across the Chickahominy River. The biggest prize, however, was word from a captured Confederate staff officer that Stuart himself had been killed. Yellow Tavern would forever be known not so much for the Union Victory but as the place where Gen. Custer's daring charge resulted in the death of legendary Gen. James Ewell Brown (J. E. B.) Stuart.

May 28, 1864   The Battle of Haw's Shop. Custer was ordered by Gen. William T. Sherman in May 1864 to provide security for the workers building a pontoon bridge over the Pamunkey River in Virginia. On May 28 at nearby Haw's Shop the 2nd Division under Gen. D. M. Gregg had encountered a large detachment of Confederate cavalry and were being overwhelmed in what was one of the bloodiest cavalry engagements of the war. Custer came to the rescue, deploying his dismounted troops against the superior force and soon routed them to clear the road to Cold Harbor. Throughout the engagement, Custer rode along his line in full view of Rebel sharpshooters, and had his horse shot out from under him.

June 11–12, 1864   The Battle of Trevilian Station, VA. Confederate Gen. Robert E. Lee attacked in retaliation for Union Gen. Phil Sheridan's destruction of the railroad at Trevilian Station. Custer and his brigade were caught between two Rebel divisions: struck from behind by his former West Point roommate, Gen. Tom Rosser. The surprise attack cost Custer 41 killed, 375 wounded, and 242 captured. The enemy also captured his adjutant, Jacob Greene; his cook, Eliza BROWN; his servant, Johnny Cisco; as well as the trappings of his headquarters—wagon, bedding, field desk, clothing, cooking outfit, spare horses, even his commission to general, and his letters from wife Libbie. Custer had to personally save his battle flag from being taken when his color bearer was shot. Needless to say, a hasty retreat was ordered, and the Union cavalry fell back and regrouped. Brown and Cisco escaped later that night and returned to friendly lines. Greene was not so fortunate: he remained a prisoner until later that year.

September 19, 1864   The Battle of Winchester, VA. Confederate Gen. Jubal Early's men were well entrenched within the town of Winchester when Gen. Phil Sheridan's Union forces approached. Custer's Michigan Brigade, reinforced by the 25th New York Cavalry, came under intense fire along Opequon Creek. Custer laid down a base of fire with the 6th Michigan, and attempted to cross the waterway. The Rebel riflemen and gunners opened up with a furious barrage and Custer's men floundered. In a surprise bold move, Custer ordered a charge across the stream. The Confederate soldiers, under Custer's West Point friend, Gen. Stephen Ramseur, decided to retreat. Custer followed, eventually coming upon a Union division under Gen. Averill who were engaged with a line of Rebels. Custer halted to await further orders. Word came that the battle in the center of town was not going well for the Union. It was Gen. Sheridan's turn for a surprise, bold move. He ordered his beleaguered troops to advance. Custer's orders were to charge the fortification on the left flank. Custer believed that a frontal assault at that time would be suicidal, so he requested that his orders be amended to allow him to choose the timing of his charge. Had most commanders made that request it would have been considered insubordination. However, Sheridan apparently trusted Custer enough to agree with the Boy General's assessment. As Sheridan's infantry pressed against the Confederate center, more and more men were taken from Custer's objective to reinforce that line. Finally, it was time, Custer ordered "Yankee Doodle" his song for the charge, be played, and off they went at a trot, then a gallop. The 400 Union horsemen routed the Confederate boys, capturing and turning their cannon to protect against a counterattack. The Rebel army fled from Winchester down the road toward Strasburg. However, more than 700 of them remained behind as Custer's prisoner, along with 7 battle flags.

September 22, 1864   The Battle of Fisher's Hill, VA. In this running battle 20 miles above Winchester, Gen. Phil Sheridan's plan to halt Confederate General Jubal Early's retreat failed. Early deployed Custer's West Point roommate Gen. Thomas Rosser's cavalry at Milford to stave off Union forces until the Rebel army had safely passed. Custer chased the enemy for 20 miles without success.

September 30, 1864   Brevet Maj. Gen. Custer was assigned to the command of the 3rd Cavalry Division, which consisted of the 1st Brigade: 2nd New York Cavalry, 2nd Ohio Cavalry, 3rd New Jersey Cavalry, 5th New York Cavalry, and 18th Pennsylvania Cavalry; and the 2nd Brigade: 1st Vermont Cavalry, two companies of the 3rd Indiana Cavalry, 8th New York Cavalry, 22nd New York Cavalry, and one battalion of the 1st New Hampshire Cavalry.

October 9, 1864   Battle of Tom's Brook (aka the Woodstock Races). The Confederate Army was determined to deny the Union forces their capital city of Richmond and had massed near the end of the Shenandoah Valley. The Rebel cavalry, however, had been harassing the Union column for some time, forcing delays and retreats that were not to Custer's liking. Custer, whose 2,500-man command had been assigned dreaded rearguard duty, finally received the order for which he had been waiting: Sheridan directed, "I want you to go out there in the morning and whip that Rebel cavalry or get whipped yourself." The morning dawned crisp and sunny as the Union cavalry advanced toward Confederate lines. Across Tom's Brook on the high ground awaited Custer's former West Point roommate, Gen. Thomas Rosser, with 3,500 troops. When all was ready for battle, Custer—in an act of bravado of which legends are made—rode out in front of his command where he could be seen by both sides. He then removed his broad-brimmed hat and swept it across himself and down in a salute. "Let's have a fair fight, boys!" he shouted. Gen. Rosser was not particularly amused by the showmanship. "You see that officer down there?" he said to his staff. "That's

General Custer, the Yanks are so proud of, and I intend to give him the best whipping today that he ever got!" Confederate artillery from the bluffs pummeled the field as the battled raged. Custer ordered a charge with 8 regiments to the front and 3 in a surprise attack at Rosser's left flank. The Rebels were outflanked and forced to retreat. Rosser halted his artillery in a stand of timber 2 miles away. Cannons opened up on the onrushing Yankees, while Rosser and his troops counterattacked. Custer's cavalry effected their own retreat. Rosser, however, could not advance against the Union guns, and deployed his men in the timber. Custer assembled his cavalry for another charge. This time he crashed through the entrenchment, and sent the Rebels running in a disorganized retreat for 10–12 miles. Rosser had not simply been defeated; he had been humiliated. Custer wrote to wife Libbie on October 10: "Darling little one, yesterday, the 9th, was a glorious day for your Boy. He signaled his accession to his new command by a brilliant victory. I attacked Gen. Rosser's Division of 3 Brigades with my Division of 2, and gained the most glorious victory. I drove Rosser in confusion ten miles, captured 6 cannon, all his advance trains, ambulance train, all Genls. Rosser, Lomax's and Wickham's headquarters wagons containing their baggage, private and official papers. I am now arrayed in Genl. Rosser's coat."

October 19, 1864   The Battle of Cedar Creek, VA. Custer's 3rd Division was camped along Cedar Creek, stretching a full 5 miles with Custer's headquarters at the western end. On the morning of October 19 confederate Gen. Jubal Early launched a surprise attack of 5 divisions against the eastern end of the encampment. The Union had been caught unawares and were in the process of being overrun and routed. The troops had been demoralized, and become disorganized. Custer and his men saved some face (and lives) by slowing the at-

tack with a stalemate face-off against a superior force of enemy soldiers commanded by his West Point roommate and friend, Confederate Maj. Gen. Tom Rosser. Then an event occurred to rally the Union forces. Gen. Phil Sheridan had halted up the road in Winchester, but heard about the battle and galloped to Cedar Creek. He rode up and down the lines to the sound of cheers, assuring his men that they would prevail. The Union troops responded, and "Sheridan's Ride" became famous. Late in the afternoon Sheridan noticed a gap in the Rebel lines, and quickly notified Custer. The 2,000-man strong 3rd Division led by the Boy General charged into the gap with sabers flashing and split the enemy in half. The Rebels began a hasty retreat, with Custer's command inflicting heavy casualties and collecting captured Confederate equipment. That night a jubilant Custer hugged his diminutive commanding officer, Gen. Phil Sheridan, and danced him around the campfire. "By God, Phil!" Custer cried, "We've cleaned them out of their guns and got ours back!" In addition, 13 enemy battle flags were captured in the battle. The following day Custer traveled to Washington, DC, with 13 of his men for a ceremony with Secretary of War Edwin Stanton. While wife Libbie proudly watched, Custer's troopers each presented the secretary with an enemy battle flag, and the secretary then presented Custer with a promotion to major general. *New York Times* reporter, E. A. Paul wrote: "Custer, young as he is, displayed judgment worthy of Napoleon."

March 2, 1865   The Battle of Waynesboro, VA. Custer's 3rd Cavalry Division was dispatched by Gen. Phil Sheridan to reconnoiter the area around Waynesboro ahead of the Union column. The going was difficult over the muddy road, and a freezing rain fell. Horses wallowed almost to their bellies. Regardless, a determined Custer kept his men struggling forward. At noon, through a pouring rain, he spied what he had been seeking. Confederate forces under Gen. Jubal Early—2 infantry brigades, artillery, and the cavalry of Custer's West Point roommate Gen. Tom Rosser—were entrenched in a bend of the South River. The position appeared insurmountable at first glance. However, further reconnaissance by Custer revealed one chink in Early's armor: a gap between his left flank and the river. He decided against waiting for the arrival of the column, and quickly ordered a diversion by sending mounted skirmishers to attract attention. He then ordered 3 regiments to dismount, and to sneak through the cover of timber in order to flank the Confederates on the left near the river. Horse artillery was brought up to soften up the Rebel lines. Custer ordered his bugler to sound the charge. The flankers left the timber to send a murderous volley into the rear of the startled enemy, while the other brigades rode over the mire straight toward Early's lines. The Rebels broke and ran, with Custer's men in hot pursuit. Three hours later the Confederate army in the Shenandoah Valley had, for all intents and purposes, been destroyed. Custer's 3rd Cavalry Division had captured 1,600 prisoners, 11 artillery pieces, over 200 wagons with supplies, and 17 battle flags. Generals Early and Rosser had been fortunate to personally escape the trap.

March 29, 1865   Brevet Maj. Gen. Custer was assigned the command of the 3rd Cavalry Division, which consisted of the 1st Brigade: 1st Connecticut Cavalry, 3rd New Jersey Cavalry, 2nd New York Cavalry, and 2nd Ohio Cavalry; the 2nd Brigade: 8th New York Cavalry, 15th New York Cavalry, and 1st Vermont Cavalry; and the 3rd Brigade: 1st New York (Lincoln) Cavalry; 1st West Virginia Cavalry, 2nd West Virginia Cavalry, (7 companies), and 3rd West Virginia Cavalry.

March 31, 1865   The Battle of Dinwiddie Court House. On this rainy af-

ternoon the head of the Union cavalry was pushed back to Dinwiddie court House by Confederate Gen. George E. Pickett's men. Custer's command, however, was detailed to the rear of the column escorting the wagon train along the sloppy, nearly impassable road. The Boy General and his troops could hear the battle raging up ahead. It was not long before Gen. Sheridan summoned Custer to bring two of this brigades forward. Custer and his aides rode ahead, one of them unfurling Custer's new personal guidon that he had received from his wife Libbie the night before. Custer wrote to his wife Libbie, March 31, 1865: "Last night Lt. Boehm arrived, with what all pronounced 'the handsomest flag in the army.' ... What renders it infinitely dear to me is that it is the work of my darling's hands. It could not have arrived at a more opportune moment. It was attached to my staff when battle was raging all along our lines. Cannon and musketry saluted it as its folds opened to the breeze. I regarded it as a happy omen." Custer found Dinwiddie Court House in turmoil; the Union troops were being driven back. Custer rode to the front, exposing himself to enemy fire, ignoring the fact that one of his orderlies was killed beside him or that his wife's name was shot out of the new guidon. The infantry attacked the Rebel lines, and Custer went with them. The Confederates counterattacked and forced the Yankees back. Custer rallied the troops, imploring them to remain behind rail barricades and hold their position. The Rebels were repulsed on one final desperate assault at sundown. Gen. Sheridan stated: "They—the Confederates—opened up, but Custer's repeating rifles poured forth such a shower of lead that nothing could stand against it."

April 1, 1865   The Battle of Five Forks, VA. Custer's division initially served as a diversion while Union infantry attacked a line of Confederate breastworks at this road junction. Then Custer was put up against Gen. George

E. Pickett's advancing troops, and he set about the business of capturing Confederate soldiers: more than 5,000 were taken that day, including Pickett.

April 3, 1865 The Battle of Namozine Church. Gen. Robert E. Lee with 80,000 retreating men had passed just north of Gen. Custer's campsite, traveling west along the Appomattox River Valley. Custer followed, moving his troops cautiously along the Namozine Road until they reached Namozine Creek. The bridge had been destroyed, and Rebel fortifications could be observed on the far bank. Gen. Custer did not know it at the time, but his men were greatly outnumbered by the enemy. He ordered one troop to outflank the position by wading the stream while a cannon battered the breastworks. Men with axes were detailed to remove the fallen trees from the stream and thereby permit the remainder of the troops to easily cross and attack. His brother, Capt. Thomas Ward Custer, however, refused to wait for the stream to be cleared. He impatiently spurred his horse and charged across Namozine Creek toward the enemy position, a course of action that inspired the troops to follow. The enemy fired volleys at the onrushing cavalrymen, but soon broke as a final result of the surprise maneuver. The battle became a running fight as the Rebels tied to elude their pursuers. When Capt. Custer's small force neared the Namozine Church, they found themselves facing a determined line of Confederate cavalry. Once more it was Tom who boldly led the charge, and he was the first cavalryman to break through. When hostilities had cooled, an elated Capt. Tom Custer presented his proud brother with the battle flag along with 14 prisoners, including 3 officers. Maj. Gen. Phil Sheridan recommended that he receive the Medal of Honor for his actions, the first of 2 he was awarded within a period of several days.

April 6, 1865 The Battle of Sayler's Creek. Gen. Robert E. Lee's retreating army was exhausted and in dire need of provisions. Early on April 6 the commander changed his order of march for the purpose of expediting their movement to stay ahead of their Union pursuers and to reach their resupply objective. Lee rode at the head of the column with Lt. Gen. James Longstreet and the infantry. They were followed by a lengthy line of wagons and then by Maj. Gen. John Gordon's II Corps acting as rear guard. Lee was approaching Farmville when the column inadvertently split into two detachments. Lee continued on as planned, but the wagon train and Gordon veered to the north, where they came under immediate Federal attack at a place called Sayler's Creek. Gen. Custer's opportunistic cavalrymen plunged right into the hottest of the engagement. The hastily entrenched Confederates put up a gallant fight, and kept the division at bay for some time. Custer had his horse shot out from beneath him, and his color bearer was killed by a bullet in the head. He realized, however, that as soon as the Union infantry arrived an effective attack could be executed. The 3rd Brigade led the charge against enemy lines. The Rebels held their fire behind the improvised breastworks until the last moment, then unleashed a furious barrage. The assaulting cavalrymen were undaunted, and soared over the fortifications. Within minutes, the gray line was sent scattering in the wake of the surging Federals. The Rebels continued to fight as they withdrew to the north. Custer formed his division and rode to the sound of the guns to seek further glory. This portion of the battle amounted to little more than putting the finishing touches on their day's work. The enemy had already been demoralized and weakened from early assaults and the withering cannon salvos, and was unable to muster any vigorous resistance. Capt. Tom Custer, although having been shot pointblank through the cheek, captured a Confederate battle flag. He was rewarded for his bravery with his second Medal of Honor in three days, thereby becoming the country's first and the Civil War's only double recipient. Over 9,000 Confederates including 7 generals—one of them Robert E. Lee's son, Custis—were taken prisoner at Sayler's Creek: more Americans than had ever before or after been captured at one time on this continent. The Army of Northern Virginia had lost a full 33 percent of its total force on the afternoon that the South long remembered as "Black Thursday." The Battle of Sayler's Creek was the final major engagement of the war.

April 8, 1865   The Battle of Appomattox Station. Custer and his division had gone into bivouac in the early evening some 2 miles from Appomattox Station when word arrived about 4 Confederate supply trains waiting at the station. Custer roused the troops, galloped into Appomattox Station, and easily captured the trains, except one engine that was uncoupled and escaped. Moments after Custer's men had assumed occupation of the station, Rebel artillery began to rain shells upon them. Custer detailed former Union engineers and stokers to move the trains to safety. He then ordered a charge on the Rebel cannons. The surprise attack drove off 2 divisions commanded by Gen. J. A. Walker, allowing Custer to seize 25 artillery pieces that moments before had been turned on his command. More importantly, he made off with the 4 railroad trains loaded with ammo and rations that were desperately needed by the Confederates.

April 9, 1865 Appomattox. Custer's command had pushed to within sight of Appomattox Court House, and held the Lynchburg Road. A force of Confederates were up ahead, and Custer was preparing his troops for a charge. Without warning, a Confederate officer appeared under a tattered white towel flag of truce, and presented himself to Custer. The officer introduced himself as Maj. Simms, a member of Gen. Longstreet's staff, and his message was good news to the Union troops. Gen. Lee requested a suspension of hostilities. Custer dispatched his chief of staff to accompany Simms behind Rebel lines to deliver the demand for unconditional surrender. The Civil War had for all intents and purposes ended at Custer's command post.

April 9, 1865   Appomattox Court House. Gen. Robert E. Lee surrendered to Gen. Ulysses S. Grant in Wilmer Mclean's parlor at 3 P.M. on Palm Sunday to end the Civil War. The writing table on which the official papers were signed was purchased for $20 by Gen. Phil Sheridan. The next day he wrote the following note to Custer's wife Libbie: "I respectfully present to you the small writing table on which the conditions for the surrender of the Army of Northern Virginia were written by Lt. General Grant—and permit me to say, Madam, that there is scarcely an individual in our service who has contributed more to bring about this desirable result than your husband."

Index

Bold page numbers indicate the main reference, and *italics* indicate photographs or maps.